Ten Lectures on Event Structure in a Network Theory of Language

Distinguished Lectures in Cognitive Linguistics

Edited by
Fuyin (Thomas) Li (*Beihang University, Beijing*)

Guest Editors
Hongxia Jia and Jinmei Li (*Beihang University*)

Editorial Assistants
Jing Du, Na Liu and Cuiying Zhang (*doctoral students at Beihang University*)

Editorial Board
Jürgen Bohnemeyer (*State University of New York, Buffalo*) – Alan Cienki (*Vrije Universiteit (VU), Amsterdam, Netherlands* and *Moscow State Linguistic University, Russia*) – William Croft (*University of New Mexico, USA*) – Ewa Dąbrowska (*Northumbria University, UK*) – Gilles Fauconnier (*University of California, San Diego, USA*) – Dirk Geeraerts (*University of Leuven, Belgium*) – Nikolas Gisborne (*The University of Edinburgh, UK*) – Cliff Goddard (*Griffith University, Australia*) – Stefan Th. Gries (*University of California, Santa Barbara, USA and Justus-Liebig-Universitat Giessen, Germany*) – Laura A. Janda (*University of Tromsø, Norway*) – Zoltan Kövecses (*Eötvös Loránd University, Hungary*) – George Lakoff (*University of California, Berkeley, USA*) – Ronald W. Langacker (*University of California, San Diego, USA*) – Chris Sinha (*Hunan University, China*) – Leonard Talmy (*State University of New York, Buffalo, USA*) – John R. Taylor (*University of Otago, New Zealand*) – Mark Turner (*Case Western Reserve University, USA*) – Sherman Wilcox (*University of New Mexico, USA*) – Phillip Wolff (*Emory University, USA*) Jeffrey M. Zacks (*Washington University, St. Louis, USA*)

Distinguished Lectures in Cognitive Linguistics publishes the keynote lectures series given by prominent international scholars at the China International Forum on Cognitive Linguistics since 2004. Each volume contains the transcripts of 10 lectures under one theme given by an acknowledged expert on a subject and readers have access to the audio recordings of the lectures through links in the e-book and QR codes in the printed volume. This series provides a unique course on the broad subject of Cognitive Linguistics. Speakers include George Lakoff, Ronald Langacker, Leonard Talmy, Laura Janda, Dirk Geeraerts, Ewa Dąbrowska and many others.

The titles published in this series are listed at *brill.com/dlcl*

Ten Lectures on Event Structure in a Network Theory of Language

By

Nikolas Gisborne

BRILL

LEIDEN | BOSTON

Library of Congress Cataloging-in-Publication Data

Names: Gisborne, Nikolas, 1966- author.
Title: Ten lectures on event structure in a network theory of language / by Nikolas Gisborne.
Description: Leiden ; Boston : Brill, 2020. | Series: Distinguished lectures in cognitive linguistics, 24684872 | Includes bibliographical references.
Identifiers: LCCN 2020024553 (print) | LCCN 2020024554 (ebook) | ISBN 9789004358966 (hardback) | ISBN 9789004375291 (ebook)
Subjects: LCSH: Grammar, Comparative and general—Verb. | Grammar, Comparative and general—Syntax. | Grammar, Comparative and general—Semantics.
Classification: LCC P281 .G555 2020 (print) | LCC P281 (ebook) | DDC 415—dc23
LC record available at https://lccn.loc.gov/2020024553
LC ebook record available at https://lccn.loc.gov/2020024554

Typeface for the Latin, Greek, and Cyrillic scripts: "Brill". See and download: brill.com/brill-typeface.

ISSN 2468-4872
ISBN 978-90-04-35896-6 (hardback)
ISBN 978-90-04-37529-1 (e-book)

Copyright 2020 by Nikolas Gisborne. Reproduced with kind permission from the author by Koninklijke Brill NV, Leiden, The Netherlands.
Koninklijke Brill NV incorporates the imprints Brill, Brill Hes & De Graaf, Brill Nijhoff, Brill Rodopi, Brill Sense, Hotei Publishing, mentis Verlag, Verlag Ferdinand Schöningh and Wilhelm Fink Verlag.
All rights reserved. No part of this publication may be reproduced, translated, stored in a retrieval system, or transmitted in any form or by any means, electronic, mechanical, photocopying, recording or otherwise, without prior written permission from the publisher. Requests for re-use and/or translations must be addressed to Koninklijke Brill NV via brill.com or copyright.com.

This book is printed on acid-free paper and produced in a sustainable manner.

Contents

Note on Supplementary Material   VII
Preface   VIII
Preface by the Author   X

1 Event Semantics: A Network Model of Language Structure   1

2 Parts, Wholes, and Networks; Idioms; Semantics—Syntax—Morphology   36

3 Evidence for Structure in Verb Meaning   65

4 Polysemy and Semantic Structure   90

5 Events and Thematic Roles   117

6 Resultatives and Causation   147

7 Ditransitives and Verbs of Buying and Selling   176

8 Classes of Events and Aspectual Class   206

9 Conflation Classes, Transitivity Alternations and Argument Realization   238

10 Situating Meaning in the Utterance   268

Bibliography   293
About the Series Editor   301
Websites for Cognitive Linguistics and CIFCL Speakers   302

Note on Supplementary Material

All original audio-recordings and other supplementary material, such as hand-outs and PowerPoint presentations for the lecture series, have been made available online and are referenced via unique DOI numbers on the website www.figshare.com. They may be accessed via a QR code for the print version of this book. In the e-book both the QR code and dynamic links will be available which can be accessed by a mouse-click.

The material can be accessed on figshare.com through a PC internet browser or via mobile devices such as a smartphone or tablet. To listen to the audio recording on hand-held devices, the QR code that appears at the beginning of each chapter should be scanned with a smart phone or tablet. A QR reader/scanner and audio player should be installed on these devices. Alternatively, for the e-book version, one can simply click on the QR code provided to be redirected to the appropriate website.

This book has been made with the intent that the book and the audio are both available and usable as separate entities. Both are complemented by the availability of the actual files of the presentations and material provided as hand-outs at the time these lectures were given. All rights and permission remain with the authors of the respective works, the audio-recording and supplementary material are made available in Open Access via a CC-BY-NC license and are reproduced with kind permission from the authors. The recordings are courtesy of the China International Forum on Cognitive Linguistics (http://cifcl.buaa.edu.cn/), funded by the Beihang University Grant for International Outstanding Scholars.

The complete collection of lectures by Nikolas Gisborne can be accessed by scanning this QR code.

Preface

The present text, entitled *Ten Lectures on Event Structure in a Network Theory of Language* by Nikolas Gisborne, is a version of the lectures given by Nikolas Gisborne in May 2016 as the forum speaker for the 15th China International Forum on Cognitive Linguistics. Nikolas Gisborne received his PhD from University College London and is currently Professor of Linguistics at the University of Edinburgh, Scotland, the United Kingdom, where he has worked since 2002. Before moving to Edinburgh, he taught at the University of Hong Kong and the University of Cambridge. Dr. Gisborne works on syntax and semantics, particularly event structure and predication, and on language change. He works with a network-based theory of language and cognitive structure, and is interested in the theoretical question of how to model a formal theory of language so that it is cognitively and psychologically plausible.

One of Dr. Gisborne's representative works is *Event Structure of Perception Verbs* (Oxford University, 2010), which analyses the event structure of perception verbs from the perspective of Word Grammar. Dr. Gisborne has also co-edited a book with Willem Hollmann entitled *Theory and Data in Cognitive Linguistics* (John Benjamin Publishing Company, 2014), which includes studies on the current theory and research methodology in Cognitive Linguistics.

The China International Forum on Cognitive Linguistics (http://cifcl.buaa.edu.cn/) provides a forum for eminent international scholars to give lectures on their original contributions to the field. It is a continuing program organized by several prestigious universities in Beijing. The following is a list of organizers for CIFCL 15.

Organizer:
Fuyin (Thomas) Li: PhD/Professor, Beihang University

Co-organizers:
Wei Wu: PhD/Professor, Tsinghua University
Yihong Gao: PhD/Professor, Peking University
Baohui Shi: PhD/Professor, Beijing Forestry University
Yuan Gao: PhD/Professor, University of Chinese Academy of Sciences
Xu Zhang: PhD/Professor, Beijing Language and Culture University

The text is published, accompanied by its audio counterpart, as one of the *Eminent Linguists Lecture Series*. The transcriptions of the video, proofreading of the text and publication of the work in its present book form, have involved many people's strenuous inputs. The initial transcripts were completed by the following: Longbo Ren, Yu Deng, Zhiyong Hu, Lin Yu, Jinmei Li, Hongxia Jia, Jing Du, Mengmin Xu, Chenxi Niu. Jing Du produced revisions of the initial transcripts. The speaker, Professor Nikolas Gisborne made the final revisions. The published version is the final version approved by the speaker.

The publication of this book is sponsored by the National Social Science Foundation Award No.13BYY012, and by the Fundamental Research Funds for the Central Universities (YMF-16-WYXY-010).

Beihang University (BUAA)

> *Thomas Fuyin Li*
> *thomasli@buaa.edu.cn*
>
> *Hongxia Jia*
> *melodyjhx@buaa.edu.cn*
>
> *Jinmei Li*
> *Ljm-hubeidaxue@163.com*

Preface by the Author

This book originated as a series of lectures that I gave in Beijing as part of the 15th China International Forum on Cognitive Linguistics in May 2016. It offers an account of events and event structure within a theory of language, Word Grammar, which assumes that language is a cognitive network with no embedding where the language network is just part of the larger cognitive network. Word Grammar's language network is a symbolic network which is designed to be as simple as possible: formally, it is just a series of arcs and nodes, classified by default inheritance. The problems that I am concerned with are to do with events and event structures. In a cognitive approach, events are just verb meanings, but an event is not (only) the sense of an individual verb. Events are individually identifiable, with times, places and participants, and these pieces of information have to be built into the linguistic representations. I look at how this information is built up, and its consequences for the representation of events, and the relationship of event semantics to sentences and utterances.

There are several issues in the analysis of events. For example, what is an event? Verb meanings make up a heterogeneous class. Intuitively, we can see that defining the meaning of the word EVENT as the class of verbs' meanings makes sense: EXPLODE, KISS, RUN, and WALK all have dynamic states of affairs as their meanings.[1] They also have pretty simple meanings. But what do we make of more complex states of affairs? Verb meanings can involve more than one event, so how should we analyse these complex event structures? Does KILL mean something like 'cause to die'? How can the meanings of stative verbs such as LOVE be "events"? Other stative verbs include modals like MAY and copular verbs such as SEEM—how do they work? How many participants can an event have? For example, there are two in transitive verbs, but what about ditransitives, or verbs with even more participants such as BUY in *he bought it from her for £50*, which appears to involve four participants. What are the limits on how events are structured? Are all results entailed? Are there restrictions on how events can combine within verb meanings?[2]

---

1 A note on representational conventions. I use SMALL CAPS for lexical entries or lexemes. I use *italics* to show examples of utterances. Single 'quotation marks' identify the conceptual structures associated with meaning. Double "quotation marks" are reserved for scare quotes and for direct quotations. The labels for syntactic relations such as Subject and semantic relations such as Agent, have a capital letter.

2 Another complexity is that the word EVENT is polysemous: it can mean what are sometimes called "eventualities," including both stative and dynamic verb meanings, and it is also sometimes restricted to the dynamic cases only. I use it in both ways in these lectures, although I have tried to make it clear which interpretation I intend.

In the course of these lectures, I tackle these and other related questions while building up a model which allows us to bring the questions to the fore and explore them in a precise way. Word Grammar views language as part of a larger cognitive network—so I explore the consequences of the network architecture and allow it to guide the analyses of event behaviour and event structure. There is some comparison with other approaches, most usually Cognitive Construction Grammar, which has a number of similarities to Word Grammar, except that it permits the recursive embedding of constructions within constructions.

The main argument in the book is that we should take the notion of language as a cognitive network seriously. I think that this obliges us to reject phrase structure, and other devices which require there to be embedding of one structure within another. I argue that knowledge of language is just part of a larger cognitive network, and that the language network is supported by social understanding, and our theory of mind. Even complex event structures can interact with the mental representations of utterances and utterance context, which suggests that language should be viewed as integrated with social cognition and is another argument for the network approach.

With the exception of Lecture 7, each lecture addresses a different theme, rather than being organized around particular data sets, which means that the same data points can recur. For example, ditransitives are discussed in Lecture 7, and then again in Lectures 8 and 9, although with a different take. However, when the data sets recur, it is in order to make a different point: in one case I am interested in the syntax of ditransitives; in another, I look at the semantic relationships between ditransitives and the related prepositional uses of the same verbs.

Lecture Titles and Summaries

1. A network model of language structure
   It is widely accepted in cognitive theory that language is a conceptual network. Often, this is understood as a network of constructions. In this lecture, I argue that it makes sense to take this position to its logical conclusion, and to treat language as a symbolic network with no part-whole relations at all: language consists of nodes, and relations, and nothing much else.
2. Parts, wholes, and networks; idioms; semantics—syntax—morphology
   This lecture explores the consequences of adopting the position in Lecture 1 for theories of syntax, semantics and morphology, and their

interactions. We look at the treatment of idioms as a case study and the lecture finishes with a discussion of WG lexical entries.

3. Evidence for structure in verb meaning

   One of the tasks of work on event structure is to establish the nature of the relationship between syntax and semantics. But there is a task that has to happen first: we need to explain why we assume that there is an event structure. What is the evidence that events are complex and that the complexity is structured? What facts can we draw on? Are we obliged to assume that there is structure, or from a theoretical point of view, is it possible to do without it? I argue that there is, indeed an event structure, but that within Word Grammar's network model, that structure does not involve recursive embedding of one concept within another.

4. Polysemy and semantic structure

   One thing a lexical semantic theory has to do is to model polysemy. Some polysemy is relevant to event structure: the polysemy to do with variation in argument realization. But there are other dimensions of polysemy, which don't affect argument realization: are they relevant to the theory of events? Are there different kinds of polysemy? How should we model polysemy?

5. Events and thematic roles

   Do different event types define different thematic role types, or is it the other way around? What diagnostics could we deploy to find out? I argue that we can distinguish fruitfully between Talmy's "force-dynamic" relations, and the other kinds of semantic role which are usually defined in terms of how language structures space.

6. Classes of event

   What categories of event are there? In this lecture we establish a type hierarchy of events, and ask how we might model event types cross-linguistically, looking at Talmy's claims about verb-framed and satellite-framed languages, and Levin and Rappaport Hovav's claims about manner/result complementarity.

7. Building structure: ditransitives and verbs of buying and selling

   Ditransitive verbs are a complex type: they involve multiple events, and an additional participant—albeit one that has a stable interpretation in the verb's meaning. Verbs of buying and selling build on the meanings of ditransitives, and here we look at how they require a fine-grained interpretation. This brings us back to the material of the second lecture, in that we explore how the network approach takes us to different conclusions from those you would arrive at by following a frame-semantic approach.

8. Events and Aktionsart—modelling the structure
   This lecture builds on the earlier lectures, and explores the issue of how the different Aktionsarten—states, simple dynamic events, semelfactives, achievements and accomplishments—are built up from the tools we have introduced so far. We look at complex events, the possible roles of different thematic role types, and the representation of polysemy.
9. Transitivity alternations and argument linking
   One of the key roles for events in linguistic theorizing is in establishing a theory of argument linking or argument realization. In this lecture we explore how a declarative theory of argument linking can be described in terms of the event structures we have established in the earlier lectures, but without recourse to phrasal constructions.
10. Situating meaning in the utterance: modality
    As an envoi, this lecture discusses how the intramental-network approach allows us to model how context interacts with the linguistic material. We explore how the subjectivity of modal meaning interacts with the speaker and the hearer, and explore whether this account is compatible with the earlier theory of event structure and argument realization that we have produced. We also look at other evidence for the communicative and social embedding of linguistic information.

The lectures I gave in China were recorded and transcribed. What follows is edited and corrected versions of the transcriptions. As well as removing the oral features of the lectures—the *ums* and the *ers*—I have also taken out the thanks to my hosts at the beginning of the lecture, stories and jokes that do not work on the written page even if they might have helped keep the audience engaged, and I have improved the exposition where I thought I was not clear enough or got things wrong. However, the organisation and structure of each lecture follows the spoken version.

I owe a debt of gratitude to many people. Professor Thomas Li Fuyin, invited me to give these lectures, and provided exemplary hospitality during my trip to China. His team of postgraduate students, particularly Jia Hongxia, Li Jinmei, and Du Jing, were very helpful and well organized. I am grateful to the authorities of Professor Li's university, Beihang University—as well as the other universities in Beijing which hosted these lectures, Beijing Forestry University, Beijing Language and Culture University, Peking University, Tsinghua University, and the University of the Chinese Academy of Sciences—for their practical support and hospitality. The lectures attracted a stimulating audience, and I would like to thank the audience members for their time and for their thoughtful questions. Maarten Frieswijk and Elisa Perotti at Brill have been very patient, and helpful, editors. And I am very grateful to Brill's indefatigable Production Editor, Fem Eggers. I also owe a debt of gratitude to Dick Hudson who read through the slides and discussed them with me before I travelled to China and who also make helpful comments on the final manuscript submission. The Moray Endowment Fund of the University of Edinburgh gave me a small grant which paid for Yueh-Hsin Kuo to work as a research assistant on this project: I am grateful both to the fund for their support, and to Yueh-Hsin for his work. Finally, I would like to thank my wife, Caroline Lewis (who sadly was not able to travel to Beijing with me as we'd planned), for her support and love.

LECTURE 1

Event Semantics: A Network Model of Language Structure

1   The Roadmap of This Lecture

This lecture is part of an introductory pair together with Lecture 2. It has two main parts. In the first part, I discuss some issues in event semantics and in the history of the study of events, and in the second I discuss the model, Word Grammar, which frames the discussion in all ten lectures. Therefore, there will be some discussion of the kinds of formalism that I adopt, and some (brief and non-technical) comparison of the Word Grammar framework with other models.

I start off by talking about events, event structure and issues in event semantics. We will think about the linguistic theory of events, verbs and their arguments and lexical semantics; word meaning and sentence meaning; polysemy; argument linking and argument realization; a little bit of typology; and the construal of events/states of affairs/things that happen. Then in the second part of the lecture, I introduce Word Grammar: the theory that my work is embedded in and which it contributes to. Word Grammar treats language as a cognitive network—Word Grammar is a cognitive theory of language, which argues that all language is just part of a vast symbolic cognitive network, and nothing else. Formally, the cognitive network is defined by classified arcs and nodes: there is no other formal apparatus.

In the second part of the lecture, therefore, I introduce the machinery we need. There are four pieces of technical equipment that I rely on in particular. The technical equipment is default inheritance (which is a model of classification); a technical innovation called the "sub-lexeme"; dependency structure; and network structure. I introduce these devices in the course of the lecture.

 All original audio-recordings and other supplementary material, such as any hand-outs and powerpoint presentations for the lecture series, have been made available online and are referenced via unique DOI numbers on the website www.figshare.com. They may be accessed via a QR code for the print version of this book. In the e-book, both the QR code and dynamic links are available, and can be accessed by a mouse-click.

© NIKOLAS GISBORNE. REPRODUCED WITH KIND PERMISSION FROM THE AUTHOR BY KONINKLIJKE BRILL NV, LEIDEN, 2020 | DOI:10.1163/9789004375291_002

Lecture 2 continues the introduction. It has three parts: (i) a defence of the network idea; (ii) a case study showing how WG treats idioms; (iii) analyses of semantics, syntax and morphology.

We will begin by looking at events and event structure.

2   Events, Event Structure, and Issues in Event Semantics

2.1   *Locating These Lectures in the Field*

In this lecture, I present a particular cognitive theory of language, Word Grammar (or WG), and its approach to event semantics and to event structure. WG is a theory of language which claims that all language can be represented as a network. This network is part of a larger cognitive network, with an architecture that consists exclusively of arcs and nodes. As well as discussing how this theory works, I also look at the research context in event semantics.

I am also concerned with matters of representation. Every theory has a representation, which is a way of showing you in its analytical model what this analysis says. Some theories, such as the different stages of Chomsky's theorizing from Transformational Grammar to the Minimalist Program, use tree diagrams to capture constituency facts, interpret grammatical functions from positions within the constituency structures, and use movement to capture complex relationships within clauses. Other theories such as Goldberg's model of Cognitive Construction Grammar use boxes to represent constructions. Moving away from syntax, Talmy has force dynamic diagrams which represent a particular understanding of causation. Langacker has various representations for his theory of Cognitive Grammar. WG also has a representation, which has a logic, which I talk about below.

There is also another reason for talking about matters of formalism: it is not just the case that I am discussing and introducing an unfamiliar theory. I am also discussing event semantics. This area of meaning has been discussed in a number of different linguistic theories, including formal semantics. The first person to talk about event semantics was the philosopher Donald Davidson in 1967 who introduced the notion of the event argument in predicate calculus as a way of understanding how verbs could be modified by adverbs (among other issues). Cognitive linguistics have also discussed event semantics. Talmy was an early researcher, with his PhD thesis in 1972 on Atsugewi. Jackendoff represents another tradition—in his case coming out of generative linguistics—where he invented his own theory and representation. There isn't an agreed theory or representation, so we need to think about representations as part of thinking about events and event structure, and in order to make sure we understand what the different representations mean. I use Word Grammar network diagrams throughout these lectures so I am concerned to make sure that you can understand and read these representations.

2.2 Events, Event Structure and Event Semantics

Where do events belong? For a cognitive theory, they belong somewhere in word meaning. But there are several theoretical traditions which set out to study events. For example, Davidson (1967, 2001) was followed by Terence Parsons (1990, 1995).[1] Dowty (1977) explored the *Aktionsarten* and event representation in Montague semantics. Jackendoff's Conceptual Semantics emerged in the early 1970s (Jackendoff 1972, 1983, 1990, 1997) following Gruber (1965). Another tradition is of course Cognitive Semantics (Talmy 1975, 1976, 1985a, 1985b, 1988; Croft 1991, 2012). So there is a rich literature and there are several themes that emerge and re-emerge, but the literature can be complex and difficult to read because of the different foundational assumptions of the various authors, alternative approaches to the various topics they analyse, different issues that are privileged in the authors' theorizing, as well as the different representations.

Some of the problems I mentioned before, which are discussed in the analysis of events—how events related to each other for example—have been analysed in different places within linguistic representations. There are theories that claim that properties of events should be discussed in the syntax and others that say that they belong in the semantics. The different theories are led by their axioms and foundational assumptions. For example, Ramchand (1997, 2008) has written on event theories within Minimalism. She puts the burden of analyzing events in the part of the syntax that has an interface with the lexicon. In a different theory, Combinatory Categorial Grammar, Steedman and Moens (1998) looked at events and *Aktionsarten* and their interactions. Other theories, such as those in the cognitive tradition, for example Goldberg's Construction Grammar (1995) and Word Grammar (Gisborne 2010, 2011; Hudson 2007, 2010; Hudson and Holmes 2005) put the work of understanding events and event structure in the semantics. Word Grammar relates its semantic representation to its syntax with associative links. There are no events in the syntax because it is a parallel-architecture theory—similar architectures are found in Lexical-Functional Grammar, Role and Reference Grammar, and Simpler Syntax.

---

1 Davidson and Parsons work with an externalist theory, where meaning is the fragment of the world that a sentence corresponds to. Therefore, for them an event is the real-world state of affairs that a sentence refers to if it is true.

The questions about representations are therefore related to larger questions of theory, particularly questions to do with how different linguistic theories conceive of the architecture of grammar. Questions about the architecture of grammar involve theoretical decisions such as whether there is mismatch between syntax and semantics, or whether they are isomorphic and how the lexicon relates to other parts of language. These questions, in turn, relate to other issues to do with learnability.

2.3   What Are Events?

On a cognitive or conceptual construal, events are verb meanings within conceptual structure. That is, they are mental representations of verb meanings. Events can be simple or complex, and have a number of different properties, such as structure (where events have sub-events), participants, causes and times.[2]

Let us take a very simple example. I dropped a battery about 20 seconds ago. This event clearly has a spatial-temporal location—20 seconds before I told you about it. It has a structure: it is a simple event. I am the participant. And the meaning of the verb DROP happens to encode no information about what causes it. When we discuss events, we need to discuss all of these properties. As I explain later, the *times* of events have been critical to theoretical discussion. Events are part of the structure of meaning—they are part of the conceptual cognitive construal of the world.

2.4   Davidson and Events in Formal Semantics

We can start by looking at Davidson and events in formal semantics. I am not following Davidson, who was in the logical tradition of Bertrand Russell and Frege, but I want to discuss aspects of Davidsonian event semantics, because this has been very influential and it gives us a context for looking at some of the issues that arise in these lectures. Davidson is very useful for thinking about representational issues: he makes us think about the formal question of how we organize meanings and their combinations. Therefore, even though Davidson has nothing to do with cognitive linguistics, his work is a starting position for thinking about events and event semantics.

---

2   I talk about event *structure* as though it is a given that events are necessarily structured. It isn't, of course: the work of Davidson and Parsons treats complex events as unstructured. But the work reported in these lectures treats events as structured mental representations of verbs' meanings.

The crucial thing to remember about formal semantics and logical semantics is that in this tradition events are bits of the actual world which can be individuated and distinguished—they are particulars. For a formal semanticist, the meaning of a sentence is the bit of the world that it corresponds to. This theory is not conceptual; it does not posit mental representations. Sentences are understood in terms of whether they are true or false. For example, if I say *I am British*, then the meaning of that sentence is whether it is true or false. *I am British* is true in this world where I have a British passport. *I am Chinese* is false in this world where I have a British passport. The truth or falsity of the sentence is what gives it meaning.

2.5   *A Simple Formal Semantic Theory of Events*

Davidson's theory was intended to explain how adverbs and prepositional phrases could modify verb meanings: he had a technical problem which he set out to solve. Let's take the following example:

(1)   Jane kissed Peter at three o'clock.

(1) is about times: how *at three o'clock* interacts with *Jane kissed Peter*. We can decide whether (1) is true or not: we can look at Jane and Peter kissing and decide if it is true that she is kissing him at three o'clock or not. (It doesn't have to be exactly true, but has to be true within reason. Hence, if it is three minutes past three, yes, it is true. But if it is half past three, it is not.)

However, there's a problem. In Davidson's theory, which uses predicate calculus, the meaning of *kissed* is a predicate. A predicate is something which has empty slots that need to be filled. Davidson's theory encounters a problem when it comes to filling empty slots. Do we need to say that there is a special lexical entry for KISS, which has an empty slot that needs a time phrase, as well as the slots for its Agent and Patient? Do all verbs have a special lexical entry for every time phrase? The word *kissed* in (1) has a time phrase of *at 3 o'clock*, but it can also have time phrases like *one minute past 3* or *two minutes past 3*. It could have thousands of time slots in its lexical entry, because sentences like *Jane kissed Peter at 3 o'clock, at 3.01, at 3.02* and so forth are grammatical. If KISS does have all of these time slots, then the theory is not a good theory, because it will make your lexicon explode and become unmanageable. An exploding lexicon is a problem—theories have to be constrained to be formally tractable, or cognitively plausible.

Why do you limit theories in various ways? As a cognitive linguist, I'm interested in limiting theories in ways that are compatible with our theories about how the human mind works. Unfortunately for us, we are just apes.

Our nearest biological relatives are gorillas, chimpanzees and bonobos, which means that we have ape brains. Therefore, our cognitive theory has to work with our ape brains (luckily, we have the best ape brains). That is how we limit a cognitive theory: how can it work given what we know about the constraints of our ape brains? We have to constrain things in various ways which are compatible with the properties of our brains, and what we have learnt from cognitive psychology. I think that there are two key properties of our brains: we have good memories, but we do not process very fast. If you want to do a complicated sum, it is better to use your phone than it is trying to do it in your head. But Davidson has different constraints on his theory, because it belongs in the larger field of logic, so it is subject to the constraints that logicians impose on their theorizing.

2.6 *Basic Formal Semantics*

Let's start with the first-order logic. It has two subsystems: one is the predicate calculus and the other is the propositional calculus. The predicate calculus shows the internal structure of propositions and says that the meaning of a declarative utterance is a proposition which is something that can be true or false. A declarative sentence is an ordinary sentence like *I am British*, not a question, or an order. The propositional calculus treats propositions as its atoms to make complex propositions. We calculate complex propositions out of atomic propositions by linking them with sentence connectives.

2.7 *Propositions and Connectives*

I won't show you the formal logic of sentence connectives here, but they are useful in this theory; they are part of the structure which makes it work. Here are four sentences, which refer to Merkel, leader of Germany, and Hollande, leader of France in 2016, when I gave these lectures.

(2)   Merkel is German. Hollande is French.
(3)   Merkel is German *and* Hollande is French.
(4)   Merkel is German *or* Hollande is French.
(5)   *If* Merkel is German *then* Hollande is French.

In (2), in July 2017, those two sentences are both true. You can say *Merkel is German. Hollande is French.* (3) is true: because *Merkel is German* is true, and *Hollande is French* is true, the whole sentence is true. (4) is also true: if both of the sentences in (4) are true, then (4) is still true, as long as something includes them all. (5) is also true. This sentence connective is called material implication, which is shown with an arrow, →. In this theory, we can work out the meaning of these connectives in something called a truth table. The whole theory is organized around whether a statement is true or false. What linguists in this tradition do is test the system, which is a little bit like maths. They use formal logic to make the theory unbreakable. The atomic propositions are evaluated for their truth value, then the complex propositions are evaluated for theirs.

I am not going into detail, but we can see how this works by looking at AND. The sentence in (3) is only true when both the atomic elements are true. If the sentence were instead *Merkel is German and Hollande is Swiss*, then the whole sentence would be false, even though it is true that Merkel is German. The logic just cares about the truth or falsity of the relationship between the two sentences. However, we can also work out the truth-based meaning of the sentence connectives themselves: the logical analogues of AND, OR and THEN, and we can use them in the system of propositional logic.

A key relationship in this theory is the relationship of entailment. This relationship is similar to logical implication in (5) above (although it is not the same thing); I will not go into the specific differences, but I will show entailment through examples. For example, if Peter smoked a cigarette, then it is entailed that Peter smoked. Or if Peter likes all dogs, then it is entailed that Peter likes your dog Fido.

2.8 Predicate Calculus

To understand how to integrate a modifier with the semantics of a verb, we need to look at the predicate calculus. Remember our problem: we are trying to integrate the modifier with the semantics of a verb. To look at the semantics of a verb, we need the predicate calculus. This is the way of looking at the internal structure of propositions, predicates, arguments and quantifiers.

For example, I have a dog named Jumble. Let's look at the following examples involving Jumble.

(6) Jumble barked.
(7) Jumble chased the ball.
(8) Jumble gave me the ball.

In (6) *barked* is the predicate, and *Jumble* is the argument. In (7) *chased* is the predicate, *Jumble* and *the ball* are the arguments. In (8), *Jumble*, *me*, and *the ball* are the arguments, while *gave* is the predicate. We can treat all of these things as constants, if we want: that is to say we can just give them names which identify the relevant individuals. But not all sentences can be understood by using constants in that way. In (7), we can identify the ball that Jumble chased because the NP is definite, but what if the sentence were *Jumble chased a ball*? Or what about the sentences in (9) and (10), which both involve quantified expressions?

(9) Everyone kicked the ball.
(10) Jumble bit someone.

(9) has a quantified expression because *everyone* means *each person* or *all people* kicked the ball. And *someone* is also a quantified expression: (10) asserts that someone exists who was bit by Jumble but that person is not identified. We will come back to (9) and (10) later.

2.9 Some Basic Issues about Verbs and Arguments

The arguments of the verb are the participants in the states of affairs that the verb denotes. This is a semantic definition. The arguments of the verb are realized as its Subject and its Object and so forth. Now confusingly, because we don't have a terminology commission, people use words in all sorts of different ways: the syntactic relations Subject, Object and so on are also called "arguments" in some traditions. We need to distinguish between semantic arguments and syntactic arguments.

2.10 Verb Meanings as Predicates

Keeping to the semantics, we need a representation for predicates, arguments and quantification. So, for (11), we have the representation in (12).

(11) Jane kissed Peter.
(12) kiss' (j,p)

Kiss' is the meaning of the verb *kissed*. It means that *kiss* is a kind of complex relationship between *p* for 'Peter' and *j* for 'Jane'; it is a kissing relationship. So how will a modifier fit in here? We will come to the modifier in a moment.

2.11 What about Quantifiers?

We need quantifiers as a way of identifying individuals. A sentence such as (13) does not have a meaning unless we can identify which ball.

(13) Jumble chased a ball.

Therefore, we have to assert the existence of the ball. This becomes clear with words like *everyone* and *someone*. *Everyone* means every single person.

Someone means some person exists. We have to have a way of actually identifying what ball we were talking about.

2.11.1 EVERYONE

Therefore, to capture *everyone kicked the ball* we need a way of saying *everyone*. There is a symbol for all things, ∀, which means 'for all'. This is the universal quantifier. In order to get from a sentence to the world, you have to quantify over the objects in the world in order to identify the referent of the particular noun phrase that you are using. We use quantification as a device for going out into the world and identifying a referent for the meaning of that word. We can write a formula that says *for all things x, if x is a person, then x kicked the ball*. That's the way of saying *everyone kicked the ball* and the formula is given in (14a) below; the universal quantifier is usually restricted by the material condition sentence connective which we saw in (5).

2.11.2 SOMEONE

For *someone*, we need a different quantifier. It doesn't mean 'for all', but it means 'there exists'. This is the *existential* quantifier, represented by ∃. ∃x means 'there exists an x'. We therefore have a way of writing the formulas expressing (9) and (10):

(14) a. $\forall x$, Person'$(x) \rightarrow$ Kick'$(x, \text{the-ball})$[3]
       b. $\exists x$, Person'(x), bit'(j,x)

(14a) says *for all things x, if x is a person, then x kicked the ball*. (14b) says *x exists, x is a person, jumble bit x* or more succinctly, 'Jumble bit someone.' One of the differences between the two quantifiers, the universal and the existential quantifier, is that they are analysed using different sentence connectives. The universal quantifier is analysed using the "material implication" connective, which vaguely means something like *if ... then* (although it does not actually map onto the meanings of *if ... then* particularly well) and which is represented with an arrow.

This business with quantification is a round-about way of talking about the meanings of noun phrases; it is important because it is the way of making sure the logic doesn't break when you are out there in the world and you are looking at the relationship between the meaning of a sentence and the meaning of the world. And the point of this discussion is that it is a preamble for getting into

---

3   I am not analysing the structure of *the ball*; I am just treating it as a name.

the question of why Davidson (1967) introduced events into his theoretical ontology and the problem with modifiers.

2.12 The Problem with Modifiers

As I mentioned above, Davidson (1967) pointed out that the standard predicate calculus treated modifiers as though they were arguments. To recapitulate, *Jane kissed Peter at 3 o'clock*, which repeats example (1) above, has to be treated as though KISS has in its lexical entry a time PP, along with the information that it takes a Subject and an Object, if the semantics of KISS is just a predicate.

But verbs can be modified by several modifiers at once. If you take this approach, then you need to have a separate lexical entry for every single possible modifier a verb can have. And this is impossible. Take, for example, *Jane kissed Peter at 3 o'clock, passionately, mindfully, enthusiastically* (etc.). There are also lots of ways of describing kissing: kissing between a husband and a wife, between a boyfriend and a girlfriend, between a parent and a child, etc. Including this large set of possible modification patterns adds up to a large, impossibly complex lexical entry. What is worse, the word order possibilities of modifiers are very flexible. *Jane kissed Peter at 3 o'clock, at 3 o'clock Jane kissed Peter* and *Jane at 3 o'clock kissed Peter* are all acceptable. The only place where a modifier cannot go is between the verb and its Direct Object. As a consequence, with longer sentences, there are many positional possibilities. Do we need a separate lexical entry for each possible modifier and combination of modifiers?

Another problem with modifiers is due to entailment. The entailments of sentences with modifiers generally include the entailments of sentences without them. For instance, *Jane kissed Peter at 3 o'clock*, entails *Jane kissed Peter*. On the other hand, *Jane almost hit the target* entails that *she did not hit the target*. Therefore, all of these complicated relationships have to be put in as well.

Davidson shows if we treat modifiers as arguments, we cannot have formal entailments because the lexical entry for each verb is different. To put the modifiers in the lexical entries requires there to be a profusion of lexical entries: KISS1 (with Subject and Object); KISS2 (with Subject, Object, and preceding time modifier); KISS3 (with Subject, Object and following time modifier); KISS4 (Subject, Object, and following manner modifier), and so on. This kind of theory means that it is not possible to capture the entailment relations across different lexical entries. Davidson had a stroke of genius: he showed that we can treat events as statements of the existence of an event, so that if we translate a sentence like (15) into a logical formula, we get something like (16).

(15) Shem kicked Shaun.
(16) $(\exists x)$ Kick' (Shem, Shaun, x)

(16) says, 'There exists an x, Shem kicked Shaun x'. The x is the event of kicking which has been quantified over—what comes to be known as the "event argument." The formula in (16) asserts the existence of an event of kicking. Essentially Davidson says that there exists an event and he makes the event argument an argument of the meaning of *kick*. (In later work, such as the work of Parsons, e is used as the event variable. That just means the same, as x is just a variable in this system and e is another way of stating this variable, which identifies that it is a variable of the event.)

As Davidson (2001: 119) points out, this approach solves the problem of entailment. Each sentence with a modifier just has the modifier intersectively taking x as its argument; as a result, each modified variant of (15) entails (15). In this way, Davidson gets around the problem of modification, because this variable can interact with other predicates and modifiers. A modifier can take that event variable as one of its own arguments. So, for example *at 3 o'clock* in *Shem kicked Shaun at 3 o'clock* takes the quantified variable x as its argument. Allowing modifiers to use the event variable as an argument solves the problem of formal entailment between different verbs. It also keeps the lexical entry of KICK simple: there is just one entry, which means that the interaction of the modifiers works in a straightforward way and the lexicon is not made over large.

2.13 *Locating Davidson in a Semantic Tradition*

As I have said, Davidson is concerned with treating sentences as descriptions of fragments of the world, which means you must be able to decide whether they are true or false. A lot of Davidson's essays talk about the existence of events and how you individuate them. (But Davidson is also concerned with causation and how events bring about other events.) There is a long tradition drawing on Davidsonian Semantics. Parsons develops Davidson's theory, while other formal semantics develop its insights. Gillian Ramchand has worked in this tradition and embedded it in Chomskyan Generative Syntax. But cognitive/conceptual semantics has also drawn on these insights, therefore it is worth introducing them. The key insight is that events can be quantified over and individuated.

2.14 *From Logic to Linguistic Semantics*

We can lay out some of the alternatives in broad terms here. Jackendoff is interested in thinking about semantics from an intramental point of view; that is, what happens in the mind. He explains verb meanings in a larger theory of language in the mind, which he develops to include Talmy's force dynamics in his theory of argument linking in Jackendoff (1990). He also draws extensively on Gruber's (1965) MIT PhD thesis.

Talmy's work is broadly typological; he starts out with descriptive linguistics and then induces generalizations from the language data. Talmy describes motion as basic to verb meaning, a premise Jackendoff also adopts. Talmy (1985a), introducing the satellite-framed and verb-framed distinction, presents a typological theory of event structure. In a different theory, Levin and Rappaport Hovav (2005) are interested in English verbs and their behavior, and the relationship between English verb classes and transitivity alternations. This tradition involves the very close analysis of verbs and verb classes. One of Levin and Rappaport Hovav's major concerns is also argument linking.

Peter Gärdenfors, a cognitive linguist working in Sweden, who has also published two books with the MIT Press which are easy to read and interesting (Gärdenfors 2000, 2014), says there are two different ways of doing semantics in general. One way of doing semantics is from a very high level. In this approach, you are like a bird looking down at the ground, and interested in all sorts of different kinds of meanings: social meaning, the meanings of individual words, the meanings of sentences, how people express politeness, etc. In the other approach, you are like a dung beetle, interested in the tiny fragments of meaning. You explore how they get buried in the ground, and pull them out. Gärdenfors believes that the bird has to work with the dung beetle, and meet in the middle in order to come up with a comprehensive description of how language works. He develops a "Geometry of Meaning" which "is organized in abstract spatial structures that are expressed in terms of *dimensions, distances, regions* and other geometric notions." (Gärdenfors 2014: 21) The idea of underlying spatial structures is related to Talmy's, Gruber's and Jackendoff's theorizing which works with the idea that the conceptual system that underlines how language works is to do with motion; the basic human idea that underlines verb meanings is motion related.

This is to do with embodiment; for cognitive linguists, motion underscores verb meanings, because of embodied experience. Therefore, a lot of verb meanings are metaphorically related back to motion. Jackendoff describes this in terms of the verb *go* and the difference between *I went to the shops* and *the traffic light went from green to red*. However, Gisborne (2010) found that the motion elements of meaning in perception verbs were attenuated. Perception is highly embodied, and arguably where metaphor starts whereas motion is perceived, so it is arguably a second-order property.

Croft is interested in many things, especially aspectual structure and causal structure in terms of a functional linguistic theory that is typologically plausible. For Croft, the main starting point is the Speech Act function of a sentence: what is the speaker trying to do with language when they say something? His approach is very top down in terms of the organization of language. This approach follows from Croft's interest in typology, and his desire to organize a theory in terms of viable objects of cross-linguistic comparison. In a different variant of Construction Grammar, Goldberg (1995, 2006) understands events in terms of frames related to constructions. Her approach is not grounded in the Speech Act Functions that drive Croft's theorizing.

This linguistic semantic tradition is the broad framework I work with.

2.15   What We Have Learned So Far

Davidson gets us to think about events as individuals, causal relationships between events, and what makes a plausible lexical entry. These are all key, but they are only part of verb meaning. We also need to think about other issues, especially polysemy, because verbs can be highly polysemous. We can take CLIMB for example. CLIMB is the subject of a paper by Jackendoff (1985), which will come up in later lectures. The basic idea of CLIMB is some kind of clambering or upward motion. But you can say *the plane climbed to 20,000 feet*, with no clambering or *the cat climbed down the tree* with no upward motion.

We also need to talk about structure in event semantics and verb meaning. What kinds of structure do we find? Are they all causal relationships? Are there different kinds of causal relationship? In later lectures, I shall argue that there are different kinds of causation, as well as a prototype.

Another topic that has to be addressed is to do with the nature of the *Aktionsarten*. (*Aktionsart* is a German word meaning 'action type'.) Some verbs denote states. For example, *has* in *Thomas has brown eyes* is a state: he was born with brown eyes, he has brown eyes now, and will die with brown eyes. *Peter is walking to the window* is not a state; it's dynamic, because it involves action and is a temporary property of Peter. We distinguish between states and dynamic situations. Dynamic situations can have different time profiles as well. Some can be punctual. If I click my fingers, then that's punctual and instantaneous. We can construe other dynamic events as being punctual changes of events. Take *dying* for example. If somebody dies, it can take a very long time, because he can be terribly ill for a long time. But up until the moment when their heart stops beating, they are still alive. They are only dead when their heart actually stops: *dying* is an instantaneous change of state. All of these different kinds of verb interact with other parts of the temporal system of the language. For example, I can say *Thomas has blue eyes*, but not **Thomas is having blue eyes*; I can say *Peter is walking to the window*, but not **Peter walks to the window* (unless I want to describe a habit of Peter's, or as part of a stage direction).

Other topics we need to think about include the temporal structure of verbs; argument linking—the relationship between the participants of events and the Subject, Object, etc. of verbs; and the relationship of "thematic roles" to events. What is an Agent, a Patient, or a Theme? How are they related to events?

2.16 What Is Lexical Semantics?

These topics are all a subpart of a larger field, Lexical Semantics, which is concerned with word meaning—the semantic structure of the lexicon or how meanings within the lexicon relate to each other. Lexical semantics can be about aspects of how words combine, properties such as how verbs select their Subjects and their Objects. For example, you cannot eat *concrete*. You can only eat *food*. But lexical semantics is not about things like reference and quantification and scope, although these can be relevant to lexical-semantic analysis.

2.17 Word Meaning and Sentence Meaning

Davidson's theory of events is a way of understanding how words behave in sentences: it is a theory of sentence meaning. But when we look at verbs, we're concerned with a range of topics, not just how they interact with modifiers, including polysemy, structure in meaning, argument realization, and cross-linguistic variation.

2.18 Polysemy

Polysemy is pervasive, and it interacts with other aspects of event behaviour, such as argument linking. For example, there are two different verbs MAKE, shown here in (17) and (18). These two verbs MAKE have different meanings.

(17) Jane made Peter a cake.
(18) Jane made Peter a hero.

In (17) there is a verb of creation: *Jane* created the cake for *Peter*. The example involves a ditransitive construction with a Beneficiary, *Peter*. But in (18), there is a very different structure: it is not a ditransitive verb. The string *Peter a hero* is a kind of predication structure which involves a verb of creation—in the past it is what has been called a "small clause". In construction grammar, the analysis might be that the different meanings come out in the construction, but the verb itself does not have different meanings. In this theory, it is the interaction with different constructions that gives rise to the different meanings. However, I will argue that MAKE does actually have two different meanings in those two different patterns and that constructions are not the way in which we are going to handle polysemy relations like this.

2.19 What Is Polysemy vs. Ambiguity, Vagueness, Homonymy?

If we are going to talk about polysemy, then we need to compare it with ambiguity, vagueness and homonymy, all of which can be difficult things to work out (see the introduction and chapter by Cruse in Ravin and Leacock 2000). We have to be aware that the boundaries between them cannot be precise, because pragmatics can drive changes in words' meaning.

If you are interested in language change, one of the things you realize is how very unstable meaning is because when we speak to each other, we invite all sorts of inferences. We do not just use words to mean exactly what they mean. We also use words to try to bring about ideas in people's minds in various ways and to induce new and exciting ways of thinking about what was said. Because of this property, meaning is not particularly stable. Here is an example. This bone around the bottom of my mouth is called the jaw. The bit of muscle and fat on the side of my face is called the cheek. But historically in English, for example, if I were living at the time of Shakespeare, my cheek was called my jaw and my jaw was called my cheek. And the etymon of *silly* in Chaucer meant 'lucky'. There is one moment in one of Chaucer's tales, where he is talking about one of his characters and he says "Oh, silly Damian" which means 'lucky Damian'. Words change their meanings because of how speakers invite inferences and how hearers interpret those inferences.

Part of the job of the semanticist is in working out whether the differences between *jaw* and *cheek* are vague differences, because they are both regions of the face, or whether there is another explanation. Likewise, what pragmatic changes have given rise to the change in meaning in *silly*?

2.20 What Are the Main Research Issues in Polysemy?

One main issue in polysemy is how to diagnose it. In the case of verbs, one way of doing this is to look for regularities between word meaning and argument realization. For example, MELT can either mean 'cause to melt' as in (19), or 'go through the melting process' as in (20).

(19) They melted the iron.
(20) The iron melted.

A verb that means has the meaning structure of the example in (19) has a Subject and an Object, a verb that has the meaning structure of (20) only has a Subject. We can use this property to probe into verb meaning. This approach obliges us to look at the relationship between different lexemes and invites us to look for structure in word meaning. Structure in meaning relates to argument realization.

2.21 *Structure in Meaning*

There is evidence for structure in verb meaning. For example, KILL means 'cause to die'. HIT has a meaning which combines 'moving' and 'touching'. If I *hit something*, I have to move my hand and then I have to touch it. Let me hit the microphone—to hit the microphone, I have to touch it; if I don't touch it, you can't hear me hit it. So 'hitting' involves 'moving' and 'touching'. We can actually use the syntactic behavior of verbs as evidence for the kind of structure HIT has, which involves 'moving' and 'touching', just as we can use our real-world understanding to help us think about verb meaning.

The claim, then, is that both KILL and HIT have complex structures in their meaning even though there isn't an intransitive verb KILL and despite the fact that HIT also lacks an intransitive. It's the job of the analyst of event structure to work out what possible structures there are and what the limits on event structure might be.

2.22 *Argument Linking/Realization*

Another topic is the mapping between syntax and semantics: how meaning maps onto the syntax of grammatical relations such as Subject, Object and Indirect Object. We can talk about (17) and (18) in these terms. In (17) *Peter* is the Indirect Object and *a cake* is the Direct Object. But in (18), *Peter* is the Direct Object and *the hero* is the predicative complement. These syntactic differences are related to semantic differences, which is part of the information we can use to understand how verb meaning works.

We also need to think about how this information is represented in the mind. One answer is in "constructions". Goldberg (1995) presents a declarative approach to argument realization, with constructions as her key theoretical tool. (A declarative approach is just an approach where you state exactly what you find and there are no transformations and no technical wizardry.) One of Goldberg's great insights is that knowledge of language is just part of knowledge and that we have a huge storage of different bits of linguistic information. We just use bits of the knowledge and put them together in ways where they fit properly to come up with grammatical sentences of any language.

I agree with that, but I don't agree that constructions are exactly the right way of modeling our grammatical knowledge. My approach is going to make use of a strict and simple network structure. I'm going to talk about a different approach, Word Grammar, that doesn't need constructions to account for (17) and (18). Word Grammar treats language as part of a larger cognitive network and keeps to the idea of a network architecture strictly, so the nodes of the network are literally just nodes, not structures.

2.23 Typology

We need to talk about cross-linguistic variation when dealing with verb meaning. Talmy famously introduced the verb-framed vs. the satellite-framed distinction. English is a satellite-framed language, exemplified in (21). The notions "satellite-framed" and "verb-framed" relate to whether the verb encodes direction or not. In satellite-framed languages, direction is not encoded in verb meanings whereas in verb-framed languages it is. In (21) *floated* is a manner of motion verb, but it does not encode directionality.

(21) *The bottle floated into the cave.*

Catalan, by contrast, is a verb-framed language: direction is encoded in the meaning of the verb.

(22) *La botella entrà a la cova flotant* (Acedo-Matellán and Mateu 2013)

This is because the verb *entrà* encodes motion and direction (with manner being separately encoded by *flotant*). (22) literally means 'the bottle entered the cave floating'.[4] Coming up in later lectures, I'm going to claim that from a typological perspective the verb-framed vs. satellite-framed distinction is too simple. English has both ways of representing both types of event: the verb ENTER has the same semantic structure as *entrà* above. A similar mixed pattern can be found in some Romance languages too. Although Italian is usually classed among the verb-framed languages, there are verb-particle patterns such as PORTARE VIA 'to carry away' and SALTARE FUORI 'to jump out' which look like manner of motion verbs with directional satellites (Iacobini and Masini 2006).

Languages also change typologically. Latin was a mixed language with many more satellite-framed verbs than modern Spanish, French and Catalan, but the latter languages, the descendants of Latin, are verb-framed and the verb-particle patterns of Italian just mentioned appear to be a modern development. Slobin (2004) argues that Chinese is an equipollent language, but it seems to me that really there is a mixed typology, because there are verbs of both kinds,

---

4 I find the verb-framed vs. satellite-framed distinction hard to keep clear. There are three semantic elements—motion, direction, and manner—so it is hard to see why a language which puts motion and direction in verb meaning, leaving manner to be expressed by a participle should be called "verb-framed" and why a language which puts motion and manner in the verb, leaving direction for a PP, should be called "satellite-framed".

and the language might well be in the middle of moving from one type to the other. I am not sure this is a stable system. Croft (2012) says this distinction is not really a typological property; it's more a property about meaning structure within verbs. To some extent I agree with that, but there are other important typological facts to keep in mind: verb-framed languages, for example, do not have structures like resultatives.

2.24   *The Relationship of Thematic Roles to Events*

Now I want to mention the relationship of thematic roles to events. Do thematic roles (also known as semantic roles) define different types of event? Or do we conceptualize them in terms of events? The Thematic Roles Hypothesis of Gruber and Jackendoff (Gruber 1965; Jackendoff 1972, 1983, 1990) understood events in terms of (basic) motion events. For example, the semantic role Theme is the participant that travels along a path. On the other hand, the Force Dynamic relations, Antagonist and Agonist make up a dyad which defines causal relationships. In the prototypical version of this dyad, the Antagonist acts on the Agonist, as a result of which the Agonist undergoes a change of state.

Therefore, there are different kinds of thematic roles. We need to think about what use we can put those roles to, and what they do for us in terms of how we understand events, verb meaning, argument realization and polysemy. I am going to claim that force dynamics is relevant to the causal prototype, but there is a lot of variation with the causal prototype. I am also going to claim that thematic roles are a way of understanding metaphor in verbs, but they do not do very much for us in terms of argument realization. That is to say, we can understand meaning extension and polysemy through semantic roles, but they do not help with understanding how meanings of verbs map onto Subject, Object, Indirect Object, and so forth.

2.25   *Key Assumptions*

Let us assume that in dealing with event semantics and event structures we are engaged with a conceptual or cognitive semantics. It is a lexical semantics, because it is about word meaning. There is encyclopedic information in the picture, because there is not any encapsulation in the type of the network Word Grammar uses. Like Goldberg and the other cognitive linguists, knowledge of language is just knowledge and it is not encapsulated; instead it interacts with the rest of knowledge. Most event semanticists are concerned with structure in verb meaning, but perhaps some parts, such as manner meanings would in other traditions be treated as encyclopedic meaning.

3 Introducing Word Grammar

Word Grammar (WG) was first reported in a book in 1984, called *Word Grammar*, by Richard Hudson who worked for all of his professional life at University College London. There have been several book publications since. The most recent books were published in 2010, one by Hudson and one by me. The main claim of the theory is the *Network Postulate* which claims that language is part of a cognitive network, and is not encapsulated. All human knowledge is also nothing else but a network.

3.1 The Network Postulate

The Network Postulate is a claim that human knowledge is a network and is nothing but a network, and that language belongs together with the rest of cognition. The networks of WG are a type of knowledge-representation system. The arcs of the network have the properties of attributes and their values, and the network is also classified by default inheritance and multiple inheritance. Therefore, we work with a network which is the same as the semantic networks in the literature. Hudson thinks that the WG network is scale-free, but nobody has actually done the maths so I cannot demonstrate that claim.

3.2 Language as a Network

In order to analyse language as a network, we need a toolkit. The toolkit requires some primitives to constrain our description of language, and it needs some principles of organization in order to constrain how the model works, and how we describe linguistic structures.

3.3 Levels of Grammar

We might decide that as long as there is evidence for the different levels of grammar, then those levels of grammar exist. One theoretical question, for example, which linguists have been exercised about for a long time, is whether morphology is independent. Is morphology part of syntax, or part of phonology? Can it be divided so that some of morphology is in the syntax, with the rest in phonology? Or do we actually need an independent level of morphology within the grammar? Our working assumption in WG is that if we see linguistic evidence for something, then we assume that thing exists as part of how human beings organize linguistic knowledge in their minds.

But one theoretical assumption has to be that we have the same minds. We have perceptual information coming in which is processed in the same ways. But we all have different experiences, so we do not expect all languages to have the same categories—and of course we see that the categories of natural language can differ from language to language. We would argue then that there is no Universal Grammar. As a point of support, we can look at a simple difference between English and Chinese. Chinese does not have tense, while English has a past/present distinction. It is not advantageous to write a grammar that forces Chinese to look like English or the other way around. I also think that Chinese probably does not have Subjects in the same way that English has. Chinese is a topic-oriented language, so we might not want to say that it has the same grammatical functions as English.

What we do is we try to work out the knowledge of the language a native speaker has, just factoring in what makes sense in terms of the particular evidence. In WG, we recognize the following levels of grammar: semantics, syntax, morphology and phonology. Semantics is complicated, because in a conceptual theory, it does not just come down to truth conditional meaning, but also involves encyclopedic information in the lexical entries of words. I would be inclined to put semantics and pragmatics together, as I am not sure what boundaries might be between semantics and pragmatics—which is a particular theoretical position.

The next claim is that the grammar of a language is a lexico-grammar: there is no ontological distinction between the lexicon and the grammar. All of the information is stored declaratively in the knowledge representation network. There are no rules in WG. WG is a constraint-based theory, so it has constraints that restrict a sentence's properties, but does not generate sentences by rule. But we can write formal descriptions so it is a formal theory and WG is therefore a formal and cognitive theory. It is a generative theory in the sense that constraint-based theories are generative, but it is not generative in the narrower sense which associates the word "generative" with Chomsky's school of linguistic theory.

3.4   *Evidence for Levels of Grammar*

Evidence for levels of grammar includes mismatch, arguments from classification, and arguments for the principled combinations of elements. Let us discuss mismatch.

We can observe all sorts of mismatches between linguistic levels. For example, in French, VILLAGE 'village' is a masculine noun and requires the masculine determiner *le*. If you want to say (*go*) *to the village* you must say, *au village*. *Au* 'to the' is one word in its morphological realization, but it combines *à* 'to' and *le* 'the'. You must have *au* instead of **à le*, which is ungrammatical. However, with the feminine determiner *la*, *à la* is the correct form. The situation with *au* involves a kind of mismatch. The research decisions about what to include and allow in the theory are led by principles and what we observe. There are a range of studies on syntax-morphology mismatches and syntax-semantics mismatches, but there has not been much work in Word Grammar on discourse or pragmatics. In its syntax, Word Grammar is a lexicalist dependency theory, and this brings us to the main features of the theory.

3.5 The Main Features of WG

WG's main features include default inheritance, sublexemes, dependency structure, and network structure. Default inheritance is a logic of classification which allows exceptions. It enables us to say that (in the general case) *birds fly* and to capture the fact that penguins are birds, even though they do not fly. We can state this exception. Default Inheritance also allows us to say *students are typically studying for an undergraduate degree*, because most students in the university are studying for undergraduate degrees. But a part-time PhD student, who is also a teacher in the university, is still a student. That is, default inheritance permits defaults and exceptions and allows us to talk about prototypes. Default inheritance classifies words and lexemes, and it also classifies the relations in the network.

In our theoretical toolkit, as well as lexemes, WG also has sublexemes, which allow us to show partial differences within a lexeme, and it has dependency structure which is one part of the network structure that allows us to relate words directly to each other. Finally, the network architecture accommodates spreading activation which is part of the explanation of linguistic behaviour. Spreading activation is just the way in which information flows through the brain in a connectionist theory, and we try to capture that in our symbolic theory.

3.6 How to Draw a Network: the Primitives

Before I come to talk about each of these features, I want to discuss how to draw a network, come back to the primitives, and discuss how WG compares with the formal theory of events discussed earlier. WG has a number of primitives: *Isa, argument* and *value, identity*, and *quantity*. Isa, 'an instance of', is the primitive of default inheritance. Arguments and value are used to define relational concepts. Identity is used to say that a given concept is identical with another.

3.7   How to Draw a Network: Isa

Some literature on how Isa works in a diagram is presented below. But here I want to use it conceptually. For example, my name is Nik. In WG we can have the following representation:

(23)   *Nik Isa man*

In (23) '*man*' is not a predicate. It's just a node in the network. It just means that I inherit all of the properties inherited from being a man. Those properties will have a prototype structure. For example, a man has to be of a certain age. Legally, in my culture, that age is over 18. But in my culture, you are probably not really a man until you are older than 18 and economically independent, and show certain types of adult behaviours, although legally you only have to be 18. Adulthood is therefore a complex prototype.

In the predicate calculus representation in (24), there is no scope for a prototype structure: the category has fixed boundaries.

(24)   Man' (n)

In this theory, there is a simple either/or kind of relationship: you are either in the category, or not.

3.8   How to Draw a Network: Argument and Value

Argument and value are ways of drawing associative links in a network. My wife is called Caro. I am married to Caro and Caro is Nik's wife. We have the relationship in (25).

(25)   Nik –wife→ Caro

There is a node, Nik, and we can draw an arrow to a node, Caro, and label the arrow —*wife*→. Then Nik is the argument of x's wife and Caro is the value of x's wife. Arguments and value are ways of understanding the relational concept *wife* or *wife of*.

3.9   Default Inheritance

Default inheritance is a system of classification. It looks like hyponymy, but it is not only word meanings that are classified. We can start off just drawing a hyponymy chain, like Figure 1. In Word Grammar diagrams, the inheritance relationship is shown as upside-down triangle which goes from the classifier to the classified concept.

EVENT SEMANTICS: A NETWORK MODEL OF LANGUAGE STRUCTURE   23

FIGURE 1   Hyponymy chain for 'dog'   FIGURE 2   Hyponymy chain for 'running'

A hyponymy chain is just a small default inheritance hierarchy. In this hyponymy chain, 'dog' Isa 'mammal' and 'mammal' Isa 'animal'. We can make it a lot more complicated if we want to. As a dog is a member of the class canidae and canidae is the name of a type of canine animal including dogs, foxes and wolves, so we could add 'canidae' to Figure 1. The category 'mammal' has different subtypes as well. We can decide whether some animals are mammals or not. You may wonder whether kangaroos or some strange egg-laying animals in Australia, like the duckbilled platypus, are mammals. Most mammals have a body temperature higher than 30 degrees Celsius, yet duckbill platypuses have a body temperature below 20 degrees C and they lay eggs. Are they mammals? They are still warm-blooded. We might therefore say that 'mammal' is a kind of prototype category as well. You might even say that 'animal' is a prototype category.

In Figure 2, I present a classification of verb meanings. One key thing to note is that in Word Grammar both verbs' meaning and nouns' meanings are nodes in the network. They are not predicates.

'Running' is a kind of 'moving' and 'moving' is a kind of 'doing'. Again, we can make that a lot more complicated. We can talk about 'running' as being a kind of 'moving' but restricted to animate Agents. (People talk about trains running, but that is a metaphorical use of the word RUN.)

3.10   *Multiple Inheritance*

Now we can look at multiple inheritance. A pet dog inherits from the category 'mammal'. It also inherits from 'pet' because as well as belonging in the category of mammals he also belongs in the category of family members, and PET is the word for non-human animals that humans keep as additional family members. This is represented in Figure 3.

Because pets are family members but not all domesticated animals are, we can see that pets are not the only kind of domestic animal. If you were a farmer, then you might have a cow, or a pig. But you do not invite the pig into your

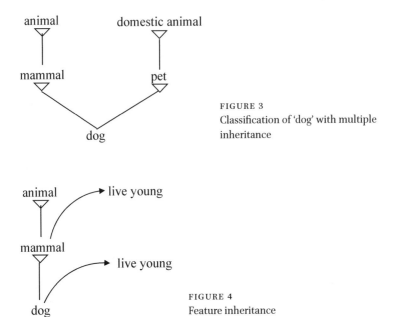

FIGURE 3
Classification of 'dog' with multiple inheritance

FIGURE 4
Feature inheritance

house, take it for a walk, talk to it, or tickle its tummy, so a domesticated pig experiences a different kind of domestication from a pet dog.

3.11 Inheriting Attributes

Hyponymy chains are one kind of inheritance hierarchy. In an inheritance hierarchy, the lower nodes inherit features from the higher nodes. One of the properties of a mammal is that they give birth to live young, so 'dog' inherits the feature 'bears live young' from 'mammal' as well. This is captured in Figure 4.

As before, the diagram shows the inheritance relationship with an upside-down triangle which goes from the classifier to the classified concept. If you like, Figure 4 says that we take properties of the classifier and we push them out to the classified concept.

3.12 Inheritance beyond Hyponymy

But inheritance is not just a hyponymy relationship. Other things can be put into an inheritance relationship as well. For example, in the lexicon, lexemes belong in hierarchies. Figure 5 shows RUN, WATER and DOG in an inheritance hierarchy. In these hierarchies, lexemes are written with capital letters.

At the top of the classification, there is the category 'lexeme' which is divided into nouns and verbs. RUN is classified as a verb. The category 'noun'

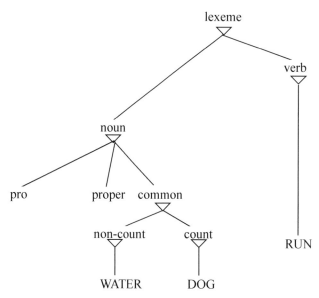

FIGURE 5   RUN, WATER and DOG in an inheritance hierarchy

is divided into 'pronoun', 'proper noun' and 'common noun', while 'common noun' is divided into 'non-count' and 'count' common nouns. WATER is classified as a non-count common noun, while DOG is a count noun.

3.13 *Words and Meaning*

Figure 5 is a classification system which shows the classification of lexemes, not word meanings. As we shall see, words are not the same thing as their meanings, which is evidence that syntax is not semantics. I said that one of the ways in which we identify differences between different levels in the grammar was by mismatch. This is an instance. The meaning 'dog' is an instance of the meaning 'mammal', but the lexeme DOG is not an instance of the lexeme MAMMAL. This is shown in Figure 6, taken from Gisborne (2010).

Both DOG and MAMMAL are instances of the category 'count noun' and the meaning of the word DOG is an instance of the meaning of the word MAMMAL.

Figure 6 makes assertions such as "the concept 'dog' Isa 'mammal'," "the lexeme DOG is a count noun" and "the lexeme MAMMAL is a count noun." Therefore, you can see that lexemes inherit in the word hierarchy and the meanings inherit in the meaning hierarchy. There is a mismatch represented here: the concept 'dog', the meaning of the lexeme DOG, inherits 'bears live young', but the lexeme DOG does not: it inherits from the category 'count noun' because lexemes inherit in the word hierarchy and meanings inherit in the

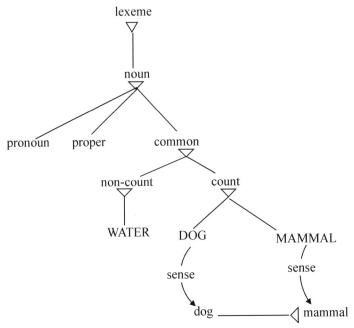

FIGURE 6   DOG, MAMMAL, 'dog' and 'mammal' in an inheritance hierarchy

meaning hierarchy. (I could also show the proposition "'dog' Isa 'pet,'" but that would make the picture too complicated.)

In sum, there are two kinds of relation: the inheritance relation, Isa, and the association relation represented by an arrow. There are also two different structures: an inheritance structure for meanings and an inheritance structure for lexemes. That is, words and meanings inhabit different systems of categorization. Furthermore, other subsystems of language such as morphology, have their own category structures.

3.14   *Default Inheritance Allows Exceptions*

Default inheritance allows exceptions, so instances can have exceptional properties. For example, *tall* overrides the default height. A tall man has greater height than usual. Typically, a dependent enriches the head's sense and can override default properties. Also, any property can be overridden. For example, *fake diamonds* look just like diamonds but are not diamonds; that is, the word *fake* overrides the categorization of *diamond*. The meaning of the word *fake* says, "I am overriding the classification of the word that *fake* is a dependent of." Overriding is just a property of language, independent of the theory.

There is a famous problem for multiple inheritance called the Nixon Diamond because of the example of feature conflicts that the famous, corrupt

American president, Richard Nixon lived with. Richard Nixon was, among other things, a member of a Christian subgroup called the Quakers. Quakers are very peaceful and cooperative. They are opposed to social hierarchies and have a very strong social ideology. However, Nixon was also a Republican American and Republican Americans don't share Quaker ideologies, as they are very individualistic. Quakers, by contrast, believe very strongly in socialism. Therefore, Nixon had a feature conflict: he was both a Republican and a Quaker. He had to decide, if you like, which features he would inherit: Republican or Quaker features? He chose Republican features. This just seems to be how things work for us: we just override things we do not like.

3.15   *Theoretical Point*

You might have heard of unification grammars. Early Construction Grammar was a type of Unification Grammar. In unification grammars, words go together like the pieces of a jigsaw puzzle. You build up a sentence chunk by chunk, until you have a grammatical sentence. But unification gets blocked by conflict. In WG, we allow both multiple inheritance and conflicts.

Default inheritance is widely accepted in artificial intelligence models of cognition. It goes back to the work in 1970s by Roger Schank and others. With WG's classified network, we can explain prototype effects found by psychologists as well.

3.16   *Type and "Token"*

There is a formal property of default inheritance systems called "non-monotonicity". If it is possible to override features, the system is non-monotonic, because it allows what you know to change as you build up structure. This is a problem, because it could arguably allow infinite searching in conceptual structure so we need a strategy for resolving possible conflicts in information. One of the things we know about human cognition is that we have limited working memory resources. Because of that, we have limited abilities to do complex calculations. Therefore, we cannot assume that in human classification we run through the total possible search space every time we classify a concept. Word Grammar's solution is that inheritance works *bottom-up* (Hudson 2007: 26). Consider the following example:

(26)   A: Can a *bird* fly?
B: Yes.
A: What if *it*'s a *penguin*?

Bird is a type, *it* is a token, and *penguin* is a type. *It* then inherits from *a penguin*, and it inherits *does not fly*, and then searching stops. You don't carry on searching on the type, because you know that penguins do not fly even though they are birds.

The idea is that, cognitively, inheritance works with a search mechanism: Search and Copy. When a node is encountered, it is classified. The inheritance search is upwards. And no value is inherited for relations that already have values. That is, once a feature is satisfied, searching stops. Humans do not override in reverse, as it were, and we do not reinstate defaults.

3.17 *Intramental Tokens*
In an intramental theory, tokens can include utterances of words. For example,

(27) *The₁* dog sat on *the₂* mat and annoyed *the₃* cat

The example has three tokens for *the*. They all instantiate the same type THE. But you know there are other things that we might identify as being different. One common property among young people in Britain is that the phonemes represented by *th*, [ð] and [θ], can be realized as [v] or [f]. This is called *th*-fronting. Somebody who has that kind of accent might pronounce *bother* as [bɒvə] and *think* as [fɪŋk]. The realizations [v] and [f] not only have different phonetic properties from the realizations [ð] and [θ], but also different intramental references: they signal different social backgrounds. Voiced *th*-fronting is rare syllable initially, but it is found in varieties of London English Tollfree (1999). In such a variety, *the₂* might be pronounced [və] with the other two instances of *the* pronounced [ðə]. We can capture this property of *th*-fronting, by distinguishing between types and tokens: the type has one default pronunciation, but some tokens instantiate another non-default pronunciation.

One of the things about a mental network in any kind of theory is that speakers and hearers are creating nodes all the time. Our minds are constantly working, through spreading activation and classification. We create nodes in our networks and classify them, but as your memory moves on they die. Some of those nodes become consolidated and they pass into permanent memory, but others do not, which we have to tolerate. We have temporary types which are created on the wing. But because tokens are all intramental, the distinction between type and token can be quite hard to see. I think, therefore, that a token is a concept whose features are all filled out in the particular utterance context.

3.18 Sublexemes

Sublexemes are a way of representing information which shows partial variation in a lexical entry. They allow us to capture polysemy and to state relationships between different senses of the same word and other linguistic properties.

3.18.1 THINK

Take the verb THINK for example. It has a stative and a dynamic use and they have different complements. Here are two examples:

(28) *I think that the square root of 9 is 3.*
(29) *I'm thinking of going to Sicily for my holiday.*

In (28) THINK has a *that* clause as its complement and is stative. But in (29) THINK takes a PP as its complementary prepositional phrase and is dynamic. Both *think* and *thinking* Isa THINK, but if our theory has sublexemes, this gives us a way of relating the syntactic differences to the different meanings and enables us to handle some of the variability that constructions and the relationships between constructions allow Goldberg to handle in her 1995 theory.

OPEN also shows similar properties. Here is a complicated conceptual representation for OPEN, taken from Gisborne (2010) in Figure 7.

Lexemes exist in a conceptual taxonomy, so we can say OPEN Isa verb Isa word. As each word token Isa some lexeme, "sub-lexeme Isa lexeme" is permitted. It then follows that we can say, in Figure 7 OPEN/tr (transitive OPEN) Isa OPEN/intr (intransitive OPEN) Isa verb. Figure 7 shows a complex event structure representation, which also shows semantic relationships of the adjective OPEN. The sense of OPEN/tr is a kind of 'causing' and the sense of OPEN/intr is a kind of becoming: it is becoming in the state of being 'open'.

Figure 7 also has the semantic relationships, Er and Ee, which will be explained later. The point of Figure 7 is that the intransitive and transitive verbs are two sublexemes which show the relevant syntactic and semantic information as well as the shared morphological information. OPEN/intr only has a Subject but OPEN/tr has a Subject and an Object. They tie that semantic and syntactic information to bits of syntactic and semantic information at the dot in the center of Figure 7. That is, the sublexeme is a way of tying syntactic information to semantic information. I have now illustrated this point with what I said about THINK, but also with this diagram for OPEN.

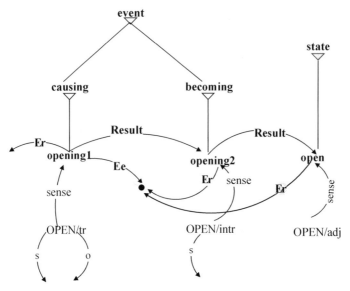

FIGURE 7   Conceptual representation for OPEN

3.19   *Linking Syntax and Semantics*

Figure 7 shows how a verb's semantic representation might work. And we might ask ourselves how argument linking should be done. Sublexemes are part of the argument linking story, but they are not the whole story. One of the claims that I want to make is that dependencies are better than phrase structure at argument linking. The reason is that dependencies can have their own meanings, which allows us to handle the relationship between syntax and semantics without having to use phrasal constructions.

3.20   *Dependencies Are Packages of Information*

Dependencies are packages of information and are not just links between word tokens. They also include positional information and semantic information. For example, Subjects come before the verb and Objects come after the verb. The Subject dependency, for example, is associated with Agent semantics. Each dependency is like an argument-linking construction in its own right. For example, consider Figure 8:

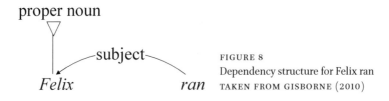

FIGURE 8
Dependency structure for Felix ran
TAKEN FROM GISBORNE (2010)

EVENT SEMANTICS: A NETWORK MODEL OF LANGUAGE STRUCTURE

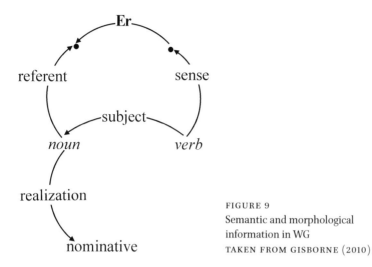

FIGURE 9
Semantic and morphological information in WG
TAKEN FROM GISBORNE (2010)

The Subject relation links *ran* to *Felix*. *Felix* is the subject of *ran*. Figure 8 shows positional information: *Felix* comes before *ran*. But there aren't any phrases at all in this theory; nor are there part-whole relationships. Should there be other information? The answer is yes: there should be semantic information and morphological information, for languages which have this kind of morphology, like Latin or Russian.

3.21 *A Linking Rule for Subjects*

This can be further illustrated in Figure 9, which adds Nominative information to the Subject relation.

Figure 9 shows a verb that has a subject. And the sense of the verb then links its Er argument, i.e. the Agent, to the referent of the noun. This is a WG argument linking construction for subjects. It includes syntactic, semantic and morphological information without needing larger conceptual constructions.

3.22 *Network Structure*

Dependencies are classified in inheritance hierarchies, too, just like meanings and lexemes. The WG representations bring permanent information and temporary information together. As I have said before, there is no lexicon-grammar divide: the system is all related through associative links and inheritance.

3.23 *Dependency and Inheritance Information Combined*

Figure 10 is the representation for *Felix ran*, with both dependency information and dependency information in place.

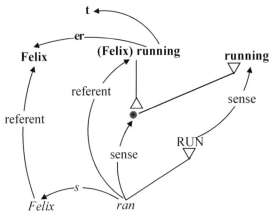
FIGURE 10 Network structure for Felix ran
TAKEN FROM GISBORNE (2010)

In Figure 10, the basic sentence is at the bottom, *Felix* is the subject of *ran*, and the sense of *ran* Isa 'running'. 'Running' is the sense of the lexeme RUN and the sense of the word *ran* inherits from the sense of the lexeme (in parallel with how the word Isa the lexeme). This then relates *ran* to RUN, and the sense of *ran* to the sense of RUN. There is another link: the Er relation which links 'running' to the referent of the noun, *Felix*: 'Felix'. The node 'running' also has a time node attached to it because events take place at times. The representation then puts together information from the lexicon into the syntax, into the semantics, and even to the semantics of reference, and adds a temporal index. The diagram looks complicated, but it is only as complex as language is, and no more. We can add in morphological information as well. If the sentence were in Latin, then the fact that *Felix* is in the nominative case would mean that it can be used as a Subject, but not as an Object.[5] I will present representations that show the morphology for the verb in the next lecture.

3.24 *Spreading Activation*

Hudson (2010: 74) asks you to imagine you have a concept 'cat': how do you retrieve this concept when you need it? How do you use it for recognizing some observed exemplar as a cat? "When a concept's current activation level reaches a certain threshold, the concept 'fires' [… and] activation spreads [… to] its neighboring nodes." Therefore, Hudson argues that we experience a certain amount of activation in the brain which corresponds to a certain amount of activation in the symbolic network that we are modeling here.

---

5 The Latin adjective FELIX 'happy, lucky' was occasionally used as a name by the Romans.

Spreading activation allows us to model this flow of information through a network, and to pay attention to other factors like context.

Context can direct flow through a network because context activates certain kind of nodes. Take [kæts] for example. This pronunciation can mean two different things: the plural of the lexeme CAT in use, or the name of somebody called Dr. Katz. Katz is a Polish name, and there is a linguist called Dovid Katz, the expert on Yiddish. Context will determine which of these two outcomes you will end up with. If you have been talking about Yiddish, and you say *I like* [kæts], then the person you are speaking to will probably understand that you mean Dr. Katz. But if you are talking about pets, and you say *I like* [kæts], then the person you are speaking to will understand you to mean the little furry felines.

Spreading activation is a little bit complicated, because human cognition is dirty and slow: we are limited by our ape brains. We have good storage capacity, which is where the default inheritance comes in. Default inheritance permits fast and efficient look up of information. But humans are not very good at working online. Therefore, our theories have to be sensitive to these kinds of limitations. That is why I do not work with derivational or algorithmic syntax: it has too many complicated computations, and I do not think that human minds can do these complicated computations all the time on line for communication to work.

3.25 *Other Cognitive Dimensions in the Theory*

There are other dimensions of cognitive psychology which are relevant, too. The taxonomic structure that I have talked about is supported by work on language acquisition by Ellen Markman, a professor at Stanford. Markman and Wachtel (1988) and Markman (1990) identify three acquisition biases that direct children to learn words: the whole object bias, the taxonomic bias and the mutual exclusivity bias.

An acquisition bias is a cognitive default which governs aspects of human behaviour which are relevant—in the case of linguistics—to how language is acquired. The whole object bias is an acquisition bias that relates to how we perceive objects. Markman studied children looking at picture books. The picture books would show, for example, a cartoon pig with a curly tail, so the word *pig* could be referring to either the pig or its tail. The children in Markman's study typically associated the word with the whole object, and not just with part of it.

Daniel Gildea and Daniel Jurafsky (1996) identified something called the community bias, a bias that you put things that look like each other together into the same taxonomy. But Markman also has the mutual exclusivity bias.

She says you might put *a pig* and *a cat* in the same category, but you don't take them as the same thing. You separate them out. Mutual exclusivity gives you something which comes from functional linguistics where Bolinger (1977) has the "one form: one meaning" constraint on languages. We classify things that look like each other together, yet we keep things separate, too, at the same time, again because we are looking for the single best-fit category.

These biases seem to be basic properties of cognitive organization, not specific to language, but relevant to it. They are, I think, actually perceptual biases: they are to do with how we organize perceptual information as it comes into our minds. For those who are not persuaded by the innateness hypothesis, cognitive biases explain how children are able to recognize and therefore manipulate certain kinds of information better than other kinds. Another example of where cognitive biases can be found is in face recognition, on which there is a lot of psychological work. Even though most of us are very good at face recognition, some people are face-blind.

Markman has applied an analysis based on cognitive biases to the learning of word meanings, but they also have a more general consequence. The taxonomic bias directs children to put things into categories, or actually to identify things which can be categorized, such as words and their meanings, phonemes, and morphs, while the mutual exclusivity directs them to factor these items out, so you will not assume that dogs and cats are the same thing, just because they both Isa 'mammal' and Isa 'pet'.

3.26   *A Potential Research Project*

Spreading activation offers a route for exploring how reference tracking in discourse happens. How do we understand the concept referred to by *it* in *the dog has a small head, and it likes to run in the woods when we go on walks. It has a bad hip, but it is very friendly*? Every time you see the word *it* in the sentences, it has more information. The first *it* isn't just for *dog*. It's the dog with a small head. The second *it* isn't just a dog with a small head. It's the dog with a small head who likes to run in the woods when we go on walks. The third *it* isn't just the dog with a small head or the dog. It's the dog with small head who likes running, who has a bad hip.

The word *it* gets more information added to every time it is used. There is not much work on discourse in WG. But reference tracking in discourse is something that needs to be done. This is the sort of things that we might think about of in terms of spreading activation relationships. And we need to ask ourselves how concepts get enriched. With each new clause, the referent of *it* becomes enriched. How do we show it? The WG answer is that this is up to spreading activation and the creation of new nodes in the network in the context of perceptual information.

3.27   *Wrap Up*

In this lecture I discussed events, and I focused on a particular theory of events, and I have introduced some aspects of WG. In the next lecture, I will talk rather more about the cognitive aspects of WG, and compare it with Construction Grammar by exploring an analysis of idioms. I will also talk about the relationship between syntax, semantics and morphology. One of the things I am going to do in that next lecture is to show you a little bit more about how we understand morphology in a sentence in use.

LECTURE 2

Parts, Wholes, and Networks; Idioms; Semantics—Syntax—Morphology

In this lecture we explore the consequences of adopting the position in lecture one—that language is a cognitive network—for theories of syntax, semantics and morphology, using idioms as a case study. The structure of the lecture has three parts.
1. Parts and wholes versus networks.
2. Idioms as a case study.
3. Analyses of semantics, syntax and morphology

1 Parts and Wholes versus Networks

1.1 *Situating WG in the Field*
WG is a cognitive theory of language structure with a formalism that embodies a number of theoretical assumptions about language and cognition. It includes a corpus of analyses of syntax, morphology, lexical semantics, and some sentence semantics. It is probably most similar to Goldberg's (1995, 2006) Cognitive Construction Grammar. But it has one major difference from that theory, which is that we do not think there are any "boxes"—that is we do not that that it is possible to embed a construction within another construction; we think that cognition is just a network, so language has to be represented in a pure network, without embedding, as well. Constructions are complex signs, and a construction grammar network is a network of information in constructions, or complex signs, which means that it is a network of information packaged up in boxes. In WG we reject the idea that language is a network of signs.

 All original audio-recordings and other supplementary material, such as any hand-outs and powerpoint presentations for the lecture series, have been made available online and are referenced via unique DOI numbers on the website www.figshare.com. They may be accessed via a QR code for the print version of this book. In the e-book, both the QR code and dynamic links are available, and can be accessed by a mouse-click.

There are several reasons for dispensing with signs or constructions from the theoretical ontology. One is to do with network flow. WG networks are entirely unencapsulated so it is straightforward to posit direct links between different nodes in a network. But if you have complex nodes, which are structured as signs, how can you have direct links from a node within a given sign to a node within another sign? It seems problematic. Another reason for dispensing with signs is that they are not necessary. We posit all sorts of things in linguistics because of our intellectual inheritance. But it is important to examine the ideas we have inherited, and when a new idea comes along we need to confront old ideas with the new, and throw away what is not helpful. The notion of constructions relies on a phrase-structure theory of syntax, because it assumes that phrasal patterns are meaningful, so it is fundamentally incompatible with WG. A classic example of rejecting old ideas in favour of new ones is the rejection of Aristotelian categories in favor of prototypes. Categorization does not exist in the real world: it is a human invention. Therefore, it exists in the human mind. Therefore, the model of categorization we need is the model of categorization that human psychology needs. We do not need the model of categorization that Aristotelian logic needs.

1.2   Why a Network?

Why should we get rid of constructions? I have three answers. The first answer comes from cognitive psychology and artificial intelligence research. My second answer is the adoption of dependencies in syntax and the rejection of phrase structure. The third one is that speech errors require a network because they are the result of spreading activation.

Because formal signs or boxes add complexity, it is incumbent on their proponents to show what function they serve. The usual argument for signs or boxes is that they capture non-compositional meaning. But we are going to see that signs, boxes, or constructions are not needed for non-compositional meaning. Later in this lecture, I discuss the non-compositional meaning of idioms, just using the machinery of default inheritance and sub-lexemes, and without relying on constructions.

1.3   Why a Network?

The WG claim is that boxes have no function: they are part of "metacognition," not cognition (Hudson 2016), and can be disposed of there, too. I said in lecture one that WG is a "lexico-grammar". Traditionally the lexicon is kept separate from the rest of grammar, but not in WG, Construction Grammar, or Cognitive Grammar. These theories all have a lot of similar assumptions, including the network idea.

I have also said that meaning in formal semantics excludes encyclopedic information. In WG, we include encyclopedic information, which actually is part of the network. For example, in lecture one I presented an analysis of 'running' which showed it with just one node, but we need to have lots of information surrounding the concept for 'running' to distinguish it from 'walking' and 'jogging', and from other senses of the word *run*, which might include the speed but not include the use of legs, for example, if you want to say that *the train is running on time*.

1.4   Why a Network?

Another reason to have a network is usage-basedness. I do not think that users know actual probabilities of usages. If you have variable realization of a particular word or linguistic concept, I do not think that you know the probabilities with which you will come out with one variant.[1] But I think the probabilities in the speech that you encounter will affect the kind of mental grammar that you create: the usage environment certainly affects our knowledge of language and it affects the shapes of the grammars that we create in our minds. But I do not think that speakers or hearers just store an inventory of the tokens of language that they encounter, so in WG we model categorization and taxonomic reasoning in Default Inheritance hierarchies.

The grammars that we create are generalizations over the perceptual data that we encounter in our linguistic environments. Therefore, we create different grammars perhaps from each other, which is inevitable, because we have different input from each other, depending on where in the country we are brought up, who we go to school with and so on. It is important if we think about language, to distinguish between language as an individual mental property and a language as a population phenomenon. A language is something that belongs to a population, but grammar is a mental property that belongs to an individual. Individuals create grammars out of the language environments they hear in the population that they inhabit.

There are various ways in which our own usage, and that of our surrounding speech environment affect us. Priming is one. I talked about priming in lecture one, using the examples of *Katz* and *cats*. Priming can cause you to interpret things in different ways, so you can interpret the sound string [kæts] either as

---

1   Yueh-Hsin Kuo (p.c) disagrees with me, suggesting that dialectal differences can be attributed to different probabilities, so speakers might have a rough idea about whether a form is more frequent. Given the difficulties involved in explaining quantitative reasoning, I think it is more likely that there are differences in activation levels, rather than speakers having any real understanding of relative frequency.

being a person's name or being the plural of an instance of CAT depending on whether you are talking about Yiddish linguistics or household pets. Priming is a kind of recency effect which means that the active network surrounding a particular concept has not died down yet. But despite all of these psychological effects, we still induce grammars.

Pieter Seuren has a very useful blog about language, where he has an interesting post in which he talks about why we definitely induce grammars. One of Seuren's examples is to do with scope variation (see https://pieterseuren.wordpress.com/2013/04/):

(1) Twice I saw someone leave.
(2) I saw someone leave twice.

(1) is not ambiguous. It has to mean that the 'seeing' takes place twice. (2), on the other hand, is ambiguous: either the 'seeing' takes place twice, or the 'leaving' takes place twice. Twice can modify either of those two verbs. There has to be structure in language for those two positions to involve different interpretations. It is a complicated structure in fact, because we need to know the 'twice' modifies verbs and refers to sets of things and sets of events. We also need to know that it can modify verbs at some distance, or locally. Finally, we need to know that we can force a particular interpretation if it is in a particular environment. All of these things we must know are quite abstract grammatical information. The chance that you learn all of that information by storing utterance tokens is quite unlikely. Learners must induce structure in language and, therefore, we need to find the structure in language that allows us to talk about properties like scope; in doing so, we have induced generalizations about linguistic data.

1.5 Why a Network?

In fact, there has to be a hierarchical structure that shows us that in (1) *twice* unambiguously scopes over *saw* semantically. There must also be a relational structure that shows us how *twice* can be attached to either *saw* or *leave*. But that structure does not need phrases. We can do it with dependencies which are adequate for representing hierarchical information and linear order. Dependencies just present a network of syntactic structure. Within a dependency grammar, the notion of a phrasal construction does not make sense because there are no phrasal nodes which can be associated with phrasal meaning.

If we adopt a network as our way of analysing language, it is possible to encode structural information like this in a way that also allows us to model associative links between different parts of language and from language to other parts of cognition. That is part of the analytical job, because the WG claim is that language is part of a seamless whole with the rest of cognition.

There is plenty of evidence in neuropsychology that language in the mind exists in a distributed neural network. But language is clearly symbolic, so no linguistic theory can work with a directly connectionist model: to have a linguistic theory, you need some kind of symbolic system. In order to make a symbolic system as close as possible to the structures of a neural network, we have not just a network theory, but a symbolic network theory, which can then hum along on top of the neural network. That is, a symbolic network gives us a model of language—and the rest of knowledge—which can be modelled so that it sits on top of the neural network in a way as closely as possible. But it makes less sense to try and put boxes of information, and part-whole structures on top of a neural network. What would the fit be?

1.6   Does a Symbolic Network Need Signs?

The brief answer is "no". A symbolic network does not need signs. WG does not have signs in its theoretical machinery. There are two main reasons why. The first reason is that signs have too little information in them, and the second is that language involves too much information for signs to be a sensible way of organizing it. We can think about this by thinking about levels of form and levels of meaning. A sign is prototypically understood as a relationship between a level of form and a level of meaning. But what is form? It includes phonology, morphology, and arguably syntax. But then what is meaning? It includes semantics, discourse, pragmatics, and arguably syntax. The problem about syntax is not just a problem of what it is, but also how we learn it.

For example, there is perceptual information, in the form of phonetics, which anchors phonology for us, so we can figure out the relationship between phonology and phonetics (relatively) straightforwardly. We seem to have ways of chunking language so that we recognize word units (this is actually part of Markman's (1990) whole object constraint). We also know what words are. A meaning is embodied, experiential, and perceptual, so we have ways of accessing meaning through our ordinary daily experience. But syntax is complicated. It is miles away from experience of the world, because it is a purely linguistic system. It is the most abstract, the least perceptually grounded part of language. That makes it really difficult to think about. It also means that it is very hard to consider it as either a unit of form or of meaning, because it has properties in common with both.

That creates two problems: where do we put syntax? And what does it mean to talk about the 'form' pole of a sign? Syntax is arguably in both parts of the sign. It is relevant to form because syntax determines word-order, which is clearly a formal property of language. *The farmer kills the duckling* means something different from *the duckling kills the farmer*. But syntax is also relevant to meaning, which we have just seen in examples (1) and (2): scope is a meaning relationship dependent on syntax—whether *twice* scoped over *saw* or *leave* in the examples. How we interpret the combinations of words is partly to do with the positional syntax of words, and the attachment syntax of words. Syntax therefore is between the two different poles of a potential sign.

Also, how do we understand the form side of the sign? This question takes us into issues about morphology, which arise in nearly every single morphological theory that I am aware of. In WG, we take it that morphology is autonomous, which means that for WG, "morphemes" do not directly have a meaning. If morphemes are parts of the formal pole, and meaningless, then how is the sign structured? Syntax, as I said, does direct links to meaning. So do bits of phonology. For example, Mandarin tones signal meaning contrasts. Intonational phonology has meaning in English, too. So if I say *he did what?* it is obvious that I am asking a question because the intonation tells you so. Intonation can derive the overall meaning of a sentence which has the syntax of a declarative (making it interrogative). Trying to put a sign into the theory makes the theory really difficult to engineer. You get a more straightforward and simpler theory if you have no signs. Every notion that we need in order to compose a theory of language is just a node in the network, with associational links to the other nodes in the network.

1.7   *What Are Constructions in WG?*

The answer is this: language just consists of nodes and relations stored in inheritance hierarchies. Lexical items are just lexemes and sub-lexemes—which are explained in the discussion of the polysemy of the word SEE in (Gisborne 2010). Constructions in this theory are just lexemes or sub-lexemes linked by dependency relations and the associated network.

1.8   *Predicative Complementation*

Predicative complementation is a case in point. It is widely recognized that the ability for a noun to occur as a predicative complement is constructional (Francis 1999). Predicative complementation is the kind of complementation where a noun can take a Subject when it is in a particular syntactic position (there are other kinds of predicative complementation, but this exemplifies the point). If we look at the lexical entry of a noun, nouns do not have Subjects in their lexical entries. On the other hand, you might say that a verb has a Subject in its lexical entry, especially a weather verb. For example, in English, the verb RAIN takes IT for its subject or in some circumstances you might say that verbs like BE of existence have a lexically specified subject: it always takes THERE as its subject. But you would not say that nouns have subjects in their lexical entries.

For example, consider (3).

(3) Jane considered Peter a fool.

Example (3) means the same as *Jane considered Peter foolish*; here *Peter* is the subject of *foolish* and in the same way in (3) *Peter* is the subject of *a fool*. How does this predication come about? Is it because nouns have a subject relation in their lexical entry? The answer must be "no". *A fool* gets a subject because of its syntactic function: it is a predicative complement. This is represented in Figure 1.

Consider takes a direct object and a predicative complement which must have a Subject, therefore the predicative complement coerces subjecthood in these situations. In (3) *a fool* has a Subject only because it is the predicative complement of the verb *considered*.

The analysis is a little bit like construction grammar, because it shows how a lexical category can be coerced into having a particular grammatical function by its syntactic environment and because there is a particular kind of form-meaning correspondence. Every lexeme is associated with a fragment of meaning, and so is every dependency—Lecture 1 showed the relationship between Subjects and Agents, for example.

However, Figure 1 is unlike a construction grammar analysis in some other ways. It just uses arcs and nodes. Essentially, it says that if this arc exists (the xcomp, or predicative complement relation), then this node must also have a subject. There is no phrase structure: no noun, verb or prepositional phrases, thus there are no signs. The associated semantics is linked to the syntax by associative links from words to meanings, and from dependencies to meanings. But nevertheless, the analysis just involves a seamless network where all of language, like all of knowledge, is shown to be just a series of arcs and nodes.

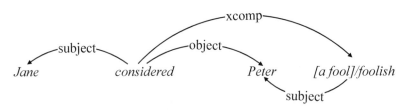

FIGURE 1   Jane considered Peter a fool/foolish

1.9 Parts and Wholes

Chomsky has argued since the 1960s that humans have an innate capacity for linguistic knowledge. Over the decades, that claim has been weakened again and again. The latest version of it (Hauser, Chomsky and Fitch 2002) is that "only recursion (in the form of Merge) is considered to be unique to human language ability" (see also Christiansen and Chater 2016). Merge is a relationship of parts and wholes. Under Merge, Chomsky creates sets. If α and β Merge, then they form a set γ, which is a part-whole relationship. But WG does not privilege part-whole relationships in this way: they are invoked where they are needed, for example in morphology, but they are not the basic building blocks of the grammar. So one claim that I would make is that language does not involve recursion, in the sense of the recursive embedding of information from one unit into another.[2]

In WG we therefore argue in line with Christiansen and Chater (2016) and many others that language is learnt. Christiansen and Chater, psychologists who are specialists in the evolution of language, argue that language is learnt, and in WG, we claim that the learnability of language follows from the network structure. The rejection of a part-whole analysis applies to Phrase Structure Grammar (PSG) and to Minimalism, as much as it applies to the rejection of the part-whole nature of signs, or of constructions. But it is notable that the network approach also makes it straightforward to reject the claim that there is a biologically unique human endowment for language. It would be kind of odd from the evolutional point of view if there were.

There is plenty of evidence that an evolutionary change which has adaptive advantages from an evolutionary perspective can have negative consequences—for example upright stance allows us to use tools, but it causes lower back problems not found in four-legged animals. This is normal in evolution. Recurring mutations confer adaptive advantages which results in them being selected over successive generations because the organism is more successful in breeding and (in animals) raising their young, and passes that change on.

---

2 Nordström (2014) makes the claim that WG does not involve any kind of embedding or recursion in a plea for a revision of minimalist syntax.

You can see how a sudden radically evolutionary adaption for language would confer an advantage. But it is actually very unlikely that there was a radical jump, because evolution typically works in terms of small changes that happen over many successful generations. For example, the other great apes can also walk on their legs and manipulate tools. But at the same time, they walk on their hands sometimes, and use their arms to swing around in trees. This means that their upright stance is not exactly like ours, which is expected because evolution is accidental and does not constitute a big jump from four-leggedness to upright stance. The idea of a unique human endowment for language involves a very big radical step, therefore it is evolutionarily unlikely.

Another argument in favor of WG's simple networks, and against parts and wholes comes from relations in Construction Grammar. Construction Grammar has relations between constructions and within constructions: Goldberg (1995, 2006) uses grammatical functions like Subject, Object, and Indirect Object within her constructions. That is to say, she has a network-like relationship between her constructions and a network-like relationship within her constructions. But why have constructions then? They will get in the way if you are a network, because information does not just flow freely through the network if there are in boxes.

Taylor (2004a) and Verhagen (2002) also argue for the explicit inclusion of other kinds of relations between subparts of constructions in formal and semantic representations. If words are constructions and if constructions can embed other constructions within them, then there are associative links between constructions—if not in the construction. So why privilege the sign? What is the function of form-meaning pairings in the sign? Recall that the network is symbolic. It just does not have formal signs in it. Therefore, I do not see what the advantage of a sign is if you have relationships between constructions, and within constructions. It makes life too complicated to do that.

2 Idioms

This section reports joint work with Dick Hudson, presented at the Annual Meeting of the Linguistics Association of Great Britain in 2010. The reason to talk about idioms is that idioms are the key case study in Fillmore and Kay's work on why you need constructions (e.g. Kay and Fillmore 1999) because of their non-compositional meaning. The easiest way to understand the non-compositional meaning of an idiom is to argue that these phrases are like words: the idiom is a complex sign or construction with an unanalysable meaning. In this section I will explain why we do not need constructions to understand non-compositional meaning. Idioms' exceptionality can be captured in terms of sub-lexemes, and it does not require constructions or relationships between constructions. Instead, I will also suggest that we can understand the exceptionality in terms of their meaning, and that the syntactic restrictions on idioms follow from the ways in which they use conceptual metaphors. Then I will argue that if we do not have constructions, or signs, then we can have a better analysis of some of the gradient information in idioms. Finally, you might recall that Nunberg, Sag and Wasow (1994), a famous paper in *Language*, distinguishes between two different kinds of idiom: idiomatic combining expressions and idiomatic phrases. I will show that this distinction is too coarse, and that we need to understand the gradient nature of idioms because they have a range of properties.

2.1 Idioms Are Exceptional
Let's take (4) for example.

(4) kick the bucket

Example (4) means 'die'. It's an exception to general compositionality because *kick* does not mean 'die', nor does *the bucket*. DIE is intransitive and signals a change of state, while *kick the bucket* is transitive. Example (4) is also an exception to general syntax. It does not have a passive. You cannot say **the bucket was kicked*. Also the idiom in (4) is different from the normal verb KICK because it does not allow TOUGH-movement.

(5) *The bucket was hard to kick.

Suppose you are trying to kill something, and it will not die. Even so, you cannot say **the bucket was hard to kick*. But it is possible to say *the ball was hard to kick* if a ball has the right properties and *the pig was hard to kill* is also grammatical.

2.2 Our Questions
First, why are such exceptions possible? Does default inheritance explain how such exceptions are possible? Second, how are idioms stored in relation to their constituent lexemes? Can we use the sub-lexemes of WG to account for how idioms are stored? This is an important question, because if language is just a cognitive network, then idioms must be stored in relation to their constituent lexemes; they cannot just exist on their own. If you make a past tense and say *her cat kicked the bucket yesterday*, then the past tense of *kick* works exactly the same whether it is in the idiom or whether it's the normal verb. So, at least to

capture the morphology, it would be a good idea to make the *kick* of *kick the bucket* inherit (via Default Inheritance) from the ordinary verb KICK. Third, how are idioms organized syntactically? Does dependency structure help the organization? Do we need phrases for that?

2.3 Kinds of Idiom

Nunberg, Sag and Wasow (1994) distinguish Idiomatic Phrases, like *kick the bucket*, which have a rigid syntax, from Idiomatically Combining Expressions, like *bury the hatchet*,[3] which have some syntactic freedom. Therefore, you can make an idiomatic-combining expression passive. You cannot say *the bucket was kicked*, but you can say *the hatchet was buried*.

2.4 More Recent Research in Linguistics

The contrast identified by Nunberg *et al.* (1994) has been explored further. Horn (2003) claimed that Idiomatically Combining Expressions are regular if their parts have regular theta roles. (Theta role is the technical term in the minimalist literature for a thematic or semantic role.) In other work, Espinal and Mateu (2010) said that the distinction between an Idiomatic Phrase and an Idiomatically Combining Expression is too rigid. They claim that *to laugh one's head off* is part Idiomatic Phrase and part Idiomatically Combining Expression because it has rigid syntax. You cannot say *his head was laughed off*. However, you can insert any pronoun to replace *one* that can refer back to the subject. You can say *John laughed his head off, Jane laughed her head off, we laughed our heads off*, and so on, so it has that kind of flexibility. Jackendoff (1997, 2011) accepted the distinction between Idiomatic Phrases and Idiomatically Combining Expressions and suggested a formal analysis.

2.5 Idiomatic Phrase or Idiomatically Combining Expression?

First of all, how do we decide if something is an Idiomatic Phrase or an Idiomatically Combining Expression? Is it really likely that there are just going to be two kinds of idiom? Perhaps there are degrees of opacity, degrees to which something is not clearly compositional. The most opaque type includes the cases which are like *kick the bucket*, a less opaque kind includes examples such as *bury the hatchet*, and the least opaque examples would be those like *laugh one's head off*, because you can see how the metaphor works in *laugh your head off*—you could laugh so hard that your head wobbles about a lot. But how do you measure opacity? Does a network analysis help?

---

3 *Bury the hatchet* means to make peace with someone after an argument.

2.6 Jackendoff: an Idiomatic Phrase

Let us take Jackendoff's (1997: 161–169) analysis as a comparative point. He has the kind of structure for Idiomatic Phrases, illustrated in Figure 2:

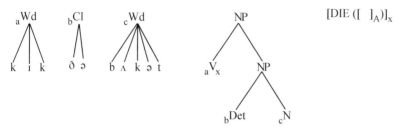

FIGURE 2   Jackendoff's (1997: 169) analysis of *kick the bucket*

Figure 2 presents a structure where there is a word, a clitic and another word on the left hand side. Below them is the sound representation [kɪk ðə bʌkɪt]. In the middle there is a phrasal syntax, and to its right, the semantics. So, each word has a label *a*, *b*, and *c*: *a* is the first word *kick*; the second word *the*, labelled *b*, is cliticized to the noun, *c*, to form *the bucket*. Then there is an *x* on the verb node, associated with the *x* in [DIE ([ ]$_A$)]$_x$. The subscript "A" means that the argument of *die* is labeled as an Agent. The subscript indices are a way of linking the word string to the phrase structure and the semantics. And so Jackendoff is saying that the meaning 'die' is attached to the word *kick*. Therefore, the head word of the VP in his analysis has a special role; the object NP in Jackendoff's analysis does not contribute to the meaning at all.

2.7 Jackendoff: an Idiomatically Combining Expression

Figure 3 represents the idiom *bury the hatchet*.

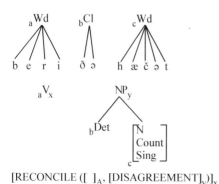

FIGURE 3
Jackendoff's (1997: 168) analysis of *bury the hatchet*

Jackendoff shows *bury* and *the hatchet* meaning 'reconcile disagreement'. The whole thing is associated with the verb, by the subscript x. The noun phrase is associated by the subscript y, with the meaning 'disagreement'. That is, the part of semantics marked by y is associated with the noun phrase, and the other part of semantics marked by x is associated with the verbal head. Essentially, Jackendoff's analysis is that an Idiomatically Combining Expression is compositional, but it has a metaphorical meaning, and its component parts have a metaphorical meaning, whereas an Idiomatic Phrase is non-compositional, and its whole meaning is just attached to the head. Finally, note also that the y subscript is the only link between *bury* and *the hatchet*.

2.8 Jackendoff's Analysis

For Jackendoff, an Idiomatic Phrase has a totally rigid syntax, although it is possible to say *he kicked the proverbial bucket*, and an Idiomatically Combining Expression has a totally free syntactic order. The analysis is not entirely right: it is not possible to say something like **they found the hatchet then buried it*, which means that an Idiomatically Combining Expression is not totally flexible. The analysis does not account for either the flexibility in *kick the proverbial bucket* or the lack of flexibility in **they found the bucket then buried it*. Jackendoff also does not capture how the phrase *buried the proverbial hatchet* works, where is the whole phrase that is proverbial, just as in *kick the proverbial bucket*. (The burying is as proverbial as the hatchet.) Jackendoff's analysis of Idiomatically Combining Expression's involves something he calls "metaphorical semantic composition". Both *burying* and *the hatchet* are metaphorical because *burying* means 'reconcile' and *the hatchet* means 'disagreement' and so the whole idiom is compositional, because the overall meaning 'reconcile disagreement' follows from composing the different elements in the idiom. This (metaphorical) compositionality is related in his analysis to the syntactic flexibility of Idiomatically Combining Expressions, because although more than one of the words in the expression might be metaphorical, it is nevertheless a compositional semantic structure.

2.9 Metaphorical Semantic Composition

Let us look at metaphorical semantic composition in a bit more depth. The argument is that metaphorical semantic composition is not sufficient for Idiomatically Combining Expressions, that it is not necessary for Idiomatically Combining Expressions, and that it is not necessary for literal meaning (as in cases such as *do a cartwheel*). I take each of these in turn.

First of all, metaphorical semantic composition is not sufficient for Idiomatically Combining Expressions. For example, Jackendoff (1997: 170) quotes a personal communication from Paul Postal who argues that *raise hell*, which is a transparent metaphor because *raise* means 'cause' and hell ('disturbance') cannot passivize, which would mean that it is not an Idiomatically Combining Expression. Also, metaphorical semantic composition is not necessary for Idiomatically Combining Expressions. If you use the idiom *let the cat out of the bag*, we can see some transparency: *let* means 'reveal' and *the cat* means 'the secret', but what about *out of the bag*? In fact, it is *let ... out of the bag* that must mean *reveal*, but that is not metaphorical composition. Instead, it is a kind of idiomatic or non-compositional meaning, therefore it does not work as an example of metaphorical semantic composition.

Finally, metaphorical semantic composition is not necessary for literal meaning. You can *do a cartwheel*, a kind of movement game that we get children to do where they put their arms and their legs up and out in a star shape and then roll on their hands and their feet with their hands and feet as spokes of a wheel. The verb *cartwheel* means to perform this action; the noun *cartwheel* denotes actions of this kind; *do a cartwheel* involves *do* and *cartwheel*, both of which mean 'cartwheel'.

2.10 *Research in Psycholinguistics*

We will now consider some evidence from psycholinguistics to see where we go with this. We can ask ourselves how activation affects idioms. How are they represented?[4] One argument is that idioms are not represented as single words, but as phrases with a single entry. We will talk about Cutting and Bock's (1997) "Hybrid theory" and "Superlemma theory" (Sprenger *et al.* 2006).

Let us look at Cutting and Bock first. They have a relationship between the syntax and the lexicon. Their representation has a conceptual level which is shown with pictorial representations in Figure 4, a lexical conceptual level which is shown in words—their examples include *pail* and *bucket*, *kick the bucket*, *pop the question*, *meet your maker*, *punk*, and *kick*, and so on. A sort of syntactic representation comes out of syntactic categories in the lower left corner, which gives a phrase structure, and there is the lexical-syntactic level on the bottom level. Their theory suggests an associative network of links, In this theory, there is a complex relationship between the lexicon and the syntax, and different levels of meaning and syntax through the system.

---

4 The reason for looking at the psycholinguistic literature is that it offers a means of evaluating the different theories of structure. If there is a choice between two theories, the better theory is the one that is most consistent with the psycholinguistic evidence.

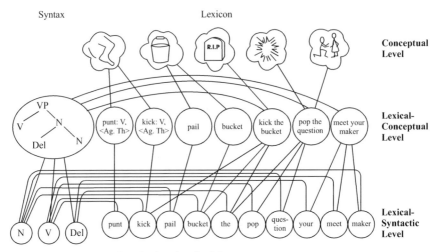

FIGURE 4   Cutting and Bock's (1997) Hybrid theory
TAKEN FROM KUIPER ET AL. (2007: 321)

If we look at *kick the bucket* in Figure 4, we can see that it is linked to a gravestone with Rest in Peace on it, so *kick the bucket* activates 'dying', but it also activates *kick*, *bucket*, and *the*. In this theory, the syntax of these words is activated, and so is the metaphorical bit of semantics. The model gives you a hybrid approach between a constructional approach and a non-constructional approach. There is the link from *kick the bucket*, all the way to the bit of phrasal syntax in the bottom left of the diagram and other idioms such as *pop the question* and *meet your maker* also link to the same phrasal syntax which links down to the syntactic categories in the very bottom left of the diagram. So syntax is independent of words in this theory but there are lots of associative links between different bits of information in conceptual structure, lexical conceptual structure, lexical syntactic structure, combinatorial syntax, and lexicon.

Now let us turn to superlemma theory (Sprenger *et al.* 2006) shown in Figure 5, which is a model of activation, not a model of structure. In Figure 5 there is a lexical concept which means 'die', which is in a bilateral relationship with the superlemma which has the form *kick the bucket*.

In the figure, *kick the bucket* is associated with simple lemmas, *a*, *b*, and *c*, which are *kick*, *the*, and *bucket*, which are in turn associated with these word forms at the bottom of the figure. Because this is an activation theory, the idea is that activation spreads through that network, triggering an association between the word forms on the one hand, and the meaning 'die' on the other. Because it is not a representational theory, the diagram implies that there are syntactic relations among the parts of the superlemma, but Sprenger *et al.* do

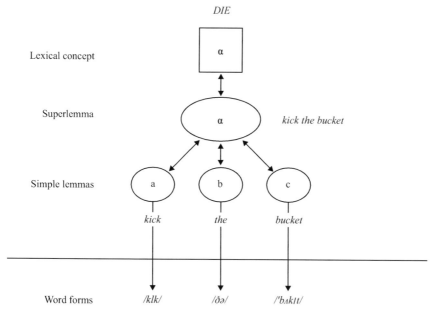

FIGURE 5   Diagrammatic representation of superlemma activation
TAKEN FROM KUIPER ET AL. (2007: 324)

not tell us how the structure works—what is the composition in the superlemma bubble in Figure 5?

Research in psycholinguistics has shown that we access conceptual metaphors in idioms. One conceptual metaphor might be ANGER IS HEAT, so for example the idiom *blow your stack*, means to explode with anger. The word *stack* refers to a chimney stack. The source of the metaphor is the fact that a chimney stack does not always take exhaust gases away efficiently, so it can overheat and explode. An idiom like *blow your stack*, then, is associated with a very simple conceptual metaphor, ANGER IS HEAT. On the other hand, ANGER IS HEAT is not the right conceptual metaphor for the angry interpersonal relationship expressed in *jump down somebody's throat*, because it involves a different conceptual metaphor—to do with an aggressive objection to what someone says—see Gibbs, Bogdanovich, Sykes and Barr (1998) for more. Peterson, Burgess, Dell and Eberhard (2001) found that we process idiom syntax normally. Sprenger, Levelt and Kempen (2006) also found that when we process idiom syntax, literal word meanings become active during idiom production. That is, we actually activate all of the normal words associated with the idiom as well.

2.11 To Summarize

Idioms have a single entry in memory. They contain ordinary lexemes and ordinary syntax. They involve ordinary metaphor. But they have an abnormal linkage to meaning. Because the linkage to meaning is abnormal, the syntax of idioms can also be abnormally restricted.

2.12 Recall what Word Grammar Offers

WG gives us a *default inheritance* which allows exceptions, *sub-lexemes* which allow partial differences within a lexeme, *dependency structure* which gives us associative relationships between words, and *network structure* which explains spreading activation and relatedness. We can try and use these tools to capture these various facts about idioms.

2.13 Content from Lecture One: Default Inheritance

Default inheritance allows exceptions. Instances can have exceptional properties. For example, *tall* overrides the default height. Typically, a dependent enriches the head's sense, so it can override default properties, and any property can be overridden. For example, fake diamonds look just like diamonds.

2.14 Exceptionality Ranges

Exceptionality ranges then from zero through partial to total. For example, there is zero exceptionality in the morphology of *walked* and *kick a ball*. Both behave precisely as you expect them to and precisely as they should. Partial exceptionality can be found in the vowel change in *run-ran*, which is regular, but which represents a very minor kind of regularity that just affects a few verbs in English, deriving from its Germanic inheritance. An example of an idiom with partial exceptionality is *kick up a fuss*. Total exceptionality can be found in *went*: the suppletive past tense of *go*, which is historically derived from a completely different verb from *go*—there is no formal morphological relationship between *went* and *go*. Among idioms, *kick the bucket* is also totally exceptional. *Kick a ball*, *kick up a fuss*, and *kick the bucket* show the same kind of variation that we can see in the morphology from *walked*, to *ran*, to *went*.

2.15 Sub-Lexemes Again

Lexemes exist in a conceptual taxonomy. TAKE Isa full verb Isa verb Isa word. Each word token Isa some lexeme. So "sub-lexeme Isa lexeme" is permitted by default inheritance. For example, TAKE/off[5] Isa TAKE Isa full verb Isa verb Isa word.

---

5 This notation represents a sublexeme.

TAKE/off is a particular instance of TAKE which regularly collocates with the preposition OFF. It means 'remove'—so it is possible to take your jacket off, or to take off part of an over-complicated analysis (it can be used metaphorically in that way) or you can take the lid off a cooking pot. But there is also a degree of idiomaticity to TAKE/off because it is a particle verb. English particle verbs are verbs that regularly collocate with prepositions, but have an idiomatic meaning to different degrees of opacity. TAKE/off is actually quite transparent because the meanings of both TAKE and OFF are transparent. Note that TAKE/off inflects to *took* in the past tense—we say *he took off his hat*—however, some of the differences are that, unlike TAKE, TAKE/off is intransitive and has a slightly different meaning. The idea of a sub-lexeme then allows us to capture a relationship between a word which is a little different from, yet still a little similar to, its lexeme.

2.16   Sub-Lexemes in Idioms

Our analysis of the idiom *kick the bucket* exploits the idea of sublexemes. KICK/bucket Isa KICK. What we are saying is there is a special sub-lexeme for KICK of KICK/bucket, and we will just call it KICK/bucket, which inherits from KICK. Like KICK, it needs an object. Unlike the normal verb KICK, its object is specified to be THE/bucket—WG assumes that the word THE is the head, so this is a way of specifying that the object of KICK/bucket has to be *the bucket*. In its semantics, unlike KICK, it has a special sense, 'die'.

2.17   Pace Jackendoff ...

I will argue against Jackendoff here, who rejected my kind of analysis. In (1997: 160), he said, "it's a notational variant of listing a lexical VP", it's "clumsy" and "collapses under its own weight". In Jackendoff (2011: 281), he said that there is "no non-theory-internal reason to concentrate the meaning in just one of the morphemes". But his own analysis locates the meaning on the head, so I think he actually does the same thing. Figure 6 is again Jackendoff's analysis. Note a special role of the head word, circled in red, where the meaning 'die' is attached to the verb KICK, circled in red as well.

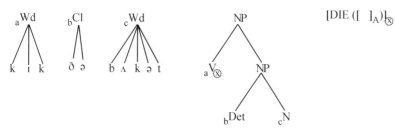

FIGURE 6   Jackendoff's (1997: 169) analysis of kick the bucket

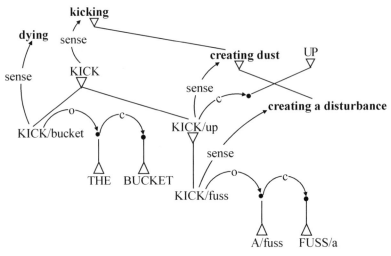

FIGURE 7   WG analysis of kick the bucket

Figure 7 presents the WG analysis.

Let us start with the lexeme KICK. Its sense is 'kick', and on the left of the diagram, there is a sub-lexeme: KICK/bucket. KICK/bucket has an object and the object has to be THE/bucket. WG adopts the determiner-as-head analysis, so the complement of THE is also specified, and it is BUCKET. *Kick the bucket* must have this kind of syntax. All of that syntax is associated in the network with the node KICK. *Kick* in *kick the bucket* has a special sense 'die'. Note that 'die' is separated from 'kick' by two links.

There is another idiom in Figure 7, *kick up*, as in *kick up a fuss*. KICK/up has a complement which is an instance of UP, and a sense which means 'create dust'. This sense is an instance of the sense 'kick'. But it has a special sub-type: KICK/fuss. *Kick up a fuss* takes as its object, A/fuss. That is also a special syntax. The sense of *kick up a fuss* is to 'create a disturbance', which I have shown you is a sub-type of 'create dust', although perhaps it would be better treated as a metaphor or a metaphorical link.

Note that there is a direct link from 'create a disturbance' and 'create dust' to 'kick', because when you kick in a dusty street, you create dust and kick up the disturbance. The idea is that the chain of meanings is much more closely related than in the case of *kick the bucket*'s meaning, *die*, where there is no direct inheritance chain of meanings. Finally, the link from 'fuss' to 'disturbance' is not shown, because the diagram would become too complicated.

2.18   *Idiomatic Phrases and Idiomatically Combining Expressions in WG*

Idiomatic Phrases and Idiomatically Combining Expressions both use ordinary syntax. Their head words have exceptional senses. The network shows how close the idiomatic sense is to the literal sense. Therefore, there's no need for any other Idiomatic Phrase/Idiomatically Combining Expression contrast. We speakers can vary the syntax as we want. But there's no point in varying it if the parts are unrelated to the idiomatic meaning. That is the constraint. We do not vary it if it breaks the idiom. We only vary it as long as it makes the idiom possible.

2.19   Intermediate Conclusion about Idioms

The idea then is that the Idiomatic Phrase/Idiomatically Combining Expression contrast has no theoretical status. The range of possibilities is as expected, given default inheritance, sub-lexemes, syntactic and semantic detail, dependents as semantic modifiers, and the network structure.

3   Semantics, Syntax and Morphology

In this part of the lecture, I talk about how we might think about analysing semantics, syntax and morphology, building on the idioms case study. We can begin with a diagram for a lexical entry. I explore what that diagram shows, and how it works. And then I will take us through how a sentence is composed. Figure 8 is an analysis of the lexeme CAT, which it is classified as a common noun.

The lexeme CAT inherits from the category Common Noun. The lexeme CAT has a sense link to its sense 'cat', classified as a mammal and a pet by multiple inheritance. We can put in a lot of associative information: for example, the sound that a cat makes is 'purring'. But other kinds of information are possible, too, because the word CAT is ambiguous. It has the sense of a domestic cat, and a second sense where it's the name of the category 'cat'. Domestic cats are one type of 'cat', 'lion' is another type, and 'puma' yet another type, and so on. Figure 8 is just a sketch, but in a complete analysis, we would need to be able to show all of that semantic richness.

In Figure 8 also shows how the morphology works, which means that it shows plural inflection, called "CAT:plural", This category inherits from the lexeme CAT, and from the category Plural. The sense of "CAT:plural" is a set of cats, because a plural noun refers to a set of the entity. Then we need to show the relationship between CAT, CAT:plural, and the forms {cats}, and {cat}. The base form of CAT is the morphological entry {cat}, realized as [cat] phonetically. It's also the base form of the plural form of CAT whose a fully inflected form is the s-variant of the base form {cat}: {cats}. The form {cats} involves a part-whole analysis, but we do that with associative arrows which link to the different parts. Therefore, part 1 of {cats} is {cat} and part 2 of {cats} is {s}, but

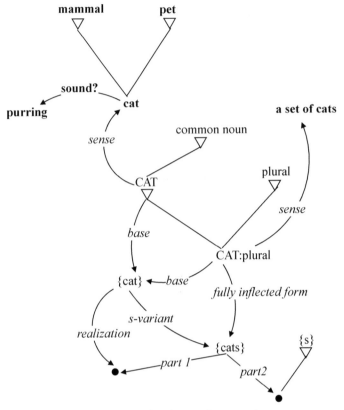

FIGURE 8   The lexeme CAT (taken from Gisborne 2017)

the semantics is not like this, because semantics is a lot richer than syntax and morphology.

Figure 8 shows the lexeme CAT is classified as a common noun, has a sense that is classified as 'mammal' and as 'pet', a plural inflection and morphological information that show how the base form and the plural form are related. There is quite a complicated pattern of morphological information, even for a simple word which involves a simple inflection contrast such as that found in an English count noun like CAT. Note that even though the morphology and syntax here are complete the meaning of CAT is left underspecified and there is no phonological information showing the variation in the way in which the plural morpheme is realized.[6] For a complete analysis, we need to show all of that as well.

---

6   The {s} form in the morphology has a variable realization depending on whether the environment it occurs in is voiced, in which case it is /z/, voiceless as it is here, or syllabic as in the case of *kisses* when it is realized as /ɪz/.

We can think about what would have to be included for the word CAT to have a more complete meaning. First, we would need to distinguish the prototype meaning from non-prototype meanings. For me the prototypical meaning of CAT is a domesticated cat. But as I have just said, *cat* is also the superordinate term for a category of animals, including wild cats, pumas and tigers. Our semantics needs to establish the difference between the superordinate term, and the difference between each of these items. The diagram is a simplification.

It is possible to factor out the two senses and to show this in the semantic structure: we could distinguish between 'cat₁' (the domestic feline) which inherits from 'cat₂' (the category name). It would also be possible to show that 'cat₁' is the prototype: in the WG language network, the prototype has a denser network associated with it, because around the prototype, there is more information. The further you get from the prototype, the less information you have. The higher up the inheritance hierarchy, the less information there is. That is, just as Lakoff (1987) says, the basic level categories are categories with the richest network surrounding them. But there is something else, which is that we need to know difference between 'cat' (the meaning of the lexeme CAT) and 'cat' (the meaning of the token *cat*), if we say *a cat walked in front of me*. This is a type/token relationship.

3.1   Type versus Token in Semantics
Consider (6):

(6)   Jane fed her cat.

In (6), the meaning of the phrase *her cat* is a hyponym of the meaning of the lexeme CAT. In the WG semantic representation of (6) there is an intramental referent. This is not a referent out there in the real world, but a mental representation of one. One of the key properties of WG is that the whole representation is intramental. Of course, this causes some problems when you are talking to formal semanticists, because for them reference is strictly to entities and events in the real world. One way of not getting confused when you are talking to formal semanticists is to say in WG, we have discourse referents, which a formal semanticist will think of also as intramental.

The key point is that WG's referents are linked to their models not by inheritance: reference in WG has a particular status. It is not just intramental, with nothing else to distinguish it; it is also the intramental model of a token of a type. Semantic tokens are like other tokens—they have a number of features which are "filled out", such as a time, and their deictic features. We can link the idea of intramental reference back to the discussion of type and token in Lecture 1.

3.2 Reference in Semantics

You might wonder how we diagnose reference in semantics. We do so by using particular pronouns and their positional variants. HE, SHE and IT and their object variants, HIM, HER and IT pick out referents. Pronouns such as SOME and ONE, on the other hand, pick out senses. We can see this in (7) and (8):

(7) My$_i$ dog is called Jumble. He$_i$ is a border-terrier.
(8) We like border terriers, so we got one.

In (7) *he* picks out the referent of the phrase *my dog*. Because of the way that the WG analysis of phrases such as *my dog* works, that's the referent of *my*. The personal pronouns are identity-of-reference pronouns, whereas SOME and ONE pick out senses; they pick out type meanings, not token meanings, so they are identity-of-sense pronouns. In (8) the phrase *border terrier* refers to a type of dog, and *one* just means we have got some border terrier or other. It does not identify Jumble. It means that we got any border-terrier. The same process works with SOME as well—*I like porcelain from China, so I bought some*—where *some* picks out the sense of *porcelain from China*. SOME and ONE are both involved in identity-of-sense anaphora.

Because verbs' meanings are nodes in the WG network, verbs can have referents as well. And like nouns, verbs' senses can be built up by being added to by the meanings of other sentence elements.

3.3 The Syntax of CAT

Let us return to Figure 8 and the analysis of the lexeme CAT. The syntax of CAT is simple. It is a count noun. Count nouns can be singular and plural, so Figure 8 shows that there is a plural inflection which is a subtype of the noun CAT. This tells us that the default form of the noun is the singular—according to the diagram, singular is default and plural is not. In the diagram, the morphosyntactic inflection node, CAT:plural, inherits both from the lexeme and from the category Plural. Morphosyntactic categories such as Plural have the same status in WG theory as lexemes do: they are just classifications.

Morphosyntactic categories are abstractions of various kinds of morphosyntactic information. Because of multiple inheritance, it is possible for an inflection to inherit from both its own lexeme, and another type, just as 'cat' inherits from both 'pet' and 'mammal'. Morphosyntactic categories such as Plural are all in the same organizational system and all part of syntax. That is, Plural is part of syntax in the same way that the lexeme CAT is part of syntax. However, even though a network node can inherit from more than one type in the same system, it cannot inherit from more than one type in two different systems. It is not possible for a node to inherit both from the lexeme CAT and from the semantic representation, 'cat'. That would break inheritance. One of the constraints on the formal system is that the inheritance mechanism must work in the right way.

One of the key properties of count nouns is that they can only occur in one position in English. They have to be the complement of a pronoun (or determiner in other theories; in WG, we consider determiners to be transitive pronouns). The difference between *the*, *a* and *every* and other pronouns is that they are always transitive, whereas *this* and *that* and so on are optionally transitive.

Count nouns have a very restricted position; they typically can only occur in that one place, while other nouns can occur in argument positions as Subject, as Object, and so on. However, count nouns can occur as a predicative complement of certain raising verbs. You can say *he became president*, but in this distribution, the count noun is not referential, it is predicative, which affects the semantic interpretation (and representation).

3.4   *The Morphology of CAT*

The morphology of CAT is slightly more complicated than the syntax. There are two key properties to the morphology. First, there is no direct link to the semantics and secondly, it is realizational. Let us go back to Figure 8 again. The morphology is in the lower half of Figure 8. Nothing in the morphology has a direct link to the semantics. The link from the morphology to the semantics is through the morphosyntactic category CAT:plural and the morphosyntactic category, the lexeme CAT. The actual morphemes have no direct relationship to the semantics at all; they only realize these different nodes in the syntactic network. *Cat* realizes the lexeme CAT, and {cats} realizes the syntactic node CAT:plural. Therefore WG is a realizational theory; it is not a morphemic theory.

Finally, the same approach is used throughout the grammar. For example, in the case of verbs, Past and Present work just as Plural does in the case of Nouns. The system creates additional subcategories, through multiple inheritance, which are the inflected subtype of the Verb lexeme.

3.5   *Moving On to Sentences*

We have seen how a simple monomorphemic noun works, and now we can look at how sentences work. Sentences work by composing together syntactic and semantic information. Apart from some special bits of language, like clitics, the analysis of sentences does not involve morphology or phonology—except for prosody. WG does not have a category "Sentence", or "Clause"; they are just emergent properties of words and their meanings combined. They arise as a side effect of words combining to satisfy their combinatory and distributional requirements. Therefore, the theory really is just word-based!

3.6 A Simple Sentence

Let us take a simple sentence:

(9) Jumble barked.

This is the simplest sentence I can think of. It requires an analysis that shows the relationships between the verb *barked* and the proper noun *Jumble*, and between the verb *barked* and the category Past. It also needs to show the relationship to the sense of *barked*, the referent of *Jumble*, and the referent of *Jumble barked*. Figure 9 is an analysis of *Jumble barked*:

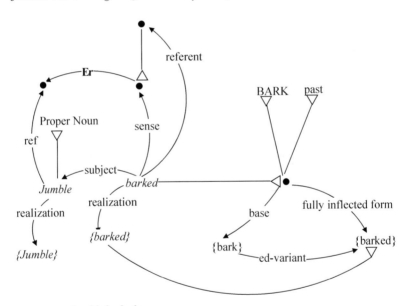

FIGURE 9   Jumble barked
TAKEN FROM GISBORNE (2019: 329)

There is *Jumble*, and *barked* in the syntax. *Jumble* is shown as the Subject of *barked* and classified as a proper noun. It has a referent: the referent of *Jumble* is the value of the *Er* of the sense of *barked*. The referent of *Jumble barked* is the referent of *barked* after it has combined with *Jumble*. That discusses how the diagram represents the syntax and the semantics. *Barked* is classified as an inflection of *bark*. It inherits from BARK and from Past. Its realization is {barked}. The realization of *Jumble* is just {Jumble} in the morphology. *Barked* is analysed as the realization of past tense of BARK which has the base {bark}. The base has an -*ed* variant, {barked}, which is the fully inflected form of this morphosyntactic node. The form {barked} realizes this fully inflected form in the morphology. The morphology is therefore a fully realizational theory, in Stump's (2001) terms.

Figure 9 gives us syntactic information, morphological information, and semantic information. But even now, I need to tell you that it is incomplete because I have not shown the semantics of tense, nor have I shown that there is a relationship between the morphosyntactic category Past tense and past time meaning. However, Figure 9 does show a considerable measure of the complexity in understanding how a two-word sentence works and in the analysis of a two-word sentence.

3.7   *Sentences*

Note that there is no sentence category in the analysis of *Jumble barked*. The nearest there is to a sentence is the referent node for the verb: this shows that the referent of the verb is the meaning of the verb with all of its arguments instantiated. In WG, verbs can also have conceptual referents, just like nouns. This is because verbs are nodes in the network and so they behave like events in Parsons' and Davidson's theories of events.

3.8   *What Else Do We Need?*

What else do we need to add to get a complete description? We need to add Tense. That is part of the semantics of verbs. Other parts of the semantics of verbs are Aspect and *Aktionsart*. Morphosyntactically, English tense is simple: Past and Present. But semantically it is not so simple, because present tense can be used to refer to past, present or future time. For example, I can tell a story using present tense to refer to past. I can say *I am walking on the road when all of a sudden, I see the police are chasing after a robber*. I can also use present tense to talk about the future; I can say *I am lecturing on polysemy tomorrow*. English present tense is a semantic mess.

3.9   *Aspect*

Aspect is quite complicated. It involves how an event is presented. We might ask ourselves what the difference is between (10) and (11).

   (10)   Jane closed the door.
   (11)   Jane was closing the door.

The answer is that (10) treats the event as encapsulated and closed. We can't look inside it. (11) treats that event as ongoing, and "looks inside" the event.

It shows us the event from the inside—it shows us a phase of the event; if you imagine an event broken down as sub-phases, there is a way of seeing a phase of the event. I have called this kind of construction "partitive". It shows us a part of an event. The English Simple Past is perfective, which is why (10) is an encapsulated event. The verb CLOSE symbolizes a complex event with subevents built in—the subject causes the closing to happen, and there is a result state where the door is closed. I discuss subevents in the next lecture. But nevertheless (10) describes an encapsulated event which is not seen to have complexity in this example. The English Progressive Aspect is imperfective, however, so (11) opens up the event so you can see inside it.

3.10 *Aktionsart*

Aktionsart, on the other hand, is the temporal contour shown by a verb's meaning or by an event; it is an event's "internal" aspect. For example, *has blue eyes* is stative, but *is running* is dynamic. We can also talk about permanent states and temporary ones. I can say *my son Tom has blue eyes*, and because he was born with blue eyes and he will die with blue eyes this is a permanent property of Tom. I can also say I live in Peebles, a small town outside Edinburgh, but this is a temporary property, and if/when we move house we will live somewhere else, making the state of living in Peebles a temporary state. States and simple dynamic events such as 'running' are simple; for these event types there is no event complexity, nor is there any event structure.

But other events that involve a change of state have an internal structure. The two main classes of complex events, both having an internal temporal structure, are "achievements" and "accomplishments". Achievements are the events that make up the meanings of verbs like *realize* and *arrive*. They involve a change of state: the subject goes from not being in the result state to being in it. *The door closed* involves an achievement: the door goes from being not-closed to being closed. But achievements also present other difficulties: it is possible to say (12) but not (13).

(12) The train is arriving at platform 2.
(13) ! He is realizing what you meant.

(12) is acceptable, although, for something to arrive, there is an instant change of state. We can talk about the "run up": (12) is called a "run up achievement". But (13) is unacceptable. Because 'realizing' is instantaneous, you can't have a "run up". For people who distinguish between these two classes of achievement, *arrive* is an achievement verb, while *realize* is semelfactive verb. One of the things that we might want to ask ourselves is why they cannot occur in the

same structures? Both 'realizing' and 'arriving' both involve a 'becoming'. One difference between them is that 'realizing' is a mental predicate, and 'arriving' is a physical one which has, in Jackendoff's terms, a Theme. We can analyse it in terms of the semantics of motion: events with Themes can include a "run up" phase whereas those that do without Themes, like 'realizing', cannot include a run-up phase.

Accomplishments are the event type found in predicates such as *build a house*. They also have internal complexity. Consider the difference between *she was running* and *she was building a house*. If someone says *she was running when she broke her ankle and had to stop*, it is nevertheless true that she has already run. But if someone says, *she was building a house when she ran out of money*, it is not true that she has already built a house. This difference reflects the relative complexity of the two events.

When we look at events, we explore event structure, different kinds of semantic relation, the relationship between events and aspect, the relationship between events and a verb's internal aspect or *aktionsart*—as well as the relationship between events and tense. This is all part of the job of trying to understand event structure.

I end this lecture with a brief glossary which summarises some of the key technical vocabulary from the lecture.

- *Reference.* First, to be able to talk about reference we need to be able to distinguish between sense and reference. A sense is a word's meaning in permanent storage. A referent is the entity in mind when a word or phrase is being used. For example, in *my dog is called Jumble*, the sense of *dog* is the permanently stored meaning 'dog'; whereas the referent is the entity under discussion—the dog I live with who has this name. We can draw a distinction between LEXEMES which have senses, and *words in utterances or texts* which have referents.
- *Sense.* The permanently stored meaning of a word: the meaning associated with a lexeme.
- *Lexeme.* An abstraction: the permanently stored entry of a word in a lexical entry. A lexeme is an abstraction away from inflections. For example, the lexeme for the word *cats* in *my cats hate dogs* is the idealized abstract entry in my mental lexicon, which has all the information I know about the word CAT associated with it.
- *Cognition.* This is a bit tough, because cognitive scientists are still working out what it is. So I will give you an ostensive definition. I think that it is what is in the brain that involves a range of activities, at both a higher and lower level, which are to do with, for example, identification of distance when we

look at things, activity planning when we go to make tea, perception of pitch when we hear a noise and the understanding of certain abstractions as we discuss the relative merits of different approaches to complex problems.
- *Concepts.* Nodes in a symbolic network which we are not always consciously aware of—the building blocks of cognition.

LECTURE 3

Evidence for Structure in Verb Meaning

In this lecture, I talk about event theory using the formalism of Word Grammar. More specifically, this lecture is concerned with the following questions:
1. What evidence is there that verb meanings are complex and that the complexity has structure?
2. How are we to determine where the structure comes from?
3. From a theoretical point of view, are we obliged to assume that there is structure, or are there theories that do without it?

1 Who Thinks What?

Within both the logic-based tradition in semantics and the less formal tradition of linguistic semantics, including cognitive semantics, most scholars assume that there is complexity in event meanings.[1] As well as these two traditions of linguistic semantics, there is also work in computational linguistics which assumes that verb meanings have structure—one example is James Pustejovsky's theory of the Generative Lexicon (Pustejovsky 1995). Because of this broad consensus, a large part of the research agenda lies in finding out what the actual structures we find in meaning look like.

---

1 One outlier is Jerry Fodor (see, for example, Fodor 1970), a leading philosopher of language who assumed that words' meanings are "indissoluble monads"; that is, for Fodor, word meanings do not have structure. Another theory, which does not admit structural relations among events, even though it admits event complexity, is the event semantics of Davidson (1967) and Parsons (1990).

 All original audio-recordings and other supplementary material, such as any hand-outs and powerpoint presentations for the lecture series, have been made available online and are referenced via unique DOI numbers on the website www.figshare.com. They may be accessed via a QR code for the print version of this book. In the e-book, both the QR code and dynamic links are available, and can be accessed by a mouse-click.

© NIKOLAS GISBORNE. REPRODUCED WITH KIND PERMISSION FROM THE AUTHOR BY KONINKLIJKE BRILL NV, LEIDEN, 2020 | DOI:10.1163/9789004375291_004

2 Evidence

Most of the literature I will talk about features a discussion of structure in verb meaning. Two classics on this topic are Jackendoff (1990), drawing in turn on Jackendoff (1972, 1983) and Levin (1993). Jackendoff argues for a highly articulated semantic structure on the basis of evidence from the behavior of verbs. His theory has a deep engagement with the cognitive linguistics literature. For example, in Jackendoff (1990) there is an extensive discussion of Talmy's force dynamics, which Jackendoff implements a version of in his own theory of conceptual semantics. Levin was part of the lexicon project at MIT in the 1980s whose work inspired investigation into verb meanings, motivations, and so on. In Levin (1993) she goes through several different classes of verbs and different diagnoses of structure, some of which have become widely used (and which I use below).

2.1 Evidence

There are three main kinds of evidence for structure in word meaning: modification, polysemy, and behavior in transitivity alternations. We will start with modification and look at these kinds of patterns to see what sort of evidence we can come up with. These three kinds of evidence can overlap, so they do not always constitute distinct kinds of evidence.

2.2 Modification

Compare the following pairs of sentences.

(1) He immediately reached the summit.
(2) *He reached the summit for three hours.
(3) *He immediately kept the book.
(4) He kept the book for three hours.

(1) is acceptable because *immediately* can modify a punctual verb. But you cannot say (2). REACH is a punctual verb, so it cannot be modified by a durative prepositional phrase like *for three hours*. Similarly, (3) is not acceptable, because *keeping the book* is durative, and cannot be modified by *immediately*, but the example in (4) is acceptable precisely because *keeping the book* has temporal duration and can therefore be modified by *for three hours*. *Immediately* and *for three hours* give us a two-way classification of events: *immediately* can modify punctual events, such as the sense of REACH, and *for three hours* goes with durative events like KEEP.

2.3 Modification of SINK

Now let us consider the verb SINK.

(5) The submarine immediately sank.
(6) The submarine sank for three minutes.
(7) The submarine immediately sank for three minutes.

The examples in (5)–(7) are all acceptable. How come? On the evidence of (1)–(4), it should not be possible for a verb to be modified both by a punctual modifier like *immediately* and by a durative modifier like *for three minutes*. We need an explanation. And what is more, there are other verbs like SINK, such as LEAVE, STOP and LEND.

(8) He immediately left the room for three minutes.
(9) He immediately stopped for three minutes.
(10) He immediately lent her the book for three minutes.

What does this mean?

2.4 What Is the Sense of SINK?

The usual answer—which I support—is that the different modifiers modify different parts of the semantic structure. In order for SINK to have this modification pattern, there must be two events in its meaning. One event is instantaneous, and the other is durative. One way of thinking about this is to say the sense of SINK Isa (=is an instance of) 'moving' whose Result Isa 'being'. Then we have an account of the data: there are two different meaning elements in the meaning of SINK: one is punctual; the other is durative, and the durative event is the Result of the punctual event. 'Moving' is an instantaneous Action and 'being' is a durative State. This is shown in Figure 1.

Figure 1 says that the lexeme SINK has a sense, 'going under', which has a Result, 'being under'. 'Being under' is classified as a State while 'going under' is classified as an Action. Both 'being under' and 'going under' share the same Er (explained below). Therefore, although there is some shared structure in the semantics, there are two distinct events. The event of 'going under' can be modified by *immediately*, while that of 'being under' can be modified by *for three minutes*. The two different kinds of modification are evidence for two different events.

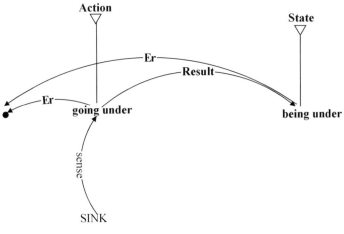

FIGURE 1   SINK

2.5   Toolkit

If we are going to talk about diagrams and use them analytically, we should understand what they mean. In Figure 1 there are two semantic relations. The Er—a term derived from the suffix -{er} in agent nouns like *driver*, *rider* and *walker*—is the semantic argument that maps onto the subject of the verb in the active voice. The Result relation is a relationship between events, which states that one event is brought about by another. I mentioned before that causation is a kind of prototype concept, so not all examples of causation are exactly the same as each other. Therefore, I will be cautious about causation, but nevertheless the Result relation is necessary in the analysis of causation: there are Results between one event and another in causation, otherwise there isn't a causation relationship. We can add another semantic relationship, the corollary of the Er, which is the Ee relation. The Ee is the semantic role that maps onto the direct object of an active voice verb. If we take the verb KISS, as in *Jane kissed Peter*, there is a *kisser*, *Jane*, and a *kissee*, *Peter*.

Another part of the toolkit is the notation which shows the Isa relation. This is the relation of default inheritance, which I introduced in Lecture 1. If x Isa y, then x inherits the properties of y, thus 'sparrow' inherits the properties of having feathers, flight, the female laying eggs and so on, from the fact that 'sparrow' Isa 'bird'. In a WG diagram, this relationship is shown with the triangle notation: the base of the triangle points to the classifying node and the apex points to the classified node. Thus, the diagram analyses 'going under' as an instance of the category 'Action' and 'being under' as an instance of the category 'State'.

2.6 What Is the Analysis in Figure 1?

Figure 1 says that the sense of the lexeme SINK is a kind of 'sinking'; that 'sinking' is a kind of 'going under'; and that it is a special kind of 'going under' because it has a Result built into its structure: a state of 'being under'. That is, 'going under' is an action, and that 'being under' is the resulting state of 'going under'. Figure 1 thus allows us to capture the different aspectual properties and account for the modification patterns. Aspectual properties are to do with *Aktionsart*, which was discussed briefly in Lecture 2 and which is discussed in more depth in Lecture 8. The first node, 'going under', can be modified by *immediately* and the second node, 'being under', can be modified by *for 3 minutes*.

2.7 Points to Take Away

The first point is that a verb can have more than one event in its meaning. When a verb has more than one event in its meaning, we need to work out how the semantic roles or relations are tied to each other. But there is something else as well, to do with Fodor: recall that for Fodor, the meaning of a verb was an atom. In a sense, the WG analysis of SINK makes the same assumption as Fodor because the meaning of SINK is just the node 'going under', a monad or atom, although it is defined by its Result. One way of thinking about this is that the node is supported by a larger network, but it is not broken down into parts.

In WG it is always possible to pick out one element in a verb's meaning as its sense, just as it is possible to pick out a head in syntax. In this case, the Er of the second event maps onto the same entity as the Er of the first event. This is something else that we have to explore when we look at a verb meaning: we have to explore how the participant relationships map when we have complex event structures, because the participant relationships do not always map in exactly the same way. In the case of SINK it is simple, because SINK just has two events and one participant, and the mapping relationship of participants and events is the same in both events. However, we have to keep in mind that it is not always so easy. We need to think about the number of events, the relationship between events, and how the participants map, whether they map onto the same concept (such as the referents of nouns or other events), or not.

2.8 Another Approach: Levin (1993)

Recall the three main kinds of evidence for structure in word meaning: modification, polysemy, and behavior in transitivity alternations. Let us now take transitivity alternations: Levin (1993: 5–10) argues that various transitivity alternations probe verb meanings. An example of a transitivity alternation is the occurrence of active-transitive verbs in the middle alternation (*she drove the car* vs. *this car drives smoothly*). In Levin's work, the middle alternation is claimed to diagnose for change of state. Another of Levin's example is the conative alternation which diagnoses for motion. For example, there is a difference between *Jane hit Peter* and *Jane hit at Peter*. If you *hit something*, you make contact with it, but if you *hit at something*, you move, but you miss it, and don't make contact. One last example is the transitive verb/body-part ascension (BPA) alternation which diagnoses for contact, such as *Jane hit Peter* (*on the nose*). Normally, if you *hit somebody* or *something*, you do not hit the whole entity, but part of the entity, so it is possible to name the part that you hit (e.g. *on the nose*). Different transitivity alternations such as these give us a way of exploring structure in verb meaning.

2.9 Transitivity Alternations and the Middle Construction

The notion of transitivity alternations is complicated. *Jane hit Peter* and *Jane hit at Peter* count as an example of alternation, but *the dog barked* and *the dog barked at Peter* do not count as an example. Likewise, with the BPA, we have to be careful to make sure that we have the right kind of diagnostic pattern—*Jane hit Peter on the nose* is an example of the BPA, but *Jane hit Peter on the island* (in a situation where they were on an island where they were having an argument) is not.

Levin says that the Middle diagnoses for a change of state but the examples from Rosta (1992) below (also see Ackema and Schoorlemmer 2006) suggest the facts are rather more complicated.

(11) We forded the river.
(12) The river fords easily.

FORD is not a change of state verb. If you ford the river, then you go through the river. If you walk through the river, you don't do anything to the river, let alone change it. But we can say *this river fords easily*, which is a middle construction, so the claim in Levin (1993) is not accurate: change-of-state verbs are a subset of verbs which can occur in the middle construction but it is not restricted to change-of-state verbs. We need additional diagnostics as well, because of these other verbs which don't involve a change of state, but which can occur in the middle construction. FORD is a simple single-event activity verb, which is the other class of transitive verb that can occur in the middle.[2]

---

2 Note that this means that the middle is still a useful diagnostic: if there is evidence of event complexity, and if the verb can occur in the middle, then the verb is a change of state verb. But you need further evidence of event complexity for the middle diagnostic to be useful in analysing changes of state.

2.10 What Do the Conative and the BPA Diagnose For?

The conative construction diagnoses for motion. The preposition AT defines a path, so the conative must have an element in its meaning that travels along a path. You can say *he kicked the ball/at the ball*. But you cannot say **his warriors heard at the ball*. As there is no movement involved in hearing something, you cannot have a conative construction with a verb of hearing. But you can have it with KICK because 'kicking' involves movement towards something. The BPA construction diagnoses for an element of contact in verb meaning. You can say *I kissed the baby on the nose* but you cannot say **I heard the baby on the nose*, as no contact is made.

2.11 The Middle

Although the Middle does not distinguish change of state verbs from simple verbs (like FORD above), all transitive change of state verbs can be made into middles. You can say *he opened the door/the door opens easily*, or *he killed the ducklings/the ducklings kill easily*.

Note that, however, you cannot say **books about swans buy easily*, although you can say *books about swans sell easily*. Obviously, BUY is a change of state verb. If someone buys a book, then the book's owner has changed. But it is an odd, complicated change of state verb, because it does not go from being active and dynamic into a particular result state. Verbs of buying and selling involve a change of state (which is a change of ownership). But they do not necessarily involve a change of state in the way that a verb like DIE involves a change of state, where the subject goes from being alive to being dead, or CLOSE, where the subject goes from being open to being shut. Therefore, we have to be quite careful about the sort of semantic structures that we find, and we cannot assume that just because a verb looks like one it should be treated as a simple change of state verb.

2.12 About AT

As I have just said, AT defines a path: *the warriors ran at the enemy*. In traditional terms, AT is a two-place predicate. It has a meaning which mediates a relationship between a Trajector—Langacker's term—or Theme—the more usual term—(they both mean something that travels along a path) and a Landmark (the reference point at the end of the path). Figure 2 demonstrates this.

We can generalize Trajector/Theme and Landmark, and call them Er and Ee as well. 'Kissing' has an Er (the kiss-er) and an Ee (the kiss-ee). In *he kissed the baby*, the referent of *he* is a kiss-er, and the referent of *the baby* the kiss-ee. Similarly, the Er of 'at' is what travels along the path it defines and its Ee is the landmark at the end of path. Hence, in *he ran at the enemy*, *he* is the Trajector/Theme, the Er, of 'at' and *the enemy* is the Landmark, the Ee of 'at'.

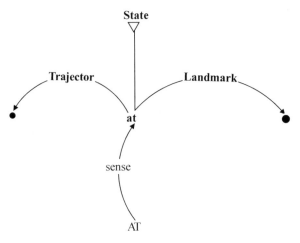

FIGURE 2   AT

2.13 *About Transitivity Alternations*

Transitivity alternations are a kind of collocation. Collocation is the property where words go together naturally and fit or fail to go together naturally. For example, you can eat an ice cream because an ice cream is a kind of food, but you cannot eat the chair because it is not a kind of food. It is a failure of collocation if you say *he ate the chair*. Of course, it is possible to interpret *he ate the chair* metaphorically, but then the meaning is moving into a new domain. What we are doing when we are talking about things like collocation is trying to work with the literal meanings, because we are using the literal meanings as a way of probing into the semantic structure.

Transitivity alternations tell us about the semantics of verbs, but they do not tell us about the semantics of all verbs, only particular classes of verbs. The conative construction tells us about transitive verbs, but collocation with AT does not always tell us that an intransitive verb has a meaning element that travels along a path (except perhaps metaphorically). Take SMILE for example: *Peter smiled at Jane*. If Peter is at one end of the room, and Jane is at the other end, he can smile at her. Nothing travels; all that happens is that she sees his smile on his face—it there is a path here, it is metaphorical. However, it is not possible to analyse this verb as meaning that there is a literal path with a Theme that travels along it, unlike the case of *he kicked at the door*, where there is a literal path and Theme.

This means if a transitivity alternation is a kind of collocation, then we do not have to assume that there are actual variant patterns where a verb can occur in both pattern (a) and pattern (b). In WG it is probably better to think of them as networks of syntactic and semantic information which is compatible with some verbs, but which is not compatible with other verbs. We would need to recognize (at least) two lexical entries for AT: one which selects for a physical entity as its Er, and one which does not. Let us call these AT/physical and AT/metaphorical. It is collocation with AT/physical that is evidence that a verb involves an element of motion in its meaning.

2.14   Levin's Case Study: the Middle

We can explore Levin's (1993) case study by looking to see how the four verbs she describes, TOUCH, HIT, CUT and BREAK, work out in the three constructions. First of all, she puts them all in the Middle.

 (13) The bread cuts easily.
 (14) Crystal vases break easily.
 (15) *Cats touch easily.
 (16) *Door frames hit easily.

Based on the examples, Levin says that CUT and BREAK are change of state verbs, while TOUCH and HIT are not a change of state verbs. However, as we have seen not all verbs that can be middles are necessarily change-of-state verbs (e.g. FORD in examples 11 and 12 above). But we can use this diagnostic as a starting point, because the two classes of verbs that can be middles are change-of-state verbs like CUT and BREAK, and simple, single-event activity verbs, like FORD.

2.15   Levin's Case Study: the Conative

The conative is exemplified in examples (17)–(20).

 (17) Margaret cut at the bread.
 (18) *Jane broke at the vase.
 (19) *Terry touched at the cat.
 (20) Carla hit at the door.

The examples indicate that neither BREAK nor TOUCH has a meaning element that travels along a path, whereas CUT and HIT both do. This tells us then that two of these verbs are predicates that conflate Path in their meaning, and two of these verbs are predicates that do not.

2.16 Levin's Case Study: the BPA

The Body-Part Ascension alternation is shown in examples (21)–(24).

(21) Margaret cut Bill on the arm.
(22) *Janet broke Bill on the finger.
(23) Terry touched Bill on the shoulder.
(24) Carla hit Bill on the back.

Whereas (21) shows that CUT has a touching element in its meaning, and (23) & (24) show the same for TOUCH and HIT, the example in (22) indicates that, perhaps counterintuitively, BREAK does not involve touching. You might think that if you break something, you really have to touch it. But that is not necessarily so. For example, we can say *the soprano broke the glass*. A soprano can vibrate the atmosphere with her voice until she makes the glass break, which does not involve touching.

2.17 Levin's Case Study: Conclusions

Table 1 is a table from Levin (1993: 7) which shows how the different verbs fit into these different diagnostic constructions.

TABLE 1

	TOUCH	HIT	CUT	BREAK
conative	no	yes	yes	no
body-part possessor ascension	yes	yes	yes	no
middle	no	no	yes	yes

2.18 What the Verbs Mean according to Levin's Diagnostics

According to Levin, TOUCH is a verb of contact, as indicated by the BPA, but not of motion, as it is incompatible with the conative. TOUCH is just a verb of pure contact. HIT involves both motion and contact; it is a verb of contact by motion. CUT involves contact, motion and a change of state in the Ee. It causes a change of state by moving something into contact with the entity of a change of state. BREAK is a not a single-activity verb, so in this case we can say that its ability to occur in the middle shows that it involves a change of state. Furthermore, as it does not occur in the other constructions, there is evidence that it is a pure change of state verb. Among the verbs in Levin's case study, CUT is the most complex, involving contact, motion, and change of state.

EVIDENCE FOR STRUCTURE IN VERB MEANING 75

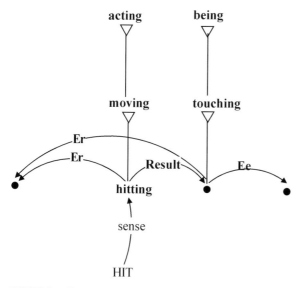

FIGURE 3   HIT

Levin's diagnoses are also evidence for structure in verb meaning and further evidence that verbs can involve more than one event in their meaning. As the meaning of HIT involves motion and contact, HIT has two events built into its sense. CUT has a network involving three events as its meaning: it involves motion, contract and a change of state. The meaning of BREAK involves a change of state, but since it has a cause as well, BREAK is a two-event verb with a cause and a change-of-state event built into its sense. Because BREAK is durative, it is not like REALIZE, for example, which is just a simple, punctual, change-of-state verb.

We can focus on event complexity by taking a closer look at HIT in Figure 3. It seems somewhat counter-intuitive to think that HIT is a verb with a complex event structure, but that is what Levin's diagnostics have indicated.

The diagram presents an analysis of HIT as a verb that has two events in its semantic structure. The sense of HIT is 'hitting', which has a Result, 'touching'. 'Hitting' isa 'moving', resulting in 'touching', and the Er of 'hitting' is the same concept as the Er of touching.

This shows a very similar structure to SINK. The main difference in the semantic structure from SINK is that the touching event also has an Ee, which is because HIT is a transitive verb. Observe that the Ee is the Ee of the Result event: it is not the case that participants in complex events must participate in all the events that make up the complex event. The Ee is the Ee of the 'touching' subevent, but not of the 'moving' one. This gives us a sense of our task in looking at event complexity: we need to explore the number of subevents and how they relate on the one hand, and we need to look at participants in events, and how they map onto the syntactic arguments of the verbs on the other.

We come back to the meaning of HIT in a later lecture, when we explore force-dynamic relations and the treatment of force-dynamics in Croft (2012).

What is left is how we diagnose change of state verbs. This raises a range of different issues which we explore further below. Change-of-state verbs have been a source of contention in lexical semantics research for several decades, and for various reasons. A famous case, dating back to the Generative Semantics debates, is whether KILL means 'cause to die' or not. On the one hand, the evidence from event complexity suggest that it does; on the other hand, Fodor (1970) presented a number of cogent arguments against that position. We will come back to this issue.

2.19 *Summing Up Levin*
The following quotation shows Levin's main idea:

> Studies of diathesis alternations show that verbs in English and other languages fall into classes on the basis of shared components of meaning. The class members have in common a range of properties, including the possible expression and interpretation of their arguments, as well as … related forms. Furthermore, the existence of a regular relationship between verb meaning and verb behavior suggests that not all aspects of a verb's behavior need to be listed in its lexical entry, […] The picture that emerges is that a verb's behavior arises from the interaction of its meaning and general principles of grammar. Thus the lexical knowledge of a speaker of a language must include knowledge of the meaning of individual verbs, the meaning components that determine the syntactic behavior of verbs and the general principles that determine behavior from verb meaning.
>
> LEVIN 1993: 11

The take-home message from this quote is that Levin thinks that the syntactic behavior of a verb can be predicted from its meaning; that is, meanings of verbs give rise to how these verbs behave syntactically.

2.20 *Levin's Case Study: Criticisms*
There are criticisms of Levin's position. Some of these criticisms are general criticisms of the approach to verb meaning which suggests that there is a complex event structure. Other criticisms are to local implementations of

the various ideas that have been explored from within this general position. One specific criticism of Levin (1993), however, is that there is no attempt to theorize the relationships between the different meaning elements. We need to ask ourselves what kind of theory we should adopt, what we want to argue about, what the different elements mean, and how they compose into more complex events. That is, what we should be looking for is a more general theory of word meaning and verb meaning. Moreover, Levin doesn't provide an explanation of what different constructions mean, and why those constructions are diagnostic of the different verb meanings, so this issue also needs further exploration.

2.21   Dowty's Criticism of Levin's Analysis of the Middle

We can look at a specific criticism of the transitivity alternation approach to verb meaning. Dowty (2001) is critical of what Levin says about the middle alternation. Dowty is famous for his work on event complexity (Dowty 1979) and also his work on a prototype approach to thematic roles (Dowty 1991).[3]

> There is no mention of any semantic effect involved in the middle alternation itself. Perhaps the treatment of the manifestation of "argument alternation" is assumed to be entirely within the syntactic component, and thus does not involve changing meaning. As far as this explanation goes, the semantics of corresponding pairs of sentences within each pattern could be exactly the same.
>
> The "analysis" of the phenomenon thus consists of A LISTING OF CORRELATIONS between features of verb meanings and participation in syntactic alternation patterns. There is no attempt to explain why each alternation pattern should be associated with its particular combination of semantic features of verb meaning, rather than with other features. In other words, Levin's analysis would have been as satisfactory if it had been the case that, the TOUCH and HIT verbs underwent the Middle Alternation while the CUT and BREAK verbs did not.
>   DOWTY 2001: 180

Dowty's criticism is really that Levin does not present a semantic theory. She needs to have one in order to be able to explain how these alternations actually

---

3   In Dowty (1991), he introduces the idea of an Incremental Theme which is an argument that measures out the event in some way. This is an important idea because it relates to the idea of scalarity, which come back in Levin's later work, and others'. We return to these ideas in later lectures.

work.[4] Dowty himself provides an analysis of the Middle. He argues that the middle construction works because it's a kind of "filter" on the verbs that can occur in it: "[the] Middle Verb Construction compares one object (implicitly) to other objects indirectly: via comparing an action performed on the first object, to the same action performed on the other objects; the actions are compared with respect to the ease, difficulty, time needed, etc. in performing them. For example: *this car drives easily*. It compares this car with other cars (or 'the average car') indirectly, by comparing the action of driving this car with the action of driving other cars, with the conclusion that the first action requires less effort than the others" (Dowty 2001: 181). Dowty further notes, "[the] meanings of the verbs of the *Break*-class and the *Cut*-class verbs all entail the causing of a physical change in all or part of the direct object referent (the Patient), cf. *break the vase, cut the bread*. Therefore, inherent physical properties of the Patient can affect the ease/difficulty of bringing about this physical change in it. Thus, the Middle Construction is meaningful with these verbs, cf. *Crystal breaks easily, The bread cuts easily*" (2001: 182). That is, what you are saying is that it is a property of the crystal by comparing it to the other objects, *or* in the case of *this bread cuts easily*, by comparing with other bread that might be less easy to cut.

Something similar applies to middles with verbs that denote activities as in *this river fords easily*: there is a quality in the river which makes it easier to ford that other rivers. The physical properties of the Direct Object referent affect the ease/difficulty of performing the action denoted by the verb. This is a useful generalization and it shows that the middle really diagnoses for properties of the Ee argument.

2.22 What Is Event Structure?

We can ask ourselves: what is event structure? To do this, we need to ask how events are related to each other. We also need to come back to Dowty and to ask ourselves what it means to say that the diagnostic "constructions" have meaning. From a pre-theoretical perspective, it is obviously true that constructions have meaning. But it is not a claim that has a great deal of meaning in WG because WG has no larger signs like constructions. If there are no larger signs in the ontology, we cannot talk about words occurring in these signs. We have to talk about words in their associative concepts collocating with each other in various ways.

---

4 Dowty has made a major contribution to the study of verb meaning, particularly in Dowty (1979) and Dowty (1991).

EVIDENCE FOR STRUCTURE IN VERB MEANING 79

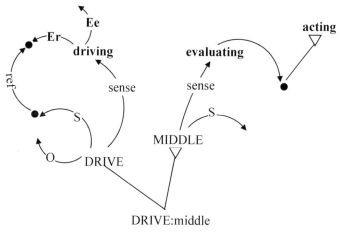

FIGURE 4   The Middle

The diagram in Figure 4 shows how to analyze the Middle in a network using a sub-lexeme-like notation, as a way of capturing the WG approach to Dowty's intuition.

In Figure 4, the WG analysis says that the Middle is like an inflection (DRIVE:middle; recall CAT:plural in lecture two). DRIVE:middle inherits from two nodes: DRIVE which has the normal syntax, semantics and morphology of the verb DRIVE, and the category Middle which affects the semantics because it only has a Subject (and so overrides the transitivity of DRIVE), and because the sense of Middle is an evaluation of the Subject-referent which is performing an action. On the left-hand side of the diagram side is the semantics of 'driving'. Essentially, the claim of the analysis in Figure 4 is that the speaker of DRIVE:middle evaluates the Ee of the action denoted by *driving*. It also shows that we can capture the interaction between a construction and a verb by using sub-types of a verb, as with sublexemes.

2.23   Discussion of Figure 4

The analysis presented in Figure 4 is schematic. I have not shown that the Er links to the Subject in the basic verb, or how the argument linking differs in the middle verb. What I have shown instead is that the middle "construction" can be treated as a simple example of a lexeme having an inflection, and this overrides the lexeme's defaults because the sub-type inherits from the category Middle. By default, verbs are Active but the category Middle overrides their default voice properties, just as Passive overrides their default voice properties. And the rest follows.

2.24 *What Do We Take from Dowty?*

The main point to take from Dowty's contribution is that variation in syntactic behavior is not enough to understand the semantics of the verbs. We have to understand the meanings of the linguistic environment as well. This is the same as when I was talking about AT. However, we don't have to understand those environments in terms of constructions and constructions as signs; we can do it with a network.

2.25 *Summary*

So far, we have looked at modification and transitivity alternations as diagnostics for event structure, but showing how they provide evidence that there are different events involved in a verb's meaning. Additionally, I have argued that transitivity alternations reduce to a kind of collocational information, because each subtype of a verb needs to be stored separately, which arguably means that they are similar to modification as a source of evidence.

2.26 *Polysemy*

We have talked about modification and behavior in transitivity alternations in order to probe into event structure. Another tool we can use is polysemy. Polysemy really is just another way of thinking about the interaction between verbs and constructions because the polysemy of verbs comes out in particular constructions. My case study is going to be the verb CLIMB which both Fillmore and Jackendoff have discussed. Discussion of CLIMB has come up again in the recent literature because CLIMB looks like a counterexample to Levin and Rappaport Hovav's theory of manner/result complementarity, recently defended in Levin and Rappaport Hovav (2013). Manner/result complementarity is the claim that a verb cannot conflate both manner and result in its meaning: if a verb has a manner meaning (like SWEEP), it cannot lexicalize a result; if it has a result in its meaning (like CLEAN) then it cannot lexicalize the manner of causing the result. Therefore, *he swept the floor* does not entail that the floor is clean and *he cleaned the floor* does not tell you how the floor was cleaned.

There have been various arguments against manner/result complentarity, including Koontz-Garboden and Beavers (2012), with more recent discussion in Gärdenfors (2014) so this is currently an on-going debate. However, here I am going to discuss the older literature on CLIMB just to show how to use polysemy as a way of thinking about diagnosing structure in verb meaning and events.

2.27 CLIMB

Let us start off by looking at Fillmore (1982) and Jackendoff (1985) and their treatments of the verb CLIMB. The basic claim is that CLIMB has what Kiparsky (1997) calls a "disjunctive" meaning: it encodes elements of clambering and of upward movement. Clambering is when you use, if you are a human, your hands and your feet in order to climb something, or if you are an animal, you will use your front feet and your back feet. Therefore, on the one hand, clambering suggests there is a manner-of-motion in CLIMB. On the other hand, there is a direction which is like a result because you end up 'above' where you started. That is, there is both manner-of-motion and path, which is a kind of result. These different elements can be factored out by using the verb in different ways. Consider the following examples.

(25) The cat climbed the tree.
(26) The train climbed to 2000 feet.
(27) The cat climbed down the tree

The example in (25) encodes both meaning elements. The example in (26) on the other hand does not have a 'clambering' element. A train can't clamber because it has wheels and stays grounded.[5] The example in (27) has no upward movement; instead there is downward movement. The prepositional phrase *down the tree* overrides the normal, upward movement. To summarize, in (25) we see the prototypical use; in (26) there is no 'clambering', while in (27) there is no directive motion. This means that, prototypically, CLIMB lexicalizes clambering and directed motion.

Levin and Rappaport Hovav (2013) claim that an example like *the snail climbs the side of the tank* shows that the 'clambering' is not part of the meaning of CLIMB. But Gärdenfors (2014: 186) argues, "However, the snail's use of suction should be seen as a metaphorical use of clambering: the force patterns involved are sufficiently similar." As this quotation shows, there is actually even an argument about what 'clambering' is and what this manner element means.

Jackendoff (1985: 275) notes that in examples such as *the plane/elevator climbed* the direction of motion is still understood as upward. Levin and Rappaport Hovav (2013) state: "Although there are undoubtedly manner-only and direction-only uses of *climb*, any account of this verb must deal with sentences [...] in which manner and direction appear to be jointly entailed"

---

5   Indeed, it is possible to say, *the aeroplane climbed more than a kilometer*, which does not involve contact, let alone clambering.

(58–59). The problem for their theoretical claim that verbs cannot have both manner and result meanings is that in the case of CLIMB you have both manner and direction conflated in the verb at the same time.

Putting manner/result complementarity aside, for our purposes it is enough to show that polysemy means that there are two elements in the verb's meaning, and those two elements both have to be built into the representation. Essentially, the polysemy of CLIMB tells us that its meaning involves a prototype which has two different events in it: a clambering event which has as a result upward motion. However, there is another issue.

Geuder and Weisgerber (2008) point out that there are examples of CLIMB which show a downward direction and an inanimate subject. The examples are taken from Levin and Rappaport Hovav (2013).

(28) Before noon the train climbed down to a green valley.
(29) Once the bus climbed down the ghat.

These are naturally occurring examples, but they are a bit odd. It seems that they are being used metaphorically to adapt the limited resources of language to untypical usage situations and Gärdenfors (2014: 186) uses a "?" against his version of (28), suggesting that for him this use is not particularly successful. But the issue is that, these non-clambering plus downward direction uses seem to extend the meaning of CLIMB a bit further, because here what CLIMB means is *to move*, with the construal being that it is movement within some kind of vertical direction. You can understand that vertical direction downwards as well as upwards, and you can remove the 'clambering' element from the meaning of the verbs. These examples show that verb meaning can get fairly complex.

Fillmore and Jackendoff both argue that the prototypical meaning of CLIMB is 'upward clambering' and 'ascending'. But (28) and (29) are possible, which indicates CLIMB can mean neither 'clambering' nor 'ascending'. CLIMB must involve a very rich network of facts—not just two meaning elements, but two meaning elements in its prototype, which can be overridden in more specific uses that extend away from that prototype. The extensions can involve motion within some kind of vertical dimension and do not even have to involve 'clambering' or 'ascending', given the right linguistic context such as the preposition *down*. The very rich network of possible meanings of CLIMB looks something like Wittgenstein's family resemblance analysis of the meaning of 'game' where chess is a game, and football is a game, and chess and football have nothing in common with each other apart from competition. And games need not even involve competition: we can play solitaire on our own, yet still call it a game.

Although a number of the event structure patterns that we look at over the course of these lectures are schematic, and the schematic patterns are the essential ones to do with argument linking, looking in detail at the lexical semantics of verbs requires attention to a range of different semantic facts. It is not possible to get a full meaning profile of every verb within a non-encyclopedic semantics. The CLIMB example demonstrates this point. There is a very rich structure of prototypical family resemblance structure that we need to explore to capture all of these different possible senses. Another example of a very rich network structure is Lakoff's (1987) analysis of OVER, and it can be argued that a similar approach needs to be brought to bear on verb meaning.

3 Event Complexity and the Theory of Grammar

In this section, we ask ourselves what event complexity means for a theory of grammar? It is probably the most basic question and the reason why people are interested in event semantics. We want to understand how form and meaning actually relate to each other and where meaning comes from. There were several different approaches to semantics and to grammar more generally, as discussed in lecture one: Cognitive grammar, Construction Grammar, Minimalism, earlier versions of Generative Grammar and various theories of formal semantics. All the theories are concerned with these questions and a theory of event structure goes someway to working out a more general theory of the relationship between form and meaning.

In lecture two, I added to this question, the question of recursive embedding in syntax, and I argued that there is no recursive embedding in a network. A network simply has active arcs and nodes, at different levels of activation. In Generative Semantics, an earlier theory of the relationships between semantics and generative grammar from the 1960s and early 1970s, the verb KILL was analyzed as involving lexical decomposition in the syntax. Similar analyses can be found in modern Minimalism. For example, Ramchand (1996, 2008) argues that there is a kind of lexical semantic structure in syntax.

3.1 Event Complexity and the Theory of Grammar
However, one of the major arguments against lexical decomposition in syntax came from Fodor (1970) which I have mentioned before, whose evidence included the examples in (30)–(33).

(30) John caused Mary to die and it surprised me that he did so.
(31) John caused Mary to die and it surprised that she did so.

(32) John killed Mary and it surprised that he did so.
(33) *John killed Mary and it surprised me that she did so.

The examples in (30)–(32) are all fine, but (33) is not. The example in (30) means that John causing Mary to die surprised the speaker. The example in (31) means that John acted in a way that resulted in Mary dying, and it surprised the speaker that she died. Maybe he pushed her, and she fell and hit her head. The speaker was then surprised that the result was that she died. Therefore, the examples in (30) and (31) show that anaphora with *do so* can pick up on the meaning of either verb in the preceding clause. In (32) *did so* picks up the whole meaning of *killed*. But the example in (33), which Fodor uses to argue that KILL cannot mean *cause to die*, is not acceptable. If KILL meant *cause to die*, then according to Fodor *do so* should be able to pick out the 'die' element in KILL, but this is not the case. In sum, the examples in (30)–(33) tell us parts of the meanings of verbs are not available for VP anaphora with *do so*.

3.2   Event Complexity and Grammar

Fodor also gives us the following examples.

(34) John caused Bill to die on Sunday by stabbing him on Saturday.
(35) *John killed Bill on Sunday by stabbing him on Saturday.

Fodor argues that (34) and (35) show the same thing: that the decomposed meaning of KILL is not available for the rest of the grammar. More specifically, (34) and (35) shows us that subparts of this verb's meanings have to take place in a temporally close way, unlike the meanings of different verbs, such as SINK discussed earlier.

3.3   Event Complexity and Grammar

There have been various replies to Fodor in the literature. One reply is that event structure is not syntactic, but semantic. Fodor was arguing against syntacticizing event structure. Jackendoff (1983) argues that "decomposed" verb become "wholes" in the human mind. He has a metaphor of playing a piece of music. If you have ever learned the piano, you will remember that when you started to learn it, you did things in 4/4 time, and then eventually you got better, and you did pieces in 6/8 time. When you first started playing 6/8 time, you counted 6 beats in a bar. But eventually you got better, and you'd just count that as two groups of three, each of which had sub-parts. You came to see this time signature structure as a kind of gestalt. Jackendoff argues that word meanings have the same kind of gestalt properties as musical phrases. But there is a different response in WG.

3.4   Event Complexity and WG

There is no event decomposition in WG. Each node in the network is just a conceptual address. Each conceptual address is linked to a network that supports it. This network does not break down into parts: there are no parts and wholes in a network, but a series of nodes and arcs. Fodor's arguments do not apply to the WG analysis because in WG we would say that in the case of VP anaphora the anaphor has to point back to the exact concept which is the verb's sense. That is, we have a way around this problem just in the logic of how networks work. The meaning of a verb in WG is just a node, the verb's sense. That node is supported by a large conceptual network, but there is not any decomposition as such. Therefore, there is a sense in which a node in a WG network is also an indissoluble monad. There can be more than one event in a word's meaning because of the Result relation, but in WG the meaning of a verb is the node which is identified as its sense, supported by its surrounding network.

The kinds of modification seen with SINK earlier suggest that Fodor's treatment of KILL is not the end of the story either. In cases like this, WG would argue that the two events of SINK have different time indices, whereas the events of KILL do not. In this way, SINK permits conflicting temporal modifiers, and KILL does not.

4   Theoretical Questions to Do with Polysemy and Event Structure

So far, I have been talking about issues like finding evidence for event structure, showing that verbs can lexicalize more than one event in their meaning, establishing what those events are, working out how events relate to other events, and what this means for a theory of language and an architecture of grammar.

4.1   Theoretical Questions

Actually, there are more basic questions that we might want to look at. They include, "How many classes of event are there?" You might want to use *Aktionsart* as your diagnostic: among the different *Aktionsarten* there are States, Activities, Achievements, Accomplishments, and Semelfactives. From this classification, we might conclude that there are five classes of events. But we might also think that the best diagnostic of event classes is found in the kinds of meaning that are conflated. For example, on this basis, it is possible to classify verbs into motion verbs, result verbs, mental-state verbs, psych-verbs, physical-state verbs, or change-of-state verbs (a sub-type of result verb). The question of how many classes of events there might be is a theoretical question, with a theoretical answer, because it is determined by our assumptions about how events and event structure work.

The next theoretical question is to ask ourselves how events interact with thematic roles. Talmy, Jackendoff, and others talk about thematic roles based on the concept of motion. In Jackendoff's work, this is called the Thematic Roles Hypothesis. This is a localist analysis of thematic roles, which is related to the localist analysis of case semantics in case languages like Russian, German and Latin. There is another kind of thematic roles as well, the force-dynamic thematic roles. Croft makes the very strong claim that the only thematic roles that are relevant to argument linking or argument are the force-dynamic thematic roles (Initiator and Endpoint in Croft's system; Agonist and Antagonist in Talmy's). But are there other types of thematic role? What about predicates such as THINK which do not appear to have motion elements or "force" in their meaning? Does motion have anything to do with thinking? Does force have anything to do with thinking? For example, force-dynamics are significant in Sweetser's (1990) treatment of the semantics of modality—include epistemic modality. Talmy also talks about force and force-dynamics playing out in the semantics of modality. What are the bounds on the system?

Another theoretical question which we need to think about is how events combine to make up complex events. Is there just a simple Result relationship in event structure such that one event causes another? In most analyses of the ditransitive construction, there is a claim that in *Bill gave Haley sweets* there is a causing event which results in the state of *Haley possessing sweets*; these analyses claim that ditransitive GIVE means '*x* causes *y* to have *z*'. But is it really the case that in a complex event, the initial event is always a causing event, or can there be any other possible relations between events? Perhaps the first event is not a causing event or perhaps the Result is not entailed.[6]

So far, I have given examples with mostly just two events in the substructure. But perhaps, there can be more than two. A simple change of state involves just two events, the changing event and the resultant stative event. In *the window broke*, there is a change of state. But in *John broke the window*,

---

6   One case in point is in sublexical modality (Koenig and Davis 2001). For example, Simon (2017) discusses a sub-class of psych-verb, the PROVOKE class, where the relationship between the two subevents is not entailed. In *Peter provoked Jane but she wasn't annoyed* we can see that although it is necessary for the Subject-referent to act in a provoking way, it is not necessary for the Object-referent to experience the psychological state that they must experience if the verb is used in the passive (*Jane was provoked*). This, then, is an intended Result rather than an actual Result.

perhaps there are three events—a causing event as well as the changing event and resultant stative event. And what about verbs of 'buying' and 'selling'? How many events are in 'buying' and 'selling'? The meanings of both BUY and SELL involve exchange, so if I sell you my car, then I give you my car, and you reciprocate by giving me money. In a verb of exchange, we might propose that 'giving' involves two events, and 'giving' goes in both directions. Or we might profile the events differently, so that they are about 'getting' not about 'giving'. Then perhaps there are four events in a verb of exchange. And how many participants are there in verbs of buying and selling? For example, take a sentence such as *I could sell you my car for £5000 pounds*; in that case there would be four participants: *I*, *you*, *car*, and *money*. We might ask ourselves how many participants are possible in complex events as well. Is there a maximum number of participants per event? Is there a maximum number of participants in the whole of a complex event?

4.2   Theoretical Questions

Moreover, how should complex events map onto structures which we know about from elsewhere? What is the relationship between causal structures and *Aktionsart*, for example? We might expect these structures to be the same. *Aktionsart* is a way of viewing an event sub-atomically in terms of its temporal profile. It is therefore expected that there is some kind of relationship between *Aktionsart* and an event structure because if an event has a temporal profile, then certain kinds of temporal profile will correlate with complexity, and other kinds of temporal profile will not. But recall that in lecture two, we saw 'arriving' and 'realizing' have a different relationship to progressive aspect, even though they are both achievements, because you can say *the train is arriving*, but you cannot say **he is realizing*. This fact suggests that there is not a simple relationship from event classes to aspectual classes.

4.3   Theoretical Questions

There is evidence from the aspectual behaviors of verbs that not all of event structure belongs directly to the verb itself; sometimes it has to do with the interaction of verbs and their arguments. Consider the examples in (36) and (37).

(36)   He drank beer *in an hour/for an hour
(37)   He drank a beer in an hour/*for an hour

(36) and (37) tell us that *Aktionsart* involves a relationship between verbs and their arguments as well. In (36), when the Direct Object of *drank* is a mass noun, the event is unbounded; but when the Direct Object is a count noun,

the event is bounded. Unbounded or atelic events cannot occur with *in an hour*; bounded or telic events cannot occur with *for an hour*. Depending on what its Direct Object is, DRINK can occur with each of these time adverbs. We therefore need to ask ourselves how the event structures should be represented, what boundedness is, and how boundedness should be put into the representation. In summary, we have two different problems when considering the relationship between event complexity and *Aktionsart*. There are different behaviors of change-of-state verbs, like *realize* and *arrive*, and there is variable behavior according to the semantic properties of the Direct Object.

Another issue is to do with Direct Objects which measure out events, and with the temporal profile and temporal contour of verbs. Take, for example, *mow the lawn*. The *mowing* event takes as long as it takes to mow a lawn. If you mow half of the lawn, you have done half of the event. This means that the Direct Object measures out the event. However, verbs of creation are different. If I am baking a cake, and there is a power cut, then it is not the case that some of the cake has been baked. If you do not finish baking the cake, there is no cake; that is, the completion only takes place at the end of the event. Part of the job of understanding the semantics of events lies in understanding how event predicates interact with other sentence elements or how event complexity causes events to interact with aspectual causes of the sentence, like BAKE, or how two verbs that do the same thing can fail to have the same aspectual class, like REALIZE and ARRIVE. Therefore, there are many things to be alert to as well as the simpler issues of what conflation classes are possible, and whether there really is manner/result complementarity. These are the various theoretical questions that we need to explore as we look at event complexity and the relationships between sub-events, and as we are exploring the lexical meaning of verbs.

4.4 *Theoretical Questions and Conclusions*

Now, let us return back to the basic questions. How many classes of event are there? That depends on how we are counting. From an aspectual point of view, as I said before, there are states, actions, achievements, semelfactives and accomplishments—although not all typologies since Vendler's (1967) pioneering work have the same set of aspectual classes (or *Aktionsarten*). But what about complex events? How many complex event types are there, and how well do they map onto the aspectual classes?

The answers to these questions depend partly on the theory that you adopt. As theoreticians, we make choices about how you think language works. We will find that there is a gross relationship between causative predicates, and accomplishments. Therefore, accomplishments involve causes. But even then, how many events are there in a causative predicate? For example, for a causative predicate like OPEN, Parsons (1990) has two events, and a result state, which—translated into WG terms—are related by a 'causing' and a 'becoming' predicate. But then what about force-dynamics? These relations are also implicated in the analysis of causation in Croft (1990, 2012), Gisborne (2010), Sweetser (1990) and Copley and Harley (2014). As well as in formal theories, causation has featured extensively and obviously in cognitive theories. In 2010, I argued that sublexical causation cannot be analyzed by exploiting the semantics of the word CAUSE alone: we also need force-dynamics, Force dynamics are part of the definitions of events that they are associated with.[7] Therefore, we would expect in a network theory that the force-dynamic relations support the event concepts that they are part of. I will talk about this in lecture 6.

Finally, another area that we will need to explore is the question of what event networks are possible. All of these theoretical questions I just have been covering in this section are questions that emerge from finding evidence that there really is event structure. By the end of the lecture series, I expect we will have some answers to some of these questions.

The theoretical questions I have just been raising frame the discussion in the remaining lectures. We will be looking at causation, event complexity and structure, the relationships between participants and events, and polysemy, among other topics. The evidence for structure that we have seen in this lecture is also evidence for polysemy—because many verbs that have complex event structures are polysemous as well. We come to polysemy in the next lecture.

---

[7] The claim that verbs with a causal meaning do not involve the same sense of CAUSE that you find in the meaning of the verb CAUSE is of course not original; it is also part of Fodor's (1970) argument about KILL not meaning 'cause to die'.

LECTURE 4

Polysemy and Semantic Structure

This lecture is concerned with the following questions about polysemy: what can polysemy tell us about event complexity? What are the different kinds of polysemy? How should we diagnose polysemy? What are the representations for different kinds of polysemy in the WG network? I will argue that WG permits a subtle approach to polysemy which captures a range of relevant phenomena.

1   Polysemy: an Introduction

1.1   *Polysemy vs. Homonymy*
When talking about polysemy, we need to start with the notion of sense disambiguation: how do we know that we have different senses of the same item, rather than different connotations or features of a meaning? We will come back to this, because before discussing sense disambiguation, I want to ask another question: how do we distinguish polysemy from homonymy (and should we)? In traditional approaches to a lexical item having multiple meanings, homonymy involves the distinction between BANK/'river' and BANK/'money'. These two senses are not related to each other and so on a homonymy analysis, BANK/'river' and BANK/'money' are two different words because they have different senses even though they are both nouns with the same form and same morphological variants. In a theory that maintains the polysemy/homonymy distinction, polysemy involves a relationship between the different senses. The examples involving two different senses of BANK in (1) and (2) exemplify polysemy: in (1) BANK means the institution, not the building; in (2), BANK means the building. These different senses are related.

 All original audio-recordings and other supplementary material, such as any hand-outs and powerpoint presentations for the lecture series, have been made available online and are referenced via unique DOI numbers on the website www.figshare.com. They may be accessed via a QR code for the print version of this book. In the e-book, both the QR code and dynamic links are available, and can be accessed by a mouse-click.

(1) My salary goes straight to the bank.
(2) I tripped up right outside the bank.

The reason why there is polysemy in (1) and (2), not homonymy, is because these two meanings of BANK are both related to the place where money goes, where money is stored and so on. The words for institutions typically show this kind of polysemy. I can say Beihang University, as an institution, invited me to give some lectures and I can also say I am lecturing in Beihang University, the location or building that houses the institution.

The reason why the distinction between polysemy and homonymy matters is that we have to work out how we want to think about these differences theoretically. We also need to think about whether there are any regularities in the ways in which senses of words can be related to each other. It is often claimed that polysemy is regular, unlike homonymy. Therefore, if we have a word for an institution, then that word will also name the physical place for the institution. But we can also say the same for words such as WINDOW and DOOR. If we focus on looking through the window, then the window is a kind of glazed aperture which we can see through. But if we open the window, then the window is a physical object that we can move. It is perhaps even more obvious with the DOOR: it can be an aperture (as in *I walk through the door*) or it can be the thing that fills the aperture (as in *I open the door*). If polysemy is regular, then we need a way of capturing that regularity, understanding it and using it in our theories of word meaning. This kind of regular polysemy is the same phenomenon as the structured polysemy I discussed in Lecture 1 when I discussed the verb THINK.

However, I will argue in this lecture that despite regularities in polysemy, there are also lots of small irregularities. In a theory such as Word Grammar, or in Construction Grammar, default inheritance allows us to state regularities at many different degrees of granularity. As Goldberg has pointed out, some generalizations are expressions of small regularities. I think polysemy is one of the cases where we might need to make generalizations at a rather fine grain. We need to ask ourselves whether we really want to privilege the big regular patterns over all of the other patterns including the less regular patterns, and whether that is the right approach to polysemy.

What does homonymy do then? It gives you sets of meanings, which are not related to each other. We have to ask ourselves, "Do the same two senses belong to the same lexeme, or do they belong to different lexemes?" This leads us to another serious theoretical question: what is a lexeme? One answer that works for European languages is that is a generalization over all of the inflectional variants of a word. If this is so, then you would expect for homonyms to share a lexeme, as long as they are in the same lexical category. For example, two nouns that are homonyms could theoretically share the same lexeme, because there would be the same generalizations over the singular and plural variants.

Before we proceed, we need to differentiate homonyms which are two words with the same sound in the same word class, from two words in different word classes. The form *drive* can instantiate two different lexemes: a noun lexeme and a verb lexeme. The verb lexeme is found in *to drive a car*, but the noun lexeme denotes a place in front of a house where the owner can park their car: *my drive is made of monobloc*. These words are distant homonyms: lexemes in different word classes that happen to have some of the same phonetic/phonological realizations. They are different lexemes because they belong in different word classes, and they involve different sets of inflectional forms.

So, coming back to nouns, what do we do with homonyms' discrete and separate senses? Does having different senses make BANK/'money' and BANK/'river' different lexemes? They are both nouns and can have some of the same modifiers (e.g. *a big bank* and *a bank in the city*). Therefore, I think they share the same lexeme, but they are different senses. For this reason, I think it makes more sense to treat homonyms that share forms, and are in the same word class together with polysemy, rather than together with the kinds of homonyms that are in different word classes. But then what would distinguish the senses of these kinds of homonym? In this case, we might want to say that BANK is a single lexeme, with a set of meanings, but where one of those meanings is associated with a larger network. This is represented in Figure 1, taken from Gisborne (2010).

However, I now think that this representation is wrong. It says the lexeme BANK has a sense which is a set of meanings where the first member is 'river

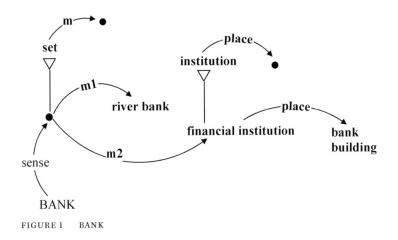

FIGURE 1   BANK

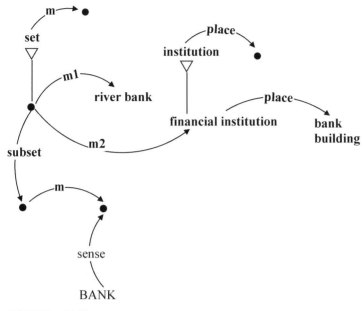

FIGURE 2   BANK

bank' ("m1," which means "member 1") and the second one is 'financial institution' (m2). But this is not correct. The meaning of the word BANK is not a set of meanings. It is one of the members of a set of meanings. In fact, the meaning of a word cannot possibly be a set, as that would mean the meaning of the word BANK was plural when it actually is not. What is needed is a way of capturing the fact that the sense of BANK is one or other of the two senses. Figure 1 does not force the choice between m1 and m2; instead, it says the whole set is the meaning. We need to have a way of forcing the choice. I give an alternative representation in Figure 2.

Figure 2 says the sense of the word BANK is the member of a subset of a set whose members are either the 'river bank' or 'financial institution'. Because members of the subset are members of the set, and the sense of BANK is an arbitrary member of a subset, which has a cardinality of 1, of this set of meanings we force BANK to mean either 'river bank' or 'financial institution'. The diagram gives us an analysis equivalent to saying "the sense of BANK is river bank or financial institution." The diagram therefore shows a way of analyzing OR.

In his discussion of the conjunction OR, Hudson (2007: 35) shows a different way of forcing the choice between the members of a set. He uses a relationship which looks like a choice-function. I think that the two analyses are probably equivalent, but I also think that the analysis I offer here is simpler, because it does not require us to posit a 3rd member of a set which is bound to one of the other members of the set, and which does not add to the cardinality of the set.

1.2 Polysemy vs. Homonymy

What about sublexemes? I have talked about sublexemes as a way of handling different relationships with the lexeme members. Rather than saying that a lexical item has different properties in different constructions, and therefore having to posit symbolic phrasal constructions, we can treat the variable behaviour of a lexeme as being due to partially regular behaviour among different subtypes of that lexeme. In Gisborne (2010), I showed a way of capturing the polysemy of SEE by having separate sublexemes which were associated with different parts of the network profiling the different senses, and where the various senses were matched to different argument-structure properties. This is necessary for verbs, because different senses are associated with different argument-taking properties. But for homonymy, sublexemes will not work. This is because either 'financial institution' or 'river bank' would need to be the main sense of the lexeme, but it is not possible for either 'river bank' or 'financial institution' to serve as the main member of the main sense of BANK, which is completely ambiguous. There is no way in which one of those senses is primary to other senses. An alternative would be to assume that homonymy involves different lexemes. Should we do that? No: the reason why that will not work is that lexemes are a way of capturing inflectional variation. If we were to have two separate lexemes for 'river bank' or 'financial institution' when these meanings are associated with precisely the same inflectional variants, we would miss important generalizations. The treatment in Figure 2 above allows us to capture all of the relevant morphosyntactic generalizations while at the same time showing that the senses are strictly different.

These observations lead to a new question: should the polysemy of nouns be represented in the same way as the polysemy of verbs (with different sublexemes associated with the separate senses), or should it be represented with the subset relation like homonymy? (In the latter case, the semantic relationships among the different senses would also need to identified.) I do not know the answer to this question, but choosing the different sublexemes approach will involve the problem that each sublexeme will have the same syntactic properties.

1.3 The Argument from Homonymy

There is an argument from homonymy which gets us to think about how we induce new lexemes in acquisition. We can use it as a start in getting us to think about representations. Here is a relevant quote from Hudson:

> When we first meet a homonym of a word that we already know, we don't treat it as a completely unfamiliar word because we do know its form, even though we don't know its meaning. For instance, if we already know the adjective ROUND (as in a round table), its form is already stored as a 'morph'—a form which is on a higher abstraction level than phonology; so when we hear *go round the corner*, we recognize this form, but find that the expected meaning doesn't fit the context. As a result, when creating a new word-concept for the preposition ROUND we are not starting from scratch. All we have to do is to link the existing form to a new word. But that means that the existing form must be conceptually distinct from the word—in other words, the morph {round} is different from the words that we might write as ROUND/adj and ROUND/prep. Wherever homonymy occurs, the same argument must apply: the normal processes of learning force us to start by recognizing a familiar form, which we must then map onto a new word, thereby reinforcing a structural distinction between the two levels of morphology (for forms) and syntax (for words), both of which are different from phonology and semantics.
>
> HUDSON 2012: 11

Essentially, what Hudson says here is that the more extreme form of homonymy which involves different lexemes, forces us to represent distinct levels of morphology, syntax, phonology and semantics. That is relevant to my discussion, because I was saying a true homonym such as BANK/'river' and BANK/'money' forces us to say we have only one lexeme. That is also an argument to do with morphology. In WG our strategy is to use linguistic evidence to tell us whether there are certain kinds of distinctions in language and whether

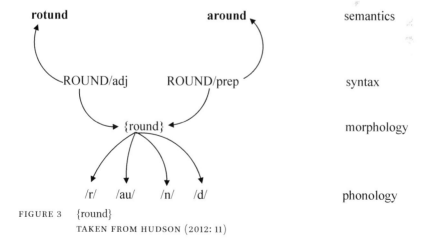

FIGURE 3 {round}
TAKEN FROM HUDSON (2012: 11)

those distinctions exist between phonology and morphology, morphology and syntax, and so forth. The research strategy is to draw conclusions from the way in which the language itself works. Figure 3 presents Hudson's representation of the homophony of *round*.

The morphological form {round} shares phonology and morphology. There are distinct lexemes because one is a preposition and the other is an adjective, and the different lexemes also have different meanings. But the different lexemes share the same realization. By the same token, I think we should treat homonymy and polysemy in the same way as each other when they must share the same lexeme, because the lexeme covers the same inflections.

1.4   Types of Polysemy

What matters in event structure is polysemy rather than homonymy. In polysemy the senses are related and as we saw in an earlier lecture in the case of OPEN a complex event structure invites an analysis of polysemy. But there are various approaches to polysemy, and they do not necessarily converge on the same analysis or the same solutions. For example, Pustejovksy (1995) has a model which deals with a small handful of related meanings—his qualia. But Pethő (2001) distinguishes between what he calls regular and irregular polysemy.

Pethő (2001) argues that the kind of polysemy we see in the case of WINDOW or DOOR is regular (it is amenable to analysis in terms of Pustejovsky's qualia). Recall the different meanings of WINDOW that I mentioned earlier: in *I looked through the window*, the window is a glazed aperture in a wall. In *I threw it through the window*, it's the aperture once you open the window. But he says that HEAD is irregular. You can say *this is a human head*, or *she is my head of department*. This difference is, according to Pethő, not regular polysemy but irregular polysemy. It seems to me, however, that in the case of the polysemy of nouns the distinction is graded rather than clearly bounded, and that it might be better to look at the networks surrounding particular senses. And there is clearly a metaphorical link from head as part of a body, and head in the sense of head of department.

My main theme for this lecture series is that several distinctions made in the research literature can be rethought. These distinctions include, for example, categorical differences between X and Y, as in regular and irregular polysemy, and idiomatic phrases and idiomatically combining expressions, or the idea that an item can occur in this construction or can't in that construction. I think these sharp distinctions are not always true. Given what we know about Rosch's (1975) results in terms of prototype structures in human categorization, we must expect there to be not just degree of goodness prototypicality as John Taylor (2004a) discusses, but also degree of category membership prototypicality as well. Therefore, there are graded boundaries in polysemy just as there are graded boundaries between different kinds of idiom. Obviously, there are some places where we have categorical boundaries. This said, perhaps we should remind ourselves that some linguistic phenomena are categorically ungrammatical. For example, it is grammatical to say in English *which dog do you like*, but **which do you like dog* is completely ungrammatical. In short, we have to be sensitive to the possibility that there are also graded boundaries around some categories, polysemy being one of them.

With verbs, it makes sense to talk about regular or structural polysemy, which clearly exists in verb meaning, especially in cases such as the causative/inchoative alternation, such as *open the door* and *the door opened*. In many cases, the transitivity alternations we discussed in the previous lecture are related to structural polysemy. Our theory also has to embed this kind of polysemy in a larger account of different kinds of polysemy as well. The research strategy is to go for the low-hanging fruit first, but it is a mistake to think that once you have done that, you have done the work.

1.5 Structured Polysemy

We can begin by looking at polysemy and event structure. I am going to explore the analyses in two papers from the literature: Pustejovsky (1991) and Rappaport Hovav and Levin (1998). The classic starting point is the relationship between causative verbs and their inchoative counterparts which is shown in the semantic distinctions between transitive and intransitive variants of the same verb as in (3) and (4), for example.

(3) The door closed.
(4) Peter closed the door.

In these examples, we see an additional element in the syntax—the example in (4) adds a syntactic argument—and an additional element in the meaning: the causative element. One of the first task we have when we are looking at polysemy and verb meaning, especially if we are interested in event structure, is to explore patterns like this and see what sense we can make of them. Other kinds of structured polysemy include (5) and (6):

(5) Jane sent Peter a present.
(6) Jane sent a present to Peter.

(5) entails that *Peter received the present* while (6) does not: (5) cannot be continued with *but he didn't get it*, but (6) can. However, there is some dispute

about the how to analyse (5). (That's another difficulty with research: if we rely too much on our own judgments without asking other people, doing experiments, or looking in corpora, it is easy to make mistake about what the facts are. We have to bear in mind that grammar exists in individual people's minds, but language exists in the population. As a result there can be a variation in a language which is not necessarily variation individual speakers' grammars.)

1.6   Structured Polysemy: Pustejovsky's Model of Events

Examples like (3) and (4) lead Pustejovsky (1991) to argue for a syntax of events. For him it is necessary to have a discrete level of event structure, which is separate from what he calls "Lexical-Conceptual Structure" which is needed in order to be able to identify the syntax of events. By the syntax of events, Pustejovsky does not mean syntax in linguistic sense; instead, he just means that there is a syntax to the combinatorial possibilities of events and he's trying to sketch what that syntax looks like. Essentially, Pustejovsky is interested in what combinations of events are possible and his theory is designed to capture the regularities between lexical semantics on the one hand and how event structure works on the other. Figure 4 gives a representation from Pustejovsky's work.

In Figure 4, Pustejovsky says that transition, represented by *T*, consists of a process which results in a state. Lexical Conceptual Structure prime (LCS′) is a lexical conceptual structure associated with each subevent. In Figure 4 the process (*P*) consists of *John acting on the door* and *the door being not closed* ([act(j, the~door) & ~closed(thedoor)]) and the LCS′ of the state (*S*) that the door is closed ([closed(door)]). Each part of the event structure has an associated meaning. If you put those two events together and compose them,

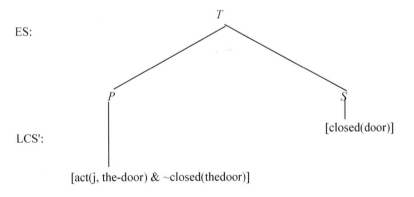

FIGURE 4   Representation for 'close the door'
TAKEN FROM PUSTEJOVSKY (1991: 58)

then you need another predicate *become*. Therefore, the overall LCS is John's action on the door causes a becoming event, and the becoming event is the door closing. Pustejovsky factors out the structure of events from the meaning of events and from the composition of the meaning of events, therefore you have a three-way analysis of looking at event structure. The basic idea of Pustejovsky's model is that there is a structure which organizes how events can be related to each other.

For Pustejovsky, the two complex event types, achievements and accomplishments, are both transitions and have the same structure. The difference in the temporal semantics is not represented. The other two event types in his event structures are processes and states. Verb meanings are therefore built up out of more basic elements which compose them into complex LCS structures, which map onto a complex event structure. Pustejovsky's theory gives us a way of thinking about analyzing structural polysemy because we can draw diagrams like Figure 4 for the different kinds of complex events to see the different relationships between them.

1.7 Rappaport Hovav and Levin

Rappaport Hovav and Levin (1998) make a similar argument but with different representations. Unlike Pustejovsky's, their representations are not layered. Rappaport Hovav and Levin (1998) are mainly concerned with intransitive and transitive verbs, and they develop a model which tries to account for a range of different verb patterns. It does not extend to ditransitive verbs or to verbs of buying and selling. Their representations, given immediately below, relate event structure to *Aktionsart*.

[x ACT$_{<MANNER>}$]	(activity)
[x $<STATE>$]	(state)
[BECOME [x $<STATE>$]]	(achievement)
[[x ACT$_{<MANNER>}$] CAUSE [BECOME [y $<STATE>$]]]	(accomplishment)
[x CAUSE [BECOME [y $<STATE>$]]]	(accomplishment)

These representations are ways of capturing complex event structures for a range of different aspectual categories or categories of *Aktionsarten*. An activity involves a participant acting in a particular manner, for example *running*. Being in a state, say being asleep, involves a participant being in the state that the relevant predicate names. An achievement involves undergoing a change which consists of entering into a state, so there is a predicate BECOME with a state predication as its argument. This state predication is a kind of result. There are two different ways of representing accomplishments: one means 'x acts in a manner which causes something (y) to become in a state', and the other one means 'x causes something (y) to become in a state'. Each of these event structures maps onto the aspectual category of an accomplishment.

The model is based around *Aktionsarten*. Each verb class corresponds to an aspectual category and the meaning of those aspectual categories is structured. There is also a relationship between meanings of one kind and meanings of another: states are embedded within achievements and achievements are embedded within accomplishments. How does this model then map onto simple argument-taking facts? There are two kinds of argument in this model: those which are licensed by the verb root—for example the *x* argument of the state predication "[x <STATE>]" or the state predicate within the event structure for an accomplishment—and those which are licensed by the template such as the *x* argument of the two kinds of accomplishment. If we look at the transitive verbs in (7)–(9), we can see how they map onto the kinds of structure that Rappaport and Hovav propose.

(7) He licked the ice-cream.
(8) He walked the dog.
(9) He made a cake.

Licking is a simple activity event. *Walking the dog* is a transitivized unergative verb. It is a kind of strange causative verb, because it is about making a participant act in the way denoted by the verb, so it wraps a causative predicate around an activity. With a verb like it, you put a cause on the outside of the representation for an activity verb like [x ACT$_{<MANNER>}$], to make, something like [x CAUSE [y ACT$_{<MANNER>}$]]. However, Rappaport Hovav and Levin do not show the representation for kind of causative and note that walking the dog collocates with *for an hour* not *in an hour*, so it is an activity verb, not a telic one. *Making a cake* is one of the two accomplishments; it is a complex event involving a verb of creation and it is telic.

Part of the theory is to do with linking to syntax. Rappaport Hovav and Levin have a system of indexing which relates semantic arguments to syntactic ones. They also place restrictions on their theory: one of the claims that they make is that each subevent can only have one argument; this claim is a way of addressing some questions we thought about in the last lecture: how many subevents are possible, and how are they related to participants?

The model allows for thinking about polysemy in terms of transitivity alternations and like Pustejovsky's makes it straightforward to capture the polysemy that certain transitivity alternations involve.

POLYSEMY AND SEMANTIC STRUCTURE 101

1.8 Prepositions and Verb Polysemy

Something we need to think about is where polysemy gets more graded. For example, adding prepositions to verbs can also change their meanings. Consider:

(10) He ran up the hill.
(11) He ran up a huge bill.
(12) He ran down the hill.
(13) The battery ran down

Up in (10) tells the direction of the verb of motion, but the same expression *ran up* in (11) is idiomatic. (12) has another directional verb of motion, but here the expression *ran down* is idiomatic, too. These examples show that "verb + preposition" combinations can be transparently compositional or idiomatic. This kind of combination tends to be more idiomatic than the combinations of other categories. (12) and (13) also show the prepositions can be transitive or intransitive.

1.9 An Alternative View

It appears to me that the distinction between regular and irregular polysemy is not helpful because it's an arbitrary distinction. Let us go back to RUN.

(14) He ran up the hill.
(15) The train ran up the hill.
(16) The train ran along the new tracks.
(17) The programme ran for 4 hours
(18) He ran up a huge bill.

In (14) RUN is a verb of manner of motion, and the prepositional phrase tells you the direction of motion. There are two parts to the manner element of the meaning of RUN in (14): the first part is that he used his legs, and the second manner-element is that it was fast. In (15), even though RUN is also a verb of manner of motion, the first manner-element is missing. In (16), *the train* might not even move fast; it could just mean that the train moved at normal train speed. This is a metaphorical extension of this meaning of RUN. We return to a representation for RUN in Figure 7, later in the lecture.

But what about a computer programme, as in the example in (17)? In this example, nothing is moving: there is just electrical activity happening very fast in the machine. (18) is also an example of an extension of the meaning of RUN, but in this case its idiomatic in the combination with UP. Someone who believes in the difference between regular and irregular polysemy would say (14) and (15) are regular, while (16)–(18) are irregular. But that misses the connections between all of them: they have a family-resemblance structure, and you can see the polysemous/metaphorical thread from (14) to (17). Rather than talking about regular or irregular polysemy, I am more inclined to talk about meaning networks of the kind of complexity that Lakoff (1987) discusses in his analysis of OVER.

There is a metaphorical extension from an animate subject running up a hill to an inanimate subject. And again, from a moving inanimate subject to an unmoving inanimate subject. The first is a generalization: 'running' loses selection restrictions on its subject so that the subject of 'running' can be anything that involves locomotion. The second though is not a generalization: it is a semantic shift, a metaphorical extension, from the running of an engine that moves to the running of something virtual—a computer programme. The last is idiomatic. It is possible to understand the relationships between these different instances of RUN.

Are any of these regular? Or irregular? If we return to the topic of the last lecture, we will see that the evidence for structure in meaning comes from lexical aspect and *Aktionsart*. We saw this as well in Levin and Rappaport Havov's paper and also from a particular set of transitivity alternations. The argument from lexical aspect is that achievements and accomplishments are more complex.

1.10 The Main Data Sets

The classic event structure data sets for regular polysemy are the causative—inchoative alternation (where the meaning of the inchoative is embedded in the meaning of the causative) and the ditransitive—double complement alternation. In the ditransitive we have various examples such as these. (See also Goldberg 1995: 75.)

(19) Jane gave Peter a cake. (Peter must receive the cake)
(20) Jane gave a cake to Peter. (Peter doesn't have to receive the cake)
(21) Jane sent Peter a letter. (Peter probably receives the letter)
(22) Jane sent a letter to Peter. (There is no guarantee Peter receives the letter)
(23) Jane baked Peter a cake. (Peter is at least the intended recipient)
(24) Jane baked a cake for Peter. (On Peter's behalf—he need not be the recipient)

There are differences in these examples all the way through. It is not the case that the Object is received by the Recipient in the prepositional cases, although it is received in the double object cases. In these cases, it looks as though there are regular differences between the ditransitive and the double complement examples, until we come across the alternation between (23) and (24). It seems to me that there is no guarantee that Peter received the cake in either case.

1.11   *Interim Conclusions*

There are clearly some patterns which correspond to event complexity, and which look highly regular. But that does not make the less regular cases any less interesting. Nor does it require us to ignore non-regular examples that fit into otherwise regular patterns (the exceptional ditransitives). Our theory has to be able to encompass all of these.

1.12   *The Place of Metaphor*

Jackendoff (1983) introduces Semantic Field Theory in which verb meanings are organized around spatial meanings, and then that these spatial meanings can be elaborated to non-spatial semantic fields. For example, take the meaning of GO in the following sentences.

(25) The car went from Edinburgh to Glasgow
(26) The road goes from Edinburgh to Glasgow
(27) The lights went from green to red.
(28) The gun went [bæŋg]

The example in (25) describes an activity, while (26) describes a state. However, (27) is about the traffic lights changing color. In (28) [bæŋg] is onomatopoeic: it represents the noise of a gun. (25) expresses simple motion, (26) is metaphorical motion, and (27) is an even more extended metaphor that doesn't involve any kind of motion at all. In (28) motion is involved, but GO there has shifted its meaning and become a verb of sound emission

These are the kinds of metaphor which we can look at when we are looking at polysemy: these examples involve the use of a single verb across different semantic fields. But in addition, Sweetser (1990) pointed out that cross-linguistically there are several different consistent metaphorical paths. For example, it is common for a verb of seeing to become a verb of understanding and a verb of hearing to become a verb of obeying. Other common metaphorical paths underlying several different grammaticalization paths can be found in Traugott and Dasher (2002): for example, the verb MAY derives from an Old English verb with the meaning 'having the ability to do *x*'.

1.13   Looking Back over These Data Sets

I do not think there is any need to privilege certain structural patterns in our investigation into polysemy. There is a range of different ways of extending a verb's meaning. Some of these include embedding a verb's meaning in a larger network like the causativization of inchoatives. Some involve regular source-to-target mappings. Others involve collocations that change their meanings. Also, we have two different kinds of causative verb that we need to be able to look at (e.g. *he walked the dog* and *he closed the door*). On the other hand, certain meaning structures recur in different places. The resultative encodes the same semantic pattern as a causative verb in the causative—inchoative alternation: the same semantics can happen within a verb meaning as in transitive OPEN, or it can occur within a larger construction type as in the resultative construction. There is also the fact that the verb CAUSE does not have a force-dynamic transfer; it is a kind of "raising to object" verb. It does not have the same meaning structures that causation does within verb meanings (assuming my position on the ditransitive, which I will elaborate below). We will also look at CAUSE and related verbs in Lecture 6.

2   Less Regular Polysemy

I will put together some of these ideas about structure in polysemy by looking at a case study from my (2010) book in which I argued that there was a degree of regularity in the senses of SEE that arise immediately around the 'physically seeing' sense as in *Jane saw the Taj Mahal* which means 'perceive visually' and the extended sense in *I see what you mean*, which means 'understand'. I did not discuss the other metaphorical extended senses such as *I'll see you to the door* ('escort') or *Jane's seeing Peter* ('dating') and I will not discuss those examples here, either.

2.1   The Polysemy of SEE

We can begin with Alm-Arvius's (1993) analysis. She proposes nine different senses of SEE.

(29) See$_1$ 'perceive visually', 'perceive with the eyes' or 'set (clap) eyes upon something'
Ravina neither saw nor heard the boat approach.

(30) See₂ 'understand', 'realize', 'grasp', or 'comprehend'
I don't see why playing the piano should be considered an intellectual pursuit.
(31) See₃ 'consider', 'judge', 'regard', 'view', or 'think of'
He sees things differently now that he's joining the management).
(32) See₄ 'experience' or 'go through'
You and I have certainly seen some good times together.
(33) See₅ 'ascertain', 'check', and 'find out'.
Let's see what's on the radio. Switch it on, will you.
(34) See₆ 'meet', 'visit', 'consult', or 'receive'.
This is the first time he's been to see us since he went blind.
(35) See₇ 'make sure', 'attend to', 'ensure', or 'look after'.
Don't worry about the rest of the food, the children will see to that.
(36) See₈ 'escort', 'accompany', 'go with'
I really should see you home, it's not safe to be out alone in this city after dark.
(37) See₉ 'take leave of', or 'send off'.
'I wanted to come and see you off,' he had told her, ...

2.2 Micropolysemy and SEE

Even though Alm-Arvius' classification is detailed, it fails to distinguish some examples of SEE involving "micropolysemy". For example:

(38) We saw the statue.
(39) We saw the statue move.
(40) She was pale the next day and he could see that she had not slept.
(41) Sarah turned to the bed to speak and saw, shockingly, that she was dead.

According to Alm-Arvius (1993), the examples in (38)–(41) all involve the physical, visual perception sense. I do not think that is true. Obviously enough, (38) and (39) involve a physical perception sense. But what you "see" is a clause expressing a position in (40), *that she had not slept*. How can you see that somebody has not slept? You can form an inference that somebody has not slept from visual information, but you cannot see it. All you can see is evidence that somebody has slept, but you cannot actually see the actual fact of someone having not slept. Therefore, (40) cannot involve the physical perception sense of SEE. Similarly, in (41) the Subject saw evidence that somebody is dead. They did not see an event; the meaning of the clause *that she was dead* is a proposition. Therefore, the example in (41) also does not involve a physical perception sense of seeing. This is an evidential use of SEE, but it is not direct perception.

Alm-Arvius also says the following examples involve visual perception, because the FROM or BY phrase gives the source of the information.

> (42) I see from your news pages that feature films and past TV shows will soon be on the market for owners of video cassette recorders.
> (43) ... and I see by the angle of the sun that the morning is almost ended.

Again, what you "see" in (42) is a proposition, which you cannot actually see physically because a proposition is not something you can perceive directly. You may indicate the source of evidence, but that does not mean you see it directly. It just means there is some kind of visual evidence for it. In (43), again, you see the evidence for the proposition, but the proposition itself is the output of a mental process. What (42) and (43) report is some kind of mental experience for which there is visual evidence.

However, it is not good semantic research or lexical semantic research to base your findings on what you feel the words mean. We need evidence. In the case of SEE, we need to ask ourselves: what linguistic evidence is there? Is this area of meaning really all about physical perception? There are two kinds of evidence here: one is selection—what kind of complement does the verb take? And the other is *Aktionsart*—what is the lexical aspect of the verb?

2.3 Micropolysemy and SEE: Evidence for Different Senses of SEE

Let us consider selection first. THAT-clauses denote propositions. Propositions are abstractions—they are intramental, not in the real world. We cannot see them and they denote a kind of idea. You cannot see an idea. Noun phrases on the other hand, can denote physical things, so you can see the referent of a noun phrase.

Let us look at the evidence from *Aktionsart*. English verbs behave differently in the present tense, depending on whether they are stative or dynamic. *I like my friend* is a stative predication, so you can't say **I am liking my friend*. On the other hand, *I am running* involves a dynamic event. If you say *I run*, then you mean that's a habit. Lexical aspect distinguishes between stative verbs and dynamic verbs. What is the *Aktionsart* of SEE? Let's consider some examples:

> (44) !Jane is seeing into the room.
> (45) !Jane sees into the room.

(46) !Jane is seeing the picture.
(47) !Jane sees the picture.
(48) Bill is seeing a vision of dancing devils.
(49) Bill sees visions of dancing devils.

Examples (44)–(47) tell us physical perception sense of SEE cannot really occur in either the progressive or simple present. In the past tense, or under CAN, they are all acceptable. The prepositional examples in (44) and (45) involve a 'gazing' sense of SEE, whereas the examples in (46) and (47) involve transitive physical-perception SEE. (44) and (46) therefore tell you that SEE when it means 'gazing' or the physical perception sense is not dynamic, and (45) and (47) show that these senses are not stative either. In this analysis I am disagreeing with Croft (2012) who says that physical perception SEE is a stative verb. The example in (47) is possible, perhaps, but only in "football commentator" style. When SEE is okay in the progressive, as in (48), it shows that there is a different sense, because this example cannot involve physical perception. The example in (49) is habitual, just like *I run*. (48) and (49) mean 'hallucinating', so more specifically (49) means 'Bill has hallucinations of dancing devils'. The default present tense way to say that you are presently experiencing visual perception is to say *I can see the statue*: there is a linguistic difference between physical perception seeing, as in (44)–(47) and *see* when it means 'hallucinating' as in (48) and (49).

What about when SEE is complemented by a THAT clause? Take the examples in (50) and (51).

(50) Jane sees that Peter was right.
(51) *Jane is seeing that Peter was right.

SEE+THAT is stative, therefore (51) is ungrammatical. This gives us three different semantic patterns: a pattern which is neither dynamic nor stative ('gazing' and physical perception SEE); a pattern which is dynamic (the 'hallucinating' meaning); and a pattern which is stative (when SEE is complemented by a THAT clause).

Are there any other semantic facts that are relevant? SEE, REALIZE, KNOW and UNDERSTAND are all so-called factive verbs, which means that they assert the factuality of the content of the THAT clause that is their complement.

(52) Peter saw/realized/knew/understood that he was in danger.
(53) Peter didn't see/realize/know/understand that he was in danger.

The examples in (52) tell you the Subject really was in danger: they mean that the content of the THAT-clause is a fact. Moreover, (53) indicates that factivity is constant under negation: Peter was in danger, whether the matrix clause is positive or negative. The shared factivity of SEE and UNDERSTAND suggests that they might share a similar sense. Note that THINK is not a factive verb: in *Peter thought that he was in danger*, he might or might not be really in danger.

So far we have evidence for different senses of SEE from *Aktionsart*, semantic selection, and factivity. That is enough evidence because that information gives us a complex network. Among other things, we also need to unpack the sense of SEE which involves physical perception into two parts, a directional part and a mental perception part. This is because the directional examples like (52) and (53) show that GAZE and SEE both behave in the same way as REACH, which that suggests SEE in some way is a directional verb.[1]

(54) Peter reached/saw/gazed into the room.
(55) Peter reached/gazed/saw as far as he could.

We can consider more examples where the mental perception part of SEE is involved:

(56) He saw the sign but he didn't notice it.
(57) He saw hordes of devils riding on horseback.

As Jackendoff (1983) originally noted, physical perception SEE involves two bits of meaning. There is a directional element and mental perception is also involved: this links metaphorically with the meaning of hallucination. This two-part structure seems to be related to folk psychology where the meaning of SEE involves some kind of a gaze leaving the eyes, which is what gives the collocation with prepositions in the examples in (44) and (45) as well as the 'mental representation' part of the meaning. We have all sorts of metaphors in English like *directing your gaze*. If you direct your gaze, then you actually orient your face in a particular direction. Or if you *look askance*, you look sideways. These metaphors of visual experience seem to imply that we direct to gaze out of our eyes when we look at things, which seems to be the folk understanding of how the meaning in this bit of the lexicon works. See also how SMILE works: if we smile at someone, we are directing our smile to them.

---

1 Note that SEE is different from SMILE, discussed in the previous lecture. It is not possible to say !*Peter smiled as far as he could* or !*Peter smiled into the room*.

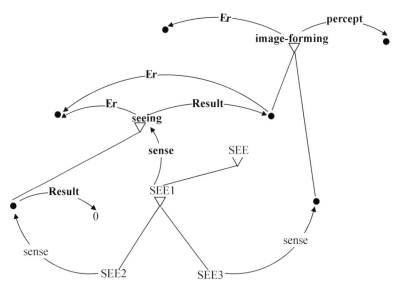

FIGURE 5 Network for the physical sense of SEE TAKEN FROM GISBORNE (2010: 138)

The physical senses of SEE have this kind of structure in Figure 5 in which sublexemes are used in order to capture these subparts of the meaning that I have been discussing. The figure is taken from Chapter 4 of Gisborne (2010).

Basic SEE has the sense 'seeing', which has an Er and result. The Er is an instance of 'image-forming'. That is, the physical perception of SEE involves casting your gaze and forming a mental image of something. 'Image-forming' also has a 'percept' (a thing which is perceived), so it has an Ee as well, which I do not show as it would make the diagram too complicated. Basic SEE has two sublexemes. One sublexeme, SEE_2, just involves 'seeing' with no result, so there is a zero at the end of result arrow.[2] The other one (SEE_3) is just the 'image-forming' meaning, and it does not involve any gazing. SEE in *I saw the blue table cloth*, is the prototypical sense of SEE. In *I saw over the audience's heads* we have the directed SEE, SEE_2. In *I saw an image of myself lecturing*, the sense is SEE_3 which is just having a mental image without actually directing your gaze anywhere in particular.

---

2 This is the published diagram, so I have included it here unchanged. However, it is possible to do better than this. The sense of SEE_2 is given as an instance of SEE_1 with an override. If, however, the sense of SEE_1 inherited from 'gazing' but without a result, adding a result to it, then the sense of SEE_2 could point directly to the 'gazing' node showing that the sublexeme had a more general sense in a direct way, without any overrides. The relationship between the sublexemes and the senses would then be the same kind of relationship as I show in Figure 7 below.

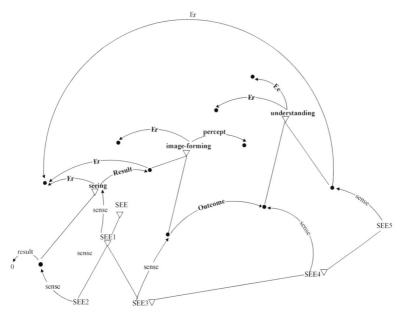

FIGURE 6   Network for the prepositional sense of SEE
TAKEN FROM GISBORNE (2010: 147)

What about the propositional senses? How should we fit the propositional senses into the meanings of these verbs? We need to capture the fact that some propositional senses do not involve physical perception at all, while some do. For example, I can say *I see from your color, you must be ill*. Figure 6 is a much more complicated network trying to capture some of those facts.

The network from Figure 5 is still in this diagram, which includes SEE$_1$ which means physical perception 'seeing'. This is the sense which Isa 'gazing' which has a Result which Isa forming a mental image ('image-forming'). There is also the 'gazing' meaning without a mental image Result (SEE$_2$) and the sense which has no 'gazing' element but which does have 'image-forming' (SEE$_3$). Those are the three physical senses of SEE. On the right-hand side of the diagram, there are two further instances of SEE each of which has a sense which Isa 'understanding'. SEE$_4$, is an instance of 'understanding' which is the outcome of 'image-forming'. If you see something then you can form conclusions about it, so there is a kind of relational link there between 'seeing something' and 'understanding something'. On the far right of the diagram, we have SEE$_5$ which means 'understanding' without there being an explicit source. *I see from your colour that you must be ill* is 'understanding with a source', SEE$_4$, while *I see why she left her husband* is 'understanding without a source', SEE$_5$.

The diagram in Figure 6 shows a tight little network, relating these different senses together and tying them to their arguments. Both diagrams are simplified: for example, I did not show in Figure 6 that SEE$_1$ has a Subject and an Object, SEE$_2$ a Subject only, SEE$_3$ a Subject and an Object, SEE$_4$ a Subject and an Object, and SEE$_5$ a Subject and an Object, and that these get tied to the Er and Ee, because it would have made the diagram too complicated.

2.4   Causative Verbs

On the account I am developing here, there is no need to privilege the kind of regular polysemy that we find with causative verbs or with ditransitive verbs, because we need to be able to understand and include other kinds of polysemy, too and these other kinds of polysemy require the same analytical tools: they are differentiated from "regular" polysemy in that there is not a simple event-structural alternation deriving them. The causative/inchoative alternation is straightforward to discuss, because it is regular and it involves a kind of structure. But we can find regularities and structure in other kinds of polysemy, such as the polysemy of perception verbs.

2.5   Logical Polysemy

Pustejovksy in his work on qualia is interested in what he calls "logical polysemy" (1995: 31). Logical polysemy is a kind of polysemy which can be captured with certain kinds of logical relations. For example, there are count/mass alternations and container/containee alternations. The count/mass alternation is the difference between 'fish$_1$' and 'fish$_2$', where 'fish$_1$' means a fish that can be found swimming in the river, while 'fish$_2$' means the fish on plate which is a mass noun meaning 'food'. Count/mass conversion is very regular in English so for example we can find the same difference between the two senses of the word CHICKEN: chicken$_1$ and chicken$_2$. There are even examples such as the unpleasant *there was dog all over the road* (imagine after an impact with a car). The container/containee alternation is a very regular conversion, too. You can "break the glass", or you can "finish the glass".

Pustejovksy is also interested in the following sort of patterns.

(58) Mary began to read the novel.
(59) Mary began the novel.

(58) denotes the beginning of a reading event. But (59) is ambiguous: it could mean that she began reading the novel, or that she began writing the novel, because they are the two main things that you do with novels.

2.6 Pustejovksy's Qualia

Pustejovksy invented the theory of Qualia in which there are four different roles that a noun's meaning can have. One of these roles is the *constitutive* role, the internal structure, and its material, weight, parts, and components. Another role it can have is its *formal* role, how it is distinguished from other objects within a larger domain, its magnitude, its orientation, its shape, its color and its position. A noun's meaning can have a *telic* role which is a different use of telic from the use in discussions of *Aktionsart*; it means its purpose and/or function. Finally, there is the *agentive* role: how it came into being. For example, a book can be considered in its relationship to its author. We can say *Lakoff is on the third shelf*, by which we mean a book written by Lakoff.

2.7 However ...

Pustejovsky's examples show, alongside the earlier data in this lecture, that the range of examples from logical to exuberant polysemy is gradient, and it does not have fixed boundaries, for all that it has clear prototypes. If we assuming a prototype semantics, we will probably not want to work with Qualia; instead we will want to work with a theory that allows us to have a gradient spread from very clear and straightforward examples of structure in meaning to these more exuberant examples of polysemy. A network is a good way of handling this kind of gradient material, because it allows you to capture the closely bound and the very different polysemes of a word. There is no need to introduce lot of new machinery. Inheritance and the notion of the sublexeme allow us to capture all of the variability that we want.

2.8 Networks and Graded Polysemy

The reason why inheritance and the notion of the sublexeme capture all of the variation that we want is because we can represent a regular alternation (causative—inchoative) as part of the prototype of a verb. But examples like *run up a bill* can be analyzed as being in a longer chain from sublexeme to sublexeme, via Isa, back to the prototype. Examples such as *run up a bill* are idiomatic, and this is the kind of pattern we saw in the discussion idioms and exceptionality in Lecture 2. But we have also seen a range of examples which look like logical polysemy.

2.9 Similar Structures to Logical Polysemy

The relationship between transitive and intransitive OPEN involves the sense of the intransitive verb being embedded in the transitive verb as an attribute of a sense of the transitive verb. The same is true for THINK, not only with intransitive and transitive but with stative and dynamic THINK. We saw diagrams for both cases in earlier lectures.

POLYSEMY AND SEMANTIC STRUCTURE

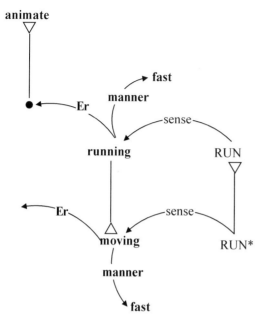

FIGURE 7   Schematic view of two senses of RUN

Earlier I was talking about RUN (see examples 10–18). Here is a diagram of *running* that captures the relationship between RUN as in *he ran up the hill* and RUN as in *the train ran up the hill*:

Figure 7 shows two lexemes of RUN—the verb RUN itself, and a sublexeme marked with an asterisk. Basic RUN has its sense 'running' which it inherits from 'moving'. 'Running' has a manner attribute 'fast' and the value of its Er has to be animate—the selection constraint is presented as an inheritance constraint on the node at the end of the Er arrow. RUN with an asterisk is a subtype (sublexeme) of RUN which does not place animacy-related selection restrictions on its subject, so RUN in *the train ran up the hill* has its sense 'moving' with a manner 'fast', but it does not put a restriction on its Er that it must be animate. Arguably, this second sublexeme is metaphorical. With basic RUN and metaphorical RUN, we can see a case of generalization, a regular pattern of semantic change whereby senses become more general—in this case by lifting a selection restriction.

However, Figure 7 is clearly incomplete, for all that it shows several relevant properties. It shows that the two sublexemes are linked by an ordinary Isa link between RUN and RUN*. The difference is between the two senses. The sense of ordinary RUN has a restriction on the referent of its Er: the Er has to be animate. The sense of RUN* has no such restriction. More interestingly, however, we see that the relationship between the two senses is Isa.

The more prototypical, conceptually richer sense Isa the more general sense. Diachronically, we saw a process of generalization which created the sense of RUN*. And a key attribute—the property of being fast—is present in both senses. But other senses of RUN will need a different analysis. There will be other kinds of relationship for the computer program running fast. A computer that runs fast is not moving, and so the 'fast' attribute itself has a different meaning. In the case of physical running, the motion is fast relative to the normal motion of the verb's Subject. But because a computer programme does not move, the 'fast' attribute also means something different.

2.10   Other Arguments

My main argument in this lecture is that there are several types of polysemy, and they can have a relationship with the way in which the verb's arguments are realized (as is the case SEE). But there are other dimensions of polysemy as well. I do not think it makes a great deal of sense to try and preserve a difference between logical and other kinds of polysemy, although homonymy does look different.

2.11   An Alternative: Construction Grammar

This brings us to the arguments of Goldberg to do with constructional polysemy. Goldberg (1995: 72–81) discusses the role of inheritance in her theory of Cognitive Construction Grammar. She explains that she is working with "Normal Mode Inheritance" (Default Inheritance) rather than Complete Inheritance and that inheritance is a static relation, and not a process. She (1995: 74–81) also discusses inheritance links as objects. She identifies four types of inheritance link: Polysemy links; Subpart links; Instance links; and Metaphorical Extension links.

   Goldberg argues, therefore, that constructions can be polysemous, and that the polysemy can be handled with a special inheritance link, which represents the fact that the constructions have a different meaning. I find the notion of different kinds of inheritance link troubling. It seems to me that this is an arbitrary decision based on Goldberg's adoption of constructions and having constructions embedded within constructions. But in WG there is no need for special links such as her polysemy link. As we see in the representations for RUN and SEE above, the sublexeme inherits everything that isn't overridden. If you have a lexeme W that has a sense S and a sublexeme W* which has a sense S*, then the statement that W* has S* as its sense is more specific than the facts that W* inherits from W, therefore overriding the sense of W. In WG there is therefore no need for a special inheritance link. However, it looks as though Goldberg does need one; indeed as just noted she posits several different kinds of inheritance link to relate her different constructions. In part, I suspect that this is because in Construction Grammar meaning is shared between constructions and the words that occur in them. But from a WG perspective, there is no need to argue that constructions have meanings that verbs fit in.

One argument for argument-linking constructions is that they allow verbs to be somewhat underspecified in their meanings. As a result, the constructions themselves have to contain meaning. But we have also seen that the verbs do have to have a meaning, because there are constraints on which verbs can and which cannot occur in a construction. This is something that comes up in the research literature, which has been discussed in one way and another (for example, Croft 2003). But rather than assuming that learners acquire abstract schemas associated with phrasal patterns of lexical items, perhaps they acquire the senses attached to given lexical items. How could learners learn the abstract meaning of a construction except by inducing it from specific verbs exemplifying the construction? With a rich, but structured lexicon, we would not need to assume constructional meaning. Such a lexicon is built around the regularities—with different degrees of granularity—that Goldberg argues for.

It is also worth bearing in mind that there are differences between Goldberg's Cognitive Construction Grammar and Croft's Radical Construction Grammar (2001). Croft is a rigorously consistent functionalist, who thinks everything begins with speech acts. Dividing language into a bunch of constructions down from speech acts privileges speech acts and suggests that the functional desire to communicate is the most significant determining factor in language. In some sense, our approach in in WG is similar, but for WG the main unit in language is the word: we claim that children learn words and how to put words together. We take the same rigorous approach, but privileging the word rather than the construction.

Goldberg claims that the templates of Rappaport Hovav and Levin (1998) are construction-like. She sets up a debate between a "projectionist" and a "constructionist" architecture of verb meanings, and suggests that Rappaport Hovav and Levin's projectionist approach is less different from a constructionist approach than it might seem at first. But I think she might be wrong about that. Rappaport Hovav and Levin are not constructionist: their complex schemas exist in the semantics, not in the syntax. They related their meaning structures to syntactic units by algorithm. Therefore, there are no constructions in their model. Goldberg's claim is tantamount to arguing that structure in meaning is equivalent to admitting constructions to your theoretical ontology. But that is not the case, as we have seen in this lecture.

2.12 *Conclusion*

There are many kinds of polysemy, but they are not sharply different from each other—the differences are gradient, and in WG accommodated through chains of inheritance links and appropriate associations in the semantic network. Polysemy can be relevant to how events are related to each other, both in terms of how lexical items are stored, and how verbs show patterns of regular sense inclusion, as in the causative-inchoative. As a result, certain patterns have been privileged in the research literature. But there is no reason to privilege these patterns—indeed doing so costs an inclusive analysis of other data. However, a network theory allows us to capture a range of facts, not just the highly systematic, highly regular bits of polysemy such as we find in the causative-inchoative transitivity alternation. I have also argued that in WG it makes sense to include homonymy together with polysemy when the homonyms are in the same word-class and only to factor homonymy and polysemy out when homonymy involves different word classes.

LECTURE 5

Events and Thematic Roles

There is a large literature on thematic roles and what they are for in lexical semantics and semantic theory. We might ask a number of questions about them: what is a thematic role? How many thematic roles are there? Are thematic roles relevant to how grammar works? Or are thematic roles just part of the encyclopedic knowledge of the meanings of words? Do thematic roles define events? Or do events define thematic roles? For example, Jackendoff (1983, 1990) defines the thematic role 'Theme' as the first argument of a 'going' event. But Fillmore (1968: 48) argues for a list of thematic roles, which he calls "cases" which define the "case frames" that verbs can occur in. It could then be argued that verb meanings (or events, in this theory) are inherently underspecified, and defined by the case frames that they occur in. The same idea is found in Goldberg (1995).

This lecture is more exploratory, than the previous one. But we are going to see what sorts of answers might work. The conclusion that I am moving towards is that thematic roles, the localist thematic roles that Jackendoff talks about, are really part of the encyclopedic knowledge of meanings of verbs. But the force-dynamic thematic roles actually help us define the meanings of events and are relevant to argument linking.[1]

---

1 Gisborne and Donaldson (2019) discusses these issues in some depth, and also addresses the history of thematic roles in the theoretical literature. We develop an account of event complexity which sees thematic roles as derivative notions which draw on our model of event structure. Our account argues that there are material differences between force-dynamic roles and other thematic roles, and that force-dynamic roles are implicated in some of the structures we come to discuss in Lecture 10. See also Croft (2012) for extensive discussion.

 All original audio-recordings and other supplementary material, such as any hand-outs and powerpoint presentations for the lecture series, have been made available online and are referenced via unique DOI numbers on the website www.figshare.com. They may be accessed via a QR code for the print version of this book. In the e-book, both the QR code and dynamic links are available, and can be accessed by a mouse-click.

1 Events, Thematic Roles, Structure

There are three different approaches to thematic roles according to Levin and Rappaport Hovav (2005)—see also Croft (1990). We can call the first approach the localist approach. This goes back to Fillmore (1968) and his case grammar, John Lyons (1977), John Anderson (1971), and the Thematic Roles Hypothesis of Gruber (1965) and Jackendoff (1972, 1983, 1990) which says that events are "decomposed" into notions such as 'going', 'being (at)'. Essentially, for these scholars, motion is the basic underlying meaning of verbs. The verbs can be metaphorically extended away from the semantic field of motion to other semantic fields, and so even in their extended uses, the thematic roles that we work with are defined in terms of location, motion and movement. As I said above, for Jackendoff, a 'Theme' thematic role is identified as the first argument of a 'going' event.

The second approach is the aspectual approach. In this approach, events are complex, because they have subevents. There are two basic categories of events: states and dynamic events. Dynamic events themselves are subdivided into activities, achievements and accomplishments, similar to the aspectual classes of Vendler (1957). In lecture 4's discussion of Pustejovsky (1991) and Rappaport Hovav and Levin (1998), we saw two aspectual approaches to event structure and the identification of thematic roles.

The third approach is the causal approach.[2] This is the idea that individuals act on individuals. In a complex event there is a causal chain from one participant to another. The relationships between events therefore can be induced from the causal chain from individual to individual. Croft is one of the developers of this approach which is an elaboration of Talmy's theory of force-dynamics. Talmy's original force-dynamic papers include Talmy (1985b, 1988); similar ideas are found in Croft's (1986) PhD thesis which turned into his first monograph (Croft 1991). Croft (2012) provides a clear overview of the current literature.

---

2 As Croft (1990) points out, there are different theories of causation in the literature: events cause events; participants cause events; and participants act on participants. As I note in the text, the causal theory of event structure draws on a particular theory of causation, the force-dynamic approach associated with Talmy. The model of Levin and Rappapot Hovav, which I discussed in Lecture 4, and which I have described here as "aspectual" involves a hybrid of events cause events (I think that this approach is built into the aspectual model) and participants cause events (see their model of accomplishment verbs). Jackendoff also has a hybrid approach, bringing together the localist approach described here and a force-dynamic approach.

We are going to think about these three different approaches and what they tell us about meaning. One important question in any kind of intellectual activity is, "Why am I doing this?"—that is, we need to understand what we are trying to work out and why. If we do not understand why and what we are attempting to explain, the research activity can be unclear and amorphous. You need to have a destination in mind, in order to shape your questions.

I think that there are two different things that people try to do when they look at event structure. One is trying to work out the relationship between syntax and semantics: is it possible to have a predictive theory of the relationship between the thematic roles of verb and its syntactic roles like Subject and Object and so on? The other is just to understand the semantics of verbs in all their complexity. This is to do with aspectual semantics, but it is also about other aspects of the semantics of verbs as well. For example, within the causal semantics approach it is possible to explore whether the causal semantics and aspectual semantics come down to one single system or not. Understanding the semantics in all its complexity is related to the first question of how thematic roles map onto syntactic functions, even though they are not exactly the same topic. This is part of the business of needing to know where your destination is. In the literature, we can see that Levin and Rappaport Hovav are interested in trying to find out how you map the relation between syntax and semantics as well as developing a coherent aspectual theory of event structure. Croft (1991, 2012) also tries to do both things: to find out how you map the relationship between semantic structure and syntactic structure and also to understand the full complexity of verb meanings. Croft privileges the causal approach. Jackendoff (1983, 1990) is mainly interested in the full complexity of the meanings of verbs, but he also works out a theory of the mapping relationship between the two.[3]

The theoretical and architectural assumptions of a theory are also relevant to how these two questions are approached. We need to decide what the basic dimensions of out theory might be: does it have a separate syntax and a semantics? It could be argued that the best (conceptually simplest) theory would not have a separate syntax, but would just map from a speech string to conceptual structure. What is the evidence for an independent syntactic level? The evidence is very indirect; essentially it is word order. Does the analysis of meaning break down into semantics, pragmatics and discourse? Is lexical semantics different from sentence semantics? We need to make principled

---

3 Jackendoff's approach to the issue of the mapping was to work with a thematic role hierarchy. See Gisborne and Donaldson (2019) for a review of the success of thematic role hierarchies in theories of argument linking.

decisions about the architecture of language if we are going to answer the question about the mapping relationship between syntax and semantics. And in the end, there isn't a right answer: we are building theories, which we have to try to break,[4] as a means of advancing our knowledge. In order to have a theory of the mapping relationship between syntax and event structure, you have to an idea about what the architecture of grammar looks like, and you have to have an idea about how different bits of the architecture interact with each other. Word Grammar argues that syntax and semantics are separate, but that they are linked because they both belong in a single associative network.

Generative theories typically approach the question of argument linking (how syntax and semantics relate to each other in the meanings of events) in terms of algorithms, where an algorithm is a procedural rule system of some kind. But like Construction Grammar, WG is a declarative theory, so there are no algorithms, just a series of declarative statements, or propositions, about language, represented in a network. These statements, of course, are subject to default inheritance, which is a logic of generalizations, so for WG, the theoretical task is to establish the right generalizations and the appropriate degree of granularity.

Each bit of language fits together piece by piece, or fails to (which gives ungrammaticality). I think that declarative theories of language are more cognitively plausible than procedural, rule-based theories with algorithms, because of how learning works. When a child learns the meaning of a word, they learn everything about the meaning of the word, so they are unlikely to learn argument linking as a discrete algorithm. They are much more likely to learn it as an established relationship. When a child hears a verb such as LOVE in use—when they hear their mother saying *I love you*—they surely learn that the verb has two semantic arguments, which map to two syntactic arguments: the Experiencer of 'loving' (its Er) maps to the Subject, and the Ee to the Object. Children do not have to run an algorithm to work that out each time he or she encounters LOVE in use.

You can see similar properties in other aspects of acquisition. For example, my older son would often announce that he was doing things while he was playing. If he was riding a bike, he would catch our attention and say, *I riding my bike*. Note that he did not use the auxiliary and did not have tense; but he did know the argument linking pattern: he knew that the Agent was linked to the Subject. When they are acquiring language, children have to learn the rules

---

4 By this I mean that the job of theory-building is to create a falsifiable theory. We try to falsify theories by breaking them. When they stop working, we can see what is wrong with them and improve them. Or reject and replace them.

of composition for syntax and for semantics—each of these systems has its own rules of composition—and then they also have to learn the associations between syntax and semantics. The association between syntax and semantics has to make sense in terms of acquisition. I think that argument linking generalizations are just learned, and then children form different generalizations at different degrees of granularity. I do not for a minute think that they learn a mapping algorithm. This makes sense in terms of human's cognitive endowment: we have more memory than we have processing capacity, so we are more likely to retrieve language from memory than we are to work out a bit of grammar on the fly.

To summarize, there are three main approaches to the semantics of events: localist, aspectual and causal. These approaches have some similarities and are related in various ways. A different dimension is whether the theory is declarative or generative. A generative theory looks for algorithms to link syntax and semantics, whereas a declarative theory makes general statements about how they relate to each other. And finally, as I said previous lectures, there are other things to consider in terms of the architecture of the grammar. For example, Croft takes the speech-act to be the basic organising unit, as a result that language divides top-down into constructions at an increasingly fine grain. WG, on the other hand, takes the word to be the basic organising unit, and language is built bottom up from words into larger units, and there are no constructions as such. A theory can be lexical, or word-based, or constructional. WG is word based.

2 Events, Thematic Roles and Structure

We can start off by thinking about what these different theories say about inchoativity. Inchoative verbs are intransitive verbs that describe the Subject as going into a result state; semantically, they are changes of state, or transitions into a result state, like DIE. If someone dies, then they become dead and the lexical semantics of a verb such as DIE must encode that change of state. The localist theory says that it is a (metaphorical) 'going' into the state. Therefore, in the localist theory, inchoativity is understood in terms of the meaning of verbs like GO: the Subject enters the result state. The aspectual theory, on the other hand, assumes a primitive conceptual predicate ('becoming') which symbolizes a change of state. This is the approach of Rappaport Hovav and Levin (1998). The causal theory assumes that there is an "offstage" Initiator which acts on the Endpoint, and which brings the change of state about in the Endpoint (Gisborne 2010). One way of thinking about these three theories is that the first, localist, theory is concerned with primitive verb meanings; the second, aspectual, theory is about structure in verbs' meanings; and the force-dynamic theory is concerned with construal.

3 Events and Thematic Roles

Before we proceed, let me remind you that first of all in this network model of grammar, we have two different pieces of network information: relational concepts which are arcs in the diagram, and non-relational concepts which are nodes in the diagram. Individuals and events are both nodes, so events are also individuals in WG, and both nodes and arcs can be classified in an inheritance hierarchy.

I will start off by reminding you how network arcs are classified and then I will talk about the hierarchy of dependency types and semantic relation types. After that, we will think about how arcs and nodes are mutually defining. From there, we can go on to think about the semantic relations that we can observe, and ask what these semantic relations do.

4 Events and Thematic Roles: the Structure of Relations

So far in these lectures, I have discussed the classification of nodes in inheritance hierarchies. In Lecture 1, I discussed topics such as the inheritance of attributes and multiple inheritance. But we can ask ourselves, "What about the relations?" As I showed in Lecture 1, in WG relations are classified too. Let us look at the classification of relations in a bit more depth. We might ask how we can classify relations when relations are relational categories. This is a technical or formal problem. What we do in WG is to say that the relations of WG are built up out of small parts, based around two primitive relations, "argument" and "value." Because it is classified, a WG network is a kind of typed feature structure—a network with classification by inheritance. By having the two primitive relations argument and value, we get past the complexities of classifying relational categories, which would oblige us to have a complex logic (a "second order" logic) to constrain our metalanguage. The justification for the primitive relations argument and value is that they keep the system (relatively) simple.

For example, see Figure 1. In Figure 1 the two smaller parts are two primitive relations, arguments and value. My wife is called Caro. We have a relation 'wife of' that says *Caro is the wife of Nik*. (There is a converse relation which goes in the opposite direction, 'husband-of'.) The relation is defined as a node, but

EVENTS AND THEMATIC ROLES

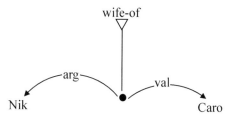

FIGURE 1   The structure of relations I

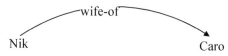

FIGURE 2   The structure of relations II

that node has two primitive relations associated with it, 'argument' and 'value'. Primitive relations are never classified; they are basic. The non-primitive relation 'wife-of' can then be classified further up the inheritance hierarchy in turn as 'partner of', which would include (classify) 'husband-of', 'wife-of' and whatever other kinds of partner you might want to identify. The idea is simple, that we can classify relations, because relations are simply a special kind of complex node with an argument-relation and a value-relation. The point is to explain that the system is formally robust—if it were not, the diagrams would be just pictures, not analyses. However, in practice we use diagrams like the one given in Figure 2 because they are more readable and lead to clearer diagrams.

Figure 1 presents a better analysis than Figure 2 because it says that the relation is classified, rather than labeling it directly. This is important because it says the relation is one instance of the 'wife-of' relation, whereas Figure 2 arguably says my wife is all wives, which cannot possibly be true because she is only my wife: I have only got one wife and she has only one husband. Therefore, we want the relation classified by a higher node, as we find in Figure 1. My wife is just the single wife of just one man, so the label of the relationship should Isa the relationship type 'wife-of'. The diagram in Figure 1 shows the structure of the function, whereas the diagram in Figure 2 explicitly shows the relationship.

5   Structure of the Function

Now for a little bit of maths. Imagine a mathematical function such as 3× ("3 times"). We can put an argument on the right of this function and then a value after the = sign. Then we get 3×(x)=y in which any number for x (the argument) gives you a different number for *y* (the value). For example, 3×1=3, 3×4=12, etc. The relation 'wife-of' works in the same way: wife-of (x)=y, wife-of (Nik)=Caro, wife-of (Rob)=Sarah and so on. The WG network relation is just a little mathematical function: each relation in the diagram is just like a function that takes you from an argument to a value. The same function gives you a different value for each different argument.

The decomposition of the relations also means that each function can be classified, but as I said, there is no need to have any tricky, or second order logic, about how to make functions into individuals so that they can be classified because each function is just an individual node. The relations, argument and value, are both primitives. They are not analysed in any other more basic terms.

6 Dependency Classification

Now we can go on to have a classification of syntactic relations, the dependencies which make WG a Dependency Grammar. Dependencies inhabit a type hierarchy and are classified by (default) inheritance, because this is how we show the properties they have in common. Figure 3 illustrates the dependency hierarchy.

In Figure 3 there is a super-type called dependent which breaks down into pre-dependent, valent, and post-dependent. Pre-dependent is the category for any dependent that can occur before its head; it includes Extractee (such as *who* in *who did the dog bite?*) and Subject; a post-dependent comes after its head, and includes the Agent BY-phrase (*the window was broken by the children*), and locative prepositions or PPs such as *in the garden* in *she was singing in the garden*. Complement is the category which classifies direct Object and

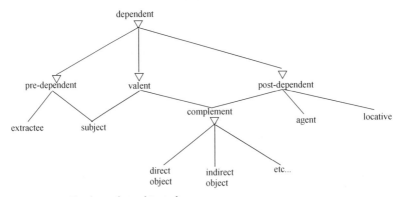

FIGURE 3   The dependency hierarchy

indirect Object and so on. The system allows multiple inheritance, so a complement is classified both as a valent and as post-dependent (because comes after its head). Inheritance is transitive, so valent is classified as a dependent. A Subject, on the other hand, is classified as a valent and as a pre-dependent. Extractee includes English WH words in the canonical distributions; extractees are just pre-dependents, not valents. The diagram in Figure 3 gives us a complex cross classification of different kinds of dependency. Because we can classify relations, we can take a similar approach to any system of relations.

All grammatical relations and all semantic relations can be classified. Why do you think we want to classify them? In order to make generalizations because generalizations allow us to have a simpler understanding of the world. If we can say something general about a category of things, then we do not have to state that fact about single instance of the category. Take the Subject relation, for example. If we can say all Subjects are valents, all Subjects are pre-dependents, then we make life really simple for ourselves. We do not have to state all the Subject properties that *John* has in *John kissed Mary*: *John* comes before the verb, *John* is the Agent of the verb, *John* agrees with the verb, and so on (and for every sentence with a Subject). We can simply say John is the Subject, and all the other properties follow from the classification. By classifying, we simplify. From the cognitive perspective, it makes it easier to understand how information is stored. This is why Langacker has schematicity as it does exactly the same job: schematicity is default inheritance. Of course, in research, the job of a linguist is to make generalizations about language. That is what we set out to do, although arguably we do not "make" generalizations, so much as find and identify them.

7   Semantic Role Classification

We can also classify semantic roles in the same way. Dependencies have word order constraints, but networks do not have a left to right word order; they can have any kind of dimensional structure you like. Therefore, semantic roles do not have word-order constraints, which dependencies do. But semantic roles are classified. The properties that define semantic roles might concern what ontological classes their arguments and values can belong to. An ontological class is a kind of category of natural types. We might distinguish between 'things' and 'ideas', for example, therefore an idea would be one kind of ontological category, and a 'thing' would be another. An 'event' would be a third kind of ontological category. Typically, in verb meanings a semantic relation is a relationship between an 'event' and a 'thing'. The relation *Agent-of*, is a relationship between an event as its argument, and a thing as its Agent. But if you believe, for example, that events cause events, then the Result relation has an event as its argument and an event as its value.

Other kinds of relations can have propositions as their value. The THAT-clause describes a proposition in *I know that the capital of Italy is Rome*, the subordinate clause *that the capital of Italy is Rome* expresses a proposition. We need a system of ontological classification in order to understand what sort of objects semantic roles relate. This is also necessary because if we do not have an ontological system for the arguments and values of semantic roles, we cannot possibly work out what semantic roles do for us. We have to understand semantic roles in terms of the relationships between events, the relationships between events and individuals, and the relationships between events and propositions.

8   Outcomes

We can start off by looking at relations between events in non-finite complementation. When a verb is complemented by a non-finite verb, as in (1) below, there is a relationship between the event symbolized by the main verb and the event symbolized by the non-finite verb. What is the semantic relation between the two different verb meanings in (1)?

(1)   She made him run away.

The event expressed by *him run away* is an argument of the 'making' event; an obvious relation to invoke is the Result relation: some events cause other events, or result in other events. (1) the event of *him running away* is in a Result relationship with *making*; responsibility is due to whoever *she* refers to. We can analyse the sense of MAKE as an event with a Result relation. This is different from (2).

(2)   They blew up the ship to destroy the enemy.

They blew up the ship symbolizes one event, while *to destroy the enemy* symbolizes a second event. The relationship between *blew up* and *destroy the enemy* is Purpose, because they might blow up the ship but fail to destroy the enemy. A Purpose is an intended Result, but it does not necessarily come about.

The situation is different again with (3).

(3) We expect you to win.

This semantic relation cannot be a Purpose because 'expecting' does not have a Purpose, nor can it be a Result because the outcome is not guaranteed. The second event, the 'winning' event, is in the future relative to the first event. The second event might not happen. The first event is mental, not physical. You might say this is some kind of Anticipation. Therefore, between events in non-finite complementation, we have at least 3 kinds of relationship: Result, Purpose, and Anticipation, as suggested by examples (1)–(3). These are different subtypes of Outcome and vary according to whether they are certain to come about (Result), a comment on why the first event happened (Purpose), or they relate to a mental state of some Agent (Anticipation).

These observations also provoke another way of thinking about these relations. Each of these relations is a relation between two events, but the argument event of a Purpose has to have an Agent. The argument event of an Intention (of which Anticipation is a subtype) has to have a Thinker because an Intention has an intramental event as its argument: 'expecting' can only take place in someone's mind.

The argument is about the complexity of the network. Some of these relations are simple. They all involve a relation between two events. But the different relations place different constraints on their arguments and values. If there is a Result relation between two events, then there are no further constraints on the events, except that the first causes the second. That is the point of the Result relationship. But if the relation between two events is the Purpose relation, then the second, argument, event must have an Agent. On the other hand, if the relation between two events is an Intention, then the first event must be an intramental event, with a conscious Er: the Intention relation places an ontological constraint on the value of its Er. We cannot say !*the stone intended to block the water.*

When I started the lecture, I raised some questions about whether events define thematic roles, or whether thematic roles define events. What I am saying now is that actually there is a complex relationship between the two, because events can be arguments or values of other events, and events can have complex little networks defining them as a range of different properties. Therefore, essentially the questions "Do arguments define events?" and "Do events define arguments?" are non-questions: they are actually mutually defining.

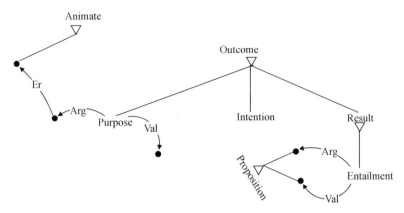

FIGURE 4   Classification of Outcomes

The Result relation is the simplest of all of these relations. It is very close to the notion from formal semantics of Entailment except that Entailment is a relationship between propositions rather than the relationship between events. We could say that Entailment was a subtype of Result which requires propositions as its argument and its value. Here is a classified set of Outcome relations.

Figure 4 shows that a subtype of Result is Entailment. Entailment has to have a proposition as its argument and value, whereas a Purpose has to have an Agent as its argument. Figure 4 analyses another relation in detail: it shows that an event which has a Purpose relation must have an animate Er. This is because its Er must be conscious (and sufficiently self-aware to intend to bring about an outcome). The reason is that only a conscious sentient being can have a purpose. If we say *the car crashed into the wall to destroy the enemy, the car* cannot be the Agent of that because it is not conscious. But if we say *He crashed the car into the wall to destroy the enemy, he* can be the conscious Agent and that relationship can be a Purpose relationship.

This exercise shows us that semantic relations must be analysed in terms of the full network that supports and defines each node. Some semantic relations will be more complex. Others, like Result, will be simpler. But semantic relations do not only link two events. Some of them link participants to events, therefore we also need to think about the relationship between participants and events.

9   Indirect Objects

One other semantic relation which is relatively simple, and which links participants to events is the relation associated with the Indirect Object.

It is relatively simple because it is associated directly with two semantic relations—Beneficiary and Recipient, often called the Beneficiary/Recipient. The semantic role associated with the Indirect Object has a more-or-less invariant semantic role. In *Peter gave Jane a cake*, Jane is the Beneficiary and Recipient. In *Peter made Jane a cake*, Jane might not be the Recipient but is the Beneficiary. In these two examples, the referent of the word *Jane* is in the Recipient semantic role in the example with *gave* and the Beneficiary role with *make*. Verbs of refusal also involve the Beneficiary relation. But they are about the Beneficiary not having the gift, or being denied the gift, so they still use the same semantic relation associated with the Indirect Object. In *she refused him another cup of tea*, the referent of *him* is still the Beneficiary. The reason why he does not receive tea is that the lexical semantics of the verb REFUSE cancel the idea that he receives the tea.

How should we capture this variation among the semantic relations associated with the Indirect Object relation? There are two sets of facts to consider: (i) the difference between verbs such as GIVE and verbs such as REFUSE; and (ii) the differences between verbs where the Indirect Object is semantically the Recipient, as in GIVE, and those where it is semantically the Beneficiary, but not the Recipient, as in MAKE.

One way might be to think about the contrast shown with GIVE and REFUSE is to think about Talmy's (1985) discussion contrasting examples in the case of force dynamics, such as *she made him leave* and *she let him leave*. The idea is that *she* is the Antagonist and *he* is Agonist in both cases. The Antagonist acts on the Agonist in order to bring about a resulting state in the Agonist. That is, in the examples just given *she* acts on *him*. Whether the event goes through or not has to do with other elements of the lexical semantics of MAKE and LET. In the case of *she made him leave* and *she let him leave*, there are two kinds of causation: one is the kind of causation where the Subject brings the event about, while the other is where the Subject allows the natural tendency of the Object to follow through. Talmy discusses the relationship between the Antagonist and the Agonist's natural tendency to movement or natural tendency toward remaining stationary. Both kinds of causation, the 'making' kind and the 'letting' type, can be captured by the generalization that the Subject referent acts directly on the Object referent.

We might ask ourselves whether there are similar generalizations with indirect objects. Indirect objects do not necessarily involve force-dynamics, so 'acting-on' will not work: in *Peter made Jane a cake*, Jane is not affected; she might just be Peter's intended Beneficiary without knowing that she is the Beneficiary and she need not even benefit, because she might not receive a cake that was made for her: *Peter made Jane a cake, but the dog ate it* is perfectly well-formed. Therefore, this is a verb of intent; it is not a verb with an entailed outcome. The fact that the benefit can be overridden is a fact about the lexical structure of MAKE. We can contrast MAKE and GIVE. With GIVE, the Result that the indirect Object actually has the gift—is entailed. See also Holmes and Hudson (2005) on DENY. Here then, we have a difference between verbs that entail the outcome and (that the intended Beneficiary/Recipient actually possesses the gift) and those that do not. As with the forced-dynamic verbs, this is to do with which subtype of the Outcome relation is chosen.

Alongside the issue of whether there is an entailed outcome of possession or not, there is co-variation with the Beneficiary/Recipient relation. When the transfer of possession is entailed, the Indirect Object's referent is the Recipient and Beneficiary. When it is not, the Indirect Object's referent is Beneficiary only.[5] What are the consequences for the semantics associated with the Indirect Object relation and how should they be modelled? Because relations can be classified, they can also be classified by multiple inheritance. So it is possible to say that the semantic relation associated with the Indirect Object inherits from both a Beneficiary and a Recipient relation.

We can go further: we can associate the Indirect Object directly with its semantic relation: because relations are nodes with primitive attribute and value relations associated with them, those nodes can themselves link to other nodes in the network. Therefore, the Indirect Object has an associated semantic relation which has a prototypical semantics, where part of the prototype can be overridden. The treatment of relations as nodes with associated Argument and Value relations also means that we can treat semantic relations as being in a direct relationship with syntactic relations. Both of these analyses are represented in Figure 5.

The grammar in Figure 5 argues that the Indirect Object has a value and an argument and a sense which is Beneficiary or Recipient. This is an innovation in Word Grammar: according to this analysis, dependencies can actually have a sense relation associated with them. That allows us to capture certain kind of linking generalization. It is a regular semantic association between a particular grammatical function and a particular meaning relationship. Because the semantic relation inherits from both Beneficiary and Recipient, either can be overridden in more specific instances.

---

5 I am ignoring ditransitive verbs that bring about a disbenefit for the indirect Object's referent.

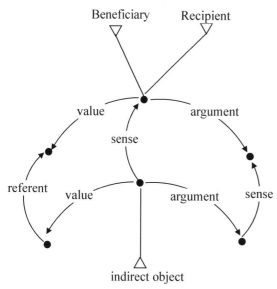

FIGURE 5   Indirect Object

10   Semantic Relations

When we move beyond semantic relations between events, and simple semantic relations such as the one associated with the Indirect Object, the picture gets more complex. The simplest semantic relation to think about—although not necessarily the simplest in its full network analysis—is the Agent of an unergative verb. Prototypical 'running' like *Jane is running* has an active Agent which is responsible, contributes force, and is aware. You might ask: how do we build this information into a network? How much of it matters? How much of it is grammatically important? Does grammar exploit the information about agency? Is agency related to the action? Is it related to causation? And is it a part of a transitive prototype? (And if it is, what is it doing in the semantics of unergative verbs?) We can explore these issues by looking at other instances of the verb RUN.

I talked about RUN in lecture 4: In *the train is running at 70 km/h, the train* is the "Agent". It is active, but it is not responsible. It contributes force but is not aware. In *the computer is running in the corner, the computer* is active, but is not responsible. It does not contribute force and is not aware. Does this tell us that there is an Agent prototype (Dowty 1991)? Or does our knowledge of language not actually rely on this kind of fine-grained detail? I do not think that this kind of variation in the property of being an Agent matters for the sake of argument linking (the relationship between lexical semantics and lexical syntax). This is encyclopedic knowledge. It is a part of the meaning of the verb, but it is not actually part of how grammar works.

But if grammar involves working out the associative relationship between different bits of form and meaning, the situation will get a little more complex with transitive verbs. Consider the following examples.

(4) Jane stroked the cat [like RUN]
(5) Jane opened the door [more than RUN: result]
(6) Jane knows the square root of 9 [less than RUN]
(7) Jane expected Peter [less than RUN]

In (4) STROKE is like RUN. Both are activity verbs. But in (5) OPEN is more complicated than RUN, because it involves at least two parts, the change of state and the resulting state. It is a complex verb with subevents. In (6) KNOW is perhaps less complicated than RUN, because nothing happens. It is a verb that symbolizes a simple state. In (7), EXPECT is also a simple mental verb. In these examples, there are different event types and different degrees of agentivity in the Subject. The annotations on the right-hand side are to do with how agentive the Subject seems to be. For example, the Subject of *running* is active. In (5) the Subject of *open* causes the subevent. In (6) the Subject of *knowing* is less active than the Subject of *running* and, in fact, entirely non-agentive. In (7) the Subject of *expecting* is less active than the Subject of *running*. There is also a difference between (4) and (5). Example (5) involves the Subject bringing a new state of affairs about.

One useful way of working out how much detail we need to include in our understanding of semantic relations is to look at verbal diathesis. Diatheses include the argument alternations we discussed in an earlier lecture, under the heading of evidence for event complexity: it includes Levin's (1993) diagnostics for different subevents in verbs' meanings. I discussed the conative alternation, the middle alternation and the Body-Part Ascension alternation in Lecture 2. Some such alternations are different ways of realizing argument properties. Others are voice distinctions, such as the distinction between active and passive. Voice changes the perspective on an event. A passive verb involves demotion of the Er of the verb; therefore in a passive, the Er of the verb is not linked to the Subject. The Er is the semantic relation that normally links to the Subject of the verb in an active voice verb, but not in passive. A key fact about passive is that passivization does not care how agentive the Er of a verb might be; therefore we can say, *the square root of 9 is known by everyone*. Verbal

EVENTS AND THEMATIC ROLES   133

diatheses, including passive, suggest that from a grammatical perspective, we
can keep semantic relations at a coarse level of granularity.

11   A WG Theory of Passive

Let us look at how passivization allows us to understand how fine-grained semantic relations should be. In WG, a passive participle is just an inflection of
a verb. It inherits from the category of a verb, and it also inherits from the category of passive. There is no rule of passivization or passive formation. Figure 6
below shows the basic argument linking pattern for the transitive verb KISS in
the active voice.

Figure 6 is the basic model for *kissing*. The lexeme *kiss* has a sense, 'kissing'
which has an Er that links to the referent of the Subject and an Ee which links
to the referent of the Object. KISS and *kissing* are both nodes in the network.
The diagram makes a simple claim which I have made before: argument realization is declarative. There is no magic and there are no rules or algorithms.
Children learn how to match one bit of structure—semantics—with another,
syntax, through their experience of language, and through their perceptual
experiences of the world. When a child learns the verb KISS, they learn all of
Figure 6; you cannot just learn that KISS is a transitive verb with Subject and
Object.

We can see this must be true, because *kissing* is one special category of
verbs, which has two different realizations. One realization is *x kisses y* and
the other realization is that you can kiss somebody who kisses you back at the
same time; see, for example, *they kissed.* KISS is a reciprocal verb, which is an
intransitive verb with a plural Subject, as well as being a transitive one. There

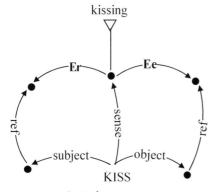

FIGURE 6   Lexical entry KISS

is a limited set of these words. We all know them and we just learn them. For example (I think this is one of Jackendoff's examples), imagine a drunk person walking down the street late at night having left the bar who sees a lamppost, wrap their arms around it and gives the lamppost a kiss. In this situation, you can say *the drunk kissed the lamppost*, but you can't say *the drunk and the lamppost kissed* because the lamppost cannot kiss the drunk back. This complicated information about verb KISS and verbs like it is just what we all acquire along the way. I do not think that there are argument linking algorithms that take us from a transitive verb to a reciprocal one, or that there is much in the way of deduction in language acquisition.

12   A Simple Argument Realization Model

This model of argument realization means that a child learns that the verb has a participant which links to its Subject—the Er. It has a participant that links to its Object—the Ee. It has a sense (a simple event, 'kissing'). The Er and the Ee are relations of the event. Subject and Object are relations of the syntactic verb. The model is symbolic like construction grammar, declarative like construction grammar, but sign-free, because it is a simple network. Otherwise it is "constructional" in that the relationship between form and meaning is profiled in the network in a complete way. The following diagram shows argument realization in usage. It is incomplete as I have left categorization facts out: the diagram does not say that the word *Jane* isa Proper Noun; the word *kissed* Isa past tense instance of KISS, which isa Verb; or that *Peter* isa Proper Noun.

Along the bottom of the diagram I have represented the syntax, a word *Jane* which is in the Subject relationship with verb *kissed*. *Kiss* is in an Object relationship with a noun *Peter*. *Peter* has a referent, the concept 'Peter'. The concept 'Peter' is classified as a thing. *Jane* has a referent, the concept 'Jane' which is also classified as a thing. The verb KISS has a sense, which is 'kiss Peter'.

13   Argument Realization in Usage

The diagram is oversimplified. I should build the structure up step by step, but I have skipped out some structure. For example, I should have a more hierarchical structure showing how the verb combines with its arguments: 'kissing' > 'kissing Peter' > 'Jane kissing Peter' in which 'kiss' combines with 'Peter', its Ee, to give you 'kiss Peter', which then combines with 'Jane'. This is given in Figure 7. However, there is no temporal information in Figure 7, which is a

EVENTS AND THEMATIC ROLES 135

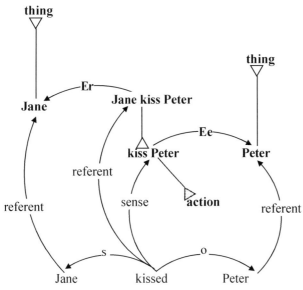

FIGURE 7   Argument realization in usage

further simplification: the verb is past tense, and in the case past tense realizes past time, so there should be a past time index on the referent of the verb.

14   Argument Realization and Passive

Figure 8 is the lexical entry for Passive. A passive verb has the same sense as the active voice verb, but it has morphosyntactic properties which override the usual argument-linking patterns: The Er is unlinked, or links to a BY-phrase, and the Ee, exceptionally, is linked to the Subject.

The ordinary active voice transitive verb KISS has a Subject and an Object. The diagram does not show the linking pattern for the lexeme in order to keep the diagram simple. KISS:passive inherits from the lexeme KISS and also from the category Passive. KISS:passive has a Subject, but not a direct Object. The Subject, however, links to the Ee of *kissing*. KISS:passive has the same sense as ordinary *kiss*, but the linking rule is different. KISS:passive also has an optional BY-phrase, and the Er of 'kissing' is what links to the BY-phrase of KISS:passive. The diagram also includes morphological information: the realization of KISS:passive is {*kissed*}.

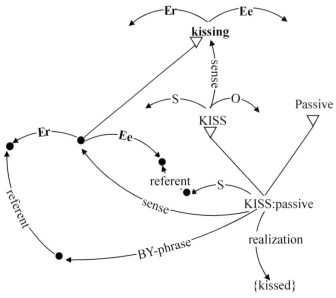

FIGURE 8   Lexical entry KISS:passive

This exemplifies the usual linking pattern for passive instances of transitive verbs. Again, when we learn English, we must learn all of these facts about how English passive verbs work. From hearing many tokens of passive verbs, we put together a schematic pattern that shows how this linking pattern is structured, which becomes information stored on the concept Passive. For any new transitive verb we encounter, it should be a straightforward step to make the passive by adding the information from the category Passive: this is simply a process of generalization.

Figure 8 presents a lexical entry for a passive participle of KISS. The passive participle inherits from KISS and from Passive. It has more specific information on it than the KISS node and it overrides the default argument linking pattern. In this respect it is like the model for Middle in lecture 3. Again, because I have chosen to simplify the model, there is missing information in Figure 8: in reality there are two passive participles—the passive participle associated with long passive which has a BY-phrase: *Jane was kissed by Peter*, and the passive participle for short passive which does not have a BY-phrase as in, *Jane was kissed*. Given the long passive *the church was destroyed by the vandals* and the short passive *the church was destroyed*, there have to be separate nodes for the two passive participles, because they include different information. I will claim that the long passive is the default and short passive overrides the default by excluding the BY-phrase. That is, short passive Isa passive and passive

Isa long passive. However, it is quite difficult to decide which passive ought to inherit from which because on the one hand KISS:passive preserves more information, but on the other hand, my hunch is that short passives are more prototypical than long passives. However, there are questions about how prototypicality should be modelled in default inheritance. One argument would be that the basic level category will be the category associated with the densest network.

15 Other Issues in the Grammar of the Passives

I have not explored all of the properties of passives here. There are prepositional passives. In English it is possible to say, *this bed has been slept in by President Obama*. Of course, the verb *sleep* does not have a direct Object, so this is a prepositional passive. There are also passives of raising-to-Object verbs: compare *we expect her to do her duty* (active voice) with *she is expected to do her duty* (passive voice). There are passives of ditransitive verbs. Ditransive verbs typically passivize the indirect Object not the direct Object. You can say *she was given a new pencil*, but *a new pencil was given her* is kind of odd. Therefore, the model is incomplete. There would be a far more complex network if I had tried to put all of the information into the diagram. It is simplified for the sake of interpretability, and to show how these phenomena are modeled.

16 Semantic Relations (Revisited)

I talked about passive bin order to want to talk about argument linking generalizations. I want to talk about which semantic properties of arguments matter in terms of the variation that we can observe in verb realization. A passive verb is a variant of an active verb. The question is what happens when we passivize, because what happens when we passivize will tell us how the semantic relations map to the grammatical functions. I have argued for the conclusion that the semantic relations that are relevant to grammar—argument realization— are very general: Er and Ee, Beneficiary/Recipient, and a handful of relations between events. The specific content of semantic roles in the behavior of various verbs is part of our knowledge of the meaning of those verbs. It does not affect how those verbs behave with respect to passivization, middle-formation and such things. This is the same conclusion that Croft (2012) arrived at. It seems like a robust conclusion to me.

17 Semantic Relations and Event Structure

This straightforward conclusion means that the semantic relations that are relevant to grammar, are very general semantic relations like Er and Ee. We do not need to be more specific; we do not have to talk about specific semantic roles such as Themes or Locations. There is not even any need to talk about Agents. We can just restrict ourselves to working with very general semantic roles which give us a difference between active and passive, and between active and middle. Therefore, from the point of view of argument linking and voice distinctions, there is no need for more detail in the typology of semantic relations. That does not of course mean that this is the end of thinking about semantic relations; we might think about semantic relations in other ways as well.

Here is what Croft says in his 2012 book, when he is discussing about Rappaport Hovav and Levin, Jackendoff and scholars with related approaches.

> Many of these theorists argue that thematic roles are not theoretical primitives but they should be defined in terms of the position of the role in event structure [...] For example, Jackendoff defines 'theme' as the first argument of his spatial event primitives GO, STAY, BE ORIENT and EXT. Although many scholars argue that thematic roles are not theoretical primitives, they in fact use thematic roles as theoretical primitives [... by positing] a thematic role hierarchy to account for the contribution of event semantics to argument realization.
> CROFT 2012: 176

Here is an example of the thematic role hierarchy (Experiencer and Instrument not included; taken from Croft 2012: 177):

Actor>Patient/Beneficiary>Theme>Location/Source/Goal

Croft also cites the hierarchy from Van Valin (1993: 75).

Agent > Effector > Experiencer/Location > Theme >Patient

Croft further notes, "[T]hematic role hierarchies include thematic roles that do not co-occur in a single event, and therefore are never realized together in a single clause [...]. For example, experiencers do not co-occur with patients" (2012: 177).

To illustrate, here is an example, LOVE. I suppose that if *Peter loves Jane* then *Peter* is the Experiencer of 'loving'. *Jane* is not the Patient of 'loving': the verb LOVE has an Experiencer as its Subject, but it does not have a Patient as its Object, because the Subject does not do not do anything to the Object by loving them. Perhaps an even better example would be FEAR. My dog, for example, is scared of fireworks. We can say *Jumble fears fireworks*. The referent of *Jumble* is the Experiencer of 'fearing'. He does not do anything to the fireworks. Fireworks are actually the Source of his fear, as *Jane* is the Source of *Peter's* love. Croft's question is why would you put them in the same hierarchy if they are not ever in the same clause? If the Experiencer is never in the same clause with the Patient, why would it be in the same hierarchy?

Table 1 is taken from Croft (2012) where he talks about the different grammatical functions that different thematic roles can be associated with.

Across the *x* axis Subject, Object and Oblique are shown (Oblique is some kind of prepositional phrase). Down the *y* axis, there are different thematic roles: Agent, Natural Force, Instrument, Patient, Experiencer, Stimulus, Beneficiary, and Figure/Theme. What the table shows us is that an Agent can be realized as a Subject or an Oblique. Natural Force can be realized as a Subject or an Oblique. And then the next four thematic roles, Instrument, Patient, Experiencer and Stimulus, can be realized as either Subject or Object. Beneficiaries can never be the Subject, but they can be the Object or an Oblique. Figure/Theme can be all three.

TABLE 1   Grammatical role and thematic role

	Grammatical role		
	Subject	Object	Oblique
Thematic role			
Agent	✓		✓
Natural Force	✓		✓
Instrument	✓	✓	✓
Patient	✓	✓	
Experiencer	✓	✓	
Stimulus	✓	✓	
Beneficiary		✓	✓
Figure/Theme	✓	✓	✓

TAKEN FROM CROFT (2012: 179)

Croft uses this table to ask a question, "Why would anybody talk about thematic role hierarchies when the realization patterns of these different thematic roles is such a complicated mess?" It is not possible to get good argument realization generalizations out of this list of thematic roles. If linguists want to have argument realization generalizations, these data are the wrong ones. They do not provide the kinds of meaningful generalizations that theoretical linguists look for. I think that is a good conclusion and I agree with Croft.

However, I think that Croft is wrong about one thing. I think that there actually are Oblique Experiencers. For example, *to me* is an Oblique Experiencer in *your car sounds like it needs a new clutch to me* and *the food tastes to me like Maud has been at the cooking sherry again*. When I talked about this data in Gisborne (2010), I argued that these Oblique Experiencers are actually different from Experiencers in examples such as *I like chocolate*. I argue that they are in a force-dynamic relationship with a modal predicate, and that *sound* and *taste* are modal predicates which express evidentiality.

This leads us to another point: if not all Experiencers are the same kind of thing why would we even try to make generalizations about Experiencers? The point is that we have to pitch our generalizations at the right level. If you try to make generalizations about thematic roles by using labels like Agent, Figure/Theme, and so on, you are making a generalization at the wrong level. You learn nothing useful from this approach about how language is organized.

18   Semantic Relations

There are also some further facts that are relevant to semantic relations, but they do not seem to be argument realization facts. Consider example (8) and (9):

(8) Jane is going from Edinburgh to Peebles.
(9) The road goes from Edinburgh to Peebles.

There is a co-occurrence restriction. In (8) *going* is dynamic, and 'Jane' is a bounded Theme that goes along the parth, starting in Edinburgh, and traveling all the way along the road to Peebles. It's an individual Jane all the way along, whereas in (9), *goes* is stative and the referent of *the road* actually extends all the way. *The road* is a path as well as the Theme; therefore in (9) the path and the Theme are coextensive all the way. Therefore, *Jane* is a bounded Theme whereas *the road* is a distributed Theme, which is distributed all the way along the path. That distinction seems to be always the case in verbs of going that have stative and dynamic realizations. In (8) and (9) there are different kinds of Theme argument and a co-occurrence relationship between the semantic role of the Subject and the Aktionsart of the predicate.

A different approach to event structure can be found in Talmy's Force Dynamic relations (Talmy 1985b). Force Dynamic relations—the Agonist and Antagonist, which are analogous to Croft's Initiator and Endpoint—have a life which is independent of the verbs whose meanings they participate in. For example, Lakoff (1977) points out that the Subject of a middle is the "primarily responsible participant" in that event. Therefore, you are blaming the page if you say *the page photocopied too low*, or you are blaming the car if you say *the car steers poorly*. You are making the Subject primarily responsible.

One of the things we need to do is to figure out how force dynamic relations fit into the typology of other relations and events, and event structures. For example, how do they fit in the Agent prototype? In a sense, they should not fit it. In Talmy's original formulation, force-dynamic participants were a kind of transitive prototype: the Antagonist acts on the Agonist. But what do we make of the primarily responsible participants in the Middle construction? And are force-dynamic participants part of the Agent prototype if they cannot be part of the semantic structure of intransitive verbs? The short answer is that they belong in a different part of the organization of language. They belong in causation, which is where Talmy originally put them: they are part of the causative prototype.

19 Force Dynamics

In Talmy's original formulation, force-dynamic participants belong to what Croft (1992) calls a "participants act on participants" view of causation. As I have noted before, Croft distinguishes three kinds of causation: "participants act on participants," which is associated with Talmy's model, "events cause events," associated with Donald Davidson, and "participants cause events," associated with Rappaport Hovav & Levin's work. Causation is not the same thing as agency. Agency seems to be related to causation in some way, but they are not identical. It is possible to have agency over an event—an action that you perform—without causing anything, except, trivially, the action that you are performing. For example, in tapping my foot, *I* am the Agent of tapping in that I am responsible for tapping, but I am not the causing any other event by tapping my foot. You can be the Agent of an event without acting on other individual or causing anything to come about.

Talmy's claim was that causation involves an Agent acting on another participant to bring about an event. Croft (2012) lists the sentences in (10)–(15) which capture all of Talmy's types of force-dynamic relations.

(10) I kicked the ball.
(11) I pushed the ball.
(12) I held the ball.
(13) I stopped the ball.
(14) I dropped/released/let go of the ball.
(15) I left the ball (in the house).

In all of these examples, the Subject acts on the ball. The idea behind force dynamics is that the Agonist has a natural tendency to movement or to rest, while the Antagonist acts on the Agonist's natural tendency. Therefore, in (10) and (11), *the ball* has a natural tendency to rest, and acting on it cause it to move. But in (12), the ball has a natural tendency to movement because if you hold it then presumably you are holding it up and gravity gives it a natural tendency to fall. Again, the Antagonist acts on the ball. In (13) the ball has a natural tendency to movement; it is moving and you stop it. Again, the Antagonist acts on the ball which is the Agonist. In each of these cases, an Antagonist acts on the Agonist to overcome the Agonist's natural tendency. Croft (2012: 205) says, "Talmy also recognizes helping and hindering force-dynamic relations in addition to causing and letting force-dynamic relations." I mentioned these different patterns earlier.

The question from the event structure point of view is, "How do these relations come together with complex event structures?" We have seen that there is independent evidence for event structure. I am not going to follow Croft directly in proposing an answer. Croft work with a model of causal chains, so he will take an example like (16) and analyse the causal chain as a series of participants acting on each other.

(16) Sue broke the coconut for Greg with a hammer.
Sue → hammer → coconut ⤑ Greg
SBJ   A.OBL   OBJ   S.OBL

Croft's analysis is that the Subject is the Agent which acts on the antecedent Oblique, *hammer*, which acts on the Object which acts on another Oblique, called the subsequent Oblique, who is the Beneficiary in some way. Subject and Object are the Initiator and Endpoint of the causal chain.

EVENTS AND THEMATIC ROLES   143

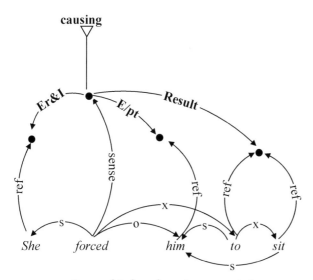

FIGURE 9   Force and its force dynamics representation

The WG approach is different, illustrated in Figure 9, which is borrowed from a later lecture.

This representation of force dynamics, uses the verb FORCE. As is usual in a WG diagram, the bottom line represents the syntax, while above it is the semantics. The sense of FORCE has an Er which is also the Initiator, and an Endpoint which is the referent of *him*. *Him* is the Object of *forced* and it is also the Subject of *to sit*. *To sit* has a semantic structure which is simplified in the diagram. The primary claim in the diagram is that force-dynamic relations are relevant in event complexity.

Figure 10 oversimplifies the semantic steps involved in building up the sense of FORCE. The key point to observe is that FORCE involves a force-dynamic dyad, from Initiator to Endpoint; the action of the Initiator on the Endpoint results in the Endpoint being in a different state, 'sitting'. In WG, we do not identify the full causal chain that Croft works with. The key question, especially for argument realization, is to establish which entity is the Initiator and which is the Endpoint.

Before we talk more about Initiator and Endpoint, I'd like to talk something that is worth thinking about but which I do not have a clear answer to. It is how we bring event complexity and force-dynamic relations together. These examples of Croft's here do not all involve complex events. *Kicking* is not complex; it is just a simple event. So is *holding*. These transitive verbs do not involve event complexity, even though according to Croft, they capture all of Talmy's types of force-dynamic relations. It looks as though force-dynamic relations are not in a perfect one-to-one correspondence with event complexity types. Even though Talmy (1985b) talked about force-dynamic relations, he did so in terms of verbs in the same class as FORCE, which take a non-finite complement (e.g. In *I force him to go*, *him to go* is a non-finite complement). There is not a perfect mapping between force-dynamics and event complexity. Therefore, there is still more work to do.

To show what sort of work is still necessary, in a personal communication Dick Hudson has asked me whether Force Dynamics may be just another way of talking about default inheritance as it applies to events, where one of the main issues that interest humans is how we react to various constraints. Force Dynamics would then be part of our "folk physics" of life, rather than being part of how we structure our conceptualization of events. Sometimes, a Force Dynamic analysis would be relevant, and sometimes not. One way of addressing this question would be to see if there are any grammatical tests for Force Dynamic relations, which would suggest that they are part of how we structure our conceptualization of events. It should be possible to devise a grammatical test. We will see in the next section that the Force Dynamic relations can link into the discourse context (to the speaker and to the addressee), an idea that recurs in later lectures. Prototypically, verbs with Force Dynamic relations that link to their Subject and Object are dynamic, whereas verbs with Force Dynamic relations that link into the discourse context are stative.

20   Initiator and Endpoint

Initiator and Endpoint are semantic relations with independent content. Their behavior affects how predicates are interpreted. We will look at resultatives and causatives in the next lecture, but we will examine modals in this lecture. The claim is that deontic modals' meanings are partly defined by the linking patterns of Initiator and Endpoint.

Force-dynamic relations have a key property. They define the events that they have as their arguments. Partly this is due to how they "link" to the context; unlike other thematic roles, force-dynamic relations can relate to the participants in the speech event. One of WG's innovations is that it represents the speech situation in its analyses. This is tantamount to saying that context is also part of the mental network in some way, which is one of its mentalist characteristics. Force-dynamic relations define modal meanings through their linking properties. Figure 11 shows the analysis of the deontic modal structure *you may leave* in WG.

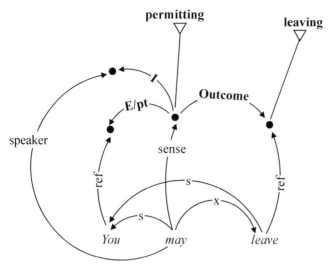

FIGURE 10   *MAY*
TAKEN FROM GISBORNE (2010: 97)

In Figure 10 *you may leave* involves the sense which has an Endpoint and outcome. The Endpoint is the referent of *you*, the Initiator is the speaker, who gives permission. This represents a force relationship through the permissive nature of the deontic modal, or in Croft's terms the Initiator acts on the Endpoint.

That is a reasonable place to end. I have run out of time—I was going to discuss causation in formal theories, such as Davidson (1967), Parsons (1994) and subsequent work by Heidi Harley and Bridget Copley. It is important to discuss this work because it is relevant to understanding how event complexity works. And it also shows an important convergence between formal and cognitive theories because Copley has been involved in bringing force-dynamics into formal semantics. However, there is no opportunity to discuss these authors' work here.

21   Summary

In this lecture, I have argued that there is a small set of relations that hold between two events: Intention, Purpose, Result and Entailment (Entailment more specifically holds between propositions). And that there are just two relations associated with Indirect Objects: Recipient and Beneficiary. I have also argued that the other semantic relations do not do a great deal of work. There are the "proto-roles" or "macro-roles", Er and Ee, that are involved in verbal diatheses. Therefore, many of the traditional semantic roles are not involved in event complexity and argument realization. These include Agent, Patient, Experiencer, Locative and so on, which are part of prototypical structure of different events and fall in that area where "dictionary" meaning shades into "encyclopedic" meaning. I have also discussed the force-dynamic relations, which I have argued are part of how different event types are defined, and which are implicated in the cognitive theory of modality.

LECTURE 6

Resultatives and Causation

In this lecture we look into resultatives and causation. I am following up Lecture 5's introduction to the role of force-dynamics in causation and previous discussions of event complexity. Resultatives are the pattern found in examples such as *Kim wiped the tools clean*, where the adjectival secondary predicate *clean* symbolizes a state which is the result of the activity that the verb symbolizes. I use resultatives as a way of exploring the nature of causation because resultatives involve a type of causative structure. There are also causative structures in the event complexity shown in the meanings of verbs such as BUILD—see examples such as *Kim built a house*—and one question is whether it is possible to generalize over the two patterns.

1 Resultatives

1.1 Secondary Predication

As I have just said, there is a secondary predicate in resultatives, which is what adds the result meaning. This resultative secondary predicate is not part of the lexical structure of a verb; rather, it is more like a construction where a resultative adjunct is attached to the verb (and its modifiers). This secondary predication structure gives us a way of understanding how causation works. One of the ideas I want to explore is something that I talked about in Lecture 5: when we look at semantic relations we must not just try to understand the semantics of the relation by itself. We also have to understand the semantics of the arguments of the relations and what sorts of properties these arguments bring with them; resultatives offer a way of doing this.

We can begin by looking at examples of two different kinds of secondary predication.

All original audio-recordings and other supplementary material, such as any hand-outs and powerpoint presentations for the lecture series, have been made available online and are referenced via unique DOI numbers on the website www.figshare.com. They may be accessed via a QR code for the print version of this book. In the e-book, both the QR code and dynamic links are available, and can be accessed by a mouse-click.

(1) The waiter served <u>the food</u> *cold.*
(2) They kissed <u>the baby</u> *silly.*

These examples illustrate two different types of secondary predication. In (1), there is a depictive secondary predicate, so the secondary predicate *cold* has as its Subject the phrase *the food*; *cold* describes a property of the food. The example in (2), however, is a resultative construction. Example (2) means they made the baby silly by kissing it. These two kinds of secondary predication are different from each other; the first is depictive and the second is resultative. A resultative secondary predication involves a kind of causative structure. Note that a depictive can also be predicated of the Subject (e.g. *naked* in *the waiter served the food naked*), but this is not possible for resultatives of transitive verbs in the active voice, which indicates that resultatives are Subject to different, and more restrictive, constraints than depictives. That is, secondary predications like (1) and (2) do not just differ in terms of their meaning; they also differ in terms of the kinds of constraints they impose on the various words and phrases that participate in these constructions.

1.2 *Basic Facts about Resultatives*

There is an immense literature on the resultative construction. We can start with Goldberg's book in which she says, "[T]he resultative can only apply to arguments that potentially (although not necessarily) undergo a change of state as a result of the action denoted by the verb" (1995: 180). Goldberg is claiming that the prototypical meaning of the resultative is that you perform an action on the Object and as a result of the performing an action on the Object, the Object undergoes some kind of change of state. For her, the arguments which can undergo this change of state are Patients. We can identify them with the acted-on participants in a force dynamic pairing; that is, in Talmy's (1988) terms, they are Agonists, or in Croft's (2012) terms, Endpoints. Goldberg argues that the semantic constraint just quoted applies even to resultatives where the verb does not normally have an Object but only has an Object in the resultative construction; we will come to these kinds of resultative construction below.

1.3 *Types of Resultative*

Transitive verbs can be made resultative:

(3) Jane kissed Peter unconscious.
(4) Peter brushed Jane's hair smooth.

The example in (3) means that Peter became unconscious as a result of Jane kissing him: she kissed him so much that she made him unconscious through kissing him. (4) means he brushed her hair so carefully that it became smooth as a result of brushing it. But notice that not all English transitive verbs can be part of a resultative construction. Neither example (5) nor example (6) is possible.

(5) *He watched the telly broken.
(6) *He believed the idea powerful.

This is despite the fact that you can imagine a plausible scenario for these examples: (5) would mean 'he watched the telly with the result that it became broken'. You can imagine that somebody could be addicted to telly watching and therefore watched it so much that it becomes broken. But (5) is not acceptable. It must also be possible to believe an idea, with the result that the idea becomes powerful. This must be a possible situation in real life: it seems to explain the delusion currently gripping a large part of the British population that leaving the European Union would be a good thing to do. But again, our language does not let us say (6).

There are other related structures as well. Example (7) is perfectly normal transitive verb and it has a resultative variant as in (8).

(7) We wiped the tools.
(8) We wiped the tools clean.
(9) The tools were wiped clean.

In (8), *clean* is predicated of *the tools*, so (8) means 'We wiped the tools with the result the tools become clean'. The example in (9) shows that a resultative construction can involve a passive voice verb and means that the tools were wiped with the result that they became clean. And so we have seen some patterns of possible and impossible resultatives, and we have shown that the resultative construction can interact with verb-changing constructions such as passive voice.

It is also possible to have resultative constructions with some intransitive verbs—the inchoative verbs which are associated with causative verbs such as BREAK (*he broke the chair*).

(10) The chair broke.
(11) The chair broke apart.

The verb in (10) is the intransitive, inchoative variant of the causative verb BREAK. It means the chair underwent a change of the state, from being not broken to being broken. Sentence (11) shows that verb in a resultative construction. The chair broke with the result that it was apart; therefore, *apart* describes the end state of the chair breaking: it is possible for something to break without it breaking apart; this is a further specification of the result state. Therefore, some intransitives can participate in the resultative construction, especially intransitives related to causatives. But we can also see that not all intransitives can have a resultative adjunct. It is possible to say (12) but not (13).

(12) He talked.
(13) *He talked hoarse.

The intended meaning of (13) is that *he talked with the result that he became hoarse,* but it is not a possible sentence of English. However, as I mentioned earlier, there are "fake Object" resultatives. These are verbs which have a suppletive Object, which is not selected for. We can illustrate with the verb RUN, which is intransitive: **Jane ran her Nikes* in (15) is ungrammatical, but (16) is a good sentence.

(15) *Jane ran his Nikes.
(16) Jane ran her Nikes threadbare.

The structure in (16) is associated with unergative verbs—that is to say intransitive verbs that are simple action verbs which do not show a change of state. To occur in the resultative construction, such verbs have to have a fake Object.

As well as fake Object resultatives, it is also possible for unergative intransitive verbs to occur in the resultative construction with a reflexive pronoun.

(17) We yelled ourselves hoarse.
(18) *We yelled ourselves.
(19) *We yelled Harry hoarse.
GOLDBERG AND JACKENDOFF 2004

The examples in (17)–(19) show a special constraint because (17) is possible, with the reflexive Object, but we cannot say (19), because the Object is not a reflexive. The example in (18) shows that the existence of the reflexive Object is related to the existence of the resultative adjunct, because the reflexive

Object is not possible in the absence of the resultative adjunct.[1] Yelling is a type of loud talking like shouting, so (17) means something similar to *we talked ourselves hoarse*.

To summarize, there are transitive verbs which can occur with resultative adjuncts as in (3)–(4), transitive verbs which cannot occur with resultative adjuncts, as in (5)–(6), intransitive verbs which can occur with resultative adjuncts, as in (11), intransitive verbs which cannot occur with resultative adjuncts, as in (13). And then there are intransitive verbs that can occur with a resultative adjunct as long as they also have fake objects, as in (16), or occur with fake reflexives, as in (17). According to Goldberg and Jackendoff (2004), the Result Phrase can be an adjective phrase (AP) or a prepositional phrase (PP). An Adjective Phrase which is the Result Phrase expresses the semantic category of 'property'. A PP resultative phrase can either express 'property' (*break the bathtub into pieces*) or spatial information (*rolled out of bed*) and the result is a kind of destination (or the end of a path), as in *we rolled out of bed*, for example, where *out of bed* describes the end result of the rolling out of bed.

Below, there are more examples from Goldberg and Jackendoff (2004). These examples show a lot of the variation in the data and also the variation in different possible resultative constructions. First there are transitive resultatives predicated of the Subject (20)–(24), then intransitive resultatives predicated of the implicit predicand (25)–(29). Predicand is Goldberg and Jackendoff's term: a predicand is a Subject and in these examples it is implicit, so the Er of the predicate is implicit in these examples. Elsewhere I have called it the resultative Subject.

(20) Bill followed the road into the forest.
(21) We drove Highway 5 from SD to SF.
(22) The sailors rode the breeze clear of the rocks.
(23) Fred tracked the leak to its source.
(24) John danced mazurkas across the room.
(25) Bill spit/urinated/sneezed out of the window.
(26) Bill sweated/bled on the floor.
(27) The toilet leaked through the floor into the kitchen below.

---

1 This is a simplification. I think that *we yelled Harry deaf* is fine. The fake reflexive is required of unergative verbs when the resultative adjunct has to be understood to be predicated of the verb's Subject. Because examples like (13) are not possible—unergatives cannot have a resultative adjunct without an explicit Object, a reflexive pronoun is required when the resultative predicate needs to be understood as predicated of the matrix verb's Subject.

(28) Bill ate off the floor.
(29) Bill drank from the hose.

The example in (20) means 'Bill followed the road with the result that he ended up in the forest'. Similarly the resultative meanings of (21) and (22) are 'with the result that we were in San Francisco', and 'with the result that the sailors were clear of the rocks'. The example in (23) means, 'Fred tracked the leak with the result that Fred found the source' and (24) means, 'John danced with the result that John was across the room'. These are all odd examples, compared to (1) and (2). Like (2) they are transitive. In (1) and (2) the Subject of the resultative is the Object of the verb, but in (20)–(24) the Subject of the result phrase is not the Object of the verb; instead, it is the Subject of the verb.

And then there are the implicit resultative Subjects in (25)–(29). The example in (25) means 'Bill spat with the result that the spit itself was out of the window'. Bill's spit is the implicit Subject of the resultative and it is not linguistically represented. It is neither the Subject of the main verb or Object of the main verb. The Subject of the result phrase is implicit in the meaning of the main verb. The same with (26). In (27) the result is that the leakage from the toilet was in the kitchen below. In (28), it is not Bill who was off the floor; it is the food that he ate. Again, the Subject of the result phrase is implicit. (20)–(29) are non-prototypical resultatives, and they are extensions of resultative construction, alongside the fake Object and fake reflexive resultatives, and they belong in a family-resemblance relationship with the prototypical example.

1.4 Rappaport Hovav and Levin's View

Rappaport Hovav and Levin (2001) observe semantic differences between fake Object and other resultatives. They claim that fake Object resultatives can be what they call "temporally discontinuous," whereas resultatives including an argument of the verb as the Subject of the resultative predicate are temporally dependent. For example, if we take (3), *Jane kisses Peter unconscious*, it must mean that his unconsciousness immediately follows the kissing. But in *he talked himself hoarse*, or *we yelled ourselves hoarse*, the meaning is not that the hoarseness has to be immediately after the talking (or yelling)—the result state could come some later time. That is, it is possible for the result phrase not to be continuous with the event in the verb but for there to be a temporal break.

1.5 Types of Resultative

We can summarize the discussion so far: there are several different dimensions of variation among resultatives.

RESULTATIVES AND CAUSATION   153

- Is the result adjunct an adjective phrase or a preposition phrase?
- Does the result adjunct express a property or some kind of spatial configuration?
- Is the main verb transitive or intransitive?
- If the main verb is transitive, is the Object selected?
- If the Object is not selected, is the suppletive Object a normal noun (phrase) or is it a fake reflexive?
- If the main verb is transitive, is the predicand (Subject) of the result adjunct the Object of the main verb (the default situation) or the Subject (an exceptional type)?
- Is the predicand of the result adjunct implicit?

I will not explain all of these different subtypes of resultatives, or give you a range of analytical diagrams showing how they all work. But I will take some examples and see what we can deduce from them. But remember that I introduced the resultative construction as a way of thinking about causation and to help us understand causation more clearly. We will be coming back to causation.

1.6   Semantics of the Resultatives

Next, we should look at the semantics of the resultative construction. Goldberg and Jackendoff (2004) say examples like (30) mean 'Willy caused the plants to become flat by watering them'.

(30) *Willy watered the plants flat*

This is because the property of the resultative has the following syntax and semantics:

Syntax: $NP_1\ V\ NP_2\ AP_3$
Semantics: $[X_1\ CAUSE\ Y_2\ [BECOME\ Z_3]]$
MEANS: $[\textit{VERBAL SUBEVENT}]$

The semantics means X_1 (which is the referent of the first noun phrase) causes Y_2 (which is the referent of the second noun phrase) to become Z_3 (which is the referent of the adjective phrase), by a certain means. They are claiming the semantics of the constructional subevent predicts the syntax of the construction. The resultative is therefore semantically the same as verbs whose meanings are X CAUSE Y BECOME Z. Goldberg and Jackendoff say, "Therefore the semantic argument structure of the constructional subevent determines the syntactic argument structure of the sentence by general principles of argument linking" (Goldberg and Jackendoff 2004: 539).

I am surprised that Goldberg could make such a claim. That is exactly the kind of the thing that Jackendoff might say because Jackendoff is interested in trying to come up with an algorithmic predictive way of organizing the relationship between syntax and semantics in argument linking. But this is very un-construction grammar like, to talk about general principles of argument linking, because in construction grammar what you do is to try to find generalizations which are represented in inheritance hierarchies. Constructions are declarative statements of grammatical properties such as linking, and so there are no general principles of argument linking: there are statements of observed patterns.

I agree that there are elements in common between the resultative construction and transitive verbs like MAKE, as in *we made a cake* which means *we cause the cake to exist*. And I agree that there is a relationship between resultative constructions and verbs with Xcomps like MAKE and FORCE as in *Jane made Peter go to school* or *Jane forced Peter to go to school*. Goldberg and Jackendoff point out that the verb MAKE with an Xcomp is a "lexical resultative," so they claim that *we made him angry* is a lexical resultative. But I think the semantics they give for the resultative construction is wrong. *We made him angry* does not mean, 'We caused him to become angry by making him'. The sentence lacks the means element of the resultative. Therefore, I think that we should conclude that the analysis, [X [CAUSE Y [BECOME Z]] by MEANS] is odd. A more natural translation of *Willy watered the plants flat*, therefore, is not 'Willy caused the plants to become flat by watering them', but 'Willy watered the plants with the result that the plants became flat'. The argument comes from the analysis of MAKE: *we made him angry* means 'we acted on him with the result that he became angry'.

Just as the verb WATER has a sense which Isa instance of the category Action and which also has a manner specification, so too does RUN in *she ran her Nikes threadbare*, which means 'she ran and as a result her Nikes became threadbare'. That is why there are fake Object resultatives—it is not that they give an Object to a verb, so much as that they supply a Subject for the resultative predication or result adjunct. And that is why fake Object resultatives are fine like that, because *she ran her Nikes threadbare* just means 'she ran, and as a result her Nikes became threadbare'.

Goldberg and Jackendoff point out some other semantic properties of resultatives: to do with the result state and the path. Property resultatives have a result state. But in path resultatives, the Subject of resultative traverses the path and then arrives at its end. Moreover, in Goldberg & Jackendoff's definition, there are causative vs. non-causative resultatives. When the Subject of the resultative is the Subject of the verb, the resultative describes a change of state, and there is no causing event. Therefore, they would say that *the pond froze solid* is a non-causative resultative because it takes the inchoative verb FREEZE which is a verb that denotes a change of state, and in this way it means that there is not a causing event.

Now we turn to looking at various different types of resultative, as laid out by Goldberg and Jackendoff (2004: 540). As before, the subscript numbers show how the semantic structures are linked to syntactic constituents.

> Noncausative property resultative, e.g. *The pond froze solid*
> Syntax: NP_1 V AP/PP_2
> Semantics: X_1 BECOME Y_2
>   MEANS: [*VERBAL SUBEVENT*]

> Noncausative path resultative (intransitive motion construction), e.g. *The ball rolled down the hill*
> Syntax: NP_1 V PP_2
> Semantics: X_1 GO $Path_2$
>   MEANS: [*VERBAL SUBEVENT*]

> Causative path resultative (caused motion construction), e.g. *Bill rolled the ball down the hill*
> Syntax: NP_1 V NP_2 PP_3
> Semantics: X_1 CAUSE [Y_2 GO $Path_3$]
>   MEANS: [*VERBAL SUBEVENT*]

The first type is a non-causative property resultative. The idea is that in a non-causative property resultative, such as *the pond froze solid*, means 'the pond becomes solid by freezing'. In a non-causative path resultative such as *the ball rolled down the hill*, the translation is 'the ball becomes down the hill by means of rolling'. In a causative path resultative, the caused motion construction, as in *Bill rolled the ball down the hill*, the translation is 'Bill caused the ball to go down the hill by means of rolling'. However, I do not agree with this analysis which exploits the notion of 'means' as I have just explained. One argument that I have just made is the argument from the verb MAKE: it is not possible to say that *we made him angry* has the meaning, 'We caused him to become angry by making'.

Another argument is that the 'means' analysis subordinates the meaning of the main verb. I think that is very strange and I do not understand why the main meaning of the lexical verbs of the construction would be subordinated to the overall meaning of the construction in this way. That seems to be an unnecessarily non-compositional analysis. I understand that construction grammar respects non-compositionality. But that does not mean you find non-compositionality everywhere you look. There is no need to force everything to be non-compositional just because you can. We need a theory that accommodates non-compositionality only when there is no other answer.

Goldberg and Jackendoff (2004: 541) also give the examples in (31) and (32) which involve an achievement verb.

(31) a. The witch vanished into the forest.
     b. Bill disappeared down the road.
(32) a. *The witch went into the forest by vanishing.
     b. The witch went into the forest and thereby vanished.

An appropriate paraphrase of (31a) is not (32a), but rather (32b). Jackendoff and Goldberg (2004: 541) say, "In short, sound emission and disappearances resultatives involve a result relation between the constructional subevent and the verbal subevent instead of a means relation." But why do they not think that all resultatives work like this? And, what is the result relation here? What is the relationship between the result relation and its cause predicate? How is a result relation different from a cause predicate? What is a result relation that makes it different from a cause predicate? I think that there is something to be thought about and challenged. It seems to me that you would want to make these examples consistent with the other examples and I do not know why you would not simply say that (31a) means, 'the witch vanished with the result that she was in the forest', or (31b), 'Bill disappeared with the result that he was down the road'. There is obviously additional constructional meaning in there, and it is a little bit complicated, but it is worth exploring this idea a little bit further.

Holmes (2005) also finds examples like SCATTER, as in *she scattered the almonds into the cake batter* which is another sort of resultative, where the result is that the almonds are in the cake batter. But there is a complication here: SCATTER is not just a manner-of-motion verb; it is a verb which expresses a path and a Result. The Result built into the meaning of SCATTER is that the almonds are spread about. SCATTER also expresses a path and *into the cake batter* is both a Path expression and a Result expression. Cases like this are also an issue for Levin and Rappaport Hovav in their theory of manner/result complementarity, which I mentioned in lecture 3 and which I will return to later.

Here is more from Holmes (2005: 217), "Many verbs, like KILL, DIE and BREAK, profile a telic event (one with a result). Sometimes, these verbs can be used with an adverbial element referring to the lexical result, and making it more specific." Consider the following examples.

(33) Billie broke the buggy up.
(34) The buggy broke up.
(35) Billie broke the safe open.
(36) The safe broke open.
(37) Billie broke the brolly in half/to pieces.
(38) The brolly broke in half/to pieces.

In (33)–(38) BREAK has the Result relation built into its meaning. *Up* is a completive particle that tells you that this event has been completely performed. You can also use completive UP in intransitive version, so in (34) *the buggy ended up completely broken*. If you break the safe, it is already open, so (35) is a way of over-specifying the result state. So is (36). In (37), the word *brolly* means 'umbrella'; (37)–(38) suggest again that it is possible to specify the specific nature of an already lexical result state.

1.7 The Result Xcomp/Adjunct Schema

Here is a diagram showing the basic way in which a Result Xcomp or Xadjunct works. *X* means the thing requires a Subject. The *x* of Xcomp and Xadjunct means that the relation has an open function that requires a Subject.

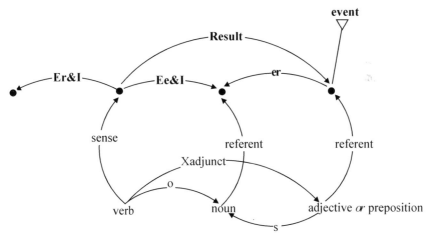

FIGURE 1   The Result Xcomp/Adjunct schema

Syntactically, the verb has an Xadjunct, the word which is the value of the Xadjunct dependency has a Subject, and this Subject is shared with the direct Object of the verb. Semantically, the verb has a sense, the sense has the result which is brought by the Xadjunct, and the result is some kind of the event. That event has Er—it has a participant. Then the meaning of a verb has both Er as an Initiator and Ee is an Endpoint. The Ee is the Agonist and Er is the Antagonist in Talmy's terms, and this is the model then for understanding how the resultative construction might work.

Figure 1 involves a force-dynamic transfer in the verb that it is a relation of. And it adds a resulting secondary predication. The next diagram shows this in action, embedded in a sentence.

1.8   Simple Transitive Resultatives

In this diagram syntactically, *Willy* is the Subject of *watered* and *the tulips* the direct Object of *watered*; *flat* is the Xadjunct of *watered*. In terms of mappings in the semantics, the Er, which is also the Initiator, maps on to the referent *Willy* and the Ee, also the Endpoint, maps onto the referent of *the tulips*. (I have shown these two words as simply having the same referent.) And then the tulips being flat is the resulting state of the action of watering. What the network analysis claims is that the interpretation of *Willy watered the tulips flat* is 'Willy watered the tulips with the result that the tulips were flat'. There is no massive overriding of the basic verb meaning, just a further result meaning element added to the verb meaning. And *Willy watered the tulips flat* does not mean 'Willy caused the tulips to become flat by watering them'.

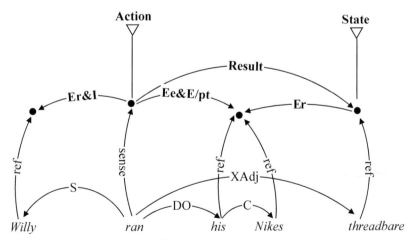

FIGURE 2   Simple transitive resultatives

One of the reasons I want to treat patterns such as the resultative as constructions that add bits of meaning to the verb meaning, rather than overriding the verb's meaning, is because of the principle of monotonicity. The idea essentially is that you cannot change structure. A theory that allows structures to be changed is non-monotonic. In a monotonic theory, when you add words to sentences and put them together, the sentences' meaning just builds up step by step. A non-monotonic theory is a disadvantage, because it is harder to control, the search space in the mind is too great, and the processing cost on the mind is too great. I think that Goldberg & Jackendoff's semantics is non-monotonic because it distorts the semantics of main verb and it does not just add a resultative predication to it.

A straightforward resultative takes a transitive activity verb. It adds an adjunct with a result meaning. It adds telicity, because the semantic value of the adjunct is a state. By default, adjuncts are predicates; typically adjuncts of verbs are predicated of the verb. But adjunct secondary predicates override the default where adjuncts are predicated of the verb and instead the adjuncts are predicated of the direct Object. This is the difference between ordinary adjuncts and resultative adjuncts—and it is why I have called resultative adjuncts "Xadjuncts." Bearing in mind the semantics of adjuncts, this pattern is fully compositional and is not constructional. It does not override anything.

1.9   Simple Intransitive Resultatives

Goldberg & Jackendoff's analysis of simple intransitive resultatives such as *the pond froze solid* or *the chair broke apart* is that they are a case of the resultative Subject (the predicand), arriving in a result state by the means denoted by the verb, i.e. the pond becomes solid as a result of freezing. But FREEZE involves a change of state. This pattern is more like the Body Part Ascension construction—the resultative AP describes the state that is the end state of the process denoted by the verb. One question is whether these are actually resultatives? I think they might be depictives, shown in Figure 3.

Figure 3 says the verb BREAK has a result state built into it. If you look at the sense of *broke*, there is a node which is classified as an action. That action has a result built into it, and the result Isa state. That is the analysis of the meaning of BREAK. This is the same structure that we find in the meaning of SINK, so what *apart* does is to add a depiction, which is the detail of that result sate in *the chair broke apart*. It tells you something more about the nature of the result state which is part of the lexical entry of BREAK. And again, I like this particular analysis, because it is compositional and there is no violation of monotonicity.

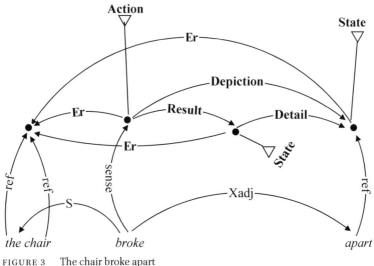

FIGURE 3 The chair broke apart

1.10 Other Approaches

According to Croft (2012: 325), Iwata (2006) treats the intransitive resultative as an "Adjunct Resultative", noting that it comes with a highly restricted set of result phrases, "[B]ecause the result state is already partly specified by the verb, which semantically selects for the type of Result phrase. Wechsler argues that this type of Resultative takes only Adjectival Result phrases that denote closed scales because the upper bound of the closed scale corresponds to the result state when combined with a verb...."

1.11 Holmes on Simple Intransitive Resultatives

Jasper Holmes (2005) offers a different analysis of intransitive resultatives. He claims that the resultative adjunct overrides the lexical network for the change of state verb, and that therefore the result link which is part of the lexical structure of change of state verbs is identified with the resultative adjunct. Figure 4 is Holmes' analysis, in which "breaking/c" is causative and transitive and "breaking/u" is the intransitive, inchoative (undergoer) variant.

In Holmes' analysis, the meaning of BREAK has two senses. The sense of causative BREAK in *Floyd broke the glass* and the sense of inchoative, intransitive, BREAK in *the glass broke*. The second sense is built into the network of the first sense; the second sense also has a result state which is *broken*, so Inchoative BREAK means *become broken*.

Figure 5 is Holmes' analysis of *it broke in half*:

RESULTATIVES AND CAUSATION

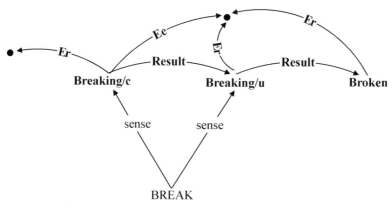

FIGURE 4 Holmes on BREAK

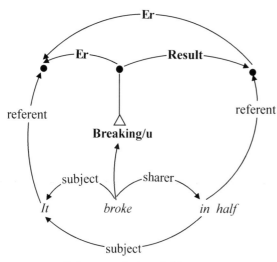

FIGURE 5 Holmes on It broke in half

The Result which is part of the meaning of BREAK, according to Holmes is replaced by *in half*. What Holmes calls 'sharer' is what I am calling the Xadjunct. Holmes' analysis involves a dependent overriding the lexical network of the verb. What happens, in the case of BREAK in the resultative construction, to the 'broken' subevent in the lexical structure of BREAK? Holmes' argument is that the addition of a dependent changes the default of a head: a dependent overrides the lexical network of the verb. This analysis requires the child to learn that there are two intransitive verbs BREAK: BREAK/intr1 and BREAK/intr2, where the second one specifically attaches to the Result adjunct. If he believes that, it gives him a compositional analysis. Otherwise, his analysis is non-monotonic and non-compositional. I find this analysis dispreferrable because it violates monotonicity and it muddles the lexical entry with the content of the adjunct. However, the depictive analysis that I give is fully compositional.

But keep in mind that there are lexical restrictions on which intransitive verbs can occur in this construction; for example, you can freeze the water solid, but you cannot melt the ice liquid. Whatever theories you come up with have to tolerate this lexical restriction. Holmes' account at least goes some way to explain it.

1.12 *Passive Resultative*

As we have seen before, examples like (7)–(9), repeated here, show how the example in (9) involves a combination of the passive structure and the resultative.

(7) We wiped the tools.
(8) We wiped the tools clean.
(9) The tools were wiped clean.

The key fact is that WIPE is not a verb that lexicalizes a result state, so the result adjunct can add one, without changing the lexical structure of WIPE. The following figure generalizes and simplifies the passive structure.

In Figure 6, I have shown a passive verb with a result, and the resultative structure just follows compositionally in the way that all these structures

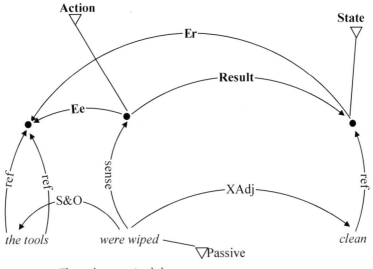

FIGURE 6   The tools were wiped clean

RESULTATIVES AND CAUSATION   163

follow. One of the key facts about the Passive is that it preserves the Er and an Ee in the semantic structure of the verb. Note that both short and long passive can occur with resultative adjuncts. In the case of the Passive, the Subject of the passive verb is linked to the verb's Ee so it is acted on. There are all sorts of complications with passives—some passive subjects have to be acted on, others do not and there are also prepositional passives. But here what makes the structure work is that the resultative is predicated of the Ee of 'wiping'. Essentially, my claim is that the analysis in Figure 6 is a well-behaved analysis, because the Er of the meaning of the resultative predicate is the same value as the Ee of WIPE. It is fully and normally compositional.

1.13   *Suppleted Object Resultatives*

Fake Object resultatives present a bigger complication. They involve intransitive verbs and event composition. For example, (16)—repeated here, and which I have argued means 'Jane ran and as a result of her running her Nikes became threadbare'—does not allow a construal where *Jane* acts on her Nikes.

(16)   Jane ran her Nikes threadbare.

Therefore, these examples do not involve force-dynamics, perhaps. Such a construal would require event composition where *running* and *threadbare* combine to form a predicate that requires an affected participant. I try to present a representation of this analysis in Figure 7. Again, I simplify the structure slightly. The diagram sets out to show that the composition of *running* and the resultative adjunct Isa the sense of RUN.

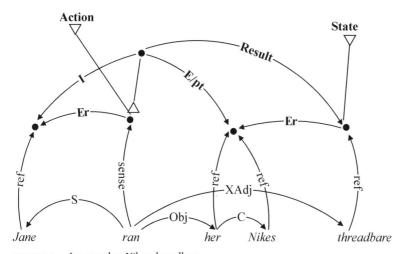

FIGURE 7   Jane ran her Nikes threadbare

The sense of *ran* combines with the result to give you a complex predicate, which Isa the sense of *ran*, where there is an Initiator and Endpoint pair, so you do get the sense of her acting on his Nikes. The idea the diagram tries to capture is that the force dynamic relationship is a kind of construal of the resultative. You construe (16) as involving *his acting on her Nikes* in some way. I am not too sure that it is necessarily the right analysis, but it gives us a way of understanding that *his Nikes* is not in a direct relationship with *run* semantically, but it is nevertheless the case that the referent of *his Nikes* is affected by the overall semantic structure. Therefore, as I said, this is a kind of complex predicate analysis. It says *his Nikes* becomes affected in the meaning of the overall event structure. I think that is probably the right way to think about it because the force dynamics affecting *his Nikes* here are probably due to the meaning of the Result adjunct composed together with the verb, and you cannot really impose them on the verbal meaning in isolation.

1.14   *Three Kinds of Result Relation*

Figure 7 requires something new. So far, the composition of the result adjunct and the verbs that it has gone together with has required nothing more than a result adjunct whose argument node has an Er relation. But Figure 7 also shows the Result relation involves a force dynamic dyad. Now I am suggesting that there are at least three different kinds of result relationship, represented in Figure 8.

At the top of the hierarchy we have a result relationship where event1 has as its result in event2. In the middle, there is a subtype of result where event1 has as its result, event2, and event1 also has a participant, an Er. The first kind of result might be something like the relationship between the following clauses:

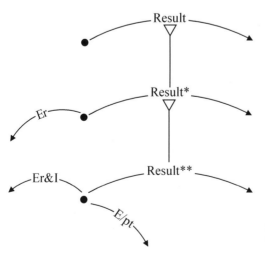

FIGURE 8
Three kinds of Result relations

it rains, the pavement became wet. That gives you a Result relation between two clauses, where the first event gives rise to the second event, but where there is no Agent, because there is no Agent of 'raining'.

The second kind of Result is something you might get in *Peter ran, his Nikes became threadbare* where Peter is the Agent of 'running', where the result is that his Nikes became threadbare. Again, I am suggesting this as a relationship between two separate, fully tensed finite clauses. The Result relation represented with two asterisks at the bottom of the diagram is the kind of Result that you get with a force dynamic pairing. That is what I am claiming we find in some types of resultative and in sublexical causation such as the causation in the meaning of transitive OPEN: that this is a Result which also brings a force dynamic pairing to it where the Subject referent acts on the Object referent.

Each one of the Result relations is more specific than the previous one. The type labeled "Result" in Figure 8 is just a relation between two events. It says that the second event is just caused by the first. The second type, Result*, is a relation between two events which has to be predicated of some entity. The third type, Result**, involves a force-dynamic pairing as well. This kind of Result relation is what is found in the event composition structures I showed earlier. Each type of Result relation can be motivated by looking at the relationships between two verbs like CAUSE and FORCE which I will talk about below. But each kind of Result relation helps in understanding the network analysis and how it compares with a constructional analysis. Fake Object resultatives, like *run his Nikes threadbare* or *yell himself hoarse*, require an analysis with additional information to capture the requirement for the fake Object or reflexive pronoun.

The patterns of the result relations give us a purely compositional treatment of the resultative construction. They require there to be symbolic dependency relations, which WG has by default. They also require it to be possible that the symbolic dependencies can be part of larger more complex networks. We saw in Lecture 1 that this is necessary in order to capture nominal predication like *she is a doctor*. But the resulting grammar is just a symbolic network. It has no parts and wholes, no boxes, and no phrasal constructions. We can capture constructional meaning, but we can do this just by using default inheritance and the ordinary categories that we find in different kinds of grammatical pattern.

2   Result Relations in Predicative Complementation

In this section, I am interested in exploring how the Result relation works, which requires us to look at the result relation in predicative complementation.

2.1 Result Relations in Non-Finite Complementation: CAUSE, FORCE and PERSUADE

There are verbs that take predicative complements as in (39)–(41), which involve the event symbolized by the verb having another event as its Result. How do the three different types of Result relation that I have just identified work with verbs like CAUSE, FORCE, and PERSUADE? Let us consider the following examples.

(39) The wind caused the roof tiles to slip.
(40) The border guard forced the refugees to wait.
(41) The doctor persuaded him to quit smoking.

These three verbs have three different kinds of causal structure associated with them. CAUSE is a raising-to-Object verb: it does not assign a semantic role to its Object; it does not affect the Object directly at all. FORCE, on the other hand, is a so-called Object control verb: it does assign a semantic role to its Object. FORCE of course can apply a semantic role to either a conscious entity or something physical, so as well as being able to force people to behave in certain ways as in (40), you can force a car door to open. PERSUADE, on the other hand, is like FORCE but it is more restricted. You can only persuade a sentient being to do something. Let us look at CAUSE first:

(42) The CIA caused it to rain.
(43) Trump caused there to be a problem

In (42) CAUSE does not affect *it*, because *it* is pleonastic, and does not have a meaning. *It* therefore cannot be acted on by any of the entities in this structure. Likewise in (43), *there* doesn't have a meaning. You cannot act on *there*: it is not in any kind of semantic relationship with CAUSE. The same is shown in (44) and (45).

(44) Being distracted caused me to burn dinner.
(45) Being distracted caused dinner to be burned.

Both sentences have the same "truth conditions," so they basically mean identical things, and CAUSE does not affect *me* or *dinner* directly. The evidence in (42)–(45) tells us that the verb CAUSE does not have any kind of semantic relation with its Object referent at all.

FORCE is different. The exclamation mark in the examples means that the example is a bad example, semantically.

(46) !The CIA forced it to rain.
(47) !Trump forced there to be a problem.
(48) Being distracted forced me to burn dinner.
(49) !Being distracted forced dinner to be burned.

Examples (46), (47) and (49) are all semantically anomalous. Furthermore, (48) and (49) are not synonymous. In (48) my distraction acts on me; in (49) it acts on *dinner* and (49) is semantically anomalous because you cannot force a dinner to be anything. These examples tell us that FORCE has different semantics from CAUSE. Note, too, the differences between *we forced him* versus !*we caused him*. The former example is acceptable but not the latter. It is the evidence of the same issue: raising-to-Object verbs such as CAUSE do not permit ellipsis of the predicative complement; Object control verbs such as FORCE do.

PERSUADE in this respective behaves just like FORCE.

(50) !The CIA persuaded it to rain.
(51) !Trump persuaded there to be a problem.
(52) His wife persuaded the doctor to see him.
(53) His wife persuaded him to be seen by the doctor.

(52) and (53) are, of course, not synonymous. In (52) *his wife* acts on *the doctor*; in (53) *his wife* acts on *him*. In short, we have the same distributional patterns again.

2.2 *Conclusions for the Result Relation*

What does this mean? The point is to see if there is further evidence about how the Result relationship works. The sense of CAUSE always has an Er, but otherwise there is no more semantic complexity. CAUSE does not involve force-dynamic transfer; it just involves an event with a resulting event, which has an Agent (so it is not possible to say *it caused it to rain*). The sense of FORCE always has an Er and an Ee, and its Initiator and Endpoint are always attached to its Er and its Ee. In the terms of Figure 8, FORCE uses the bottom kind of Result, Result**, in the hierarchy of Results, because it has a force-dynamic pairing. The same is true for PERSUADE which also involves that kind of Result and a force-dynamic pairing. However, CAUSE involves Result*, which is a more abstract Result relation which can obtain between two independent clauses and which does not require there to be any sort of agency at all on the participant in the initiating clause.

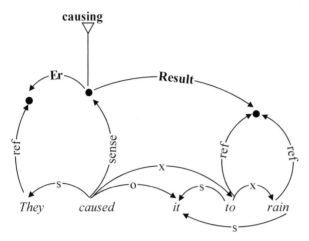

FIGURE 9   A diagram for CAUSE

2.3   *An Analysis of* CAUSE

Figure 9 says that CAUSE has an Er and a Result, and that is it. There is no force dynamic transfer; there is just an Agent and a Result. The rest of it follows compositionally.

In the analysis of CAUSE, I have taken the simplest state of affairs, where the Xcomp has a non-referential Subject. In the diagram, *it* has to be non-referential because *it* in (42) is meaningless. The only reason *it* is there is because Xcomps have to have a Subject; this is just a grammatical rule of English. This makes it very clear that 'causing' does not assign any kind of semantic role to its Object. The Object of CAUSE must be its direct Object, because it can be passivized. We therefore can say *it was caused to rain*, which shows that CAUSE is not like WANT and can be passivized. All of this is evidence that 'causing' involves the kind of Result relation that has an Er but no other participant—Result* in the diagram.

2.4   *An Analysis of* FORCE

The next diagram, for FORCE, was presented in the last lecture.

FORCE is like CAUSE, but more complicated, because the Object of 'forcing' is also the Endpoint of the force-dynamic dyad. The meaning of FORCE involves Result**: there is a force-dynamic dyad involving the Subject-referent acting on the Object-referent. This kind of Result is what you get with a verb like FORCE, it requires there to be a force-dynamic pairing between two different entities. However, apart from the force-dynamics, which is what sets it apart from CAUSE, FORCE is otherwise quite simple, and we can now contrast it with PERSUADE.

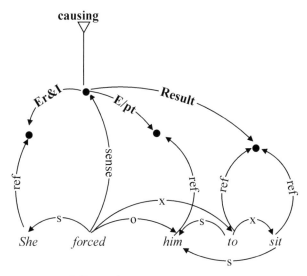

FIGURE 10   A diagram for FORCE

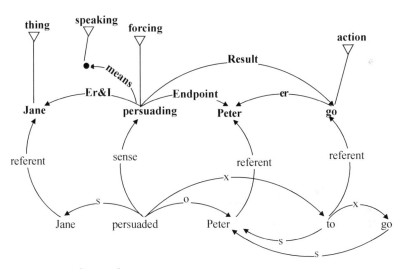

FIGURE 11   A diagram for PERSUADE

2.5   An Analysis of PERSUADE

Figure 11 says that 'persuading' is a kind of 'forcing', which has means of speaking, so you 'force' somebody to do something by speaking to them. That places an ontological constraint on the Endpoint because it means that the Endpoint has to be conscious and able to understand speech: I cannot persuade my dog to do anything (although I can order him, for example, to sit) because the dog does not understand language. Basically, the referent of the Object of

PERSUADE has to be human. That is, PERSUADE has a little bit more semantic content than FORCE, and this additional content places constraints on its object's referent. Otherwise, PERSUADE has the same Result relationship, as FORCE.

Of course, metaphorically you can use PERSUADE in other ways. You might say, for example, a thief could persuade the car door to open with a special tool. But in the core, non-metaphorical sense, PERSUADE is a kind of 'forcing' which has 'speaking' as a means. I have not analysed PERSUADE as involving multiple inheritance from 'speaking' as well as 'forcing' because you speak *to* someone. There is still a force-dynamic dyad here, so it involves the network described for Result**. However, it is not typically physical. FORCE, on the other hand, can use a physical threat or a nonphysical threat.

2.6   So What Is Causation?

It seems to me that causation is quite complicated. It involves a prototype structure surrounding the Result relation. Not all uses of the Result relation involve participants acting on each other. That is, from a force-dynamic point of view, participants acting on each other would be the prototype. "Causal" relations that don't involve participants acting on each other (force-dynamics), therefore, would be non-prototypical.

This has the rather strange consequence that sublexical causation—causation within verb meanings—involves more structure than the meaning of the verb CAUSE. This is a position I have argued for in print: I argued for it in Gisborne (2008) and (2010). It did raise some quite odd responses from some of the reviewers; however, I cannot see any way around it. There is causation with force-dynamics, which is what we see in verb meaning, and there is more abstract or underspecified causation with no force-dynamics which is the meaning of the verb CAUSE when it takes a non-finite complement.

I think this is an interesting research result because it shows causation itself involves a range of complex patterns of different kinds. Some can be physical, some can be non-physical, some involve some kind of relation between events, and others also involve a layer of participants acting on participants. The claim I am making is that causation is complex and involves a lot of different subtypes. There is a prototype which involves both a Result relationship between events and participants acting on participants. But these things can also be factored out. Therefore, we can see non-prototypical kinds of causation as well. One non-prototypical kind of causation might be a relationship between two events where the participants do not act on each other. This will be what we find in examples such as *he caused her to leave* or *the CIA caused it to rain*, where the Subject referent does not act on the Object referent. Another kind of non-prototypical "causation," might not even be causation as such, but it might be where you get force-dynamic relations and no subevents, which would be the case in modality; or alternatively another kind of non-prototypical causation might be found in the semantic structure of verbs such as HIT, as in *Peter hitting Jean*, where the force-dynamics do not cause the subevent to happen. There is something else involved as well. We will talk about 'hitting' in the next section.

This view of causation certainly raises issues for the meanings of verbs that involve more than one event. If there is a verb meaning which involves a Result relation between two events, but that verb meaning does not involve a force-dynamic transfer, is the verb really "causative"? In Gisborne (2010) I argued not. Copley and Wolff (2014), Copley and Harley (2014) have explored the role of force dynamics in causation from a formal semantics point of view. Of course, there is a great deal of variation in the philosophical literature about causation and what causation is. Copley and Harley are particularly concerned with causes that can be cancelled. For example, when you are building a house if you are stopped, then the house does not get built. But on the other hand, 'building' involves a causal relation: the Result of building is that something exists. This problem of the cancellability of the Result is a problem with any accomplishment verb. The phenomenon is called the imperfective paradox: if you have an accomplishment verb in the English progressive aspect, then the Result, which is part of the lexical semantics of that accomplishment verb, might not come about. This is because the progressive is partitive; it gives you a window on the inside of the event only and accomplishments involve successive stages leading to a final completion of the overall state-of-affairs. We might ask ourselves about the relationship between causation, verbs of creation, and Results that might not come about. And this is a general problem, it is not only a problem to do with accomplishment verbs; it also applies to ditransitives. Because if *I send him a parcel*, I am not sure whether it is entailed that he receives the parcel or not. Certainly, in *I made him a cake* it is absolutely not entailed whether he receives it: I can make the cake, and he can receive it or not receive it. We are not sure about that before we actually use that verb.[2]

There is another issue I have left aside: what evidence is there for a bare Result relation, which does not have an Er, and which does not have a force-dynamic association? The clearest evidence is from inter-clause relations with dethematized Agents. One example is *it rained until there were puddles everywhere*. The first event, the rain event, has as its Result the puddles being

---

2   In the case of ditransitives, the phenomenon is often discussed as "sub-lexical modality." See Gisborne and Donaldson (2019) for an account in terms of WG.

everywhere, so there is a relationship between these two events but there is no agency involved in either of these two events.

So having explored some general ideas about how causation might work, I now want to move on to talk about sublexical causation.

3   Sublexical Causation

Let us think about the verb HIT. If the sense of the verb HIT involves two different events, a 'moving' event and a 'touching' event, what is the Result relation between them? If the 'touching' event is entailed, then there is a Result relation. The conative—*hit at*—shows that the entailment (that there is a 'touching' event which is the Result of the 'moving' event) can be overridden. This tells us that there is an event structure, involving two discrete events. We can also see that the semantic structure of HIT is force-dynamic. If somebody hits another person, then there is force dynamic transfer between the two people. And that is shown in Figure 12, where force dynamics are a relation of construal.

'Hitting' in Figure 12 has a subordinate event, which Isa touching event, which is the Result of the 'moving' event. Both 'touching' and 'moving' have the same Er. The diagram also shows an Initiator and an Endpoint. Figure 12 says that the Initiator of hitting has as its Endpoint the person who is hit. This is something Croft (2012) says, too. He says that HIT is a force-dynamic verb, and the Subject affects the Object. But I want to think about it for a moment,

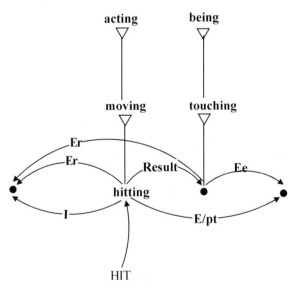

FIGURE 12   'Hitting'

about whether it is force-dynamic verb in Talmy's sense. Because when Talmy talks about force dynamics, he talks about the Antagonist overcoming a natural tendency of the Agonist. And that is not what happens in 'hitting' here. Croft says this is a force dynamic transfer verb because the Subject referent acts on the Object referent, and this claim is true: the Subject referent does act on the Object referent. But it is not force dynamic, I think, in Talmy's sense, because the Subject does not overcome a natural tendency of the Object: the Antagonist does not overcome a natural tendency of the Agonist. Talmy's force dynamics is more restricted than Croft's kind of force dynamics. This is something to explore: in Talmy's force-dynamics, there has to be a subevent that the Agonist is, in my terms, the Er of. We do not have Talmy's force-dynamics unless the Agonist, or Endpoint, is the Er of the subordinate event. This obliges us to think further about how force-dynamics interacts with event decomposition, and with other relationships among the participants in events. It is odd that although HIT necessarily involves a force-transfer in its semantics, this aspect of its meaning is not consistent with Talmy's ideas about force-dynamics.

We can take the analysis in Figure 12 further with other two-event achievement verbs. These involve changes of state. Intransitive MELT means 'x become (x liquid)'. In WG there is a 'changing' event which has a Result relation. The value of the Result relation is the state of being liquid. Such verbs are also instantaneous. In Rappaport Hovav and Levin's approach, these relationships between events are shown as non-causal as they are in every other theory. But in a theory like WG, they need a relation. If one event is brought about by another, that relation will be the Result relation. Therefore, perhaps, the Result relation is not enough by itself to show that there is a cause. Perhaps the Result relation just shows that the second event comes about as a Result of the first event in some way. In complex events where the second event is not necessarily entailed, and might not happen, I have argued for the outcome relation. The outcome relation is relevant in the meaning of predicates like ditransitive SEND, as in *we sent a present to him*. In examples like this, it is possible for the present not to arrive. This fact opens up the issue that perhaps not all ditransitives are causative. I made this point in Gisborne (2010), and I will take it up again lecture seven.

The prototype of sublexical causation is found in the set of force-dynamic verbs from Croft which I discussed in the last lecture. Each example from (10) to (15) in lecture five, according to Croft, involves a force-dynamic dyad; I repeat these examples here as (54)–(58).

(54) I kicked the ball.
(55) I pushed the ball.
(56) I held the ball.

(56) I stopped the ball.
(57) I dropped/released/let go of the ball.
(58) I left the ball (in the house).

Talmy (1985b), on the other hand, motivates his theory of force-dynamics relationships using verbs like FORCE, LET, and MAKE which have non-finite clausal complements. The examples in (55)–(58) show that Croft adopts a force dynamic analysis of verbs which just require a single verbal predicate.

I think we can conclude that prototypical sublexical causation pattern involves something like what I have argued for Result**: the event which is the argument of the Result relation also involves a force-dynamic dyad between the Subject-referent and the Object-referent.

3.1   *Conclusions*

We explored the resultative construction to find out what the Result relation looked like. Along the way, we found that resultatives do not need to be treated as a construction type: they are a simple case of monotonic composition between a predicate and an adjunct. We also found that the most problematic case of the basic resultative patterns was the intransitive resultative: I suggested that this really was not resultative at all, but was a kind of depictive, which spelled out the nature of the final Result state. We found that resultatives used two different kinds of resultative relation. And I justified the third kind, simple Result relations, by looking at the relationships between two finite clauses. From this we looked at resultative patterns in predicative complementation. We saw further justification for the different types of Result relation that I argued for.

I have finished by arguing that I think causation is a cluster concept, a similar analysis to Jackendoff and Goldberg's for the resultative construction itself. Causation involves lots of different subtypes in a family resemblance pattern. It can just involve entailed Results, but it can also be more complex, especially within lexical meaning. Causation can just be a relationship between events, but it can also involve affectedness. We find Result relations in sublexical complex events like HIT, but I am not sure that these are necessarily causal patterns. For example, there is an argument to be had about whether 'hitting' involves force-dynamic relations or not; but if it does, the force-dynamic relations cannot exist if the result state is not present. This suggests that there is a sublexical prototype for a causal pattern which involves the force-dynamic relations of the previous lecture. But it also suggests that there is a clausal prototype related to the transitive prototype, which has very different subtypes in a family resemblance pattern.

Ultimately, to come back to the overall theme of the set of lectures, what I am arguing for is that there is a range of ways of thinking about all sorts of things, from idioms to patterns of causation to the resultative construction. We should not expect to have just a single analysis which fits all cases. But we should expect a range of family resemblance analyses, organized around a prototype in a kind of cluster concept, which captures the range of different possibilities, and the network allows us to show some density in some concepts, but maybe less density in others. Also, by being classified, it allows us to understand typicality, and the various kinds of relationship that we have with these different types of causation.

LECTURE 7

Ditransitives and Verbs of Buying and Selling

In this lecture I will talk about ditransitive verbs, such as verbs of giving, and I am also going to be talking about verbs of buying and selling. As you might anticipate, the themes are going to be consistent with those of earlier lectures: I will be arguing that we do not want to have too rigid distinctions between categories—that we see clustering properties and that we see prototypes emerging. As a result, there are occasions where we have to break the analyses down. Particularly in the verbs of buying and selling, we will see that Fillmore's original, single-frame proposal for verbs of buying and selling oversimplifies the data, in fact there are different subgeneralizations in the case of these verbs. Sometimes we have to allow the data to be complicated, because it really is.

Ditransitives have been analyzed in Word Grammar by Gisborne (2010), Holmes and Hudson (2005) and Hudson (1992). The analysis of verbs of buying and selling relies on work by Richard Hudson presented in an unpublished paper, Hudson (2008). The key arguments in this lecture are first, that there is a complex network of relations that makes up the ditransitive; and second, that verbs of buying and selling are better understood in fine-grained network terms. I will argue that attempting to account for them within a single frame of commercial transactions does not capture the details in their properties.[1]

---

1 In one sense, the WG approach is a frame-based approach: in its classified network, WG adopts a knowledge-representation system which is compatible with an interpretation of "frame" that locates it in the same set of theoretical concepts as "Idealized Cognitive Model" and "script", "scene", "schema" and "cognitive model". In this lecture, I am using the term in a more restricted sense, where I am arguing against Fillmore's relatively coarse-grained frame approach, in favour of WG's more fine-grained network approach. See Gisborne and Donaldson (2019) for further discussion.

 All original audio-recordings and other supplementary material, such as any hand-outs and powerpoint presentations for the lecture series, have been made available online and are referenced via unique DOI numbers on the website www.figshare.com. They may be accessed via a QR code for the print version of this book. In the e-book, both the QR code and dynamic links are available, and can be accessed by a mouse-click.

1   Ditransitives

As part of the discussion of causation in Gisborne (2010) I explored the issue of whether ditransitives were actually causative or not, given that they are often analysed as having the semantics of CAUSE-HAVE in representations such as Goldberg's. The reason I was interested in this is because of the various arguments that I presented in the previous lecture to do with the causation prototype. If there is a causation prototype, and if the causation prototype involves both one event bringing about another event and also one force-dynamic participant acting on another force-dynamic participant, is it true to say that ditransitives are in some sense causative, in the way that a verb like BUILD in *build a house* or MAKE in *make a cake*, is causative? Because there is a significant degree of variation within the meanings of different ditransitive verbs, and some of them do not entail any kind of Result at all. In Gisborne (2010), I argued that ditransitives do not involve the causative prototype which involves a Result relationship and an Initiator/Endpoint dyad (or the Agonist/Antagonist dyad). As we saw in the last lecture, I think that within verb meaning, causation typically involves a force-dynamic transfer and a change of state in the Endpoint, and we do not always see a force-dynamic transfer with ditransitives.

However, this brings us back to how force-dynamic relations work semantically. Let us think again about Croft's claim that HIT is force dynamic, which I mentioned in lecture 6. It is not obvious how HIT is force dynamic: Croft's claim is that the Subject's referent acts on the Object's referent. But if *x* hits *y*, it is not the case that *y* undergoes a change of state: the lexical semantics of HIT do not specify how the Object is affected. Ditransitives on the other hand involve a different semantic issue: semantically, the Direct Object is the Er of the Result event. There are clearly cases where ditransitives do seem to involve some kind of causative prototype, but it is not true of all ditransitive verbs that they are clearly causative.

Another thing I worry about is how we might approach the meaning of the verb together with the meaning of the Indirect Object, which has its own sense: Beneficiary or Recipient. The claim I want to develop is that a ditransitive verb is just a verb with more than one event built into it, which also has an Indirect Object where the Indirect Object has a particular semantics. On this approach, it is not the case that verb meanings are underspecified, and that the semantics are built into the phrasal patterns. The meanings that we explore are still the meanings of the (classes of) verbs.

1.1 *The Main Data Sets*

The main data sets are the ditransitive, in comparison with the double complement construction:

(1) Jane gave Peter a cake.
(2) Jane gave a cake to Peter.

(3) Jane sent Peter a letter.
(4) Jane sent a letter to Peter.

(5) Jane baked Peter a cake.
(6) Jane baked a cake for Peter.

The examples in (1), (3), and (5) are ditransitive, while the rest are double complement constructions. In the literature, two different ditransitives are distinguished, exemplified in (1)–(6): ditransitives in a pair with the double complement construction with *to* (e.g. 2 and 4); and ditransitives that are in a pair with the double complement constructions with *for* (e.g. 6). Because of the different pairing of ditransitive verbs, they fall into different categories. There are clear semantic differences in (1)–(6).

The most obvious semantic difference is between double complement constructions and ditransitive constructions. For example, with GIVE it is not the case the Object is received by the Recipient in the prepositional case (2), although it is received in the double Object case (1). That is, ditransitive GIVE entails that the Beneficiary actually receives the cake: if I gave Peter a cake, Peter gets the cake. On the other hand, in the example in (2) it is not entailed that Peter receives the cake. However, in the examples in (3)–(6), it is more complicated than that, although I am not entirely sure of my own judgments. I think in the case of SEND and BAKE with prepositional complements, it is clear that the resulting possession is not entailed, but even in the double Object cases (3) and (5), arguably the Result is not necessarily entailed. You can say, *Jane sent Peter a letter, but he didn't get it* and it is possible to say *Jane baked Peter a cake but he didn't get it*. On the other hand, if you say *Jane gave Peter a cake*, the continuation *but he didn't get it* is ungrammatical. There is some variability in the data set and there are some things to think about, in terms of how these data work. It seems that ditransitives that alternate with a FOR-preposition double-complement construction are the least likely among these verbs to have an entailed Result.

1.2 Verbs Found in the Ditransitive Construction

There are various verbs which are found in the ditransitive construction and various verbs which are also claimed to not to occur in the ditransitive construction—although in the case of verbs claimed to not occur in the construction, some of the claims have been falsified. Here are some verbs that do, taken from Gropen et al. (1989: 243–244).

> Verbs that inherently signify acts of giving: GIVE, PASS, HAND, SELL, PAY, TRADE, LEND, LOAN, SERVE, FEED—*he passed her a pen*
> Verbs of sending: SEND, MAIL, SHIP—*she sent him a bunch of flowers*
> Verbs of instantaneous causation of ballistic motion (verbs of throwing): THROW, TOSS, FLIP, SLAP, KICK, POKE, FLING, SHOOT, BLAST—*he threw her the ball*
> Verbs of continuous causation of accompanied motion in a deictically specified direction:[2] BRING, TAKE—*she took him a pen*
> Verbs of future having: OFFER, PROMISE, BEQUEATH, LEAVE, REFER, FORWARD, ALLOCATE, GUARANTEE, ALLOT, ASSIGN, ALLOW, ADVANCE, AWARD, RESERVE, GRANT—*he offered her a pen*
> Verbs of type of communicated message: TELL, SHOW, ASK, TEACH, POSE, WRITE, SPIN, READ, QUOTE, CITE—*she told him a story*
> Verbs of instrument of communication: RADIO, E-MAIL, TELEGRAPH, WIRE, TELEPHONE, NETMAIL, FAX—*he emailed her the report*

1.3 Verbs Claimed to Be Not Found in the Ditransitive Construction

These are verbs that are claimed to be not found in the ditransitive construction (Gropen et al. 1989: 244):

> Verbs of fulfilling: CREDIT, PRESENT, ENTRUST, SUPPLY, TRUST
> Verbs of continuous causation of accompanied motion in some manner: CARRY, PULL, PUSH, SCHLEP, LIFT, LOWER, HAUL
> Verbs of manner of speaking: SHOUT, SCREAM, MURMUR, WHISPER, SHRIEK, YODEL, YELL, BELLOW, GRUNT, BARK
> Verbs of communication of propositions and propositional attitudes: SAY, ASSERT, QUESTION, CLAIM, THINK ALOUD, DOUBT

Verbs of communication of propositions and propositional attitudes are verbs of communication whose complements are full propositions. It is notable that

---

2 *Deictically specified* means that the verbs are oriented to the speech situation and who the speaker is, and have meanings which relate to whether they are oriented towards the speaker or away from the speaker.

verbs of manner-of-speaking can actually occur in the ditransitive construction, e.g. *can I shout you the solution* and *can I whisper you the answer*. You can imagine a situation where students are cheating in an exam, and one student whispers the other student the answer.

We can see that some verbs can be in a ditransitive and others cannot. Coming back to Levin's arguments about event complexity which I discussed in Lecture 2, you learn something about the semantics of verbs from the syntactic patterns that they can occur in, so our job will be to look for some generalizations to establish whether there is something about the semantics of the first set of verbs that allows them to occur in the ditransitive construction, and something else in the second set (apart from the manner-of-speaking verbs) that prevents them from occurring in the ditransitive construction.

1.4   *Diversity in Ditransitives*

It is not true that all ditransitives are the same. Some of these differences are due to the lexical nature of the verbs, but Goldberg (1995: 37–39) also argues that they are due to variation in the semantics of the ditransitive construction, and she identifies 5 different ditransitive construction types.

> X CAUSES Y TO RECEIVE Z.
> X CAUSES Y not to RECEIVE Z.
> X ACTS TO CAUSE Y TO RECEIVE Z in the future.
>   (e.g. *I promise you my house in my will*)
> X ENABLES Y TO RECEIVE Z.
>   (that is, enabling is a weaker form of causing)
> X INTENDS TO CAUSE Y TO RECEIVE Z.

Part of the task in Goldberg's account is to see how different verbs are selected by different constructions.

Boas (2013: 246) says, "Positing constructional polysemy has a number of advantages, such as not having to posit lexical rules in order to account for sense extensions of verbs whose various senses are not predictable on general grounds and must be conventionally associated with the construction." I want to unpack that quotation a little. Boas is claiming that polysemy is a problem: ideally we would have a predictive theory of polysemy if it is at all possible. Some kinds of polysemy can be predicted, but other kinds are harder to predict. Then he goes on to say, if we assume that constructions exist, then we can use the existence of constructions as a way of explaining certain patterns of polysemy. With that, we can talk about the meaning of the construction and the meaning of the verb, and we can identify some polysemous patterns as coming out of the interaction between the verb meaning and the construction meaning, which Boas thinks simplifies the lexicon. Part of what he is trying to do is to make the lexical storage system simpler. But perhaps there is another way to look at constructional polysemy and also to look at the variability in verb argument types which we saw earlier.

Boas assumes that constructional polysemy is better, because then it is not necessary to have lexical rules to account for sense extension. But why would we want to have lexical rules? The idea that you would have lexical rules in the first place seems to be a strange assumption. In a declarative system, which construction grammar is, you would not expect that there to be lexical rules; you would expect there to be certain patterns of sense extension that are predictable. Therefore, I think what we actually want to have is just patterns of sense networks, which allow us to identify some of the usual ways in which meanings develop. I have talked about some of these in previous lectures; for example, in Lecture 4 and Lecture 5, when I was talking about RUN I talked about one possible development. I am not sure that Boas is attacking the right thing with his criticism. In a network approach, there is no need for lexical rules, even in a theory that does not have constructions, because of the architectural property the theory has of being organized in terms of default inheritance hierarchies. The WG architecture is a classified network in which there is no need to have lexical rules to get you from one meaning to another.

1.5   More Data

Levin (2004) has a set of examples that show that verbs which are alleged to not occur in the ditransitive actually do occur in it. Green (1974) includes verbs of continuous causation of accompanied motion in some manner among the verbs found in the ditransitive construction; however, Pesetsky (1995: 137) and Pinker (1989: 103, 110–111) exclude them. Can we say, *carry me the ball*, or *pull me the truck*, or—if we are at a table together with food that we are sharing—*push me the noodles*? I think that those are all alright. As is *lower me the rice* if you are working in a warehouse and you ask someone to pass it down to you from above. Here are some examples from Bresnan and Nikitina (2009).

(7)   As player A pushed him the chips, all hell broke loose at the card table.

(8)   He pulled himself a steaming piece of pie.

(9)   'Well ... it started like this ...' Shinbo explained while Sumomo dragged him a can of beer and opened it for him.

One thing about these verbs is that they are not frequent, so people think they are excluded because it is hard to think of good examples. But if you are going to look at a corpus then you end up finding examples that work. Verbs of manner-of-speaking are also claimed not to occur in ditransitive construction, but they are attested on the Web (Levin 2004). Some examples include the following.

(10) Shooting the Urasian a surprised look, she muttered him a hurried apology.
(11) You just mumble him an answer.
(12) Finally a kind few (three to be exact) came forward and whispered me the answer (Bresnan and Nikitina 2009: 7–8, (11)).

Moreover, some verbs appear in the ditransitive construction with special constraints on their Indirect Objects. Each of the examples in (13)–(15) shows that the Indirect Object referent has to be animate in the basic case.

(13) Jones sent Smith/*London the package.
(14) Robin threw Marion/*the basket the ball.
(15) Sam brought Terry/*the party a cake.

These examples show us that inanimate Indirect Objects are ungrammatical: you can throw a person the ball, but even if you are playing basketball, you cannot throw the basket the ball. However, note that in (13) London can be interpreted in two different ways: (13) does not work when it means the city, but if London is a metonym for the London office of your organization, then it is fine for *London* to be the Indirect Object, so if we have a branch campus of our university in London, we can say *I sent London 5 students last year*; that is, (13) works if London is understood metonymically to stand for a community of people.

1.6 The Approach

Ditransitives involve a complex structure which is built around a Result relation but which does not always involve a force-dynamic relationship. It involves the addition of information from the Indirect Object. I do not think it involves a construction or a constructional schema. I think the variation is found in the different verbs' senses, and in the different subtypes of the Indirect Object that they occur with. That gives us a set of claims about how ditransitives work. We will see that there is a family resemblance pattern between different subtypes of ditransitive, depending on whether they have got Beneficiary-and-Recipient Indirect Objects or whether they have Beneficiary-only Indirect Objects, and depending on the verb meaning itself. The different types of Indirect Object semantics are associated with the different event structures.

1.7   Key Points from Holmes and Hudson

Holmes and Hudson (2005) present a WG analysis of ditransitives. First of all, they agree with a lot of Goldberg's analysis, particularly the semantics. But they note that Goldberg ignores syntax in her analysis, and they think that she therefore misses a lot of important facts and generalizations about how the ditransitive construction works. Here are some basic facts about the syntax of Indirect Objects that Goldberg misses: they follow their heads (like other typical valents); they are limited to one Indirect Object per head—it is not possible to have two and it is not possible therefore to combine a Beneficiary Indirect Object with a Recipient one; Indirect Objects have to have nouns or noun phrases as their values, and they are easily passivized and therefore you can say *she was given a cake*. However, **a cake was given her* is less grammatical, because in ditransitives Indirect Objects passivize more easily than Direct Objects.

1.8   Key Points about Indirect Objects and GIVE

Here are some more facts about Indirect Objects from Hudson (1992). First, an Indirect Object only occur together with a Direct Object. You never get an Indirect Object on its own. With GIVE you can miss the Indirect Object out, but you can never miss the Direct Object out. You can say *I gave her a present*, or *I gave a present*, but not **I gave her*. Second, Indirect Objects precede Direct Objects. Third, Indirect Objects do not participate in heavy noun phrase shift. Heavy noun phrase shift is the property where a noun phrase which is very long, and has lots of content, is moved to the right-hand side of the sentence. There is a functional explanation of heavy noun phrase shift: long noun phrases are hard to process and cause a lot of memory burden, so by moving them to the end of the clause, you make it easier to process the contents of the clause.

A simple example is *look up*: you can say *I looked the answer up* or *I looked up the answer*. But if you extend *the answer* to *the complicated answer in the Encyclopedia Britannica*, you cannot say *!I looked the complicated example in the Encyclopedia Britannica up*; you have to say *I looked up the complicated example in the encyclopedia Britannica*. That is an example of heavy noun phrase shift—where the heavy noun phrase gets moved to the end of the sentence or clause. However, Indirect Objects do not participate in heavy NP shift. Therefore, you cannot say **I gave the book <u>the student who was working on syntax for a final year project</u>*, where the Indirect Object NP is shifted to the end of the sentence because Indirect Objects cannot undergo heavy noun phrase shift. You would actually have to say *I gave <u>the student who was working on syntax for a final year project</u> the book*, even though that long noun phrase makes that sentence hard to process. Finally, Indirect Objects do not extract easily. Extraction is when you move an expression from its normal position for its grammatical function. In English, we find it in interrogative and relative clauses. For example, you might say *he stole the book* in a declarative clause, but if you want to ask a question, you say *what did he steal__?*[3] English is unlike Chinese in this respect, because in Chinese the question word remains in the usual place. In English we also have extraction in relative clauses: if you want to form a relative clause, you say *the book which he stole__*. But in relative clauses, extraction with Indirect Objects is also difficult (e.g. **the student who you lent the book*). In sum, Indirect Objects have a lot of strange syntactic properties which makes them different from ordinary Objects, and that is actually a really useful thing to be aware of. I do not think that this set of syntactic properties had been properly identified before Hudson (1992); in the earlier literature, the double Object construction was just treated as involving two Objects.

GIVE is the prototypical example of the ditransitive construction (Goldberg 1995; Holmes and Hudson 2005). The semantics of Indirect Objects is set up by GIVE and recycled elsewhere in the lexicon. Therefore, the first thing to do to analyze GIVE is to establish the semantics for the verb GIVE, and then to develop the analysis to account for the rest of the verbs.

1.9 *GIVE: Jackendoff's Analysis*

Let us start by looking at Jackendoff's (1990) analysis. The following representation is the semantics of the verb GIVE in *Harry gave Sam a book*.

Jackendoff's analysis has two tiers in the semantics: the lexical-conceptual tier (CS+) which talks about meaning in terms of his localist theory of semantics, and the affecting tier (AFF+) which talks about meaning in terms of force dynamics. The analysis in the CS+ tier in the representation says 'Harry causes the book to go from Harry to Sam'. The other part of the analysis is that Harry

$$\begin{bmatrix} \text{CS+ ([HARRY], [GO/poss ([BOOK],} & \begin{bmatrix} \text{FROM [HARRY]} \\ \text{TO [SAM]} \end{bmatrix})]) \\ \text{AFF+ ([HARRY], [SAM])} & \end{bmatrix}$$

FIGURE 1   Jackendoff's (1990: 135) analysis of GIVE

---

3 The underline shows the usual place of the Direct Object.

affects Sam by doing this: the AFF+ tier says that *Harry affects Sam by doing this*. *Sam* is affected because now he possesses *the book*. In short, GIVE causes the Direct Object referent to go from the Subject to the Indirect Object and the Subject affects the Indirect Object.

Note that Jackendoff assumes there are two different events in the structure: a 'causing' event and a 'going' event: [FROM [HARRY] TO [SAM]] defines a path. He also assumes a force dynamic dyad where the Subject affects the Direct Object. For Jackendoff, the analysis of GIVE includes the analysis of path which the Direct Object reference takes from Er to Ee. Therefore, for him, analyzing the meaning of GIVE also includes defining the path from the Subject referent to the Indirect Object referent. Part of the semantics also relies on Jackendoff's semantic fields approach which labels GO in this case as belonging to the possession semantic field. Hence this kind of GO is a regular metaphorical extension of motion GO: it is a change of possession from one entity to another.

1.10   *GIVE: Goldberg's Analysis*

Figure 2 shows Goldberg's analysis.

Goldberg's analysis says that the Agent is linked to the Subject, the Recipient to the Object, and the Patient to the second Object, Object2. However, she does not actually distinguish these different Objects from each other. Therefore, the fact that the Indirect Object cannot participate in heavy noun phrase shift or that it cannot extract easily does not feature in her analysis. She does not justify labelling the Direct and Indirect Objects as Objects. There is no real analysis of the differences in syntax.

Moving on to the semantics we can see that Goldberg uses the semantic role labels Agent, Recipient and Patient, which might or might not be primitives, in this CAUSE-RECEIVE construction. Goldberg says that the semantics of the ditransitive construction are "the agent causes the recipient to receive the patient". Note that Goldberg's analysis is apparently a simple event analysis, CAUSE-RECEIVE, which has three participants. It implies however two different event nodes in a WG analysis: one for causing and the other

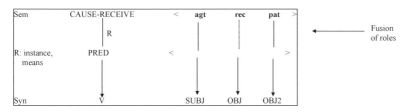

FIGURE 2   Goldberg's (1995: 50) analysis of GIVE

one for receiving. Later diagrams in her book include CAUSE-MOVE and CAUSE-BECOME which suggests a two-node analysis. Holmes and Hudson (2005) argue that this analysis is not fine-grained enough to explain examples like ENVY, because it needs to include enough detail to explain extensions of the GIVE prototype. ENVY is an emotional state which does not involve any transfer of possession, but does involve ownership. Imagine that you have a very nice house but you cousin does not. It is possible then to say *their cousin envied them their house*. The point is that the person who is envied possesses their house, but there is no transfer—the Indirect Object referent already possesses the house that they are envied for possessing. I also want to note that Goldberg's approach is causative, a point which I will examine in detail.

1.11   *GIVE Is Not Causative*

On the force-dynamic account of causation we saw in Lecture 6, we need to ask whether GIVE actually involves force-dynamics or not. I suggested that sub-lexical causation prototypically involves force-dynamics as well as the Result relation, so does the Result relation involve an argument which has an Initiator and an Endpoint? Is there a force-dynamic dyad? Jackendoff says that there is a force dynamic dyad between the Subject referent and the Indirect Object referent. But I have said, in Gisborne (2010), there are cases involving verbs other than GIVE where this does not happen—we see an example in the next section.

The issues to do with GIVE, and whether Jackendoff is right to say that the Indirect Object is affected, have in part to do with our analysis of force-dynamics, and if it matters whether the Endpoint undergoes a change of state or not. If Croft (2012) is right, that HIT involves a force-dynamic relationship between the Subject-referent and the Object-referent, then that analysis can be extended to the semantics of GIVE. On the other hand, if we were to come to the theoretical conclusion that there is no force-dynamic relationship unless the Endpoint undergoes a change of state, then HIT would not involve a force-dynamic relationship. And it would be hard to decide whether GIVE does. On Jackendoff's analysis, if x causes y to have z, then x affects y. But is having something that you have not had before a change of state? It seems to me that it is not, at least not necessarily: in *Kim gave Alex flowers*, does possessing flowers constitute a change of state? Surely not in the way that going from being 'not open' to being 'open' does, in *Kim opened the door*.

We could also look at whether the Direct Object is affected; if it were, there would be a force-dynamic dyad, even though it would be different from the one Jackendoff identifies. However, there need not be affecting relationship between the Subject referent and the Direct Object referent. If I give you my house, the house is not affected although you are affected by receiving a house, because you get somewhere to live or you benefit from the capital value, even though nothing physical happens. This is consistent with Jackendoff's analysis earlier. But what about the other ditransitive verbs?

1.12   SEND

Verbs like SEND are different from GIVE. The Result of SEND is not entailed, even in the ditransitive. Unlike GIVE, the Subject does not affect the Indirect Object even on the construal that HIT is force-dynamic. If I s*end her some flowers*, the referent of *her* is not affected by being sent some flowers although the flowers are affected, because the flowers are moved. Earlier in this lecture, I have talked about whether ditransitive verbs entail the Indirect Object actually receives the goods. In the case of SEND, if I send her flowers, she might never receive them. She is not affected if she does not receive them. It is only possible for *her* to be a participant in a force-dynamic dyad if the possession of the flowers is entailed. If it is not entailed, there is no force dynamics relationship. Consider also *send her my love*: the referent of *her* is not affected by being sent love and *my love* also is not affected by being sent to her. The same, of course, applies to GIVE: if someone says *Kim gave Alex her love*, is it reasonable to say that Alex is affected? In my culture, at least, utterances like this are part of politeness-related behaviour, and not expressions of strong feeling.

1.13   *An Argument*

It might be argued that the prototype of ditransitive involves some kind of force dynamic relationship, and that the variants which extend further from the prototype lose their force-dynamic pattern, and that the prototypical, force-dynamic, pattern involves an animate sentient Indirect Object, and a material Thing as Direct Object. But think back to FORCE itself.

(16)   Scipio forced Hannibal to concede defeat.
(17)   'Don't think of an elephant' forced me to think of elephants.

Hannibal was the Carthaginian who invaded Italy at the time of Romans. He marched his elephants all the way from north Africa around Europe down through Italy and to Rome which he held to ransom for a long time. Scipio was the Roman leader who eventually defeated Hannibal: (16) refers to an act of war and so *forced* in the example is physical, not mental. However, *forced* is mental in (17): if someone tells you *don't think of an elephant* of course the first thing that will happen is that you will think of an elephant—it is impossible to not think of one, and we could even say *the expression "don't think of an elephant" forced me to think of elephants*—which tells us even intra-mental force involves a force-dynamic transfer. However, rather different from FORCE, the prototype of GIVE can lose its force dynamics very rapidly once we move away from the core part of the meaning.

On the other hand, Jackendoff says, GIVE means the Indirect Object is affected. But why is GIVE different from SEND? And why is GIVE different from the other achievement verbs which involve force dynamic relationship in which the Subject is the Initiator and the Direct Object is the Endpoint? These are just open questions at the moment. I do not know the answer to them but what is suggested to me is that these verbs are open to further analysis in terms of the sorts of semantic structures that they have. I am not sure that they mean Goldberg's CAUSE-RECEIVE—their event structures are more complex and subtle than that, and I think adjudicating whether there is a force-dynamic dyad in the meaning of core GIVE or not will depend in part of how we choose to analyse the meaning of HIT.

Therefore, the verb GIVE involves the Result relation but its force dynamic pattern might not even be typical. In fact, perhaps prototypically, both the Indirect Object and Direct Object are affected. In *Give her some flowers*, you affect the flowers, then the flowers affect her with a causal chain via a subevent. Aspectually GIVE is like HIT, at least sometimes. For example, *she is giving him a letter* behaves like a run-up achievement in the same way as *the train is arriving at platform one*.

Here is a model of the semantics of GIVE; it does not include any syntactic information. There is a 'giving' event which has a Recipient, an Ee, an Er and a Result which is a 'having' event, which itself has an Er and Ee. This would seem to be the basic schema for a 'giving' event. Because this is an imperative structure, the diagram shows the Er of the 'giving' event linking to the addressee. We can see that 'giving' has a Result, but perhaps that is not enough for this pattern to be causal. If we were adopting Jackendoff's analysis, we would also say that Addressee is the Initiator and the Recipient is the Endpoint: recall that Jackendoff builds force-dynamics into his model with his affecting tier.

As Holmes and Hudson (2005) point out, this analysis permits "deep" analyses in Frame Semantics. In Frame Semantics, meanings are embedded in rich conceptual frames. In WG, we have an inheritance structure which classifies the network and which permit similar effects: both 'giving' and 'having' inherit from more general categories. We can classify 'giving' as 'achieving', and the node which is the Result of 'giving' as an instance of 'having': there is scope for further development of the analysis.

DITRANSITIVES AND VERBS OF BUYING AND SELLING

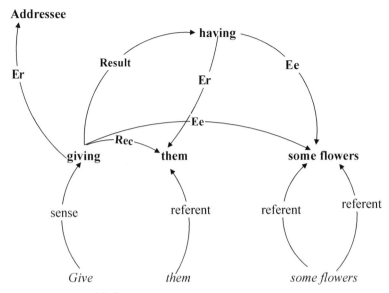

FIGURE 3 A model of GIVE

Analyzing the Result element of 'giving' as 'having' involves two parts of the 'having' prototype. So 'having' itself involves a prototypical structure. If you have something, then you possess it and also you benefit from it. That is, the have-er has socially recognized rights over the have-ee and it benefits from the have-ee. For example, I own a house, which means I can go into it, I can lock it, I can prevent other people from coming inside, I can sell it, or invite people to come and stay in it. I have socially agreed rights over my house as does everybody who has a house. Once these parts of the prototype are in place, then other extensions of the meaning of HAVE can be built. The diagram in Figure 3 makes the claim that we can enrich our understanding of 'having', to include the various things that possession involves. Once we enrich our understanding of 'having', then it is possible for us to have a deeper understanding of the variability in the different verbs that can occur in the ditransitive construction. Once the prototype is in place, other extensions of the meaning of GIVE, including the nature of 'having', can be built.

My conclusion from this discussion is that the fact that GIVE has a Result relation in its semantic structure is not enough to claim that it is causative. It is not causative in the say in which OPEN/tr clearly is. Given the claim in Lecture 6 that there are different kinds of Result relation, I would claim that ditransitive GIVE is a verb which lexicalizes a Result, but where the fact of its having a lexicalized Result is not sufficient for it to be classed as a prototypically causative verb. I would therefore challenge both Goldberg's and Jackendoff's analyses.

1.14 Ditransitive MAKE

This is about structures like *make me a cake.* In Gisborne (2010), I presented a model for transitive MAKE and elaborated it for ditransitive MAKE. Transitive MAKE is a verb of creation; it has a Result built into its meaning. Ditransitive MAKE does not have a second Result as its argument, but has a Purpose. As I have said before in these lectures, there is a theoretical claim that it is not possible for a node to have two relations that are the same: an event cannot have two Result relations, or two Ers or two Ees.[4] As Rappaport Hovav and Levin (2008) point out, there are two gross categories of ditransitive: TO ditransitives and FOR ditransitives. The examples tell us that MAKE is a FOR ditransitive, while GIVE can be either.

(18) We made a cake for/*to Jane.
(19) We gave a cake to Jane.
(20) We gave a party for Jane.

One of the reasons to have *for* in (20) is because the Beneficiary does not receive the party so much as the party-goers do: it takes a lot of people to make a party, and in a sense they all benefit. We need to build an analysis of ditransitive MAKE around one of transitive MAKE. Here is my analysis for *We made cakes*.

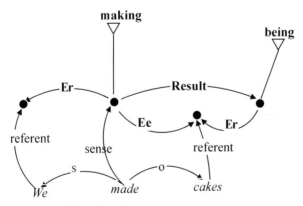

FIGURE 4   We made cakes

---

4   To put this more technically, a node cannot be the argument of two different instances of the same relation type.

In Figure 4, MAKE has a sense which is a kind of 'making' and it has an Er, an Ee and the Result is a kind of 'being'. The result of making a cake is that a cake exists. According to Gisborne (2010), the main point of difference between transitive MAKE and ditransitive MAKE is that the ditransitive variant adds a 'Beneficiary' Indirect Object. This shows that ditransitive MAKE adds conceptual structure to transitive MAKE, but it also retains the structure of the transitive variant. In addition, I argue that Rappaport Hovav and Levin's two main classes of ditransitives break down into Result and Purpose subtypes of ditransitive. This is a further justification for the elaboration of various kinds of Outcome that we have seen in earlier lectures. Purpose is one kind of Outcome and Result is another. Figure 4 illustrates the lexical structure of transitive MAKE. Figure 5 shows that of ditransitive MAKE.

MAKE becomes more complex in the ditransitive network as it involves this 'having' node which is the purpose of 'making'. Of course, if you make a cake for me, I might not receive it, so it is certainly defeasible—it can be cancelled.

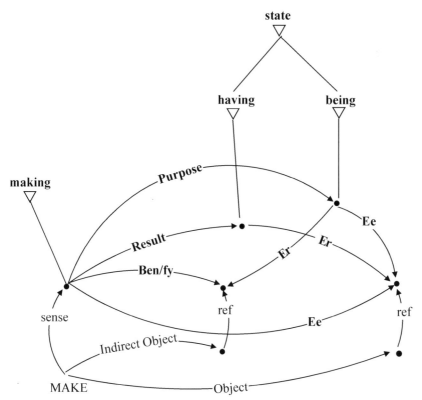

FIGURE 5   Ditransitive MAKE

1.15   Holmes and Hudson (2005)

Holmes and Hudson discuss DENY which I mentioned earlier. Their analysis is that the verb DENY uses the same semantic schema as the other ditransitive verbs, but it recycles a notation for counting, which says that the Result of DENY has a zero value. Essentially, DENY means that there is no possession. In this way, it keeps the semantic structure, which is clearly part of the definition of 'denying', while showing that the verb entails that the Indirect Object referent does not receive the Direct Object. The idea behind this analysis is the same as the idea behind the analysis of *fake diamond*, mentioned in lecture 1. In *fake diamond*, *fake* does not override the classification of *diamond*. It does not cancel the classification—fake adds extra meaning that says, 'but in this case it is not a diamond'.

Let us also consider various other examples, such as ALLOW, as in *I will allow them a break*. This is similar to DENY but it involves a second negative: if you allow somebody a break, it means you do not deny them a break. Second, we can also think about WRITE, as in *I wrote her a letter but never posted it*. WRITE is a verb of creation, and the example shows that such verbs can describe a purpose which is only partly fulfilled. The thing comes into existence but does not reach the intended Recipient. It is clear why the Indirect Object is used for the intended Recipient. Some Recipients can be only intended, not actual, thus it is not entailed that the Recipient receives the letter that is written for them.

Third, POST, as in *if you're going up to town, could you post me a letter*? The point of examples like this, which is also discussed by Goldberg (1995), is that the Indirect Object defines the Beneficiary of the whole action; I will not have the letter (on the contrary, the letter has to go away from me), less still benefit from the letter itself. What will benefit me is the action of posting. This use of the Indirect Object makes some sense if we remember that having implies benefit, so the owner is also the Beneficiary. Although the total semantic structure of *post me a letter* is very different from that of *give me a letter*, the Beneficiary relationship is enough to justify the Indirect Object. Therefore, the claim here is the Beneficiary relation itself brings with it a complex semantic schema which allows it to interact with various verbs that might not look as though they would make sense in this structure on first inspection.

Fourth, ENVY as in *I envy him his brains*. Unlike all of the other examples this does not even describe an action, because 'envying' is a state of mind. However, we can explain the use of the Indirect Object on the grounds that 'he' is the owner of his brains. No doubt this valency pattern is also supported by the possibility of using a Direct Object to define the person envied, as in *I envy him*.

1.16 *Interim Conclusions*

We see a range of family-resemblance patterns, just as we saw in the case of idioms and resultatives. Ditransitives cause some difficulties of analysis, because the force-dynamics are hard to fathom. Different ditransitives might have different force-dynamic patterns. Perhaps ditransitives can embed lexical causative structures within their meanings. But currently it looks as though they do not embed prototypical sublexical causation of the kind found with verbs such as OPEN and it is not clear that even the most prototypical sense of GIVE involves force dynamics. That then takes us to the next section.

2 Commercial Transactions

The second part of the lecture is about commercial transaction verbs: verbs of buying and selling. In this section I draw extensively on an unpublished paper, Hudson (2008). That paper is an attempt to explore the differences between the networks that I am advocating in these lectures, and Fillmore's frames. Fillmore says, "A word's meaning can be understood only with reference to a structured background of experience, beliefs, or practices, constituting a kind of conceptual prerequisite for understanding the meaning" (Fillmore and Atkins 1992: 76–77). I think that is right. Essentially Fillmore argues that word meaning is encyclopedic in some way and that part of the encyclopedic knowledge that comes with word meaning involves understanding a host of things the speaker has inherited from their experiences—perceptual, linguistic, cultural, social, and so on. But Fillmore wants to structure all of that in a single frame which is in some way supposed to encapsulate all of that information. But I think that those beliefs and cultural practices are best not understood in terms of relatively shallow "frames" and that they are better conceived of in terms of networks of information, including some higher-level information. In this section, I discuss the meanings of the verbs of buying and selling—the verbs that make up the Commercial Transaction Frame as Fillmore conceives it—in a way which does not privilege a single conceptual frame, where the verbs' meaning is addressed at different levels of granularity. The approach is different from a Fillmorean frame analysis, even though I agree actually with the content of the quotation above.

Gisborne and Donaldson (2019) explain Fillmore's perspective with a quotation from Fillmore (1976) which introduces the idea that several different verbs can be related to the same frame.

> There is in English, and presumably in every language spoken by a people with a money economy, a semantic domain connected with what we might call the commercial event. The frame for such an event has the form of a scenario containing roles that we can identify as the buyer, the seller, the goods, and the money; containing subevents within which the buyer surrenders the money and takes the goods and the seller surrenders the goods and takes the money; and having certain institutional understandings associated with the ownership changes that take place between the beginning and the end of each such events. Any one of the many words in our language that relate to this frame is capable of accessing the entire frame. Thus, the whole commercial event scenario is available or "activated" in the mind of anybody who comes across and understands any of the words "buy", "sell", "pay", "cost", "spend", "charge", etc., even though each of these highlights or foregrounds only one small section of the frame.

As Gisborne and Donaldson (2019) put it, for Fillmore, "[T]here is a single commercial-transaction event-type and that the names of the different verbs—BUY, COST and so on—are names for different figure-ground articulations of commercial-transaction events."

The Word Grammar approach of Hudson (2008) is different. We have to make our generalizations at the right level. Goldberg (2006) says that many generalizations in language are smaller than is widely believed or assumed. She advocates very powerfully (and correctly) the idea that we should be looking to make generalizations at the level at which they really exist and sometimes these generalizations are quite small. If we are to understand commercial transactions, then we need to understand them in terms of smaller generalizations. Saying that commercial transaction verbs can all be analyzed as figure-ground variation understood against a single frame fails to capture a number of relevant linguistic facts. There turn out to be three different subtypes of commercial transaction verb. Each of those three different subtypes has its own properties, and they do not all share all of the same properties. The verbs we are looking at are: BUY, SELL, CHARGE, SPEND, PAY and COST. But even though it looks as though these verbs can all be used to describe the same scene—we can buy a house for £500,000, sell a house for £500,000, charge £500,000 for the house, spend £500,000 on the house, pay £500,000 for the house, and say that the house cost £500,000—there are generalizations that apply to BUY and SELL that do not apply to PAY and COST, for example, so we end up with three subclasses of commercial transaction verb that do not all behave like each other.[5]

Here are some examples taken from Hudson (2008), where Bert is 'B' for the buyer and Sam is 'S' for the seller:

(21) Bert bought the apples from Sam for a pound.
(22) Sam sold Bert the apples for a pound.
(23) Sam charged Bert a pound for the apples.
(24) Bert spent a pound on the apples.
(25) Bert paid Sam a pound for the apples.
(26) The apples cost Bert a pound.

Do these verbs all belong in the same Commercial Transaction frame? We are going to start with the syntax. In the table, *C1–3* means "Complement 1–3":

TABLE 1   The structure of commercial transaction verbs

Lexeme	Subject	verb	C1	C2	C3
BUY	Buyer	*buys*	Goods	*from* Seller	*for* Money
SELL	Seller	*sells*	Goods	*to* Buyer	*for* Money
or:	Seller	*sells*	Buyer	Goods	*for* Money
CHARGE	Seller	*charges*	Buyer	Money	*for* Goods
SPEND	Buyer	*spends*	Money	*on* Goods	
PAY	Buyer	*pays*	Money	*to* Seller	*for* Goods
or:	Buyer	*pays*	Seller	Money	*for* Goods
COST	Goods	*cost*	Buyer	Money	

FROM HUDSON (2008)

Table 1 summarizes key facts about each of the verbs of buying and selling. The lexeme BUY has a Subject whose semantics is 'Buyer'. The verb is *buys*, C1 is *the goods*, C2 is a from-phrase, *from the seller*, C3 is *for money*. The first row therefore represents a sentence such as *Bert bought the apples from Sam for 10 dollars*. We can look at the way in which the semantic roles vary through these different verbs. BUY and SELL have Money as their C3. CHARGE has Goods as

---
5 There is a similar presentation of these verbs in Gisborne and Donaldson (2019).

its C3. SPEND does not have a C3. PAY has goods for its C3. COST does not have a C3. There is quite a lot of variability in terms of what is realized in these complements. BUY and SELL, though, seem to be inverses. With BUY, the Subject is the Buyer, and C2 the Seller; with SELL, the Subject is the Seller, and C2 the Buyer. SELL also has an Indirect Object variant here, as in *Sam sold Bert apples*. BUY can occur in the Indirect Object construction. But when BUY occurs in the Indirect Object construction, it does not vary the arguments in the table above. For example, you can *buy your children a bike*, then your children are the Beneficiary of *buying*, but they are not the Goods or the Money. You cannot put the Goods, the Seller or the Money in the Indirect Object position, because it is not possible for any of them to be the Beneficiary of *buying*.

With CHARGE, the Seller charges Money. With 'buying', the Buyer spends Money on Goods. CHARGE can also have an Indirect Object pattern, so you can say *Sam charged Bert a pound for the apples*. That involves some kind of possession transfer. Again, it is not possible to do this with SPEND because you can't get a Beneficiary Indirect Object from the participants of Buyer, Seller, Money and Goods. With PAY, it is possible so you can say *Bert pays Sam money*. There is, again, variability in how things are realized in these verbs.

The various questions we need to ask ourselves include: Is this a single frame? Do these verbs all share the same meaning? Do they differ only in how they map this meaning via the four roles onto their syntactic dependents? Or are there other dimensions of difference? We also need to compare the analysis not just with Fillmore's analysis but also with Jackendoff's. Jackendoff makes a similar claim about BUY, PAY and SELL. He distinguishes them slightly in terms of the internal organization of the shared semantic structure (Jackendoff 1990: 189–91), but he also suggests that these three verbs should be treated together. Semantically though, these verbs do not seem to all apply to the same range of situations. Syntactically, they have different valencies which cannot be explained if they share the same meaning.

2.1 *Premise*

Recall the claim in Lecture 2 that syntactic distributions can be evidence for semantic structure: Beth Levin argues that semantics explains the different argument-taking patterns of verbs, and therefore that syntax is a window on lexico-conceptual semantics. This has the corollary that syntax is set up by semantics. As these verbs have different syntactic patterns, we should expect them to have different meanings, and if they share the same defining frame, then they should all have the same range of possible applications and they should entail one another: the argument is that if they really belong in the same frame, then there should be mutual entailment patterns between them. But actually, as Hudson shows, they do not belong to the same frame.

2.2 Three Frames for Commercial Transactions

If Bert buys something from Sam, then Sam sold it to Bert. BUY and SELL are mutually entailing. They can apply to the same total range of scenes. Every scene of selling is also a scene of buying. If Bert pays Sam a pound then Sam charges Bert a pound. PAY and CHARGE are mutually entailing. If Bert spends a pound (on the apples) then the apples cost (Bert) a pound. SPEND and COST are mutually entailing. But the argument is that the mutual entailment comes in these pairs BUY and SELL, PAY and CHARGE, SPEND and COST, but not COST and SELL, and not COST and BUY, which are not mutually entailing. The mutual entailing pairs do not involve patterns from the larger system. Therefore, we can see that there are actually three frames for commercial transactions, as detailed in Table 2.

BUY and SELL share the trading frame where only ownership of Goods passes from Seller to Buyer, in exchange for Money. But the paying frame is where the ownership of money passes from Payer to Charger in exchange for Benefit provided by Charger. But of course, the kinds of things that you can *pay* or *charge* for are a larger set of things than the things you can *buy* or *sell*. Imagine you are providing a tutorial service for young kids in your community to qualify for university entrance exams. You go to their house and they pay you money to help them pass this exam. Are you *selling* a tutorial? That is not idiomatic English. But are you *charging* money for a tutorial? Yes. Are they *paying* you money for a tutorial? Yes. Are they *buying* a tutorial? No. You do actually buy services, but you probably would not normally say *I bought a tutorial*. You would say: *I charged them £20 for a tutorial*, and *the tutorial cost £20*, and *they paid £20 for a tutorial*. The same applies with other services: you pay for a hotel room, but you do not own it. That is to say that the benefit which can be charged for, have money spent on it, potentially involves a larger set of things

TABLE 2   Three frames for commercial transactions

Verbs	Shared frame	Rough definition
BUY, SELL	trading	Ownership of Goods passes from Seller to Buyer in exchange for money
PAY, CHARGE	paying	Ownership of Money passes from Payer to Charger in exchange for Benefit provided by Charger
SPEND, COST	resource management	Spender uses Resource to get Benefit, and the Cost is the Resource

FROM HUDSON (2008)

than the Goods that participate in in buying and selling scenarios, even though you can buy and sell services in various ways.

According to Hudson, SPEND and COST share a frame of resource management. In spending, the Spender uses the Resource in order to get a Benefit, and the Cost is the Resource that you use. I can say for example that *my car cost so many thousand pounds*. The Resource I used to get a car was so much money. Or I can say *I want to get a favor out of my boss* and in order to do it, I have to *trade* something; I agree to be on a really boring committee. Therefore, I can say that *my Sabbatical leave cost me being on this really boring committee*. The willingness to be on this boring committee is my resource which I am giving in order to get the benefit of the Sabbatical leave.

It looks therefore as though there are three different frames and across those three different frames we do not really have patterns of mutual entailment. Of course, it's possible to say *I spent 20 pounds on the tutorial*, or *the tutorial cost me 20 pounds*. But there is not a perfect match across these different frames.

2.3   *Verbs of Giving and Verbs of Getting*

There is a cross-classification schema which intersects with the three subtypes of commercial transaction verb: 'giving' and 'getting'. SELL and PAY are verbs of giving. BUY is a verb of getting. But CHARGE, SPEND, and COST do not fit this classification. When I say *I spend five pounds*, there is nothing entailed about giving it to somebody. If *something costs five pounds*, there is no 'getting' or 'giving'. As Gisborne and Donaldson (2019) point out,

> Fillmore and Baker (2015) treat the frame as being perspectivised by whether the verbs are giving or getting verbs. This leads to a further conflict with Hudson's analysis. Hudson analyses 'buying' as inheriting from 'getting' and 'selling' as inheriting from 'giving'. These classifications are not a way of establishing perspective in a frame: they literally are how the verbs need to be analysed. On Hudson's account, by default inheritance 'buying' is a special kind of 'getting' and the appropriate "frame" is the frame of verbs of receiving. The same arguments apply to 'selling' and 'giving'. This approach successfully accounts for the relationship of the syntactic to the semantic facts. Croft *et al.* (2001) also note that several verbs in the commercial transaction frame are verbs of giving and that buying is a verb of getting.

On a Word Grammar approach, because 'buying' Isa 'getting', these facts do not "perspectivize" the frame: they are the analysis. In fact, analyzing these verbs against a commercial transaction frame loses key information. We return to this in a moment.

2.4 Syntactic Behavior as Supporting Evidence

Levin and Rappaport Hovav (1991) distinguish resultative verbs such as CLEAN from manner-of-action verbs such as WIPE. This explains why *wipe it clear* is possible but **clean it clear* is not. That is, *wipe* is a manner-of-action verb and does not lexicalize a Result, whereas CLEAN is a result verb, therefore it is not possible for it to occur in this kind of result construction.[6] If we reorganize the semantic categories in the way we did above in Table 1, then the syntactic mapping looks less arbitrary. The three semantic classes of commercial transaction verbs are each associated with a different syntax.

2.5 More Facts

There is another cross-classification. BUY and SELL are also verbs of trading. PAY and CHARGE are verbs of paying, so we can say X *buys/sells* Goods *for* Money or X *pays/charges* Money *for* Goods. But SPEND is different; it takes the preposition ON, so we say X *spends* Money *on* Goods.

(27) Bert bought some apples from Sam for a pound.
(28) Bert bought some apples from Sam.
(29) Bert bought some apples for a pound.
(30) Bert bought some apples.
(31) *Bert bought (from Sam) (for a pound).

Bert bought is not possible, expect perhaps (31) might be ok in very specialized context. We can compare (27)–(31) to GET which means 'becomes the owner of':

(32) Bert got some apples from Sam for a pound.
(33) Bert got some apples from Sam.
(34) Bert got some apples for a pound.
(35) Bert got some apples.
(36) *Bert got (from Sam) (for a pound).

Based on the similar patterns shown by BUY and GET in (27)–(36), we can say 'buying' involves 'getting'. However, one difference between 'buying' and 'getting' is that 'buying' always involves money, whereas 'getting' does not always involve money. We may say 'buying' is a subtype of 'getting' which involves money.

---

6 Although note the discussion in Lecture 5 about examples such as *the chair broke apart*: any theory needs an account of when a result-specifying depiction can occur and when it cannot.

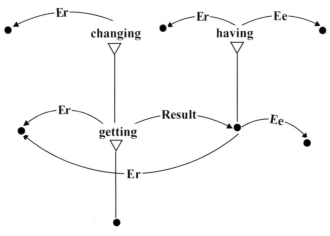

FIGURE 6   'Getting'

What is 'getting'? 'Getting' is kind of 'having' as the Result of a transfer. In WG, a concept can be defined either as the argument of the relation or as its value. In this case, 'having' is the Result of 'moving'. 'Buying' could just be an instance of 'getting' (e.g. *I bought/got a bike*). But it is also kind of 'exchanging', so the model has to include a way of understanding 'exchanging' as well as 'getting'. We can start by understanding 'getting': Figure 6, analyzes 'getting'.

'Getting' is an instance of 'changing' which has an Er. But it adds structure to 'changing' so it is an instance of 'changing' which has both an Er and a Result. The Er of the Result is linked to the same node as the Er of 'getting'. There is an Ee of 'having' because the Result of 'getting' is 'having' and HAVE is a 2-place predicate.

2.6   'Trading'

Let's look at 'trading'. Hudson treats 'buying' as involving mutual inheritance from both 'getting' and 'trading', as shown in Figure 7. The presence of these two meanings accounts for the prepositions which are associated with BUY.

'Buying' inherits from two different meanings: 'getting' and 'trading'. The involvement of 'getting' and 'trading' accounts for the prepositions which are associated with 'buying'. From 'getting', 'buying' gets its Source, which is realized by FROM. From 'trading' it gets its transferred Goods, which is realized by FOR. In short, 'getting' triggers one preposition and 'trading' triggers another preposition. 'Getting' has an Actor, a Patient and a Source. 'Trading' involves a reward which is expressed by FOR, with the semantics of the reward classified as money. The idea is that with mutual inheritance for 'buying' from 'getting' and 'trading' we can capture the syntactic facts about which prepositions are allowed or required.

DITRANSITIVES AND VERBS OF BUYING AND SELLING 201

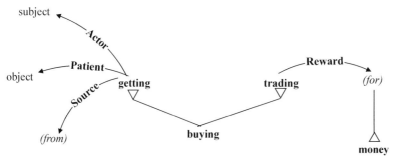

FIGURE 7 'Buying'

2.7   'Selling'
Consider the following examples.

(37) Sam sold some apples to Bert.
(38) Sam sold Bert some apples.
(39) Sam sold some apples.
(40) *Sam sold Bert.
(41) *Sam sold to Bert.
(42) Sam sold.

The obvious model for this pattern is the verb GIVE because it also displays the same grammaticality pattern: *Sam gave some apples to Bert* and so on, but not *Sam gave*. Note that SELL is ok in the middle construction—*the apples sold well*—but you cannot say **the apples bought well*, just as it is not possible to say *the present gave easily* so there is some local variability.

The idea then is that 'selling' involves 'giving' and 'trading' rather than 'getting' and 'trading'. As before, this accounts for the prepositional uses. It also accounts for the differences in the syntactic frames between BUY and SELL. This is shown in Figure 8. The point to take away is that even BUY and SELL do not involve a perfect single frame: there are lexical differences between them. We can also see where the patterns of mutual entailment come from: they are located in the converse pattern between 'giving' and 'getting'.

Figure 8 shows that 'selling' inherits from 'giving' and 'trading'. From 'trading' it inherits its reward which is expressed by the preposition FOR, which is money. From 'giving', it inherits an Actor, a Patient, a Goal and a Beneficiary which is expressed as Indirect Object. 'Buying' and 'selling' are actually subtly different from each other. The difference is explained by the inheritance of 'buying' and 'getting'. 'Buying' inherits from 'getting' but not from 'giving' and therefore can't have Indirect Object, while 'selling' inherits from 'giving' which explains why 'selling' can have an Indirect Object and 'buying' cannot have one.

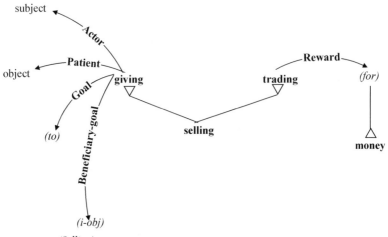

FIGURE 8   'Selling'

2.8   'Paying'
Next, let us look at PAY.

>   (43)   Bert paid a pound to Sam (for some apples).
>   (44)   Bert paid Sam a pound (for some apples).
>   (45)   Bert paid a pound (for some apples).
>   (46)   Bert paid Sam (for some apples).
>   (47)   *Bert paid to Sam (for some apples).
>   (48)   Bert paid (for some apples).

There is an interesting complication to do with the Direct Object, which can be omitted as long as the Indirect Object is present, as in (46), or if neither Direct nor Indirect Object is present (48) but not otherwise. Exceptionally the Indirect Object to be able to occur on its own, as in *Bert paid Sam*; this is not possible with GIVE: *Peter gave Jane a party, Peter gave a party, *Peter gave Jane*.

2.9   'Charging'
Let's compare (43)–(48) and (49)–(54):

>   (49)   *Sam charged a pound to Bert (for some apples).
>   (50)   Sam charged Bert a pound (for some apples).
>   (51)   Sam charged a pound (for some apples).
>   (52)   Sam charged Bert (for some apples).
>   (53)   *Sam charged to Bert (for some apples).
>   (54)   Sam charged (for some apples).

The only difference from PAY is the example in (49). *Pay* and *charge* go together. 'Seller charges Buyer Money' is like REFUSE, DENY and FINE (*Sam refused Bert a pound*, but **Sam refused a pound to Bert*). 'Seller charges Money' is like DEMAND and ASK (*Sam demanded a pound*). 'Seller Charges Buyer' is like PUNISH (*Sam charged Bert. Sam punished Bert*).

With CHARGE, there are actually three different models for the valency patterns. It looks as though the complexity in the valency of CHARGE follows not from some larger property of a conceptual frame, but from CHARGE being polysemous and having three different models giving rise to its various meanings. That makes CHARGE really quite complex in a way that BUY and SELL are not. BUY and SELL on the other hand each have very simple models but they involve different higher taxonomic nodes that they inherit from, explaining their different prepositional sources. As we look more closely at the detail, what we see is an increasing number of differences and subtleties in the various possible meanings of these verbs. That is important because that means trying to understand them in terms of a single frame misses significant facts and generalizations which identify the similarities between these verbs within this set of related meanings, but which can also identify similarities between these verbs and other verbs which are not part of the frame.

2.10 'Spending'

SPEND is different from the other commercial transaction verbs. We *buy* and *sell something*, *pay* and *charge for something*, but we *spend money on something*.

(55) Bert spent a pound on some apples.
(56) Bert spent a pound.
(57) *Bert spent on some apples.
(58) *Bert spent.

SPEND is like verbs of resource-management, like WASTE, USE, TAKE (time) and SQUANDER. We can contrast SPEND with WASTE: *Bert wasted a pound on some apples, Bert wasted a pound, *Bert wasted on some applies, *Bert wasted.* WASTE and SPEND occur in the same patterns.

2.11 'Costing'

COST is the most exceptional of all the commercial transaction verbs. Its Subject is not one of the human participants, but the goods.

(59) The apples cost Bert a pound.
(60) The apples cost a pound.

(61) *The apples cost.
(62) *The apples cost from/to Sam.

Exceptionally, neither of the Objects of COST can be passivized (Lawler 1989), although it is normally a property of Objects that they can be passivized.

(63) *Bert was cost a pound.
(64) *A pound was cost Bert.
(65) *A pound was cost.

(63)–(65) suggests that the apparent Objects are not Objects because of the passivization facts. Therefore, as it does not behave in the way in which you expect it to behave, it looks as though COST does not actually occur in the ditransitive construction, but some other kind of construction with two post verbal noun phrases. COST is like TAKE: both are verbs with two noun phrase complements after them, but they are not ditransitive verbs.

(66) The project took Bert an hour.
(67) The project took an hour.
(68) *An hour was taken by the project.
(69) *Bert was taken an hour by the project.

To summarize: using a simple frame to capture the commercial transaction verbs misses a lot of important facts. Given that Goldberg (2006) argues that our job is to capture generalizations at the right level of granularity and not to make sweeping generalizations which are insufficiently precise, it seems to be an unhelpful research strategy to put these verbs into a single commercial transaction frame, because this research strategy obliges us to miss smaller generalizations which are real, and it also causes us to miss the equally real relationships with other verbs not even in the commercial transaction frame. There are of course many similarities between WG and Cognitive Construction Grammar, but I would argue that the WG approach to verb meaning—particularly not locking bits of meaning away in frames or constructions—allows for a more accurate account of verbs' behaviour.

2.12   *Conclusions*

One main argument in this lecture has been to develop the claims of Lecture 6 and its analysis of causation. I have suggested that to treat ditransitive verbs as causative, as though they shared obvious semantic properties with causative verbs such as transitive OPEN, missed some key facts about the variation in the semantic network(s) of causation, which are built up around the Result relation. I have also suggested that there is a lot of fine-grained subtle variation in the meanings of ditransitive verbs, even within single sub-classes. This claim sets up the discussion of the so-called commercial transaction verbs.

Another main argument in this lecture is that verb meanings can overlap, and can invoke each other. We can use patterns of inheritance to show the various ways in which these meanings are set up. But verb meanings do not often fall into neat territories which can be analyzed in terms of small semantic fields. The network analysis allows us to understand verb meanings in a range of ways with different associative links and different patterns of multiple inheritance, and at the right level of granularity, while avoiding overgeneralization.

In the case of the verbs of buying and selling, the most important conclusion is that a single frame for these verbs is too general. It misses various important facts, and means that we cannot see the similarities and dissimilarities that we should look for. Like ditransitive verbs, verbs of buying and selling form a dense network of family resemblance patterns. They do not instantiate a single frame. Of course, versions of this this have been my general conclusion throughout the lecture series. Instead of trying to say that we have got a construction or a frame which captures the meaning variation that we are looking at, we actually have a kind of family-resemblance network, typically, where there are cross-classifications in the inheritance system and various kinds of associative link tie things together. But I do not think we can segment language up and partition it into boxes and say this bit of language belongs to this box and that bit of language belongs to that box and factor them out in that way.

LECTURE 8

Classes of Events and Aspectual Class

1   Introduction

Throughout this lecture series, one of my general themes has been that we do not need to put boxes around little bits of information and say they are encapsulated, because the tendrils of information spread out through a cognitive or a mental network. Another theme has been that there are obviously constellations of dense, tight information which are more pertinent to certain kinds of phenomena than others. For example, clearly there is a prototype of causation, and another of 'giving'; clearly there is a prototype of words which go on elsewhere to become (part of) idioms, which are themselves less prototypical. Therefore, we need to understand both the more prototypical structures, and how they relate to the less prototypical structures. But my last main theme has been that I do not suppose that we have predictive accounts of how a more distant, less prototypical usage will arise, relative to the more prototypical usage—there is a sort of gradient or cline of typicality.

But some sorts of semantic extension can be predicted: there are certain kinds of metaphorical extension which are regular, which we need to be able to accommodate in our description and our theory; for example, the idea that the word WINDOW can refer to the glazing that fills the window-frame or the aperture made by the window-frame, or DOOR can symbolize either the wooden structure that closes the door or the aperture that we walk through. These patterns are predictable. In the same way it is clearly predicable that a causative event will typically embed an inchoative event, which denotes a transition. We need to be able to state these generalizations at the right level. Default inheritance makes it possible to state generalizations accurately. There is a low level of generalization for small phenomena, and a high level of generalization for larger scale phenomena.

 All original audio-recordings and other supplementary material, such as any hand-outs and powerpoint presentations for the lecture series, have been made available online and are referenced via unique DOI numbers on the website www.figshare.com. They may be accessed via a QR code for the print version of this book. In the e-book, both the QR code and dynamic links are available, and can be accessed by a mouse-click.

There are all sorts of things to try and put together, though. This kind of semantics is not just about case-by-case studies, which set out to put small bits of meaning together, or to establish the relationship between literal meaning and metaphoric meaning, or the relationship between this kind of verb and this kind of construction, or that kind of verb and that kind of construction. We also need to see if we can come up with a more general account of event relationships and what we can use that more general account to try and understand. This is the topic of today's lecture.

In this lecture we discuss the inherent temporal properties of events and complex event structures, and think about how those temporal properties are implicated, or not, in the nature of event complexity and the mapping of complex events to subclasses of verbs. It is predictable that a causative event will typically embed an inchoative event, which symbolizes some kind of transition, and some aspects of event complexity are predictable. But what about the temporal properties of verbs?

There are several things to put together. First, we need to be able to state the various generalizations at the right level. Default inheritance is the tool that allows us to state generalizations very schematically or very locally. Secondly, we also need to understand the relationship between literal meaning and metaphorical meaning, and the relationships between different classes of verb and different construction types. Finally, we also need to work out the most general patterns of event relationship and see what we can use those general patterns of event relationships to understand. This is the topic of today's lecture, which is focused on *Aktionsarten* (also known as the aspectual classes of predicates). We need to look at *Aktionsart* because not only it is inherently part of verb meaning, but also because it has been claimed to be central to the nature of event structure. Levin and Rappaport Hovav (2005: 96–117) discuss a number of approaches which have placed it at the heart of argument realization. In this lecture, I argue that *Aktionsarten* add a layer of complexity to event structures, in a case study of the temporal differences between the meaning of HIT and the meaning of SINK.

Aktionsart concerns the dimensions of verb meaning that tell you about the temporal contour of an event. By the temporal contour, I mean such issues as whether an event is always the same, or whether it involves change; and whether it culminates in an endpoint, or whether it is temporally unbounded. For example, *the air conditioner stands by the wall* symbolizes a state: it is always the same. It is also possible for an event to involve change, but not necessarily directed change. For example, I am talking, and talking is an event which involves change, but that change is not directed. Verbs like TALK contrast with verbs such as DIE which is a change of state of verb where there is directed change: a living being that dies undergoes a change of state from alive to dead. The directed change is therefore scalar in some way (even though the scale only has two points on it). We need to think about the temporal contour of events because it is relevant to event semantics and argument linking or realization—the question of how the semantic arguments, what I have in these lectures called the Er and the Ee and the force dynamic participants, relate to the syntactic arguments: the Subject, the Object, the Indirect Object, and so forth.

The other kind of research question coming back to Lecture 3 is, "What sorts of patterns of event complexity do we see?" Of course, if you look for possible patterns of complexity in event structures, then you must surely also be looking for impossible patterns of complexity or unlikely patterns of complexity. Part of thinking about these questions involves an investigation into *Aktionsart* because it is a property of all event types, ranging from simple events to much more complex event structures, and I want to use some of the differences in *Aktionsarten* to understand some of the dimensions of event complexity. This means that in this lecture today, we will be modeling an event hierarchy. What I am going to be thinking about is the very top of an event hierarchy where high-level concepts—the most schematic concepts—are found. (Hierarchies become increasingly specific as towards the bottom.)

The plan of today's lecture is that we look at for main points.
- How transitive and intransitive verbs map onto different classes of *Aktionsarten*.
- How the different *Aktionsarten* can be analysed.
- Complex events and mapping to syntax and to different *Aktionsarten*.
- And, briefly, the "imperfective paradox".

The reason for taking the first point is that it shows that there is evidence for event complexity from the temporal structures of even some very simple intransitive verbs. The basic *Aktionsarten* types are states, simple dynamic events (activities), semelfactives, achievements, and accomplishments. When we look at complex events and how the different *Aktionsarten* should be analysed, we will see that *Aktionsarten* are more complex than being just simple patterns of event relationship because of how the different events' temporal indices play out in complex events.

We will also explore the imperfective paradox in the case of accomplishments. This is the observation that the interaction between an accomplishment verb and the progressive aspect in English can give rise to the interpretation that the inherent Result in the meaning of the verb is not realized. For example, BUILD in *he was building a house* is a verb of creation, so the result of building a house is that a house is built. However, the English progressive offers a window on the inside of an event: we do not see the whole event, we see a phase of it—a segment of the event—which means that when the progressive combines with an accomplishment predicate like *build a house*, it overrides the semantics of a completed result. Conversely, in the case of other classes of verb, such as the activity verbs TEACH and WALK the progressive entails that the subject has already taught or walked. This is not so in the case of *build a house*: if we say *he was building a house* it does not entail that he has already built a house. The imperfective paradox offers another window onto event complexity, and so these are the various phenomena that I discuss in today's lecture.

In the first part of this lecture, I explore the relationship between verb types by their syntactic argument structures and different event complexities. For example, we know that intransitive verbs typically symbolize activities (RUN), achievements or changes of state (DIE) but not states unless they are a verb such as STAND and are also complemented by an appropriate prepositional phrase (*Rome stands on the Tiber*). As I have argued that we can use syntactic behavior as a probe into event/semantic structure, it seems apt to work out the limits on the relationship between syntax and semantics, at least in terms of syntactic argument-structure complexity and event complexity.

I go through various kinds of verb, by looking at differences among intransitive and transitive verbs. I show that there is not a simple direct one-to-one relationship between syntactic verb classes such as transitive verbs and intransitive verbs on the one hand, and semantic classes of event and event complexity on the other. There can be mismatches between verb types and event categorizations with *Aktionsart* being related to event-types. This set of issues is worth exploring because they are relevant to the question of in what ways it is possible for aspectual class to be relevant to argument realization (which I do not explore further in these lectures) and they also apply to the question of what kinds of syntactic information we can use to form generalizations about semantic structures. Some aspects of semantic structure are just semantic.

1.1   *Verb Types: Intransitive Verbs*

If we use argument-taking patterns as a way to think about event structures, we find various categories of intransitive verbs and also categories of transitive verbs. First, intransitive verbs which divide into two different event classes: unaccusative verbs as in (1), which denote a change of state, and unergative verbs as in (2).

(1)   The ice-cream melted.
(2)   The choir sang.

In (1), there is a change of state: the ice-cream goes from being solid to being liquid. The unergative verb in (2) is just a simple activity: there is no change of state. In the literature, unaccusative verbs are also called anticausative, or inchoative verbs.[1] Similarly, unergative verbs are sometimes called simple intransitive verbs. The difference between unaccusative verbs and unergative verbs was first laid out by Perlmutter (1978). Rosen (1981) and Burzio (1981) later identified various properties of unaccusativity in Italian. For example, English only has the perfect auxiliary HAVE as in *the ice-cream has melted* whereas in Italian and languages like it in this regard, such as Dutch, unergative verbs have the verb HAVE as their perfective auxiliary, while unaccusative verbs have the verb BE as their perfect auxiliary. French has a similar split (although it does not perfectly map onto the same classes of verbs as in Italian) between intransitive verbs that have auxiliary ETRE rather than AVOIR in the perfect, so there is a difference between *je suis tombé* 'I have fallen', and *j'ai dansé* 'I have danced'. In languages with split auxiliary choice like this, there can be other grammatical facts that are also relevant.

1.2   *Transitive Verb Types*

Transitive verbs also divide into several types. We can look at them in terms of certain semantic classes, and explore how the different temporal structures work.

1.3   *Agent-Acts-on-Patient Verbs*

These verbs are not telic. They can be undirected activities with unlimited duration and no built-in endpoint as in (3).

(3)   He stroked the cat.

The example in (4) on the other hand is punctual: once you throw the ball, the ball has left your hand and the event is over.

(4)   He threw the ball.

Although both (3) and (4) involve semantic structures where the Agent acts on the Patient, they have different temporal profiles: *stroked* in (3) is a verb

---

[1] In these lectures, I have typically referred to them as "inchoative verbs" because I have been focused on their change-of-state semantics, rather than the syntactic properties of unaccusativity.

of unlimited duration, whereas *threw* in (4) is punctual. Both types are atelic, because neither instantaneous events nor events of unlimited duration have built-in endpoints.

1.4   Reciprocal Verbs

Reciprocal verbs are predicates where if there is a coordinated subject, the two coordinates are simultaneously acting on each other. I mentioned them in the lecture on thematic roles. Both *Jane kissed Peter* and *Peter kissed Jane* are possible, but it is also possible to have the example in (5).

(5)   Jane and Peter kissed.

Jackendoff has an example where he points out that *Jane kissed Peter* has the same structure as *the drunk kissed the lamppost*, but whereas (5) is possible, *the drunk and the lamppost kissed* is not. These verbs are like the example in (3) in that they have an unlimited duration, and no built-in endpoint.

1.5   Change of State Verbs

Change of state verbs have a result-state built into their meaning, where the direct object referent ends up in a different state from the state it started in, and so they involve complex events.

(6)   Kim broke the glass.

In (6), the glass has ended up in a different state from its beginning state; the semantic structure involves two or three subevents, depending on your preferred analysis: Kim has to act, which causes the glass to enter a state of being broken. Such verbs symbolize a bounded event. There is debate about whether they are achievements or accomplishments.

1.6   Verbs of Creation

Verbs of creation are like change of state verbs, in that they have a result-state built into their meaning.

(7)   Kim built a house/made a cake.

However, examples like (7) differ from example like (6) in that the change of state is from 'not-being' to 'being'. But like the example in (6) this class of verb involves at least two, and probably more, subevents.

1.7 Mental and Emotional State Verbs

Other transitive verb types include examples such as (8) and (9) which involve stative verbs; there is no change of state: if you know Latin, then you know Latin. Nothing changes—it is much like knowing the square root of 9. This is just a property of the number system which we learn in primary school maths, which we then know throughout our lives.

(8) Jane knows Latin.
(9) Peter loves Jane.

In the same way, loving somebody is a state; it is just a condition of your being. Of course, it is possible to fall in love and it is possible to fall out of love, so a state can have a beginning and an end. It is not necessarily permanent. In fact, we distinguish between stage-level states, and individual-level states, where the individual-level state is a permanent condition of its subject, and a stage-level state is a temporary state: it is true of a stage of its subject. Verbs like those in (8) and (9) are simple in terms of their temporal structure and there is not much to say about them in terms of their internal structure, but we can discuss how they interact with the English aspectual system. For example, these verbs cannot occur in the English progressive: it is not possible to say *!Jane is knowing Latin* or *!Peter is loving Jane*.

1.8 Verbs of Receiving and Sending

Among other transitive verb types, there are verbs of receiving and sending, as in (10) and (11).

(10) Kim got a present.
(11) The ambassador sent a messenger.

These are also change of state verbs; more specifically, they are instantaneous change of state verbs. The sentence in (10) describes a transition where Kim goes from not having a present to having a present, and the sentence in (11) describes one where the ambassador goes from not having sent a messenger to having sent a messenger. Even though they are transitive, these verbs have the same temporal properties as intransitive MELT in the *ice-cream melted*. The examples in (10) and (11) are achievements, the class of achievement being an instantaneous change of state predicate with a simpler event structure than an accomplishment.

1.9 Intransitive and Transitive Verbs vs. Aspectual Classes

We can think then about the relationship between transitive and intransitive verbs and aspectual class: states, activities, achievements, and accomplishments. The aspectual categorization of verbs intersects with these two classes of verb: transitive and intransitive. An achievement verb can be transitive or intransitive. DIE is an achievement verb and intransitive. Intransitive DROWN is a manner-of-dying verb which is also an achievement. *Win a race*, is also an achievement, but it is transitive—WIN is always an achievement but can be either transitive or intransitive. Verbs with the temporal contour of processes—activity verbs—can be transitive or intransitive as well. Activities or processes are a simple event type that denotes some unbounded activity, with no change of state. Some examples include RUN and SWIM, which are intransitive and denote unbounded events, and PUSH in *push a cart*, which is transitive and unbounded, so it is an activity or process.

The generalization from achievements and activities is that there is not a perfect match between these two categories of verb and the transitive or intransitive category. That is important because this means although these aspectual distinctions might have some relevance to how arguments are realized, on their own they will not give us the argument realization analysis that people want when they look into an event structure. This is an important finding, given that one of the main reasons for exploring event structure is to see whether it is possible to predict the syntactic arguments that a verb has from its semantic structure. It means that we need to find other ways of exploring event complexity. We are not going to get that from transitivity because both achievements and processes can be either transitive or intransitive

In fact, stative verbs also can be transitive or intransitive. 'Knowing', 'having' or 'being' are states. 'Standing' is a state, but in English STAND usually comes with a place expression. For example, we usually say *the statue stands in Tian'anmen square* so *Tian'anmen square* is therefore the permanent place of statue. Accomplishments are the one class of verbs that involves a clear mapping to transitivity: accomplishments are always transitive. I think the reason why accomplishments are always transitive is that the event structure which corresponds to an accomplishment's temporal contour forces transitivity: in an accomplishment, there are minimally at least two events. The first event causes the second event and the Agent of the first event acts on the participant of the second event. This is the accomplishment prototype: they are either verbs of causation or verbs of creation, and for this reason they are always transitive.

1.10 Intransitive and Transitive Verbs and Other Complements

We can look at other argument-taking properties as well. Many intransitive verbs can be transitivized, so the following examples are all grammatical:

(12) The dog walked.
(13) He walked the dog.
(14) The door closed.
(15) He closed the door.

WALK in (12) is a simple activity, but the transitive version in (13) involves a kind of causative semantics as well. However, transitive WALK is not a causative verb in the same way as transitive OPEN because there is no result state. If you *walked the dog*, the dog did not enter a result state. Therefore, like (12), the example in (13) is an activity, despite the additional causative element in its meaning. The next pair of examples show the inchoative-causative alternation: as is usual in this alternation, the intransitive (14) is an achievement, but the transitive example (15) is an accomplishment. These examples show that embedding an achievement within causation gives you an accomplishment as in (14) and (15), but embedding an activity within causation just gives you another activity, as in (12) and (13). They also tell us that we have to be sensitive not only to the transitive or intransitive contrast, we also have to be sensitive to the aspectual class of the verb that we are looking at. But we can also see that aspectual class is evidence of event structure and event complexity.

Both intransitive and transitive verbs can have other non-nominal complements:

(16) He was sitting in the corner.
(17) The water froze solid.

There is very clear lexical restriction on sentences like (17), because you cannot say **the ice-cream melted liquid*. But it makes as much sense and it should be as possible as *the ice-cream froze solid*. We can see therefore that there is an element of lexical variability, even among the achievement verbs denoting a change of state.

1.11 Transitive and Intransitive Verbs with Other Complements

Some intransitive verbs must have non-nominal complements. Take *she seemed happy* for example, you can't say **she seemed*. The adjective *happy* is the predicative complement of *seemed*. Some transitive verbs can also have additional arguments. Ditransitives are built on transitives. You can say both *the ambassador sent a message* and *the ambassador sent the president a message*: SEND is either transitive or ditransitive. There are other constructions that affect valency and event structure. For example, it is possible to add a place expression to SLICE, as in *Kim sliced the apple into the pie-dish*, which denotes a kind of result state, and is therefore a resultative.

Some transitive verbs seem to have an obligatory further complement. It is not possible to say **Jane bolted the bookcase*; you must say *she bolted the bookcase to (something)*. And at the same time, it is not possible to have BOLT as a ditransitive, as you can't say **Jane bolted the wall the bookcase*.

1.12 Rappaport Hovav and Levin's (1998) Model

Recall that I discussed Rappaport Hovav and Levin (1998) in some detail in Lecture 4, when I explored how their event structures help in an analysis of polysemy. We can ask how Rappaport Hovav and Levin's model maps onto simple argument-taking facts. Here are examples (7)–(9) from Lecture 4.

   (18) He licked the ice-cream.
   (19) He walked the dog.
   (20) He made a cake.

(18) symbolizes an activity, (19) is an activity embedding the meaning of an unergative verb, and (20) is a complex event involving a verb of creation. Rappaport Hovav and Levin say that verbs' roots can be intransitive or transitive, and that roots can be embedded within larger event structure templates. As I said in Lecture 4, Rappaport Hovav and Levin's approach is to divide verb meaning up into two parts: they call one part the verb root, which is the inherent dictionary meaning of the verb—whatever the verb must mean. In the template, they identify the overall temporal structure of that verb, which is its *Aktionsart*. Therefore, they have a template for each of states, achievements, activities and accomplishments, which I return to in the next section.

2 Aktionsarten

This is a recap of the Vendler-Dowty classes (see the seminal paper, Vendler 1967). As we have seen, aspectual classes or *Aktionsarten* include states such as *be British*, *have green eyes*, and *love one's children*; activities, *run*, *ride a bike*, *drive a car*; achievements, *arrive*, *realize*; and accomplishments, like *build a house*, and *drink a beer*. Susan Rothstein has written a useful textbook on these (Rothstein 2004). The different temporal categories are not necessary fixed: in different research traditions, achievements are divided into achievements and "semelfactives" on the basis of a further temporal distinction.

2.1   Aktionsarten—*Rothstein* (2004)

Rothstein (2004) argues that there are two dimensions to aspectual meaning: "telicity" and "stages." She uses these two features to classify different aspectual classes. Each of the aspectual classes can be understood as [±telic, ±stages]. Telicity is boundedness: we can see the difference between a bounded event and an unbounded event in the verb DRINK with different objects. With a count NP as the object, as in *drink a beer*, the drinking event is bounded because it has a terminus. When the beer is finished, the event is finished. However, in *drink beer* with a mass noun object the event is not bounded, and it does not have a terminus. There is no endpoint built into the event structure of *drink beer*.

Let us talk about boundedness first of all, with this quotation from Rothstein (2004: 7), "Eventualities of the first kind are [+telic] or *telic*, and are movements towards an endpoint where the properties of the endpoint are determined by the description of the event.[2] Eventualities of the second kind are [-telic] or *atelic*; once they have started, they can go on indefinitely, since the nature of the eventuality itself does not determine its endpoint. The telic point is often called the culmination or set terminal point. Achievements and accomplishments are [+telic], and states and activities are [-telic]." That is to say, telicity distinguishes two broad classes of *Aktionsarten*. States and activities are both [-telic], while achievements and accomplishments are [+telic]. If there were a single property that distinguished states from activities and achievements from accomplishments, then the two properties or features would be enough to analyse all four event types.

Rothstein goes on to say, "The second property which is important in characterizing the Vendlerian classes, in addition to [±telic], is whether the verbs can occur in the progressive. [...] States do not go on or progress because they are inherently non-dynamic. Achievements do not go on or progress, because they are instantaneous, and they are over as soon as they have begun. Landman's (1992) account of the progressive allows an insightful formulation. He argues that the meaning of a progressive sentence is that a stage of the eventuality given by the verb occurred, or is occurring, where e is a stage of e′ if e develops

---

[2] "Eventuality" is Rothstein's superordinate term for the categories of states and dynamic events, including activities, achievements and accomplishments.

into e″." (Rothstein 2004: 11–12). What this means is that a complex event which has duration can be understood as a sequence of little micro-events, one after the other, and each micro-event is a stage where the stages are successive.

Rothstein (2004: 12) presents a table which distinguishes states, activities, achievements and accomplishments from each other, in terms of whether they are [±stage] or [±telic]. We can see this in Table 1.

States are [−stages], because they do not change. Because of this, they cannot occur in the English progressive: you cannot say *she is loving her mother* because there are no stages in 'loving'. Activities, on the other hand, are [+stages], because they do involve change from one micro-sub-event to the next. For example, 'talking' involves stages. When you are talking, it is construed as involving a successive series of events of talking. Achievements are [−stages], because they involve instantaneous change, for example in the case of 'dying' there is an instantaneous change from 'not dead' to 'dead': it is the change from 'not in the state' to 'being in the state', that makes achievements telic. Finally, accomplishments are [+stages]. There is a successive number of stages leading up to the change of state.

In the analysis of the event types in terms of telicity, states are [−telic], because they do not finish. Activities are [−telic], because they do not finish, or do not have a natural endpoint built into the meaning of the verb. Achievements are [+telic], because once the Ee has undergone a change of state, that is it—event over! Finally, accomplishments are [+telic]. The features [±stages] and [±telic] give us a representation of the different event types, from the simplest to the most complex. The simplest (states) has neither of these features, but next two the simplest have one each of these features (activities and achievements), and the most complex has both of these features (accomplishments). This feature analysis of the different *Aktionsarten* of English is therefore also iconic.

TABLE 1 Rothstein's (2004: 12) feature analysis of the *Aktionsarten*

	[± stages]	[±telic]
States	−	−
Activities	+	−
Achievements	−	+
Accomplishments	+	+

2.2 A Hierarchical Tree Approach

Rothstein's feature-based cross-classification is one approach. Another approach is to use a hierarchical tree. I have taken this hierarchical tree from Rothstein (2004: 13)—Rothstein contrasts it with her own feature-based approach—but it ultimately draws on work by Emmon Bach (1986). There is a huge literature on *Aktionsart* that goes back a very long way, at least to since Vendler (1957).

Figure 1 shows a Bach-style taxonomic hierarchy. Eventualities are at the top, and they are differentiated into states and non-states. Non-states are differentiated between processes (i.e. activities) and events. Events can be protracted or momentaneous (i.e. instantaneous), while momentaneous events can be happenings or culminations. I am not going to go through all of these categories, but I will talk about briefly the difference between a dynamic state and a static state, because you might think that the idea of the dynamic state is a contradiction. This is just the stage-level state vs. individual-level state that I mentioned earlier in the discussion of examples (8) and (9). The idea is that there are states which are permanent, and those which are not. For example, *Hong Kong is on the Pearl River Delta* is permanent but *I own a dark grey car* is temporary, even though it is a state (note that *own* is in the simple present), because at some point I will get rid of my car. Figure 1 captures this distinction between permanent states and impermanent states, with its claim that there are two subtypes of state. There is linguistic evidence for this partition of states into two subtypes, for example because the distinction between dynamic and static states is relevant in the semantics of perception verb complements particularly with dynamic adjectives. Bach's representation is like the inheritance hierarchies that we have seen elsewhere in these lectures.

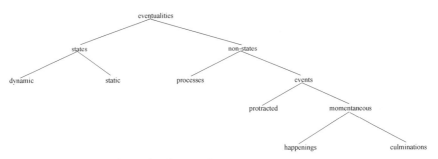

FIGURE 1   Taxonomic hierarchy of eventualities
ROTHSTEIN (2004: 13)

2.3 Diagnostics

We diagnose for telicity by using adverbial phrases such as *in an hour* and *for an hour*. *In an hour* is acceptable with verbs describing bounded events; that is, telic verbs, while *for an hour* is acceptable with verbs describing an unbounded event, that is atelic verbs.[3] This gives us the following data:

(21) He ran for an hour.
(22) *He died for an hour.
(23) He built a trainset in an hour.
(24) *He had blue eyes in an hour.

Example (21) is acceptable because RUN is atelic, but (22) is not, because DIE is telic and *for an hour* diagnoses for an atelic event. Similarly, (23) is acceptable because *built a trainset* is telic and *in an hour* is good with a telic event, but (24) is not because *had blue eyes* is atelic.

It is possible to diagnose for [±stages] by the ability to occur in the progressive:

(25) *She is loving the baby.
(26) She is running.
(27) *She is realizing the answer.
(28) She is building a house.

(25) is a state and (27) is an achievement, therefore they cannot occur in the progressive. (26) and (28) are respectively an activity and accomplishment, so they are acceptable. Examples (25) and (27) are bad, because they are [−stages] and therefore cannot occur in the progressive; (26) and (28) are ok because they are [+stages] and can occur in the progressive.

There are, of course, problems with the diagnostics. One problem is to do with so-called "run-up" achievements which are acceptable in the progressive. For example, *the train is arriving at Platform 9* is okay even though achievement verbs are instantaneous changes of state. Strictly speaking, the train is not "arriving" at Platform 9: the passengers are still on the train and the train is still moving. But it is possible to construe this event as having a kind of run-up before it actually happens and it is possible to use the progressive to describe

---

3   We need to get the time-frame right. *In an hour* might be appropriate for a predicate such as *cook dinner*, but will not fit events that naturally have a much shorter duration. In those cases, we would use an adverbial such as *in a minute,* or *in a second.*

that run-up period. Likewise, it is grammatical to say *she is dying in the hospice* even though 'dying' is instantaneous. In an example such as *she is dying in the hospice*, the speaker is predicting the instantaneous change of event symbolized by 'dying' because the person they are talking about is terminally ill. This is another run-up achievement. One question is whether there are any generalizations about these verbs that allow them to work in this way. One way of accounting for achievements that allow a run-up interpretation might be that run-up achievements are verbs that have a kind of metaphorical or literal motion built into their meaning, but verbs like *realize*, which have no metaphorical or literal motion in their meaning, are not interpretable as run-up achievements. Because of the existence of run-up achievements, some people divide achievements into two classes: achievements like ARRIVE and DIE, and semelfactives like REALIZE, which can never occur in the progressive.

Another issue to be aware of is that language use changes. Shakespeare had very few, if any, progressives: in the time of Shakespeare I would say *I lecture* to describe what I am doing now, not *I am lecturing*. And there are varieties of contemporary English which use the progressive for states where I would use the simple present. For example, when I have bought things over the telephone, I have been asked, "How are you spelling your name?" where I would use, "How do you spell your name?". This is change in progress and a dialectal difference and we have to be careful that diagnostics such as the progressive will not always work in every dialect.

When we use the progressive as a diagnostic, another problem that I have mentioned before, is the imperfective paradox. This is to do with the interpretation of accomplishments in the progressive. In *he was building a house when he went bankrupt*, the house is not finished, so in the case of an accomplishment, the progressive does not mean that the event denoted by the verb happens again and again as it does in 'running'. The stages in an activity and in an accomplishment are different. In an activity, the ordering of the stages does not matter. In an accomplishment, the temporal profile is directed, and the ordering of the stages does matter. This is why some scholars (Rappaport Hovav and Levin 2010) make a distinction between scalar and non-scalar events. Scalar events have ordered stages. Another issue to be aware of in using the progressive as a diagnostic is that that *Aktionsart* is not necessarily a property of verbs on their own; there are cases where it is clearly a property of verbs together with their arguments, particularly the object. For example, we have seen this in the discussion above about the difference between *drink a beer* and *drink beer*: it is possible to *drink beer for an hour* and to *drink a beer in an hour*, but it is not possible to *drink a beer for an hour* or to *drink beer in an hour*.

2.4 The Verb Hierarchy of Gisborne (2010)

In Gisborne (2010), I presented hierarchies of verb types and event types, for English. The verb-type hierarchy is simple, and given in Figure 2.

The diagram makes a number of claims the main one being that a ditransitive is a subtype of transitive which is a subtype of verb. But we should also note that this hierarchy invites criticism. For example, if a ditransitive is subtype of the transitive type, why is the transitive not a sub-type of intransitive? Why split the category verb in this way? After all, at the top of the hierarchy, it claims that all verbs of English have subjects so what is the difference between the node 'intransitive verb' and the node 'verb'? For example, even though weather verbs do not have a semantic argument, they must have a syntactic subject (the *it* in *it rains* is completely meaningless). No verb in English can be less than intransitive. And also where should I have put verbs that take infinitival complements or predicative complements? The diagram does not accommodate verbs such as SEEM and EXPECT in *she seemed to agree* or *we expected him to win*.

There are more questions to ask about the verb hierarchy. How does it map onto the different semantic classes that we have been discussing? It is not the case that all ditransitive verbs have the same semantic structure, nor is it the case that all transitive verbs have the same semantic structure, or even intransitive verbs. One task is to see how we map the verb hierarchy onto an event hierarchy.

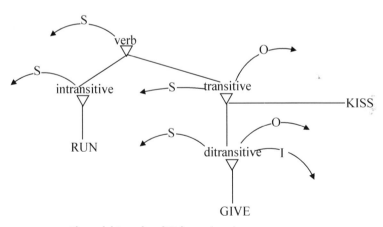

FIGURE 2   The verb hierarchy of Gisborne (2010)

2.5 The Event Hierarchy of Gisborne (2010)

How can we map the verb hierarchy onto the event hierarchy? Figure 3 presents the representation of the event hierarchy from Gisborne (2010). Like Figure 2, Figure 3 is open to improvement.

At the top of Figure 3, I have given the highest or most abstract event type the name 'situation', which is another word for Rothstein's term, eventuality. The diagram subclassifies situation into 'state' and what I have called 'happening'. There are differences in how we approach the classifications shown in the event hierarchy from how we approach the verb hierarchy, because it does not seem possible to say that states are more basic than other event types, and therefore that activities and so forth are subtypes of states. I have analyzed 'happening' as having a number of subtypes: 'acting', 'doing' and 'becoming' which in turn have properties to do with what participant relations they have, how many participant relations they have, whether they have Results, and so

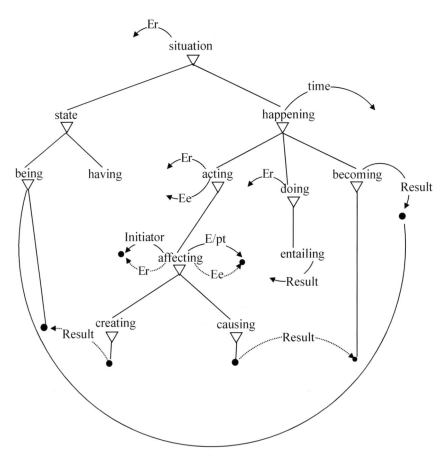

FIGURE 3   The event hierarchy of Gisborne (2010)

on. There are analyses in Figure 3 that I might now do differently; as in the changes I would make to Figure 2, these are also to do with how I have organized the type information. For example, the analysis would be improved if there were a single-argument 'doing' as a type which two-argument 'acting' inherited from, so the hierarchy would be taller. It should be possible to show various key associations between different events. Looking at the diagram now, I am not sure what the difference is meant to be between 'becoming' and 'entailing'. They have the same structure in that they both involve dynamic events with a Result; the main difference is in terms of the restrictions on the value of the Result relation: 'becoming' (the predicate of a change of state) must have a 'being' as its Result. This implies that I should have set up 'becoming' as a subtype of 'entailing'.

Within the context of understanding that it is possible to improve the analysis, Figure 3 represents a way of trying to capture the relationship between event complexity on the one hand, and *Aktionsart* on the other. In part this is done by having an augmented ontology of participant types: Figure 3 shows both WG's general semantic participants, Er and the Ee, and force-dynamic participants, the Initiator and the Endpoint. It also shows whether an event type will have a resulting event type. We can think this through in more detail by looking at how the representation analyses one or two example cases.

In the diagram, there are three subtypes of 'happening': 'acting' is an activity with two participants. It does not have a Result, and it does not have to be the case that one participant acts on the other: for example in 'sniffing', the sense of SNIFF in *I was sniffing the flowers*, there are two participants, but the subject does not act on the direct object in any way. 'Doing' is an activity with just one participant; it does not have a Result. An example would be RUN in *he was running*; the difference between 'acting' and 'doing' is the presence or absence of an Ee. As I said above, 'becoming' is the predicate for a change of state. It has a Result which is an example of 'being'. The diagram represents an attempt at capturing different types of event complexity within a single network.

There is a sub-type of 'acting', which I have called 'affecting', where the participants act on each other. There does not need to be a Result—an example would be LICK as in *Jane licked the ice-cream*. If you lick the ice-cream, then you affect the ice-cream. But there is no Result built in; no change of state is built in the meaning of the verb LICK. Another subtype of 'acting' is 'creating', within which the Result is an instance of 'being'—an example is MAKE in *we made a cake*—and 'causing', of course, in the sense of a classic causative verb such as KILL. There is also a subtype of 'doing' which I have unhelpfully called 'entailing'. This is a highly attenuated sense, which simply consists of an action with an entailed Result. We will come to this pattern when we examine HIT below.

The diagram is necessarily partial. I have also left out the analysis of ditransitive verbs which are verbs that can either have a Result or a Purpose. The diagram does not show any event types which exploit the Purpose relation, and I have avoided using labels which correspond to the different event types or *Aktionsarten*. But there is some iconicity in the hierarchy. The simplest event types are at the top of the hierarchy. These event types have fewer associative links. The more complex event types are nearer the bottom of the hierarchy. The state/event distinction is given at the top. States then divided into two classes which relate to two types of stative meaning rather than the static/dynamic distinction. 'Acting' and 'doing' are both activities (the simplest type of event) because they do not have Results. 'Becoming' is the label for an achievement. 'Becoming' is an achievement because it is a 'happening' with a Result and it is also instantaneous. One of the missing elements from this hierarchy is time indices: to be complete it should show the time relations of complex events.

I have also shown two different kinds of accomplishment in this hierarchy. In Figure 3 I have shown a distinction between 'creating' and 'causing'. 'Creating' has something 'being' as its Result, whereas 'causing' has a 'becoming' as its Result, and then 'becoming' has something 'being' as its Result. This distinction is intended to capture the different semantics of MAKE in *make a cake*, which means 'cause to exist', and OPEN, which means 'cause to become not-closed'.

The network approach represented in Figure 4 presents a hierarchical event structure which allows us to show some of the properties of the different aspectual types that Rothstein discusses. In certain cases, this is obvious: within this model, some event types are composed out of others, so 'becoming' can be the Result of 'causing'. But other facts can also be accommodated. As we have seen, in *he was drinking beer*, there is an unbounded event, whereas *he was drinking a beer* is bounded and interacts in different ways with time adverbs. This is about the verbs' semantics interacts with the referent of their object, and whether the object has mass or count properties. The network gives a suggestion about why DRINK might behave like this. Verb meanings such as 'drinking' are high in the hierarchy, and therefore relatively underspecified, so they are more likely to have variable grammatical behavior than verb meanings which are lower in the hierarchy and more specified. The less specified a verb meaning, the more likely it is that it will be affected by the semantics of its arguments.

The event hierarchy shows some simple conclusions that can be made about the mapping from the event hierarchy onto the verb hierarchy. Simple events map to intransitives if they only have an Er argument; to transitives if they have an Er and an Ee. Verbs with Results are more complex: SINK is a verb with a Result in its semantics, but it is intransitive, whereas HIT also has a Result, but is transitive. However, there are three complex event types where there are some straightforward generalizations about the mapping: verbs whose Result Isa 'being' or 'becoming' are always transitive. These are the verbs of creation or change of state. And verbs whose Result (or other outcome relation) Isa 'having' will be ditransitive.

These conclusions mean that it should be possible to learn the mapping relations between syntax and semantics. And although event complexity, whether determined by *Aktionsart* or by other means, is a confound, because it introduces a mismatch between syntax and semantics, there are some generalizations which apply in a straightforward way in some cases of event complexity.

2.6 Gisborne's (2010) *Event Hierarchy and* Aktionsart

We might then ask how this event hierarchy maps onto Rothstein's account of the different *Aktionsarten*. Let us put states aside (they are just modelled as 'being' or 'having' in Figure 3), and focus on the grammar of activities, achievements, and accomplishments.

In Figure 4, I revise the original event hierarchy and try to give a better analysis.

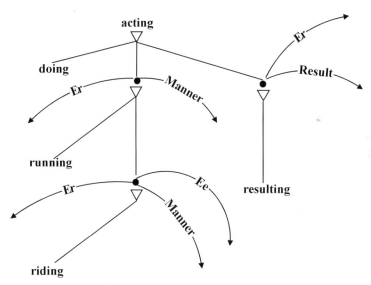

FIGURE 4 Revised event hierarchy
Note: In the diagram I use a 'manner' attribute to capture the differences between, for example, 'running' and 'jogging'. But it might be better to represent this with multiple inheritance so that rather than manner being a feature, it is a classification.

2.7 Activities

Let us begin with activities, which just have a single participant. Activities are unbounded and have stages. We can distinguish activities into activities which are just 'doing' (e.g. 'running'), activities which have two participants (e.g. 'riding') and activities which have a Result (that is change of state verbs). Figure 4 presents a different analysis from Figure 3 in that it brings 'acting', 'doing' and 'resulting' under the same hierarchy and shows that by default 'acting' verbs only have an Er, but there is a subtype with an Er and an Ee. It also claims that 'manner' verbs are a subtype of 'acting' verbs.[4]

We can map these predicates onto the verb-type hierarchy of Figure 2 very easily. Because dependencies are verb-linking prototypes, by default the Er of the sense of the verb maps onto the Subject of the verb, and the Ee maps onto its Direct Object. There are, of course, non-default linking patterns, where Ees maps onto other syntactic arguments. For example, in *I know that Scipio defeated Hannibal*, the clause *that Scipio defeated Hannibal* is not a direct object, so the Ee maps on the clause referent, not a direct object. (Clausal complements are not direct objects because they do not passivize.) However, we can put these non-default examples aside for now.

2.8 Achievements

Achievements, of course, are just simple changes of state. We need to be able to capture the two kinds, as in *she realized the answer* and *the train arrived at Platform 9*. We have also seen the relevant temporal structure with HIT and SINK. Although Figure 5, which analyzes achievements, is for intransitive verbs, bear in mind that not all achievements are intransitive.

An achievement Isa 'becoming' which has a Result, which Isa resulting state. And the Agent of the 'becoming' event is also the participant in the resulting state. The participants, the Er of 'becoming' and that of 'state' map onto the same entity. Figure 5 captures Rappaport Hovav and Levin's (1998) "internally caused changes of state" as well as their achievements. The internally caused change of state verbs are verbs like BLOOM and BLOSSOM, where an entity undergoes a change from one state to another for internal reasons.[5] They also argue that a stative verb can be coerced into participating in an achievement

---

[4] I have used the event type name 'resulting' rather than 'causing', because as I have said before there is a 'causing' prototype, which 'resulting' is just part of—fully fledged causation involves participants acting on participants, but it is possible for an event to have another event as its Result without it being the case that participants are involved in a force-dynamic transfer.

[5] In terms of their temporal structures, these verbs are just achievements, so it is not clear why Rappaport Hovav and Levin set them up as a separate category of verb.

CLASSES OF EVENTS AND ASPECTUAL CLASS

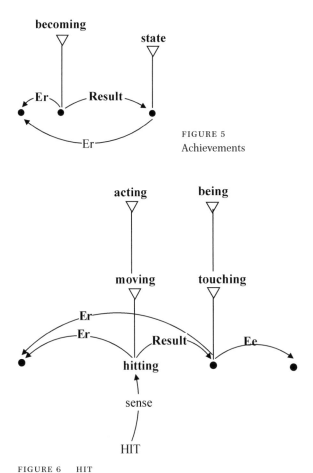

FIGURE 5
Achievements

FIGURE 6   HIT

structure by having a 'becoming' predicate added to its structure. On the evidence of SINK which I talked about in Lecture 3, we can take it that verbs like BLOSSOM are simple achievements. But what about HIT?

2.9   HIT (*Semelfactives*)

With HIT, there is a state as the value of the Result relation, which is 'touching': the diagram says that HIT means 'touching as a result of moving'. Therefore, HIT has the same semantic structure as the model for an achievement, except that 'touching' also has a second argument: it has an Ee and an Er. There has to be an Ee because there has to be a landmark of 'touching': the toucher has to touch something. However, HIT is not a change of state verb: it does not entail that the Er of the 'touching' second event undergoes a change of state. Aspectually, it is just a punctual verb, with a complex structure; it is just an achievement. But in the progressive HIT goes through the same aspectual coercion that applies to any punctual verb which is not a change of state verb: it is the construed repetitively: *he was hitting the dog* means that he was repeatedly hitting the dog, that there were several different instances of contact. This means that the WG analysis does not just limit itself to an account of event structure, and hierarchical relations between events. The aspectual differences also involve argument-mapping patterns among the different subevents.

I have also simplified Figure 6 by leaving the force-dynamic relations out. Figure 6 shows the same kind of semantic structure as the diagram for SINK (see Figure 1 in Lecture 3). The main difference is that HIT has the second participant, the Ee, shown as the Ee of 'touching'. I have classified 'touching' as a kind of 'being' which is a stative verb. But perhaps the classification of 'touching' is wrong. Certainly, Figure 6 is incomplete because HIT can also be classed as a semelfactive verb, in systems that divide the achievement class into two subtypes. The only way that you can use the progressive with HIT is on this repeated iteration interpretation (DROP is another similar verb). Semelfactives are instantaneous; there is no durative result state. As a result, a better analysis will show HIT as involving two events that share a temporal index. Therefore, one argument could be that the difference between a semelfactive and an achievement is that subevents of semelfactives are both punctual and co-temporal, whereas achievements' subevents have different time indices, and the second event is stative. A revised analysis of HIT is given in Figure 7.

Figure 7 shows HIT with a time index, showing that both events have to happen at the same time.

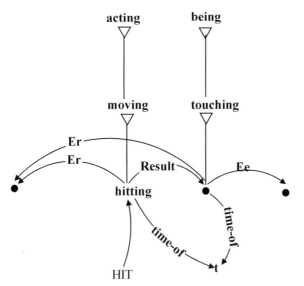

FIGURE 7
A revised analysis of HIT

2.10 What Kind of Verb Is GIVE?

Because I am talking about double-object verbs, one question that I want to ask is what kind of verb GIVE might be? Is GIVE an achievement or is GIVE a semelfactive? I think it must be an achievement, not a semelfactive because the sub-events can be factored out from each other. You can say that s*he gave him the toy for half an hour*, where *half an hour* modifies the result state 'having', not the transfer of ownership. The transfer of ownership can have its own modifier, so you can say *she immediately gave him the toy for half an hour*. This kind of structure is the same as SINK; it is not the same as HIT.

It seems reasonable to say that GIVE is an achievement. However, consider the data in (29) and (30)

(29) ?She stopped giving him the present.
(30) She is giving him the toy.

(29) suggests some kind of duration, but I think it is weird. Bear in mind that even achievements can have their aspectual structure changed depending on how they interact with their arguments. If you make the direct object plural, then *giving* becomes an activity. Therefore, if you give a lot of presents to a child, then that event is an activity; that is, it has stages. If you give only one present to a child, that event is an achievement. In this respect, then, GIVE behaves like DRINK in *drinking a beer* vs. *drinking beer*, which shows that the difference between a count noun object and a mass noun one can change the *Aktionsart* of achievements by changing the direct object's semantics. The same is true with GIVE as in *she stopped giving him money* because, like the plural, the mass noun coerces the event into an event with stages. Achievements are instantaneous and do not have stages.

2.11 Revised Intransitive Achievements

Here is a revised way of thinking about achievements.

Figure 8 claims that the two subevents are not exactly co-temporal. They must be immediately one after the other, so they can be factored out very slightly. Whereas in an accomplishment, the sub-events can be more temporally apart. With a transitive achievement, the diagram would be the same, except that there is an Ee.

This diagram looks the same as the diagram for HIT except that there is also an Ee. An example would be REACH in *the climber reached the summit*—note that there is a "run-up" in *the climber is reaching the summit*.

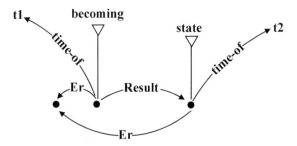

FIGURE 8   Revised (intransitive) achievements

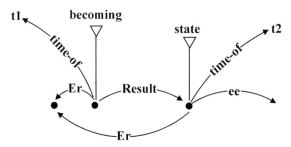

FIGURE 9   Transitive achievements

2.12   Accomplishments

In the original event hierarchy, I claimed that verbs of creating involved a different semantic structure from verbs of causing. Verbs of creating, like *make (a model aeroplane)*, *build (a house)*, *bake (a cake)* can be distinguished from verbs of causing, like *break (the glass)*, *open (the door)*, *lock (the door)*. The claim was that both kinds of event involve a kind of action with a force-dynamic transfer, but verbs of creating only have two subevents whereas verbs of causing have three. Figure 10 analyzes verbs of creating.

Verbs of creating cause something to be, so the causing event has an Agent and a Patient, or an Initiator and an Endpoint, or an Antagonist and an Agonist. The Agonist is the Er of the state of 'being'. Figure 11 says if you make a cake, then the result is that the cake exists.

Note the difference between the structure in Figure 9 and the structure in Figure 10. The issue is whether this is a good model for verbs of creation or not; we need a notion of temporal subinterval. Figure 10 works as long as the 'making' node has stages. As we have seen in the discussion of activities, the event structure can be very simple, whereas the temporal structure is more complex. We need to think about two things at the same time: one is the relationship between the events, and the other is the temporal contours of the events, their durations, whether they have stages or not, and how we represent these different things. They are all part of the analysis of *Aktionsart*.

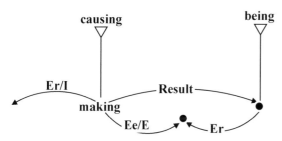

FIGURE 10 Verbs of creating

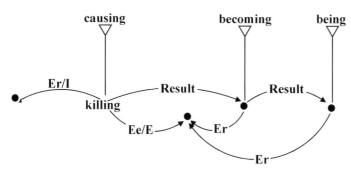

FIGURE 11 Verbs of causing

Here in Figure 11 is a representation for the semantic structure of verbs of causing, exemplified with 'killing'. A verb of causing embeds the event structure of an achievement under a causing node. There is a debate about whether verbs of change of state are accomplishments or achievements. They collocate with AT as in *he killed the pig at 5 o'clock* which indicates that they are punctual like achievements. However, Rappaport Hovav and Levin 1998 include them in the class of accomplishment (see §1.7 of Lecture 4).

There are three nodes of the events of causing: the causing event, the becoming event, and the state of being event at the end. At the bottom of Figure 11, you can see the ways which the participants are in this event are mapped onto those different relationships. The claim here is that verbs of causing are actually more complex than verbs of creating, while the apparent complexity of verbs of creating comes from is the way in which we understand the stages of the creating event. We have to have a way of thinking about the temporal structure of the different subevents as well as the relationships between the different subevents.

The crucial thing in order to understand the *Aktionsart* is the relationship between the subevents and then the participants in these subevents. Then we have to understand the temporal properties of each of the subevents. The subevents can have different temporal properties along the way. The analysis that I have just given you is a satisfactory analysis, because it embeds an achievement under a 'causing' event. Because different subevents can share temporal indices, this model works for instantaneous causation as well as more durative causation, so for example verbs like DRINK in *drink the beer* need to have stages built into them as well.

2.13   *Interim Conclusions*

We learn from this exercise that it is not only event structure that is relevant to *Aktionsart*. This is certainly one issue, but it also matters what kind of temporal structure that the different events have. This means that for aspectual purposes, we need some kind of representation of temporal structure—and in fact this goes beyond the temporal indices I have already used, because we also need a way of representing stages. One possibility is that we adapt a representation from Holmes (2005). I will not take you all the way through Holmes' analysis of 'galloping', but I want to show you that 'galloping' is temporally structured.

'Galloping' has bits that occur one time and then at successive times one after the other. Each successive part of the galloping event has its own time index, and each part of the event is a stage: 'galloping' has been broken down into a series of stepping events and in this way, Figure 12 builds the stages of 'galloping' into a WG network diagram. This analysis models how 'galloping' is a complex event where a horse has to move each of its 4 legs recurringly in a special sequence with the sequencing adds up to the event involving discrete stages—in this case shown by the movement of each leg. Because each stage

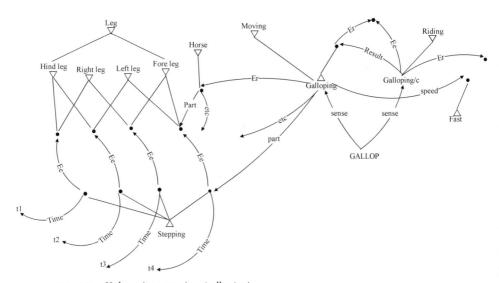

FIGURE 12   Holmes (2005: 170) on 'galloping'

CLASSES OF EVENTS AND ASPECTUAL CLASS   233

has own temporal index, the diagram permits an analysis of the relationship of the stages. We could take such an approach and use it in the model of the *Aktionsart* of the event structure of verbs of creation, which needs stages too. We can compare this approach with Rappaport Hovav and Levin (1998).

2.14   *Comparison with Rappaport Hovav and Levin's (1998) Approach*
Let us take another look at Rappaport Hovav and Levin's analysis of different event types, which they claim corresponds to different *Aktionsarten*. I discussed this model in Lecture 4, as part of looking at theories of structured polysemy. Here, I am interested in the model as a way of thinking about how event structures map onto different *Aktionsarten*.

manner → [x ACT$_{<MANNER>}$]
    (e.g., *job, run, creak, whistle, ...*)
instrument → [x ACT$_{<INSTRUMENT>}$]
    (e.g., *brush, hammer, saw, shovel, ...*)
placeable object → [x CAUSE [BECOME [Y WITH *<THING>*]]]
    (e.g., *butter, oil, paper, tile, wax, ...*)
place → [x CAUSE [BECOME, [y *<PLACE>*]]]
    (e.g., *bag, box, cage, crate, garage, pocket, ...*)
Internally caused state → [x *<STATE>*]
    (e.g. *bloom, blossom, decay, flower, rot, rust, sprout, ...*)
externally caused state → [[x ACT] CAUSE [BECOME [y *<STATE>*]]]
    (e.g. *break, dry, harden, melt, open, ...*)

FIGURE 13   Rappaport Hovav and Levin's (1998: 109) templates

This approach takes a verb meaning, and embeds it in a larger template of meaning. For example, activity verbs like JOG, or RUN, or CREAK, or WHISTLE, fit into a manner template, which says [x ACT] and there is a manner modifier on how *x* acts. That is how they would analyze the meaning of RUN. Then, the next template also contains simple activity verb, such as *the brush the floor*, or *they hammer the nail*, or *they saw the wood*. These events are just actions with a single participant with an instrument index, and an instrument modifier. A placeable object verb, is more complicated. Its structure is '*x* causes *y* to become with something', which is supposed to capture the meaning of *butter the bread*. The sentence *he buttered the bread* means 'he caused bread to become with butter'. Placement verbs are like *bag the apples, box the toys*, and *cage the dangerous lion*, whose structure is '*x* causes *y* to become at a place'. *John bags the apples* means 'John causes the apples to become in the bag': the result location of the event is the name of the verb. The internally caused state in this representation, like, BLOOM or BLOSSOM, is '*x* moves into a certain state', and the externally caused state is '*x* acted, and in their action they caused y to become a state'.

There are aspects of Rappaport Hovav and Levin's model I find it hard to understand. How is it possible to justify the distribution of verb roots in the templates? Verb roots appear in two different positions in the event structure template: as modifiers in the case of manner verbs, and as predicates in the case of result verbs. It is not clear why there is this different distribution. In Word Grammar, event names inherit from an event type and although the event that a verb is named for can occur in different positions in the network, it does not occur in relations as different as modifier vs. predicate. Another challenge in the Rappaport Hovav and Levin model is why placeable object verbs are less complex than externally caused state verbs. If you 'cause bread become with butter', you are acting, and you are doing something, but the template does not accommodate the fact that the Agent is acting. I do not understand why placeable object verbs do not have an action in their template but, in this model, externally caused state verbs do. The templates involve different theories of causation: events cause events, in the case of externally caused state verbs; individuals cause events in the case of placeable object verbs.

3   The Role of Arguments

This section is about the role of arguments in an event structure. I have already mentioned that arguments can change aspectuality. Previously, I have discussed how this affects the meaning of DRINK which has an unbounded (atelic) interpretation when its object is mass and a bounded (telic) interpretation when its object is countable. However, there are other semantic contributions that arguments can make. One of them is that the object can "measure out" the event. Consider these examples.

(31)   She was combing her hair.
(32)   She was mowing the lawn.

In (31) and (32) the direct object measures out the event, so for example if you have somebody with lots of hair, then there is lots of combing and the event is not complete until all of the hair has been combed. Likewise, the event of mowing the lawn is only half complete if only half of the lawn has been mown and complete once all of the lawn is mown.

(33) Kit ran into the room.
(34) Children ran into the room.

The examples in (33) and (34) indicate that subjects can also change aspectuality. The event described in (33) is instantaneous: Kit starts outside of the room, and ends up inside of the room and there is an instantaneous change as Kit enters the room. However, (34) is durative; the event duration depends on how many children there are. Example (34) involves an event with stages—one stage for each child. These examples tell us subjects and objects can both change aspectuality.

According to Carlota Smith (1997), (31) and (32) are vague.[6] Both have an activity reading: some lawn-mowing/hair-combing got done. But they also have an accomplishment reading: both events have natural final endpoints. This means that both examples can occur with both *for an hour* and *in an hour* modifiers: you can say *Kit mowed the lawn for an hour* or *Kit mowed the lawn in an hour*, as *mow the lawn* is vague between the activity and accomplishment interpretations.

Why are both okay? The reason why must be something to do with what we know about *combing hair* and *mowing the lawn*. The difference is one of construal. On the accomplishment interpretation, the *lawn* is a bounded space, which makes up a scale—you mow a small part, and then larger and larger parts of the lawn until it has all been mown. On the activity reading the lawn is just a space where mowing can happen.

The difference between (33) and (34) comes out clearly with temporal adverbials.

(35) !Kit ran into the room for an hour.
(36) Children ran into the room for an hour.
(37) Kit ran into the room in less than a minute.
(38) !Children ran into the room in less than a minute.

The example in (35) is only possible if *Kit* recurringly runs into the room. It is like *hitting your hand*. If the event repeats, then the modifier is fine. The examples in (33) and (34) show how the referent of the subject can affect the temporal interpretation of a verb, just as the object can in the familiar *beer* examples: *drinking a beer* and *drinking beer*. This is the difference between subject or

---

6 Vagueness is distinguished from ambiguity: if an expression is ambiguous it is polysemous but if it is vague, it is not, so the examples in (31) and (32) do not involve polysemy.

objects which are singular count nouns and subject or objects which are mass or plural nouns. Singular count nouns are inherently bounded, but mass or plural nouns are not. Therefore, singular count nouns can provide an event with a terminus. Because *Kit* is a single entity, when *Kit* traverses a path, as in (33), the event is complete. The same applies to *drinking a beer* and example (37): *a beer* and *Kit* are singular count nouns, thus they are both bounded, whereas *beer* in *beer* in *drinking beer* and *children* in (38) are unbounded. In order to capture these sorts of effects, we need a semantics of nouns, but this would take us too far from events. Therefore, we are just going to satisfy ourselves by distinguishing between stuff and entities: mass and plural nouns are stuff, entities are singular count nouns which are construed as bounded objects.

This leaves us with one problem left to address: the imperfective paradox. This is the observation that for every subinterval or stage of *I am drinking tea*, I have drunk some tea, but for every subinterval or stage of *I am building a house*, I have not built a house—each stage involves progression towards a house being built. How are we going to make sense of this? Also, how do we make sense of these facts in *he was drinking tea when he died* versus *he was building a house when he died*. In the former example, he has drunk tea whereas in the latter example, he has not built a house. We can address this by coming back to Holmes' analysis of GALLOP above.

The analysis of GALLOP gave us a way of thinking about the different stages of an event. If we think about tea-drinking and house-building in terms of their stages, we see that tea-drinking (more or less) involves stages, each of which is itself an instance of tea-drinking. But house-building is cumulative: each stage cumulatively brings you closer to the building of a house. Therefore, we have to distinguish between stages which are the same, and stages which cumulate along the way.

This means then that the representation for accomplishments is too crude. The Result is not the Result of a 'causing' event; it's the Result of the final subinterval of the 'causing' event. We thus need to have a more subtle way of representing cumulation.

3.1   Conclusion

This a good place to conclude because it reminds us how complex some of our construals of the world can be, and how oversimplified many linguistic representations can be. We need to bear in mind that linguistic representations are not necessarily subtle enough. This brings us back to my general main theme, which is that, as well as finding the prototypes of our categories, we linguists also have to state generalizations at the right level. We have to get enough information in our generalizations, and sometimes the generalizations we find are very small and highly detailed, with the analysis of accomplishment verbs showing how there is a lot of detail in just one small area of grammar.

But we have also seen a significant degree of complexity. Aspectual class is obviously related to event complexity, but nevertheless, semelfactives and achievements need to be distinguished by other aspects of their temporal properties, particularly the configuration of the subevents' temporal indices. In another way, we need to distinguish between states and activities and here the distinction is one of complexity: activities, achievements, and accomplishments have stages, whereas states do not.

We have also made some tentative first steps towards modeling the relationship between the hierarchy of event types, and the hierarchy of verb types. Here the results are provisional, not least because I only partially revised the event hierarchy from Gisborne (2010). But the results were suggestive that it should be possible to define some learnable generalizations, which indicates that this area should not require argument-linking algorithms. And it looks as though aspectual class, being derived from event complexity rather than driving it, will not be implicated in argument realization.

One element of event structure which is widely exploited which I have not brought to bear on this discussion is the issue of scalarity. In recent work by Levin and Rappaport Hovav, see Wechsler (2015), and other scholars, event structures that involve changes of state are analysed in terms of scales, where a scale consists of a directed set of stages. We look at scalarity in the next lecture.

LECTURE 9

Conflation Classes, Transitivity Alternations and Argument Realization

In this lecture I am interested in exploring argument realization by thinking about possible and impossible verb meanings. I argue that we can use the device of sublexeme to capture argument realization facts and extend it to transitivity alternations, because sublexemes capture variability within a lexeme. I will also explore the issue of what it is possible to include in a verb meaning and what it is not possible to include. First, I discuss conflation classes: Talmy's typology with its differentiation of verb-framed and satellite-framed languages, together with Levin and Rappaport Hovav's arguments about manner/result complementarity; second, I look at transitivity alternations: do verbs preserve their meanings in different argument configurations? And finally, I come to argument realization: how do we model argument-linking between syntax and semantics? WG approaches argument realization in a declarative account using the device of the sublexeme in its default inheritance classified network. In building up the WG account, I return to some data sets we have seen before: for example, in looking at how to model transitivity alternations I return to ditransitive verbs in order to compare them with their double complement counterparts.

1   Conflation Classes

1.1   *How Do We Model Conflation Classes?*
How do we model conflation classes? Rappaport Hovav and Levin (2010), among other papers, talk about "manner" meanings being incompatible with "result" meanings within a single verb. A manner verb is a verb that lexicalizes the manner of an event; for example, RUN is a manner-of-motion verb. Their

All original audio-recordings and other supplementary material, such as any hand-outs and powerpoint presentations for the lecture series, have been made available online and are referenced via unique DOI numbers on the website www.figshare.com. They may be accessed via a QR code for the print version of this book. In the e-book, both the QR code and dynamic links are available, and can be accessed by a mouse-click.

© NIKOLAS GISBORNE. REPRODUCED WITH KIND PERMISSION FROM THE AUTHOR BY KONINKLIJKE
BRILL NV, LEIDEN, 2020 | DOI:10.1163/9789004375291_010

claim is that manner verbs are incompatible with lexicalized results. Actually, I do not think that this can be true. There is a tendency in the data for verbs to exclude manner meanings if they have a result in their meaning, and to exclude results if they have a manner element (and that is a research problem in its own right) but it is not an absolute restriction. We can think about this claim by thinking about manner-of-killing verbs. KILL lexicalizes a result, therefore a manner-of-killing verb must lexicalize a manner and a result. If you *behead someone*, then you have killed them in a particular manner—chopping their head off. Moreover, if you remove someone's head, it is entailed that they have been killed. There are various classes of verb in the literature which have been claimed to falsify manner/result complementarity: others include manner-of-cooking verbs.[1] Even though Levin and Rappaport Hovav's claim that manner meanings are incompatible with result meanings faces a number of challenges in the literature on the basis of manner-of-killing, manner-of-cooking and manner-of-changing-location verbs (such as CLIMB), it is not straightforward to prove wrong, as we shall see later.[2]

1.2 Talmy's Typological Split

Talmy (1985a) claims that there is a typological split between verb-framed and satellite-framed languages. Talmy's categories involve the non-conflation of path and manner. English is satellite-framed. It conflates motion and manner in verbs such as RUN, JOG, and HOP, but excludes path. Path is usually expressed by a preposition: RUN INTO, GO OUT, FALL DOWN—this is the Germanic pattern. Spanish is verb-framed: motion and path are conflated but manner is not. For example, ENTRAR means *go in*, SALIR *go out*, SUBIR *go up* and BAJAR means *go down*. The Romance languages have shifted from the Latin pattern which was nearer being satellite-framed, like English, to this verb-framed pattern.[3] If a Spanish speaker wants to express a manner, then they would use a participle to express the manner as in *entró corriendo* which means *he entered running*.

Actually, English is mixed in terms of Talmy's typology, because English has a lot of Latinate vocabulary. For example, English has verbs like ENTER, DESCEND and so on. Talmy's claim relates to Levin and Rappaport Hovav's

---

1 Manner-of-cooking verbs are perhaps even more robust examples: if you bake something, you put it in dry heat in an oven until it has undergone the required change of state.
2 I discussed CLIMB in Lecture 1, where I quoted Gärdenfors (2014: 186) who defended an approach where manner and result are seen as both being present in the meaning of CLIMB simultaneously.
3 Italian has particle verbs, so is more satellite-framed than the other Romance languages.

claim about manner/result complementarity because a path arguably expresses a kind of result, especially paths encoded with prepositions such as INTO in English, which involve traversing a boundary. Effectively, Talmy is also saying that there is a split between manner and result and that verbs can only conflate two out of three meaning elements. Perhaps Talmy's claim is only in part typological claim. There are typological tendencies, but these tendencies are not hard and fast. They are facts about verbs rather than facts about languages. And as the case of Latin>Romance shows, the vocabulary of a language can drift from one type to another. However, in another sense, Talmy's claim is typological and relevant: Talmy shows that cross linguistically there is a strong tendency for languages not to conflate more than two out of the three meaning elements, 'manner', 'motion' and 'direction'. And his results also suggest that we do not typically see 'manner' and 'result' conflated in the same verb meaning.

Therefore, we are exploring the sorts of meaning elements that can converge on particular verbs, and those that cannot. We are also looking to see whether there are patterns across a language—for example whether the majority of the verb vocabulary was of a particular kind. And also we are looking at the question of whether there are patterns in language families: are the Germanic languages inclined to be like English? Or the Romance languages like Spanish?

1.3   *Back to Conflation Classes*

Talmy's typology also relates to questions of event structure research I talked about in lecture three. Among the research questions I identified, one was, "What are the relations between events?" I have said there are different kinds of results. There are also relations that are more abstract than results, certain kinds of outcome that might be possible or that might not be entailed. And another research question that I have discussed was, "What are the relationships between events and their participants?" How do the participants of events affect the event and affect each other? So, partly, this is force dynamics; partly, this is also a question about the thematic roles that we see playing out in certain kinds of event structure. The third question is: "What sorts of events can we identify? And what sorts of complex event patterns emerge?" These questions are also related to the issue of how many subevents an event can conflate. Levin and Rappaport Hovav's claim is a question about how many subevents an event can conflate as well as being about the constraints on the cooccurrence of event classes.[4] They derive the restriction that manner and result cannot cooccur from how their theoretical architecture works. A manner verb has

---

4   Although there is another way of construing their claim: that it is a restriction on multiple inheritance.

stages without scales, whereas a result verb is scalar, and in their theory it is impossible to mix the two kinds of event.

But it is possible in the Word Grammar network, with multiple inheritance, to have manner and motion in a single verb meaning—so in this theory at least, the conflation is not excluded by the formalism. Also, given that manner-of-killing verbs exist, we clearly have to find a way of accounting for verbs that conflate manner and result in some appropriate theoretical way. Beavers and Koontz-Garboden (2012) present a number of arguments concerning key classes of verb including verbs of manner-of-killing, verbs of cooking, and verbs such as CLIMB, all of which have been discussed in these debates.

1.4 Levin and Rappaport Hovav

From an exploration of CLEAR-class and WIPE-class verbs, Levin and Rappaport Hovav (1991) say manner and result are in complementary distribution. For example, CLEAR is a result verb: if you clear the table, then the result is that the table is clear—the name of the verb names the result. On the other hand, WIPE is a manner verb: if you wipe the table, it is possible to wipe the table without necessarily clearing it. It is possible that all you do is spread mess around on the table.

Later, Levin and Rappaport Hovav (2005) investigated BREAK versus HIT. For example, BREAK in *the boy broke the window with a ball* is a result verb, but HIT in *the boy hit the window with a ball* is not a result verb, as far as they are concerned. And it is possible to have *the window broke*, but the example **the window hit* is not possible. That is, inchoative of BREAK is grammatical, but not the inchoative of HIT, which also rejects the middle, although BREAK accepts it: *the window breaks easily* is acceptable, whereas **this window hits easily* is not.

In the terms I've been developing here, Levin and Rappaport Hovav's claim is that BREAK can participate in the causative-inchoative alternation because 'breaking' has an extra subevent. But in the analysis here, that is not possible: following Levin (1993) I have argued that the semantics of HIT involves subevents, just like SINK, and I have used different modifier attachment as a way of capturing the different subevents of HIT. Given that HIT has two subevents one of which is a result of the other, the claim that result verbs can go through the middle alternation does not work. We have to refine the claim somehow.[5] Because BREAK is a result verb for Levin and Rappaport Hovav, it

---

5   HIT is not causative even though, according to Croft (2012), it involves a force-dynamic transfer from the subject referent to the object referent. However, the network of 'hitting' is different from the prototypical causative network, with the causative network involving different

involves a causative network in its lexical structure. Verbs like BREAK include BEND, FOLD, SHATTER, and CRACK.[6] On the other hand, verbs like HIT would include SLAP, STRIKE, BUMP and STROKE. And, as we have seen, BREAK verbs participate in the causative-inchoative alternation (*he broke the stick* and *the stick broke*) but HIT verbs do not.

Note also that HIT verbs do go through the Body Part Ascension structure which BREAK verbs do not.

(1) I hit his leg.
(2) I hit him on the leg.
(3) I broke his leg.
(4) *I broke him on the leg.

BREAK and HIT then, take part in different transitivity alternations. But why? What is it about their meaning that means that HIT cannot occur in the middle construction? What is it about their meaning that BREAK cannot occur in the Body Part Ascension? Croft (2012) claims that HIT and BREAK have the same force-dynamic structure (in both cases, the subject acts on the direct object) but why are there these differences?

I will give my answer in the next section. Rappaport Hovav and Levin (2010) say these differences follow from manner/result complementarity. In their terms, manner verbs cannot be part of a causative network. Verbs that are part of a causative network cannot include manner information. They handle these differences with a theory of scalar versus non-scalar change. So now we need to remind ourselves of the differences between these two kinds of change.

When I was discussing *Aktionsart* in the last lecture, I said that Landsman had a theory of *Aktionsart* that talks about the stages of an event. Verbs that can occur in the progressive were verbs that have stages. The verbs that cannot occur in the progressive are verbs that do not have stages. Therefore, states—verbs which do not have stages—cannot occur in the progressive. Levin and Rappaport Hovav work with a version of this idea; they have also talked about verbs involving change or not involving change. An activity verb is a change verb: if I am talking, then there are different stages to the talking as I talk. If I am running, then there are different stages to the running as I run. Therefore,

---

relations from the network for 'hitting'. The differences between HIT and BREAK are not merely due to the existence of subevents, one of which is a result of the other, but also have to do with the nature of the networks that support the sense of each verb.

6 It is surely possible to argue on the basis of the differences between SHATTER and CRACK that these are verbs that conflate a 'manner' element as well, but where the 'manner' is displayed on the result rather than on the action that gives rise to the result.

these change verbs can be progressive. But then they go on to distinguish between two different kinds of change verbs: there are non-scalar change verbs opposed to scalar change verbs. A scale is just an ordered set of possible changes. For example, we can take everybody in this room and line them up along the corridor according to who is the tallest and who is the shortest. That is a scale. As well as being able to find scales in the ordinary physical domain, Levin and Rappaport Hovav think that it is possible to see scalar properties in events.[7] An event that involves a change of state has a scale, because it has an endpoint. If it has an endpoint, then it has a scale towards the endpoint. If somebody is killed, then there is an event leading up to the killing. Scalarity is, if you like, directed change in verbs.

For Levin and Rappaport Hovav, it is possible for scale to have only two values: zero and one, or $\sim x$ and x. For them therefore, an achievement verb is a scalar verb, even though it cannot occur in the progressive. On the other hand, Landman, whom I cited in Lecture 8, argues that an achievement verb is not a stage verb because it is an instantaneous change of state and it cannot occur in the progressive—which puts Landman at odds with Rappaport Hovav and Levin because verbs with scalar meanings are a subtype of verbs with stages and for Levin and Rappaport Hovav, an achievement verb is a scale verb because it has two values: take *the door* opened. There is a value of [0] in the initial state (where the door is closed) and a value of [1] in the result state (where the door is open).

For Levin and Rappaport Hovav, there are non-scalar verbs which are non-change verbs. These are states. There are non-scalar change verbs. These are activities. There are scalar change verbs, with a two-point scale. These are achievements. And there are scalar verbs with a multi-point scale: these are accomplishments. And they try to capture the theory of manner/result complementarity in terms of their theory of scalar or non-scalar change. They say, "results involve scalar changes while manners involve non-scalar changes. We propose a verb may only lexicalize one type of change, giving rise to manner/result complementarity" (Rappaport Hovav and Levin 2010: 21).

Their claim is that a verb can be either scalar or non-scalar, but not both. And anything that has a result in it is a scalar (directed) change. That is, a verb cannot involve both non-directed change and directed change and because it cannot involve both non-directed change and directed change, it is not possible for a verb to be both a manner verb and a result verb. Once they have

---

[7] One of the reasons for this is to do with arguments that "measure out" the event so that the event is "quantized." The classic example is *mowing the lawn*. In this case if half the lawn has been mowed, then the event is half complete.

made this theoretical decision, they then have to argue that all of the (apparent) counterexamples, such as BEHEAD and CLIMB, are not really counterexamples to manner/result complementarity, otherwise the theory fails.

The discussion around this idea has produced a really interesting and significant literature. Scalarity is an important topic in semantics currently, which has produced a lot of interesting work, not just in verb meanings. Therefore, if you are interested in Talmy's typological theory, it is a good idea to step a little bit closer into the detail of the verb meanings and to explore the manner versus result literature. You can start with Levin and Rappaport Hovav (1991) on CLEAR and WIPE verbs and move through to the debate that followed. As the result of this debate, we know a lot more about verb meanings than we did 25 years ago.

1.5 *Rappaport Hovav and Levin 2010*

As well as the manner/result complementarity hypothesis, which is an interesting hypothesis to explore, Rappaport Hovav and Levin (2010: 25) have a theory of "canonical realization rules" which I mentioned yesterday. In this system, verb meanings have "roots" which occur in larger schematic templates, with the structure of the template being responsible for the *Aktionsart* of the verb, when it is an achievement or accomplishment. They further note, "there's a generalization implicit in the canonical realization rules … which leads us to formulate a lexicalization constraint," which is, "a root can only be associated with one primitive predicate in an event schema, as an argument or a modifier."

Again, with this theoretical claim, they are trying to restrict possible verb meanings. They say verb meanings can only occur within certain templates (or if you will, certain kinds of construction) and they are not unconstrained. We might want to think about why we would want to constrain possible verb meanings. The reason is learnability: if there are limits on the possible patterns, it is easier for a child to learn the vocabulary of their language. The child's task is to learn the possible patterns. And then once they have learned the possible patterns, with every new verb thereafter they just have to figure out how it fits one of the existing possible patterns that they have already learned. Whether Levin and Rappaport Hovav's constraint is the right constraint or not, that is something else to argue about. But essentially, what they say is that verb meanings have a structure within which only one basic verb meaning is embedded.

Rappaport Hovav and Levin (2010: 25) further add that their "constraint is similar in spirit to the constraint with the same name … proposed by Kiparsky

(1997) in a study of denominal verbs, in that semantic roles are often taken to be labels for positions in an event schema (Jackendoff 1972)." I think that this idea is right: we can understand Jackendoff as saying that the semantic role label, whether it is Agent, Patient, Theme or whatever, is not theoretically useful. On the other hand, the issue of whether an argument is the First Argument of a verb's sense, or the Second Argument (Er or Ee in WG terms) is theoretically important. The claim is that this area of meaning is structured (Gisborne and Donaldson 2019).

Kiparksy's lexical constraint is formulated as, "A verb can inherently express at most one semantic role (theme, instrument, direction, manner, path)" (Kiparsky 1997: 30, quoted in Rappaport Hovav and Levin 2010: 25). Kiparsky's claim is that the basic verb meaning can bring one semantic role with it, while the other semantic roles come from the larger template of structure in which the events fit together to form the inchoative, the causative, or whatever.

This idea is an interesting one because it explains why thematic roles do not seem to matter. In a previous lecture, quoting Croft (2012), I talked about how the very specific thematic role meanings like Theme, Experiencer, Locative and so on appear not to do a great deal of work for us in the grammar, particularly in terms of argument realization. Kiparsky's idea suggests that constraints on lexicalization patterns come from the properties and the nature of verb roots themselves and the ways in which they are allowed to interact with larger event structure patterns or templates.

Figure 1, which is nearly the same as Figure 14 in the previous lecture, shows Levin and Rappaport Hovav's (2010) template structure. It shows the same sorts of patterns that we were looking at in the previous lecture, when we were discussing *Aktionsart*.

manner → [x ACT$_{<MANNER>}$]
   (e.g., *job, run, creak, whistle*, ...)
instrument → [x ACT$_{<INSTRUMENT>}$]
   (e.g., *brush, chisel, saw, shovel*, ...)
container → [x CAUSE [y BECOME AT <CONTAINER>]]
   (e.g., *bag, box, cage, crate, garage, pocket*, ...)
Internally caused state → [x <STATE>]
   (e.g. *bloom, blossom, decay, flower, rot, rust, sprout*, ...)
externally caused state → [[x ACT] CAUSE [BECOME [y <STATE>]]]
   (e.g. *break, dry, harden, melt, open*, ...)

FIGURE 1   Levin and Rappaport Hovav's (2010: 24) template structure

The same issues arise. They say a manner verb consists of an action which has a manner label on it as a kind of modifier. This is the explanation for JOG, RUN, CREAK and WHISTLE. Instrument verbs like SAW in *saw the wood* are the same: *x* performs an action which has an instrument label on it. I want to draw your attention to the claim that it is only possible to have one label in the event structure. This works in two ways: each slot can only have one verb label in it. Therefore, it is possible to put 'jogging' in the manner slot, but you cannot put 'creaking' in the manner slot at the same time. For example, if I were to jog, my joints might creak and we might think that there should be a verb *CREAK-JOG which means 'to jog with creaking joints' but it is not possible to say **I creak-jogged*. According to Levin and Rappaport Hovav, there is a reason why verbs such as *CREAK-JOG do not exist, and that is because we cannot put both 'jogging' and 'creaking' in this single manner slot. This constraint is an attempt to limit the bounds of the theory in order to make the theory more accurately predictive of possible verbs.

The same constraint works with result verbs too. For example, there is a schema for the verb BOX, as in *we boxed the leftover food*. In Figure 1, this is: [*x CAUSE* [*y BECOME-AT* <CONTAINER>]]. Assume the food has a sauce: you might want to put the boxed food into a bag to minimize the risk of leaks. But it is not possible to invent a verb BOX-BAG or BAG-BOX to describe the process of boxing and then bagging the food, because there is only one CONTAINER slot in the template. In this way, Levin and Rappaport Hovav set out to explain the constraints on possible verb meanings.

Manner/result complementarity follows. According to the lexicalization constraint, because a verb can only have one label, it is not possible for a verb meaning to express manner and result at the same time. Although the predicate ACT can have a manner label, as in [*x ACT$_{<MANNER>}$*], the following event structure is not licensed, according to Levin and Rappaport Hovav: [[*x ACT$_{<MANNER>}$*] *CAUSE* [*y BECOME* <RESULT-STATE>]].

In Levin and Rappaport Hovav's own words (2010: 26), "Assuming the event schemas of [Figure 1], and assuming that manner roots modify the predicate ACT and result roots are arguments of BECOME, a root can modify ACT or be an argument to BECOME in a given event schema. A root cannot modify both these predicates at once without violating the lexicalization constraint. Thus, there can be no root which expresses both manner and result, and manner/result complementarity follows." To sum up, Levin and Rappaport Hovav have two theories: one theory is to do with change being directed, or scalar, or being non-directed, non-scalar; the other theory is to do with where in the event template the manner or the result fits. But actually, these two theories have the same consequences, because Levin and Rappaport Hovav say that only non-scalar change can be a manner, i.e. can be the modifier of an action. And only scalar change can be the predicate argument of BECOMING. Their research agenda is to find the patterns which show the generalizations that apply to the data, and also to find reasons for those patterns.

1.6 "Roots"

As I said in the previous lecture, the verb "root" or "constant" in Rappaport Hovav and Levin's theory is its core meaning. The "root" can appear in two different positions in their event structure: it can occur as a modifier of an action, or as a result state. This is one of the sources of the theoretical claim that there is manner/result complementarity: it is argued that it is not possible for an event structure to include two roots. Rappaport Hovav and Levin's agenda is to identify possible event templates and what relationships are possible in the event templates. This is the same agenda as the WG equivalent of trying to work out what categories of events there can be, and what the relationships between events might look like, even though there are differences in the representations, in terms of how predicates are understood, and also in several details. But we should note that there are many similarities between the approaches.

1.7 *Rappaport Hovav and Levin* (2010)

One question to ask about Rappaport Hovav and Levin's (2010) theory is whether result verbs are necessarily telic. Their answer is that they are not, and the reason is to do with how scalarity plays out in their theory. We saw in the previous lecture that differences in the arguments of a verb can affect its *Aktionsart*—the difference between *drink beer* and *drink a beer* or between *Jane ran into the* room and *children ran into the room*. In the examples in (5) and (6) we look at another dimension of complexity, to do with the way in which degree achievements can have different *Aktionsarten*. Degree achievements are result verbs which have both telic and atelic uses. Consider the verb COOL with a direct object and bear in mind that FOR is the modifier of an atelic event, and IN is the modifier of a telic event.

(5) The chemist cooled the solution for three minutes.
(6) The chemist cooled the solution in three minutes; it was now at the desired temperature.

Suppose you want to dissolve salt in some distilled water. In order to do this, you have to bring the water up to a certain temperature because it is easier to dissolve salt in hot water. But now imagine that you need to use this solution in order to wash your face—it is a treatment for a skin condition—so you have to reduce the temperature to one that is cool enough to bathe your face. It is possible to say (5), which might describe the situation where the solution has reached the right temperature, or might not. It is also possible to say (6), if the desired temperature is achieved. Both (5) and (6) are achievements but (5) shows that the result is not necessarily telic because of the presence of the FOR modifier, whereas (5) is telic because it occurs with IN. We can factor out telicity and degree of change. And the same is true with other verbs.

1.8 What Is Scalar Change?

Rappaport Hovav and Levin also talked about WARM as well as COOL, which also involves a scale (e.g. *they warmed the milk*, and *they cooled the dinks*). Scales can go into opposite directions, so WARM goes up the scale, but COOL goes down the scale. Rappaport Hovav and Levin (2010: 29) say, "We suggest that the relevant attribute whose values make up the scale is the location of a theme with respect to a 'ground'—a reference object. In the motion domain, the predicates which lexicalize such scalar attributes without a notion of change are prepositions like *above, below, far*, and *near*, which also locate a theme with respect to a ground." Jackendoff (1983), Talmy (1983) and Vandeloise (1991) have all made similar remarks. The idea is that we can understand scales in terms of other more basic cognitive notions. We can understand scales in terms of some basic properties to do with Figure and Ground. Therefore, we can use Figure and Ground as a way of saying how scales can be composed, and in this way, we can bring scalarity back to motion. We can see *climbing up* and *climbing down* the scale as being like traveling along a path in one direction, or in another direction.

As I said previously, scalar change can involve a multi-point scale or a two-point scale. ARRIVE and CRACK are both two-point scale verbs. Multiple point scale verbs include ADVANCE and DESCEND. Scales can be closed as in EMPTY or open as in LENGTHEN. When you *empty the water bottle*, there is nothing left in it. That is a closed scale. When you *lengthen something*, you do not see the end of the scale: that is an open scale.

The key idea is that paths and telic meaning elements introduce scales. A path is like a scale, a directed change. An unbounded path symbolizes an atelic scale whereas a bounded path (a path with an endpoint) symbolizes a telic scale. And change-of-state telic meanings are also scalar.

And then what are non-scalar changes? Non-scalar changes are activities like JOG, FLAP, FLUTTER. They are activities in terms of their *Aktionsart*. They are changes because they are dynamic. They are non-scalar because the

CONFLATION CLASSES, TRANSITIVITY ALTERNATIONS   249

changes are just temporary changes in their Er. Non-scalar changes work like GALLOP from Lecture 8.

1.9   How Does This Work with the Event Hierarchy?

The event hierarchy in Figure 2 repeats Figure 3 of Lecture 8. I am not going to go over it in great deal of detail. But we could ask ourselves how such an event hierarchy might relate to scalar change in the Rappaport Hovav and Levin sense.

With the version of the event hierarchy presented in the previous lecture, the idea of scale and scalarity does not work very well. But with the event hierarchy for activities, in Figure 3, perhaps we can make more sense of the dichotomy.

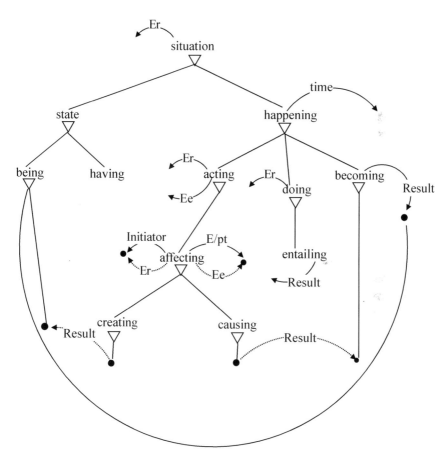

FIGURE 2   The event hierarchy

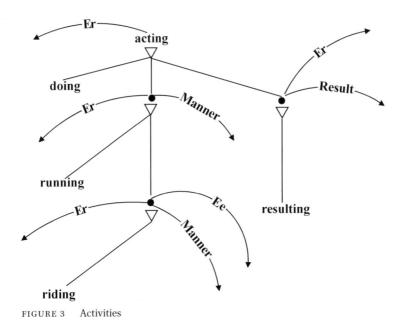

FIGURE 3   Activities

The diagram in Figure 3 splits activity verbs into two kinds right at the top of the hierarchy: those that have a manner attribute and those that have a Result attribute. And by including stage information with both of these classes of verbs which we can do by Holmes' analysis of GALLOP, we can include and describe the scalar information that Levin and Rappaport Hovav discuss.

The scalar properties that Rappaport Hovav and Levin discuss can be accommodated with a combination of the Result attribute, and the model of stages that I presented in Lecture 8, drawing on from Holmes' (2005) analysis of GALLOP. One of the things we can do with the stages that we can take from the analysis of GALLOP is to order them, so that the theory has both unordered stages and ordered stages, so Stage 1 is before stage 2, stage 2 is before stage 3, and so on. This gives us directionality and a scale.[8] By including stage information with both of these classes of verbs, as it is done by Holme's analysis of 'galloping', we can include and describe the scalar information that Levin and Rappaport Hovav discuss. We can illustrate this with RISE.

First, though, let us think about representations. How can we integrate stages into a model that essentially relies on networks of event structure to explain how some events involve results, in Rappaport Hovav and Levin's (2010) terms

---

8   I am not implying that GALLOP is a scalar predicate: I am saying that we can build scalarity into the theory of change that we can derive from Holmes' analysis of GALLOP.

and others do not? An important point is that Rappaport Hovav and Levin's result verbs are not the same as verbs with Results in their lexical entries. HIT has a Result built into its meaning, but it is not one of their result verbs: it meets their diagnostics for a manner verb: it can occur in the conative construction; and it does not undergo the causative alternation. *Kim hit at Chris* is fine; *Kim hit Chris* is the usual transitive use of HIT; **Chris hit* is ungrammatical. This is consistent with manner/result complementarity, because there are manner of hitting verbs: PUNCH, BEAT, BATTER.

Beavers and Koontz-Garboden (2012) give a test for a result verb (in Rappaport Hovav and Levin's definition of "result"): does adding *but nothing is different about it* trigger a contradiction? In the case of *!Kim killed the pig, but nothing is different about it*, it does. But in the case of *Kim hit Chris but nothing is different about him*, it does not. Event complexity, then, is not the same as being a result verb, at least in Rappaport Hovav and Levin's terms.

Is there a reason for this? One possible reason is that temporal structure is implicated. Recall the discussion in Lecture 8 about the differences between achievement verbs and semelfactives. I argued that they different in terms of how the subevents are temporally related to each other. In particular, verbs like HIT involve the two events being co-temporal, whereas the two events of inchoative, achievement verbs such as intransitive SINK are temporally ordered. Temporal ordering is relevant to Rappaport Hovav and Levin's manner/result distinction: to form a scale, the different events have to occur at *successive* times.

1.10 RISE

The sense of RISE Isa 'moving', which also lexicalizes a result. The result of the sense of RISE is that the subject referent ends up higher than before. Holmes has shown that the result can be explained by analyzing the path as in Figure 4.

Holmes breaks the path down into two different parts. He then gives the two different parts different times and makes one before the other. In this way, he gets a scale. This shows that we can actually write scales into the network. The diagram in Figure 4 captures one possible analysis of scalarity. RISE is a directed motion verb and its meaning involves an unbounded scale. A bounded scale would involve a path with an endpoint.

The analysis of RISE should make it possible to have an accurate representation of CLIMB which involves the directed motion that we see in the event structure of RISE and, in several analyses, a manner element (clambering') as well. Now the question is, "How does CLIMB work?" It has a 'rising' element in it, with this scalar change but it also has a manner element. How do we make it possible for the prototype meaning of CLIMB to work? Holmes' diagram

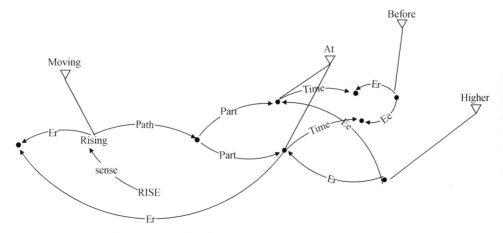

FIGURE 4   Holmes' (2005: 171) analysis of RISE

includes information that constitutes a scale, the path that RISE lexicalizes is defined as having parts, and those parts are defined as being traversed in a temporal sequence, so RISE is like DESCEND—a multiple-point scale verb.

1.11   Activities

Rappaport Hovav and Levin's claim about manner/result complementarity then can be reduced to the height on the inheritance tree: the division into manner vs. result verbs takes place right at the top of the tree, except that their 'result' includes paths and telic aspect, so it is more general than WG's Result relation. They also make the argument that there is a complexity constraint: conflating manner and result in a single verb would give rise to a great deal of information complexity, hence there is manner/result complementarity. And what about counterexamples?

1.12   Counterexamples and Counterarguments

The main counterexamples to the manner/result complementarity claim are verbs like CLIMB and CUT. Rappaport Hovav and Levin claim that these verbs do not lexicalize both manner and result; they argue that CLIMB has different senses which lexicalize one or the other, so it is polysemous, and CUT does not specify the nature of the manner element. Goldberg (2010) on the other hand, argues against manner/result complementarity with her argument coming from cooking verbs like FRY.[9] As we have noted, manner-of-cooking verbs entail a change of state in the food item.

---

9   Goldberg also argues against Rappaport Hovav and Levin's template approach in favor of an approach which explores the lexical meanings of verbs in different construction frames.

Other than CLIMB and CUT, Beavers and Koontz-Garboden (2012), who argue against manner/result complementarity, in a limited way, explore the structures of manner-of-killing verbs and manner-of-cooking verbs such as ELECTROCUTE and BEHEAD on the one hand, and FRY, ROAST and BAKE on the other. SCATTER is another—and different—manner-and-result verb. When you *scatter seed on the ground*, it has a manner because you have to throw the seed in a way that spreads it. When you scatter something, the thing you scatter also ends up in a place, so there is also a result. Beavers and Koontz-Garboden argue that these various verbs answer Rappaport Hovav and Levin's defence of manner/result complementarity, but they have an additional diagnostic which suggest that there is more to say.

The additional diagnostic concerns the scope of the adverb AGAIN. Wechsler (2015: 119) explains Beavers and Koontz-Garboden's argument with this example, "*John drowned the zombie again* presupposes that the zombie dies specifically by drowning before, and not by just any method." He says that they conclude that DROWN cannot have the complex structure of an accomplishment, and must have the simpler structure of a manner verb. However, as Wechsler points out, this conclusion cannot be correct, because DROWN participates in the causative alternation: *Kim drowned the zombie*, vs. *the zombie drowned.* This must mean that it involves a similar semantic structure to KILL, although Weschler thinks that it is different from KILL in that what is needed for DROWN is a resulting event rather than a resulting state.

1.13   *Talmy*

We can also ask ourselves where this thinking about manner/result complementarity leaves Talmy's theory of lexicalization patterns. Talmy's verb-framed vs. satellite-framed distinction is about how the predicates of languages lexicalize different meaning elements: motion, direction and manner. Verb-framed languages conflate motion and direction in a single verb-meaning; satellite-framed languages conflate motion and manner. Talmy makes a typological claim: for him it is not verbs but languages which are verb- or satellite-framed. But this typological claim is not quite right, because English has verb-framed event denoting verbs such as ENTER as well as being generally a satellite-framed language. English also has non-borrowed verb-framed vocabulary with verbs such as COME, GO, BRING and TAKE. COME means 'towards the position of the speaker', while GO means 'away from the position of the speaker'. These verbs conflate direction within the meaning of the verb. Therefore, they are like the verbs of verb-framed, not satellite-framed, languages.

As Croft (2012: 294) summarizes it, Talmy distinguishes between three language types. The first is manner-incorporating type languages, such as English: *He ran into the cave*. The second is path-incorporating type languages, like the

Spanish *Entró corriendo a la cuevo* (from Talmy 1985: 111), which means 'he entered running into the cave'. The third is ground-incorporating type languages, such as Atsugewi (the Native American language Talmy investigated for his PhD) as in (7).

(7) '-w>   uh- **st'aq'** –ik   <-ᵃ
     <3sg.fact> by.gravity **lie.runny.icky.material** on.ground
     'runny icky material (e.g. guts) is lying on the ground'

In addition, Talmy's typology has been extended by Slobin (2004) to include equipollent languages—Slobin claims that Chinese is equipollent. Talmy (2000) goes on to update his framework to talk about framing, which is a generalized concept of a result state, including notions such as path and telic aspect, corresponding to Rappaport Hovav & Levin's result.

Croft provides a summary: "It is clear that Talmy and Levin and Rappaport Hovav are describing the same broad lexical semantic contrast in terms of the lexicalization of event structure in simple verbs." (2012: 296). One question following from this is, "Is it better to understand these differences in terms of typology or in terms of lexical semantics?" It seems best to do this in terms of lexical semantics, because languages can change their type and they can be of a mixed type. For example, as I said before, Latin was more like English than the verb-framed, modern Romance languages: there must have been a period in the history of the Romance languages when they were mixed.

1.14 *Manner/Result—How to Evaluate the Claims*

It seems to me that manner/result complementarity is not a robust constraint on lexical-semantic representations: the evidence from manner-of-cooking verbs, manner-of-killing verbs, and verbs such as SCATTER, as well as the behavior of CLIMB and CUT all suggests that there are conditions when both of these elements can co-occur. On the other hand, there is clearly a strong dispreference for both elements being co-present in a single verb meaning. How should we accommodate these facts? It seems to me that the issue is one of complexity. There appears to be a threshold of complexity which disprefers a verb conflating both manner and result in the same local network. Recall that Rappaport Hovav and Leven (2010) move beyond an account of manner/result complexity in terms of the templates to one organized around scales. Scales involve a degree of complexity which is beyond the complexity of a Result relation, because they require there to be ordered relationships among meaning elements. I suspect that the manner/result complementarity claim is an insufficiently worked through, and too local, variant of a claim which ought to be about degree of network complexity in verb meanings. But deciding the case will require carefully worked out models of manner-of-killing and manner-of-cooking verbs, SCATTER, and an evaluation metric which allows us to establish the different complexity of these event types.

2   Transitivity Alternations

How do we model transitivity alternations? In this section, we are concerned with the semantics of transitivity alternations, and how the different semantic structures are related. In the next section, we come back to argument realization. Consider the following examples.

(8) a. Give him a book.
b. Give a book to him.
(9) a. Jane opened the door.
b. The door opened.
c. The door is open.
(10) a. Ali hit Foreman.
b. Foreman hit at Ali.
c. Ali hit Foreman on the face.
(11) a. Helen wiped the fingerprints off the wall.
b. Helen wiped the wall.

In Word Grammar we use sublexemes to model transitivity alternations. The verbs have subtypes, each of which is associated with different semantics. Each different semantics is associated with a different syntactic configuration.

The WG answer is that part of the network for one sense can be found in the network of the other sense. We saw this in the analysis of OPEN which I gave in the first lecture. There are two different verbs that mean OPEN, and an adjective. And they each map onto a different part of the associative network. Here is the representation of OPEN again.

Inchoative 'opening' ('opening2') inherits from 'becoming' and has a Result: the meaning of adjective 'open'. Inchoative 'opening' is the sense of intransitive OPEN (OPEN/intr). Linking is stated declaratively, and by default an Er links to Subject. Therefore linking follows. Transitive OPEN (OPEN/tr) has causing 'opening1' as its sense which has 'opening2' as its Result. There is therefore a link between the meanings of the different sublexemes. The Er of 'opening1' links to the subject of OPEN/tr and the Ee to the object. OPEN/tr and OPEN/intr are two sublexemes of OPEN, whose default is OPEN/intr, while OPEN/tr

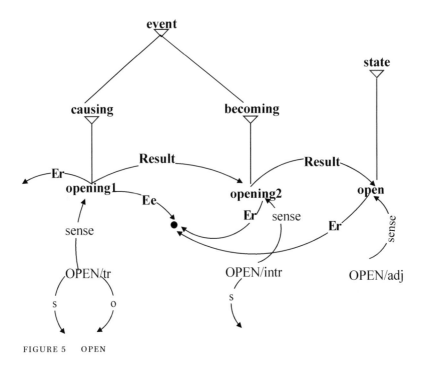

FIGURE 5   OPEN

is the extension of the default—the claim building that the more complex structure is built up around the less complex one.

Transitivity alternations involve just two different properties: polysemy and collocation. Either the two variants in a transitivity alternation are just two different senses of the same item, or the item collocates with other sentence elements. We can take collocation first.

2.1   *Collocation*

Collocation is a very simple idea. It is the idea that you can say *I ate a hotdog* but not *I ate a hot dog*. This contrast is grammatical: you can eat a *hotdog* because you can eat a sausage, but you cannot eat a *hot dog*—because then you would be eating a live animal that needed to cool down: in order to eat a *hot dog*, it would be necessary to kill the dog and cook it, in which case it would no longer be a *hot dog* but food. This is collocation: EAT collocates with a noun or noun phrase that symbolizes food, but it cannot collocate with a noun or noun phrase that does not. Collocation can also vary across languages. In English, it is normal to say *eat soup* whereas Chinese prefers *drink soup*.

Moreover, some predicates cannot collocate with other sentence elements. Verbs of perception select particular prepositions. It is possible to *look at the* *picture* but not to **listen at the music*. The linguistics of English verbs of perception seem to claim that it is possible for us to direct our gaze but not to direct our hearing, even though hearing can be directional, because hearing involves a figure-ground distinction.

It is possible to think about the Body-Part Ascension alternation in terms of collocation. It is possible to say *Jane hit Peter on the nose* but not **Jane broke Peter on the nose*. How come? The claim is that the Body-Part Ascension alternation only works with verbs that have a 'touching' element in their meanings and 'breaking' does not necessarily involve touching. For example, Jane can break Peter's nose by driving her car badly and being involved in an accident in which Peter's nose is broken.

2.2   *HIT, BREAK* and the BPA

Is collocation only to do with lexical structure? The evidence from the BPA would suggest that it is, but I think Levin's (1993) claim that the BPA diagnoses for a 'touching' element in a verb meaning is not quite right, so I want to challenge it as a diagnostic. Normally when you break something, you touch it. I wonder if Body Part Ascension construction is to do with metonymy rather than anything else and that what is at stake here is the scope of the action's effect. If person x hits person y then it is impossible for x to hit all of y. If I hit you, I can only hit part of you (because although I have big hands, my fist is only so big). This is true even if we are talking about a situation such as an adult hitting a baby. But it is not possible for x to break y by breaking some part of y. If x breaks y's leg, they have not broken y but part of y—their leg. And therefore, y is still in some sense intact.

This looks like metonymic transitivity: if you do something to a part of y, then you necessarily do that thing to y itself. If I hit the window, I only hit *part* of the window. If I break the window, then all of the window is necessarily broken. Therefore, I wonder if BPA construction is more about construal than it is about 'touching'. The BPA is allowed where the meaning of the verb requires the action to apply to a part of the Ee entity. This transitivity alternation will automatically go together with a 'touching' element in a verb's meaning because most of the time, when you touch something, you really only touch part of it. Likewise, the BPA will not automatically go together with 'breaking' because when you break something, the whole object is affected. The idea of metonymic transitivity explains why the BPA goes together with 'touching' rather than just asserting that the BPA is a diagnostic of 'touching' in a verb's meaning.

We might also ask whether there are examples of the BPA construction that clearly do not require an element of 'touching' in a verb's meaning. I think it is possible: here is a context: parents often sniff their babies—for example to find out if the baby needs a new nappy—but also because it is nice to smell a clean baby: you often see people having a little sniff on their baby's head. And if *having a little sniff on their baby's head* is acceptable what about *he smelt the baby on her head*? This is also grammatical. But when you smell or sniff the baby, you do not touch them. In fact, if you get too close to the baby's head, then you will not get enough air up and you will not be able to actually sniff or smell it. As smelling does not involve 'touching', there is at least one example involving the BPA construction that does not require 'touching'. Therefore, as I have said, I think that the BPA is more to do with metonymy than it is to do with 'touching' in verbs' meanings. Specifically, it appears to specify a default metonymy: *he touched the glass* involves him touching a part of the glass, but the expression just takes it that the glass is touched. The BPA specifies the subpart of the object that is implicated in the event.

2.3   Polysemy and Transitivity Alternations

Either way, a transitivity alternation involves either a different network, or a restriction on collocation. We look at the polysemy of MAKE in Figure 6, which comes from Gisborne (2010). MAKE has three key uses. It has a transitive verb use, as in *make a cake*. That is a verb of creation, so it has a built-in Result. It also has a ditransitive use: *make me a cup of tea*. That is an act of creation: the tea goes from not being made to being made and it is also a Beneficiary event because the Indirect Object is the Beneficiary of the event denoted by MAKE. Finally, it has a predicative complement use: *make him a good man* which means something like *make him into a good man*, or *turn him into a good citizen*. Figure 5 analyzes MAKE. There is a default lexeme, MAKE/tr, and two further sublexemes. Each sublexeme is associated with a slightly different semantic structure, and because they have different semantic structures, they also have different syntactic structures. The diagram is primarily concerned with the semantic structure.

In the middle of the diagram, MAKE/tr has a sense, which is 'making'. 'Making' is a kind of 'causing'—it Isa 'causing'. 'Making' has a Result, which is 'being'. MAKE/tr has an object and the referent of the object of MAKE is the Er of the Result of 'making'. This is the structure of meaning in a verb of creation and it is the default lexeme for MAKE. The sense of MAKE/ditrans takes the syntactic and semantic core of MAKE/tr and adds a Beneficiary and a Purpose relation, which links to another event. The Purpose is part of the meaning of the Beneficiary relationship and it adds the necessary semantic structure for MAKE to occur with an indirect object. Therefore, MAKE/ditrans

CONFLATION CLASSES, TRANSITIVITY ALTERNATIONS 259

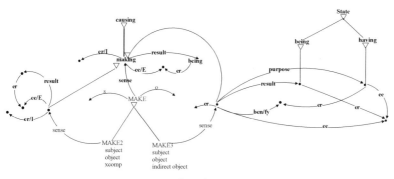

FIGURE 6   MAKE. FROM GISBORNE (2010)

is another sublexeme with an additional dependency and some additional semantic structure.

MAKE/xcomp is also slightly different, with a different syntactic pattern and sense. MAKE/xcomp and MAKE/distrans inherit from MAKE1 and their sense inherits from its sense. The semantics of MAKE/tr are entirely embedded in the semantics of MAKE/ditrans, and the semantics of the Xcomp form unpack and reassign the semantic structures associated with MAKE/tr.

The simple claim is that a transitivity alternation just involves a sublexeme which inherits from the default lexeme which has got some additional different semantic structure in the case of the ditransitive, and a different mapping of semantic structure to syntax in the case of the predicative complement sublexeme, MAKE/xcomp, which has the same semantic structure as transitive MAKE. In this way, we can see that there is a range of possible argument linking patterns but the argument linking is very straightforward. There is just a little network of verbs with an associated semantic network.

To summarize: MAKE/tr is the basic form. The ditransitive variant and the xcomp variant both inherit from the transitive. The semantics of MAKE/tr are entirely embedded in the semantics of ditransitive MAKE, whereas the semantics of MAKE/xcomp are the same as the semantics of MAKE/tr but with a different linking pattern. Therefore, MAKE/xcomp and MAKE/ditrans inherit from MAKE1 and their senses inherit from its sense. Linking from syntax to semantics is declarative, and follows default patterns. Linking is negotiated via the sublexemes, and default linking patterns, such as the Er of declaratives links to the Subject.

2.4   *GIVE*

Now we should look at GIVE, because I have not discussed the contrasts between double object and double complement GIVE: are the different patterns reflected in its argument-taking properties? For example, you can say *give her some flowers* and *give some flowers to her*. The double object and double complement instances of GIVE have different event structures. These different senses are witnessed in an ontological constraint on the direct object. (We have seen these data before.)

(12) a. The scandal gave the reporter an idea.
b. *The scandal gave an idea to the reporter.
(13) a. Bright lights give Amy migraines.
b. *Bright lights give migraines to Amy.

We can see that the direct objects in (12b) and (13b) are abstract nouns, so we can ask why the direct object can be an abstract noun in the double object construction, but not in the double complement construction. The answer must involve there being two different senses, each with different selection restrictions, so our task is to establish those two senses and to work out how they should be represented.

The two senses of GIVE differ in terms of their result event. Ditransitive GIVE, as we have seen, has 'having' as its result event. Double complement GIVE, on the other hand, has to be compatible with the preposition which it has to collocate with. As we can see, in (12b), TO defines a path. If TO defines a path, then the second event in double complement GIVE must be 'moving', not 'having'. That is, collocation is evidence for the semantic structure of GIVE. The path expression tells us that the second event in (12b) must be a 'moving' event, not a 'having' event because 'moving' is compatible with 'to', but 'having' is not.[10]

The sense of double object GIVE is represented in Figure 6 which we have seen before. Figure 7 just shows the semantic structure of the sentence *Jane gave her some flowers*.

Figure 7 says that 'giving' has four relations: an Er (with 'Jane' as its value), an Ee (with 'some flowers' as its value), a Result ('having' is the value), and a Recipient ('her' is the value). The second event, 'having' is the Result of 'giving'; 'having' has 'her' as the value of its Er and 'some flowers' as the value of its Ee in *Jane gave her some flowers*.

---

10 Although we should note the challenges of examples such as *he denied food to all of the prisoners* which has *to* but which does not involve 'moving'.

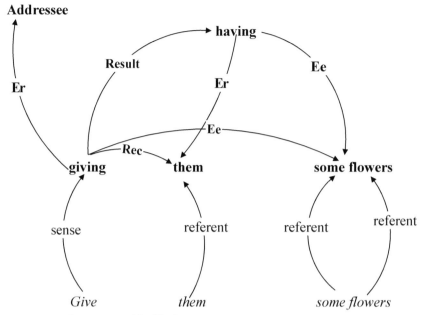

FIGURE 7   The structure of double object GIVE

The structure of double complement GIVE is represented in Figure 8.

Figure 8 says that 'moving' is the Result, not 'having', so it has a different sense with a different resulting event from GIVE in Figure 7. It also has a simpler semantic structure because the path defines its own relationship to its predicate.

The explanation of the ontological constraint is that the Er of 'moving' has to be physically capable of 'moving', the Ee of 'having' does not have to be a physical thing. This is a constraint on the categories of things that can be Ers and Ees of different event types. We can show ontological constraints very easily: by just putting a restriction on the category of whatever concept can occur in this position in the network: it is simply a matter of identifying the classification of certain nodes. And we should note that this is just collocation. Figure 8 shows the ontological constraint on double object GIVE: 'some flowers', has to be capable of moving; this node is classified as 'animate thing'. Therefore, it is not possible to *give an idea to her*, because an idea is abstract and cannot move. This constraint is really a constraint on the Er of 'moving' as represented in Figure 9.

There is another ontological constraint, which we have seen in Lecture 6. This is found on the indirect object in the double object pattern: it is not

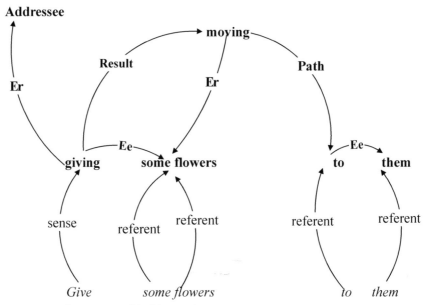

FIGURE 8 The structure of double complement GIVE

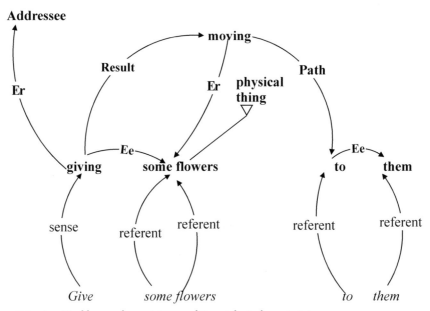

FIGURE 9 Double complement GIVE and its ontological constraint

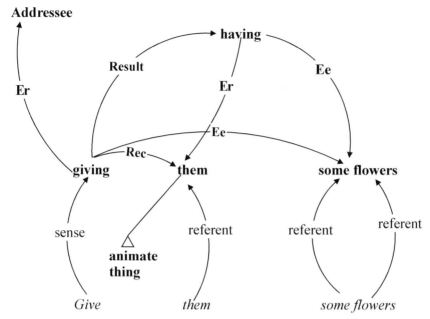

FIGURE 10   GIVE and the indirect object ontological constraint

possible to *give the table a vase*. By default, indirect objects have to be animate: the Recipient of 'giving' is more restricted than the Ee of 'giving'. In the diagram in Figure 10, the indirect object referent is classified as a subtype of 'thing'. Again, this is a matter of collocation. The Recipient of 'giving' is more restricted than the Ee of 'giving', so it is classed as a subtype of thing and because it has to be animate we cannot *give the table a vase*. This ontological constraint is represented in Figure 10 as a classification on the node filled by 'her'. The diagram says that the Recipient must be animate.

These constraints we captured above indicate that certain kinds of event select their subjects and objects, or more precisely select their subjects' and objects' categories of meaning.

2.5   More Data

We can see how well such diagrams extend to further data sets. Recall the ontological constraint on Indirect Objects: in *Jane sent Peter a letter*, the letter has to be sent to an actual person, so **Jane sent the post office a letter* is not acceptable. Again, the Recipient has to be animate. But here is something to think about: in this case, is this really a restriction on the Recipient, or is it actually a restriction on the Er of 'having'? We could construe it as a constraint that the Er of 'having' must be capable of possession? Or, because they converge on the same node, do we really need to do distinguish? Perhaps it does not matter.

Do the representations in Figures 7 and 8 explain the grammaticality difference in *break me the contract and break the contract for me? The Result in the former is a kind of 'having'. But if someone breaks something, they cannot possess it. Therefore, it is not possible to say *break me the contract because you cannot not have something and have it at the same time. But it is possible to say break the contract for me, because it is possible to add a Beneficiary FOR phrase to any intransitive or transitive verb. The FOR phrase is flexible: *dance for me, skip for me, kiss your mother for me, eat this cake for me*, etc. All of these are possible.

We can also ask ourselves whether the representations also explain the following grammaticality differences. Is there another ontological constraint that explains the facts about the double complement constructions below.

(14) a. Jane gave Peter a present.
 b. Jane gave Peter a kiss.
 c. Jane gave Peter flu.
 d. Jane gave a present to Peter.
 e. ? Jane gave a kiss to Peter.
 f. ? Jane gave flu to Peter.

The answer again is, "Yes." *Kisses* and *flu* cannot be Ers of 'moving' because of the ontological constraint on the Er of 'moving'. For those people for whom these examples are grammatical, it is probably the case that the Result of 'giving' is a different sense, something like 'going', which is more relaxed about the ontological class of its Er: all sorts of things can be the Er of 'going', but not the Er of 'moving'. 'Going' is a general event type which does not place restrictions on its Er, while 'moving' is a special subtype of 'going' that was we have seen, does place restrictions on its Er.

3 Argument Realization

How do we relate the arguments of a verb's sense to its syntactic arguments? What are the mechanisms? Are there algorithms? The answer is that there are not any algorithms in Word Grammar: argument-linking patterns are just learnt as part of learning the verb and learning the usual patterns of learning

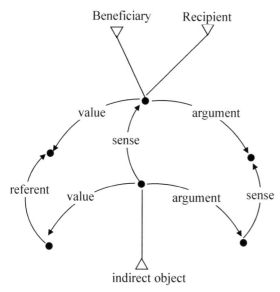

FIGURE 11 Indirect Object's sense

generalizations. The WG account of argument linking is strictly declarative, and exploits the device of the sublexemes, which we have already introduced to account for polysemy. I think that this point is obvious, but it's not obvious to everybody who studies these issues. But as with other grammatical patterns we learn generalizations, so we would expect that language-learners are capable, in the same way, of learning argument-linking generalizations. Therefore, the linguist's job is to describe the argument-linking patterns that they can see and establish the generalizations. For example, I said in lecture five that the Indirect Object had a sense which Isa both Recipient and Beneficiary, represented in Figure 10 below.

Now we can look at argument linking by examining OPEN again. On the left of the diagram is the sublexeme for transitive OPEN (OPEN/tr). The argument linking pattern is that the subject has a referent which is the Er and the object has the referent which is the Ee. And if I showed these arcs as attribute-value features, with an attribute arc and a value arc and node in the middle, as in Figure 11, then I would say that the sense of subject is 'Er', and the sense of object is 'Ee'. This is how we do argument linking in Word Grammar. It could not be any simpler. It is just a statement of the relevant generalizations.

In argument linking, the concept of the sublexeme comes into its own and becomes very useful. Taking OPEN for example, we can see that each sense

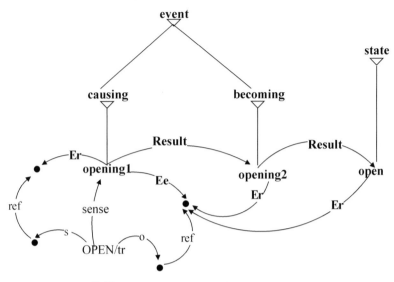

FIGURE 12   OPEN linking

of OPEN is associated with a separate sublexeme with its own particular linking pattern. The senses that we have just seen, 'opening 1' and 'opening2', each have their own little bit of form associated with them—OPEN/tr and OPEN/intr respectively. Figure 13 illustrates this by taking the content of Figure 12, and adding the argument linking pattern for intransitive OPEN to the model in the diagram.

The Er of 'opening 2' is the Er of 'open'. (I have updated this part of the diagram to show that the Ee of 'opening1' isn't exactly the Er of 'opening2', because not every instance of the Ee of 'opening1' is the Er of 'opening2': 'opening2' is both part of the semantic structure of transitive OPEN and the sense of intransitive OPEN and we need to show that difference with Default Inheritance. Sublexemes allow us to state the linking patterns directly; this is compatible with the claim that, knowledge of language is knowledge, as Goldberg says. Or more specifically, it is learnt knowledge. Humans do not actually apply rules or algorithms and try to figure it out; we just learn language as it comes.

The analysis in Figure 13 shows that Ers link to subjects; Ees link to objects; and indirect objects link to recipients/beneficiaries. But there are other patterns. For example, what links to predicative complements (xcomps)? How do complement PPs combine with the meanings of verbs? I have no time or space to discuss these, but the point is that variation within single verbs can be negotiated via the concept of sublexeme.

CONFLATION CLASSES, TRANSITIVITY ALTERNATIONS

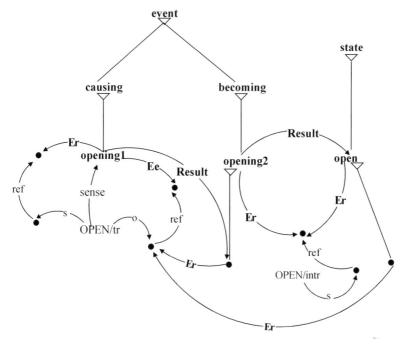

FIGURE 13   OPEN Linking

3.1   *Conclusions*

It is not clear that the manner/result dichotomy is settled. But it is clear that the verb-frame/satellite-frame distinction is overstated. Languages are not one or the other; verbs are. Argument linking is done in the network by explicit links between the semantic relations Er and Ee to Subject and Object and so on, with the device of the sublexemes being the pivot between the semantic representation and the syntactic one. And variable verb behavior is captured by degree of distance from the verb's prototype. Essentially, we can say that there are prototypical concepts and then variable behavior is simply captured by a series of inheritance links in the same way that idioms were accounted for in lecture 2. An idiom is just a subtype of a normal verb with lots of additional special information and restrictions on it. The same approach accommodates all the variation we find in the verbal lexicon.

LECTURE 10

Situating Meaning in the Utterance

I have been looking at the inside of verb meanings and breaking them down into their subatomic components. In this lecture I will argue that in fact, this verb-internal approach is not, by itself, good enough. Verb meanings inhabit a much larger cognitive ecology where we form mental representations of not just the utterance that we come out with, but also the speech context. To understand verb meaning, it is actually necessary to understand that larger conceptual and cognitive ecology, including who is speaking and listening, what the power relations are between the speaker and the hearer, the nature of the social context, the social dynamic between the participants and so on. I will argue that this is necessary even for understanding the subatomic parts of verb meaning.

This is, in some ways, an old argument. Fillmore in his *Lectures on Deixis* (1997) identifies some of the things I will be talking about today. Another person who has made similar observations is Halliday. Therefore, this lecture is very Fillmorean and Hallidayan.

1   Introduction

Have you seen ET? It is a movie by Steven Spielberg from many years ago. There is a poor little alien in the movie who gets stuck on earth and wants to phone home—he needs to get back home. The alien makes friends with a child. In the movie, there is a very touching image in which the alien's and the child's fingertips are touching. In the world of this film, aliens can communicate like that, just by touching fingers. Imagine you met a pair of Martians and they communicated by putting their fingertips together and vibrating them

All original audio-recordings and other supplementary material, such as any hand-outs and powerpoint presentations for the lecture series, have been made available online and are referenced via unique DOI numbers on the website www.figshare.com. They may be accessed via a QR code for the print version of this book. In the e-book, both the QR code and dynamic links are available, and can be accessed by a mouse-click.

gently and making new ideas emerge in each other's minds. I imagine that you would agree that it would be amazing. But I think human beings do something far more amazing.

In the imaginary world where Martians could communicate by touching, they could only speak to one person at a time. But every time we open our mouths, we make the atmosphere vibrate. The vibrations in the atmosphere make your eardrums vibrate, your eardrums send sensory information through your auditory nerve, and then the information gets processed in your brains. As a result of that, you get all sorts of experiences that otherwise you would not have. We make new ideas form in each other's minds. We can communicate all sorts of ideas by vibrating the atmosphere: more precisely, by using language. Moreover, human language is complicated: it allows us to express difficult, conceptual rich thoughts that encompass a wide range of ideas—other animals communicated by vibrating the atmosphere. But although they can signal that there is danger nearby, or that they want food, they cannot express what we can.

2   Pinker (1994)

Steven Pinker is an impressive writer, and the following quote, from his *Language Instinct*, is probably the single best beginning of a book about language I am aware of.

> As you are reading these words, you are taking part in one of the wonders of the natural world. For you and I belong to a species with a remarkable ability: we can shape events in each other's brains with exquisite precision. I am not referring to telepathy or mind control or the other obsessions of fringe science; even in the depictions of believers these are blunt instruments compared to an ability that is uncontroversially present in every one of us. That ability is language. Simply by making noises with our mouths, we can reliably cause new combinations of ideas to arise in each other's minds.
> PINKER (1994: 15)

One of the things we need to think about when we are trying to understand how language works is how all the different parts of the package work that we need to put together for this to happen. It is astonishing to me that I can travel six thousand miles from Edinburgh to Beijing, to very different culture, and for twenty hours I can speak English and be understood by all of the people in the audience. So not only do we make noises with our mouths but those noises have a system and it is possible for those of us who grow up in different communities to learn each other's systems. We are not just stuck with the system that we inherit at birth but we can acquire each other's. We can understand our own system and its relationship to our own culture. We can translate that into somebody else's system and somebody else's culture. All of this follows from the fact that language is organized and structured. One other relevant property of language is that it is social. Language is not just a cognitive system. If it were, then it would just be literally a way of organizing our own thoughts in our own minds. But we communicate using language, so it is clearly also social.

3 So What Is the Mind? And What Is in It?

If we are going to talk about making new thoughts arise in each other's minds, perhaps we ought to have a view of what the mind is. But I do not know what the mind is. That is much too complicated and difficult and I am not a philosopher. But we can have a guess about what the mind is. The crucial thing is that for a linguist's purposes, we do not have to know what the "real" mind is according to a cognitive scientist, a neuroscientist or a philosopher. We just need to know what our folk theory of the mind is. With our folk theory of the mind, we can work out what we need to have in terms of mental representations, because language is embedded in a theory of mind and an empathic understanding of the person we are speaking to.

In order to make new ideas arise in your mind, I have to have a theory of what might be in your mind, and I have to coordinate my social actions to yours. And in this coordination of social behavior, we have the basic idea of the language network which I have been talking about throughout the lectures. Social relations, like *x*'s wife or husband, are all semantically relational. As children we acquire these social relations very fast. Children know who their mothers are and they see the relationships in other family members. They induce these network relationships and the network of relationships can scaffold the larger network—the language network—that we build in our minds.

However, I do not just coordinate my social behavior towards yours. We also share the same perceptual experiences. We all see and hear the same things and we have to organize what we see and hear, especially the language data, because we need to impose the structure of words on the continuous speech stream we produce and hear. We have to be able to segment the speech stream in order to abstract out the words and knowledge of words, and build a linguistic structure. We use clues such as intonation in order to make it possible to do this. After all, we do not actually speak in the way that we write with spaces between each word that we say.

4 Social Meaning and Learning Biases

How do we do this? In the developmental psychology literature and the language acquisition literature, people talk about cognitive biases. Cognitive biases are a kind of mental property that direct us to interpret the perceptual data of our experiences in certain ways. We are in the business of trying to understand how it is the children organize and understand the world as information comes into their minds through this messy continuous perceptual input—how they make it into segments, into discrete units, and how they analyze the input. Biases were first discussed in the developmental psychology literature and the language acquisition literature, where they were used to explain aspects of language acquisition. All humans must share the same cognitive biases. We need to figure out how children use their biases to organize and understand linguistic data as the language data comes into their minds through the messy perceptual input they experience.

Children learn language fast and many grow up bilingual. They have to interpret their bilingual data, somehow, organize two language systems in their minds, and then be able to put words together in order to communicate with different people, so they need to know which word goes with which language and to know which language goes with which parent, and to know what language goes with which social situation outside of the family home, and so on. I know children who have this sorted by 2½ years old. And that is a miracle—a miracle of the human being. Our nearest genetic relatives—gorillas, bonobos and chimpanzees—cannot do what humans can. Language is a unique property of our species. We have to share the same cognitive biases. We have some kind of kit in our heads that allows us to interpret this perceptual data and build a language out of it.

Social meaning is part of the package. I think social meaning is learnt early and it works as a scaffold that we then use to help us learn other elements in language. That is, social meaning scaffolds other parts of the linguistic experience, and it interacts with learning, and it interacts with cognitive biases. Here are three cognitive biases. One of these cognitive biases is the community bias of Gildea and Jurafsky (1996). The other two are the whole object bias of Markman (1990) and the mutual exclusivity bias of Markman and Wachtel (1988). I previously mentioned these authors and cognitive biases in Lecture 1.

Let us talk about the community bias of Gildea and Jurafsky first. They say that as a learning animal, which is what we are, what we like to do with information and data is to put things that look the same into the same categories. We build communities of things and we do not care if they are not exactly the same: they do not have to be identical. In short, Gildea and Jurafsky claim that there is a categorization bias, that we are cognitively biased to put our experiences into categories. The whole object bias is related to the categorization bias because it is packaged together with Markman's taxonomic bias, and a taxonomy is a categorization system, but whole object bias is about how, when a child is learning a word, they are organizing that word into the rest of their meaning system. If you draw a picture of a bottle and you say that it is a bottle, the child will understand the whole object to be the bottle. They understand the word BOTTLE to mean the whole thing and not just the lid, the base, the material or the contents. Markman therefore claims that when children learn word meanings they are cognitively biased to learn word meanings as whole objects. Finally, the mutual exclusivity bias says if the child encounters two words, they assume that they mean different things.

We can illustrate this by thinking about animal names. When a child learns an animal name, let us say PIG, for the first time, they learn it and assume PIG goes together with DOG, CAT, COW and HORSE because they are all animal names. That is the community bias. The whole object bias means that the child learns the word PIG and assumes that it means the whole animal, not (for example) just the snout. That is the whole object bias. And finally, the mutual exclusivity bias means that when the child learns the word PIG, they assume that it means, 'Not dog, not cat, not horse, not cow'.

Those three biases together give us a very powerful way of understanding how the learning of word meaning happens. And if I have these cognitive biases, if you have these cognitive biases, and if everybody else in the room has these cognitive biases, then we are going to learn our language in the same kind of way. We are going to learn our languages looking for words, looking for word meanings to assign to these words, assuming that word meanings are mutually exclusive in various ways, and grouping word meanings together into organizational units and ultimately into taxonomies. That is quite useful because it means that we can assume that language is built up out of a social scaffold on the one hand. But it is also directed by these cognitive biases on the other. Cognitive biases shape our theory of mind, but the theory of mind is central in negotiating the social dimensions of language.

Here is an argument that tells us that our cognitive abilities may not be about innateness, but development, built on certain biases. There are stories of people who were blind from birth, or early on in life, having treatment to restore their sight. Many of these people still cannot see after treatment, because their vision loss happens relatively early and there are consequences for the parts of their brains where vision gets processed which did not develop properly. That is, they have the ability to process light in their eyes, but their brains do not allow them to form representations of those images—at least not the same representations that people who have normal vision from birth have. One conclusion we can draw from that is that seeing is not innate—it is at least partly experiential and thereby developmental. Now let us imagine that Markman's whole object bias is a perceptual bias. The biases would apply to learning how to see, as well as applying to language learning and interact with experience. This would suggest that very general biases are innate, but that they do not apply to specific cognitive domains such as language: the whole object bias could just be a general perceptual bias. And then human experience plays a crucial role in how those biases guide human development. The same argument goes for language acquisition: it is not completely innate; it is actually about the way in which perceptual experience builds up into a larger cognitive system, because language is perceptual as well, but guided by general perceptual biases.

5 Social Meaning

To summarize the argument, I think that social meaning is learnt early, scaffolds other parts of linguistic experience, and interacts with learning and other cognitive biases such as:
- The community bias of Gildea and Jurafsky (1996)
- The whole object bias of Markman (1990)
- The mutual exclusivity bias of Markman and Wachtel (1993)

The structure provided by social meaning helps us build a theory of mind, which language inhabits and which underlies the structuring of the language network.

6 Language, Mind and Communication ...

Semantics then, at least in its relationship to communication, involves a *meeting of minds*. Back in the 1960s and 1970s, there was a heated debate about what meaning was. Hilary Putnam who was a philosopher at Harvard said, *meanings ain't in the head* (1975). Instead, he, a logician, argued that the meaning of the sentence is the fragment of the real world the sentence refers to, and that people who said that meanings are in the mind are just guilty of circularity.

My answer to this question is, however, that mind gets meaning from social experience and from perceptual experience. Social experience and perceptual experience are where meaning comes from. My views echoes that of the Swedish cognitive scientist, Peter Gärdenfors. He criticizes Putnam in his book, saying, "image schemas emerge from the communicative interactions of language users" (2014: 18). That is, the question of how language means is interactive and social, so we have social meaning which scaffolds language, and perceptual biases which direct us to understand that words have certain kinds of meaning in certain ways during the acquisition process, and through communicating with people we build up an interactive understanding of how language means. So the question of how language means is interactive and social.

Putting this in the network terms of Word Grammar, then, we can claim that mental networks are constantly updated. There is always spreading activation and node-creation. There are constant activities, some of which are more active, while others are a bit less active. This activity is not just language related, it is general cognitive activity, but language is embedded within that activity. Therefore, if you like, meaning comes from social and perceptual experience and from an empathic understanding of the other people that we interact with. That is to say, in order to be able to communicate with somebody else, we have to have a mental representation of that person's mind in our own mind. Later in the lecture, I present an example—just a verb—but in order to use that verb properly you have to have a mental understanding of the other person's reality.

Richard Hudson (2007, 2010) has also argued that social meaning underlies other areas of meaning. He makes a version of the argument that I have just developed. But these ideas are not just a fantasy of how language works. They have consequences for how it works and how it should be analyzed.

7   **Social Meaning Embeds Meaning**

Social relations provide exemplars of relational concepts—this is one way social meaning embeds meaning. Word Grammar distinguishes between relational concepts and nonrelationship concepts. Nonrelational concepts include the meaning of a word like DOG, which just symbolizes a thing. A relational concept is the meaning of a word like MOTHER. The word MOTHER in fact is polysemous: it can either mean the woman or it can mean the relationship. We can factor out the woman from the relationship. For example, in the case of adoption, one might distinguish between one's birth mother and one's adoptive mother, and the mothering relationship goes with the adoptive mother. That is one way in which social meaning embeds meaning.

But we also have to create social contexts for what we say and hear because every single utterance has a grammar, a semantics based on the meanings of the words, and a sociolinguistic in-group meaning. Let us just think for a moment about the latter point. If you are British, you will be able to make all sorts of assumptions about me from the way in which I pronounce certain words. I pronounce the word *bath* [bɑːθ] and *transitive* ['trɑːnsɪtɪv], which tells you that I come from the south of England. If I came from the north of England, I would pronounce them [bæθ] and ['trænsɪtɪv]. That is a kind of sociolinguistic meaning that tells you where I am from. The city of Bath is near the city of Bristol in the southwest of England and it has a name which is pronounced by its local inhabitants as [bæːθ]. I was born very near [bæːθ], but I don't say [bæːθ] because my parents moved to the south-east of England when I was very young. But other people from Bath use my pronunciation because of their social class. How things are pronounced gives you quite a lot of social information.

8   Utterances in the Mind

Here is the main thesis for this lecture. Utterances have their context surrounding them in our mental representations. When we say a sentence, we have that sentence in our mind, together with its meaning, and its social context. That is, it is not just sentences, but utterances and the utterance context.

Our mental representations are very complex. They include social information, interpersonal behaviors and planning decisions. If you are going to open your mouth to say something, you have to plan it. The planning decisions are already part of the speaking process of what is coming next. But we also have to include ideas such as who is speaking to whom. How do we do that? We have to introduce ourselves. We have to identify the power dynamics. We have to identify the respect dynamics. In my culture, parents are called *mummy* and *daddy* when you are very young. When you are older, they are *mum* and *dad*. My children are now grown up and they call my wife and me *mum* and *dad*. However, some religious communities, such as the Quakers, do not believe in power hierarchies. (Quakers are a protestant Christian group.) Because of this, Quakers avoid using terms like *mum* or *mummy* and call their parents by their names. These sorts of social information affect all kinds of things. We also have to think about immediate local context like where you are—I mean this not in terms of the social class you come from, but in terms of expressions such as *can you bring me some water* when the water is over there, and I am over here, so just spatial orientation. Time has to be built into the meaning of utterances as well. For example, if you are telling a story, the relative time of the events in the story matters.

9 Utterance Context

Utterance context interacts with grammatical information. It exploits the semantic structures that we have found in our lexical semantic investigations. Therefore, a theory of language has to include information about how meaning interacts with context and how the building blocks of meaning work in the larger linguistic context.

The evidence that we need to include social information in verb meaning is very easy to find in the meanings of COME and GO. Their lexical semantics refers to the speech situation. COME means toward the speaker and GO means away from the speaker. It is part of the lexical semantics of these verbs that the speech situation is wrapped up in their dictionary meaning. These are deictic words. Other deictic words include the first and second pronouns: I and YOU are speaker oriented and addressee oriented respectively and related to the speech situation. The lexical semantics of COME relates to the position of the speaker and it means that another entity, the Er-entity moved or moves towards the speaker. GO means away from the speaker. The meanings of deictic words are unknowable unless you have a mental representation of the speech context and locate the deictic words in that representation.

Fillmore (1997: 61) says, "*Come* and *bring* indicate motion towards the location of either the speaker or the addressee at either the coding time or the reference time, or towards the location of the home base of either the speaker or the hearer at reference time." First of all, we know who the speaker and the addressee are. The coding time is the time of speaking and the reference time is the time that is being spoken about. If I say *Can you come over here?* then the speaking time and the reference time are the same. If I say—talking about my location—*my friend came to Beida to meet me after the lecture*, then the reference time is in the past, but the coding time is now and COME is towards me.[1] We can say then *Beida* is my home base. However, I can also use COME in an empathic way where I am using it from your perspective. This is really complicated, and we typically do not even think about it. I have never been to Thomas's flat: I do not know where it is. But I can say to Thomas, *When you came home last night did you speak to your son or to your wife first?* In this case, I understand the meaning of *come* from Thomas' perspective, not from mine. In this example, the home base is Thomas' home. Notice that if the home base is not mine, COME has to be at reference time only; it cannot be at coding time. When I am using my own home base, however, COME can be at reference time or coding time. That is what Fillmore's quote means. Observe

---

1 This lecture was given at Peking University. *Beida* is the colloquial name of the university.

SITUATING MEANING IN THE UTTERANCE 277

that we use verbs like COME and GO all the time and if you think about it, the Chinese verbs for COME and GO work in the same way. They each have a really complicated definition, which requires a sense of relative location, an empathic engagement with somebody else's mind, and social understanding of your interlocutor. That information is just there in your head from the moment the first time you use COME as a child. Language has to be socially embedded, because even lexical semantics relies on that social embedding, as we see in these deictic words. We cannot use a verb like COME without all that information in place.

10 Tensed Clauses

Here is another example of deixis. Tensed clauses have a deictic anchor in the speech act. They anchor the time of the event relative to the time of speaking. English only has two tenses: past and present. Past tense is past relative to the time of speaking. Present tense includes the time of speaking. All of this information has to be modeled in the representation of the sentence. For any language that has tense, the time of the utterance event and the reference time of the event are part of the mental model as well: they are included in the representation of the sentence and utterance.

11 Imperatives

Imperatives interact directly with the utterance context, like COME and GO. They embed the speaker and the hearer in their meaning, and the utterance time, and the situation type. Here is a simple example. If I say *stand up*, then I am telling my interlocutor, the person who is hearing me, to do something. It assumes all sorts of things: that I have the authority to tell somebody to stand up, and that they will stand up if I tell them to. There is also a power relation built into the meaning of this kind of utterance. It is quite funny that I have talked about these sorts of things in my lectures over the years, and I have noticed that as I get older and older, my undergraduate students are more and more likely to stand up if I tell them to in a lecture. That is something to do with power dynamics and the relationship of age to power.

Here is a simple explanation about imperatives. Imperatives embed the speaker and the hearer in their meaning, the utterance time, and the situation type. If I said *stand up* in a lecture you probably would not, because of the context of a lecture and the imperative I gave was just an example, not a real imperative directed you. But if we were in another environment and I told you to stand up, then you might. Imperatives are often included as finite verbs in typologies of finiteness. The reason is that they are located at the time of speaking and like tensed clauses they are anchored in the utterance event.

12   Coordination of Utterance and Context

One of the key facts about imperatives is that they make the point very strongly about how an utterance has to be located in a mental model of the speech context and the model must include the speaker and the hearer and the social dynamic between them. That is, the mental model of the utterance and its context have to be coordinated in the minds of both the speaker and the hearer. This is the point coming back to Gärdenfors about meaning being understood as a social interaction. An imperative only works if the speaker's mind and the hearer's mind are coordinated with each other. If the speaker and the hearer have not managed to coordinate their minds with each other, the imperative will fail. The imperative demonstrates very strongly that the mental model of the utterance has to include the speaker and the hearer and the social dynamic between them. It also shows very strongly that understanding is socially coordinated. Therefore meaning therefore is socially coordinated.

Imperatives are deictic in the same way that COME and GO are deictic. They locate the addressee whom they point to, relative to the speaker. They also have social meaning that encodes power relations as I already said. This combination of deictic properties and power relations makes an argument that imperatives show how language is part of an integrated unbounded cognitive network. This is something that is one of the main themes of these lectures. When I say the language network is unbounded, I mean language is not encapsulated in boxes, in terms of a language acquisition device, or constructions which can be embedded within constructions. I think that language is part of a much larger cognitive network because of this ecology that utterances must inhabit, which includes the social situation. The bits of the network flow out to the mental representations of who is speaking to whom, what they are saying, what the social relationships are. It goes backwards towards the social relationships that scaffold it. It is directed in terms of how we segment the speech stream in terms of various cognitive biases and so forth.

I said that the model of an imperative has to include the speech event, the time of speaking, the speaker, the addressee, the power dynamic and the event which is named by the verb. In some ways I think that imperatives are more embedded in the speech event than tensed clauses. What is more, the contextual information interacts with the semantics of the verbs in the imperative. The Er of the verb is linked to the addressee. If I say *stand up*, then the addressee is the stander. That means that semantic relations have to be able to point to concepts that belong to the speech event, not just to concepts that are the referents associated with the words in the sentence. That is complicated when we think of the structures of the different event types that we have been looking at. For instance, let us think about the complexity with achievement verbs: if I tell you, *hit the target*, then both the Er of 'moving' and the Er of 'touching' have to link to the Addressee because, as we have seen there are two events in the sense of HIT. This is a further argument against encapsulation. The event structure of 'hitting' cannot be encapsulated, because if it were, imperatives with verbs like this would not be meaningful.

This is part of the more general property where word meanings can interact with nonlinguistic information. For example, some non-syntactic elements can be included in a syntactic structure. If we say as a child *the train went [woo-woo]*, we have made an onomatopoetic attempt to represent the sound the train makes. What comes after *went* is not a word; it is nonlinguistic. This indicates that nonlinguistic information can get embedded in sentences as well.

13   Dangling Participles

Here is another more complex set of examples that involve the meeting of minds: dangling participles.

(1)   Driving home, I took a wrong turn and got lost.
(2)   Driving home, a kid ran in front of my car.

Traditionally, dangling participles are supposed to be predicated of the Subject of the main clause—clearly in (1) *I* is the driver. It is also the case that the speaker (*I*) must be the driver in (2). However, traditional grammar will tell you that (2) is not grammatical, because the subject of driving has to be the subject of the main clause. But, in fact, this is just a prescriptive rule; (2) is grammatical for most speakers. Dangling participles like the one found in (2) involve a lot of pragmatic resolution on the part of the hearer as they are trying to process that information. They have to imagine what the speaker means and imagine it from the speaker's perspective. From the speaker's perspective, if you are driving and a child runs in front of your car, the situation is terrifying, because the last thing you want to do is run somebody over. Therefore, in order to process the words *driving home*, you have to have empathic access to the speaker's mind. That is, in the case of dangling participles, you have to find an Er and resolve uncertainty about what the Er is, and you use pragmatic principles for this; you also have to coordinate your mind with the speaker's in order to figure out what they mean. This comes back to Grice's cooperative principle, which is a very good first principle for the coordination of communication. (This is not to say that Gricean pragmatics is "true" but that it is useful to keep in mind as a heuristic.)

14 Back to Imperatives

In the case of imperatives, the hearer has to find a value for the Er of the verb, and assign it within the speech event. It relates to both the speaker and the addressee. This is a case of event structure interacting directly with the context of the utterance. As I have said, that is also an argument against boxes or encapsulation, and an argument for seeing language as a network and only as a network, which is continuous with the rest of cognition.

15 Mood and Modality

Imperatives are one way of looking at how power relations are established in language. Another way would be deontic modality. In lecture 5, I gave you an analysis of deontic MAY and the force-dynamic relations between the speaker and the hearer. While modality involves force-dynamic relations, the imperative is a mood construction which involves the Er of an event linking to the addressee.

Modals, of course, also require the same kind of coordination between the speaker and the hearer. Modality is a kind of meta-predicate applied to a proposition. *You may go* means something like *it is possible for you to go*, or *POSSIBLE[you go]*. In this kind of modality, the content of the proposition remains intact. It is not the proposition that involves the utterance context: what involves the utterance context is the modality itself—in an utterance like *you may go*, the utterance context is involved in establishing *why* it is possible for you to go.

The following figure is an analysis of a deontic modal which involves a force-dynamic transfer between speaker and hearer. You have seen it before.

SITUATING MEANING IN THE UTTERANCE 281

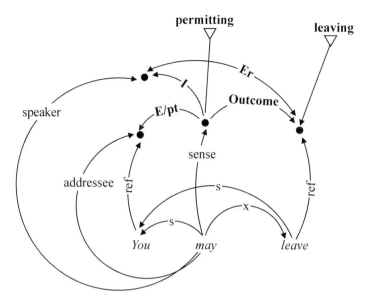

FIGURE 1   You may leave

The speaker acts on the hearer who is grammatically represented directly. The possible outcome or result of the interaction is that the leaving event comes about. Modality is "outside" the propositional meaning of the sentence. Deontic modality is usually understood as an event modality, so I have labeled the referent of *leave* as an event in the diagram.

The sense of *may* is 'permitting' which has as its outcome an event which is the 'leaving' event. The 'leaving' event has its Er argument, which is also the referent of *you*. In *you may leave*, the Antagonist, or Initiator, is the speaker acting on the addressee. You see that the deontic modality actually causes there to be an argument linking interaction between the utterance and the referent within one of the words in the utterance and the speaker. Deontic modality is another kind of speech event that requires the speaker and hearer to coordinate their mental models and to understand the power relations that play out in this kind of permission giving. The argument linking pattern of deontic modality takes you into the speech event.

Another complication in the case of *you may leave* is that the second person pronoun YOU also invokes the utterance context. The default meaning of YOU is the addressee, and that is what it means here. However, YOU can also mean 'one' as it has a usage as an indefinite pronoun. The key fact, however, is that both first and second person pronouns invoke the utterance context, because like tense and the verbs COME and GO they are deictic.

16   Epistemic Modals

Sweetser (1990) argues that it is possible to understand epistemic modality in terms of force dynamic transfer as well as dynamic modality. She says that if you use an epistemic modal like MUST, as in *he must be there by now*, "*must* is taken as indicating an *epistemic force* applied by some *body of premises* (the only thing that can apply epistemic force), which compels the *speaker* or people in general to reach the *conclusion* embodied in the sentence" (Sweetser 1990: 64). This is a force dynamic analysis of epistemic modality. Her argument is that the Agonist (Endpoint in my terms) is the speaker and/or all people in general on which the Antagonist (Initiator), the body of premises, acts.

Let us look at *he must be there by now* in more detail. We can include the following in our understanding of epistemic modality. There is a layered structure in the case of epistemic modality. We can see this in (3) and (4), where (3) lays out the schematic structure, and (4) is an analysis of *he must be there by now* in the terms of this schematic structure. The embedded proposition in (4) is *he be there by now* and the modal is *must*.

(3)   [The warrant for the modality [the modal [the proposition]]]
(4)   [Warrant [PROBABLE [he be there by now]]]

The warrant for the modality, or Sweetser's body of premises, is whatever licenses you to form the relevant inference. For example, imagine that you live in Edinburgh. Your friend is going to York. You know the train to York takes two and half hours and it takes twenty minutes to get from his place to the station. If you know your friend left his place three hours ago, you can say *he must be there by now*. What makes it possible to say is the background information that you know about how long it takes to get from his place to the railway station, and how long it takes to get on the train in the railway station if you already had a ticket, and so on. All that knowledge makes it possible for you to form the right kind of inference. We can represent it as a warrant for the modality, which in the case of epistemic modality is the basic knowledge state of the speaker. That is how this kind of modality seems to work.

What I am calling the warrant is Sweetser's shared body of premises. The warrant for the modality is the shared context. It is also the world view that makes it possible to evaluate the likelihood or otherwise, of the proposition. It is our knowledge in general, which epistemic modality requires us to deploy in some way. This is also a further argument that our representations of sentences do not only include the meanings of the words; they also include our understanding of the general state of the world as part of the context for the things that we say. Therefore, it is possible for us to be wrong when we form an epistemic inference. If I say *my friend must be there by now*, of course I do not know for sure that he is. I do not know if he actually tripped on the stairs and broke his ankle when he left his place, or if the train has been delayed—both situations which would make me wrong. Epistemic modality also involves a calculation about likelihood. It is also possible for modality, especially epistemic modality, to go wrong because our context of knowledge can be wrong.

We can understand the force dynamics like this. Let us take a deontic example first. Somebody says *you must work hard!* Here the Initiator is the speaker, who has authority, and who acts against the default inertia of the Endpoint. For example, let us assume that the default ambition of a student is to get the best mark for the least work, so if you, as a teacher, say to a student *you must work hard*, then you are pushing against the student's inertia. In *they must be there by now*, the Initiator is the speaker's knowledge about other things and the Endpoint is the speaker's ignorance about this particular issue. There is a construal, if you like, of one mind acting on another mind.

Is this force dynamic? It certainly moves far beyond thinking about individuals acting on other individuals in Talmy's sense. But I can see why Sweetser would want to say that epistemic modals are force-dynamic. This approach provides a way of capturing historical changes. Epistemic modals develop out of deontic modals, and when they do, we can say what happens is that the force dynamic relations move in terms of what they link to what. This way, we account for the fact that meanings change in small incremental steps and we do not have to have a radical theory of semantic change. This approach is also a way of minimizing polysemy, and relating the different senses of the modals to each other, making it possible to say they are intimately bound up to each other. But on the other hand, in other force-dynamic domains we see participants acting on each other. But in this domain, it is not so straightforward to see.

However, something else I want to take from Sweetser's analysis is that this kind of analysis of epistemic modality does involve the mind of the speaker and that of the hearer. It explicitly induces a theory of mind and it certainly involves the mind of the speaker.[2] My main point of this lecture is that language inhabits a wide ecology which includes mental representations of your own mind and those who you are speaking to and background contextual knowledge. Epistemic modality again reinforces this point.

---

[2] Although the context—the warrant for the modality—can involve a number of different elements and does not have to be social. If I utter *he must be there by now*, having just looked at my watch, the warrant includes my knowledge of the time and my knowledge of how long the journey takes. But this is not necessarily shared.

17 Evidential Modality

There is another area of modality. This is a third area of modality where it is easy to see how force-dynamics are relevant to the modal evaluation of a proposition. This is evidential meaning. Evidentials are a much less widely explored domain of meaning than other areas of modality. One of the reasons for this is that evidentiality is considered by some linguists like Aikhenvald (2004) for example, to be only a morphological phenomenon, as it is in Amazonian languages. There is also a debate about whether evidentiality is outside or inside the clause. Martina Faller wrote her PhD on this (Faller 2002).

But let us look at evidentiality in English. There are certainly some kinds of evidential modality in English: they are lexical and belong to meanings of various verbs. Rooryck (2001: 125) says, "Evidential markers are defined as grammatical categories which indicate how and to what extent speakers stand for the truth of the statements they make.... [e]videntials involve both *source* and *reliability* of the information. They put in perspective or evaluate the truth value of a sentence both with respect to source of the information contained in the sentence and with respect to the degree to which this truth can be verified or justified." Faller (2002: 79) claims that evidential modality and epistemic modality are distinct: "As Dendale and Tasmowski (2001) observe, most researchers would agree that there is a conceptual difference between indicating the type of one's source of information and indicating one's judgment as to how likely it is that that information is true. It is equally clear that one's judgment of the truth of a proposition is at least in part influenced by one's source of information. Thus, for Frajzyngier (1995), "it appears rather obvious that the different manners of acquiring knowledge correspond to different degrees of certainty about the truth of the proposition". It is therefore reasonable to say that there is a close relationship between the two concepts."

The idea is that with evidentiality or with evidentials, you express the source of information. If I say *I read it in the newspaper that Johnny Depp is getting divorced*, the newspaper is the evidential source. If I say *I heard it*, then it is a bit weaker. If I say *I overheard it*, perhaps I was not told directly, but was eavesdropping on somebody else's conversation. That is an even weaker evidential source. Therefore, alongside different sources of information there are different "strengths" of reliability.

Palmer (2001) says evidentiality and epistemic modality are two types of propositional modality. Evidentiality contrasts with epistemic modality because in epistemic modality speakers judge the factual status of a proposition, whereas in evidential modality speakers indicate the source for factual status of proposition. There are, according to Palmer, two main kinds of evidential: reported and sensory. Reported evidentiality involves some kind of claim that someone has passed the information on, as in *I was told*, in *I was told Johnny Depp is getting divorced*. Sensory evidentiality involves information from the senses as in, *Johnny Depp is getting divorced; I saw the petition his wife filed in the court*.

Evidential modality can also be highly subjective. We can compare *Peter looks drunk to his boss* with *Peter looks drunk*. The first example is not directly subjective, because it is reporting that a third party thinks Peter looks drunk. But if we say *Peter looks drunk* the example is subjective because it means that it is the speaker's opinion that Peter looks drunk. Subjectivity expresses the speaker's opinion, so it is the speaker's opinion that Peter looks drunk. Subjectivity is another case where speech context is part of the utterance, and where the speaker is related to the content of the utterance. I have argued in the past (Gisborne 2010) that examples like *Peter looks drunk* involve a force-dynamic transfer from proposition to speaker and that this captures the subjectivity. The modal warrant is given in the meaning of the main verb: it is the subject's appearance. In evidentiality the modal warrant is actually expressed and identified. And in evidential modality, the evidence is interpreted by a speaker, against his or her body of knowledge. For example, in *he sounds foreign* the idea is, first of all, it is subjective. The speaker says 'I think he is foreign'. Secondly, the speaker says the modal warrant for thinking he is foreign is his sound. Thirdly, the body of knowledge is what a foreign accent sounds like compared with what a native accent sounds like.

Now we are going to examine evidential verbs of appearance in more detail. The first evidential use is where the subject's referent has properties that provide the evidence for the evaluation. For example, in *he sounds foreign*, his sound is responsible for the speaker thinking he is foreign;[3] in *he looks ill*, his appearance makes the speaker think he is ill. In *the fabric feels old*, the sensation of touching the fabric makes the speaker think that it is probably old. *The wine smells delicious* and *the food tastes fantastic* work in similar ways. Given that smell is part of the experience of eating and drinking, if the wine smells delicious, it probably is delicious; likewise for *the food tastes fantastic*. This is what I have called 'evidential-1' use. The patterning of syntactic and semantic relations is similar to examples like *Jane tried to go*: it involves subject control. There is a thematic relationship between the SOUND-class verb and its sub-

---

[3] SOUND is ambiguous—it can either indicate the source of the evidential as I have just said, or it can be the predicate of a reported evidential: *from what you've said, he sounds angry*.

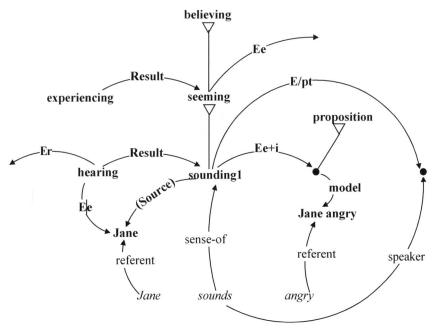

FIGURE 2   Jane sounds angry

ject. This is a perceptual evidential: the subject-referent is the percept, and it is the stimulus for the sensory evidence. Figure 2 shows my previous analysis (Gisborne 2010).

The sense of SOUND is an instance of 'sounding'. The Ee of SOUND is a proposition. In *Jane sounds angry*, the model for the proposition is Jane is angry. There is a force dynamic exchange, where the proposition is acting on the speaker. However, this analysis presented in my book is actually wrong. What is acting on the speaker should be the sound of Jane, the Source—it is Jane that the speaker hears, where Jane's sound is the evidence. Therefore, in fact the force dynamic transfer is between the Source and the Endpoint, the speaker.

In the second evidential use, the subject is not the Source of the evidence for the proposition that the Xcomp expresses. The evidence is more abstract, or ambient in these constructions. It is more like epistemic modality. One of the odd things about evidentials is that you might think epistemic modals actually develop out of evidentials, which would make some kind of sense because you could imagine it just involves the bleaching of meaning which is very usual in semantic change. But actually the semantic change can go the other way: German has a modal, SOLLEN, which has developed a reported evidential use from its original epistemic sense.

SITUATING MEANING IN THE UTTERANCE 287

Let us consider the following examples.

(3) (I've heard the forecast and) tomorrow's weather sounds fine.
(4) (I've seen the forecast and) tomorrow's weather looks fine.

Obviously, you cannot see or hear tomorrow's weather, therefore this is telling us that you have heard or seen evidence for the proposition, but the evidence is ambient. This is yet again evidence that interpreting a sentence involves a mental model which is a lot more complex than just the meanings of the word in the sentence. The proposition expressed in the clause in (3) and (4) follows from a contextual Source, which is expressed in the brackets. This is a reported evidential. In the case of SOUND-class verbs, it is only LOOK/P and SOUND that can express reported evidential.

Figure 3 is a representation of a reported evidential. It has the same mistake as Figure 2. It should be the Ee of 'hearing' which is the Initiator who acts on the speaker in some way (so the Endpoint is the speaker). But you can see again quite a lot of complex information involving context. This is the point to take away: complex information involving context is relevant to the interpretation of such verbs.

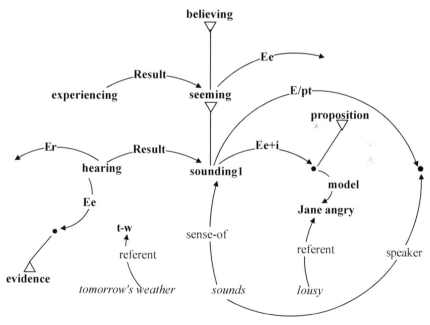

FIGURE 3   Tomorrow's weather sounds lousy

18   The Evidential Senses

The evidential senses of verbs of appearance are more embedded in the speech situation than epistemic modality which is more embedded in a broader picture or understanding of how the world works. Here are some other examples. Imagine that you are driving me somewhere. Your car is making a dreadful noise, and I hear the dreadful noise and I say *your car sounds like it needs a new clutch*. Or if you are telling me about your car, I can also say *your car sounds like it needs a new clutch* but what is heard is your report. The first one is a sensory evidential, while the second one is a reported one. But both are more related to the speech context than epistemic modality.[4]

19   *May We Come In?*

Our next discussion comes back to Charles Fillmore's work, and COME and GO. Here is a quotation from Fillmore (1997: 8): "Rather than go into such matters for these sentences, I would like to build my discussion of the explanatory domain of linguistics around a sentence which cannot be understood at all apart from considerations of its being anchored in some social context. The sentence I have chosen for this demonstration is simple and short and extremely easy to understand. It is the four-syllable question 'May we come in?' I would like to approach our examination of this sentence by way of a thought experiment. What I have in mind is this: I ask you to assume that you know, about some real-world situation, only one single fact, and that is that somebody used the sentence 'May we come in?'".

Suppose you know nothing else about the speech situation; all you know is that somebody asked the words: *May we come in*. Is that interpretable? The answer is going to be *no*. The sentences are uninterpretable unless you have the social and contextual knowledge: each word is deictically anchored: *may* asks permission; *we* refers to the speaker (and others); *come* is a verb of orientation; and *in* denotes the addressee's location.

This sentence is even more complicated than I suggested. I said earlier, that *come* oriented to the speaker's position. But at the same time the sentence is asking permission. *May we come in* is also empathically oriented to the addressee's position: it is *us* moving towards *you*. I have talked before about *come in* and you might recall that Fillmore distinguished between coding time and reference time. Here *may we come in* is actually situated at the time of the

---

[4] This example is due to Heycock (1994).

speech event. The rules for *come* that I gave earlier do not work perfectly for this situation. The sentence is asking for permission to move towards the addressee. It looks like *go*, asking to moving towards you. By using the verb *come*, the request is structured around the addressee's perspective and gives power to the addressee.

20   More on Questions

In questions, you are setting out to coordinate your mental model with your interlocutor's. You address your interlocutor directly. You ask them to fill in some question for you and you are asking them how the world is. This relies on the speech time, the speech event and the relationship between the speaker and the hearer. In addition, it also relies on the power relationship between the two.

Consider a simple question like *can you come to my party?* This is a yes-no question, so it is easier to get a one-word answer. But it uses a modal *can*, which links to the speech situation, a second person pronoun *you*, which links to the speech situation, a deictic verb *come*, and a first-person pronoun *my*. *You*, *come*, and *my* are all deictic elements, requiring the speaker and hearer to coordinate their mental organization of the world and to have an understanding that deictic words shift their meanings according to who is speaking. I have a friend whose wife is Icelandic. When his oldest child was very young, he went to pick him up from nursery school (they were living in Iceland) and there were two little boys standing at nursery school. One of the little boys pointed to his father and said *pabbi minn* ('my daddy'). And the other little boy got cross and said *nei, pabbi minn* ('no, my daddy'). And they went *nei, pabbi minn* at each other until their fathers picked them up. The point of the story is that these kids didn't understand the meaning of MY varies depending on who is speaking. It was too developmentally early for them. This is an area of understanding that comes developmentally later. You have to have a mental model that allows you to coordinate that sort of information and that allows you to bring that sort of information to bear on how you interact with these people whom you are speaking to.

May we come in is a closed interrogative with a yes-no answer. Understanding questions gets even harder with open interrogatives, such as *who bought your mother's old house?* Let us put aside items that we have already explained: deictic elements behave as we have seen, and note that this question also has a relational noun: MOTHER. But the key word is *who*. The word *who* is asking the hearer to quantify over a set of candidates and find the answer. But it does not define the set of candidates: the speaker does not know who is in the set of candidates. The question is saying that there is a set of possible candidates of people in your mind that I might be talking about. I do not know who they are, but you do know who they are: I want you to quantify over them and tell me the identity of the person or people who bought the house. This is a really complicated task.

Here is another example: *which dog do you want to get?* Let us say you want to buy a dog. In your investigations into dogs, you have come down to two different types of dog that you think it will be all right to have in your house. A poodle, because they are very intelligent and they do not lose their fur all over the house, and a border terrier, because they are wild, charming and good fun. In a situation like this, *which* does not mean 'from all the dogs in the world', but 'out of the dogs we have talked about (or that we have seen)'. The word *which* narrows down the possible candidates: it is asking you to identify the member of the choice set that you have established. Asking a question such as this involves a lot of mental coordination and explicitly requires you to coordinate your mental world with mine, by recalling our shared experience, and locating your experiences in the same place as mine. In technical terms, WHICH is a variable relative to a choice set. The effort of mental coordination involves agreeing on the choice set, without actually discussing its contents.

Of course, as we have already seen, and as you might expect, questions with modals can involve the kinds of epistemic modality I have just been discussing or deontic modality. For example, *what should I do after I have washed up?* specifically asks the hearer to give instructions. If I ask this question, what I am saying is *please tell me what to do next*. In that question, *should* is deontic, so the question assigns the Initiator role to the hearer. We can also say that the question gives power to the hearer or at least recognizes it in the hearer. Power relations fall out of argument linking which is a challenging thought. But the force dynamic relations argument link to the speech context and power relations fall out of that. We cannot understand questions without understanding the speech situation. We have to assume that the person we are speaking to understands what we are asking about. And we can use questions for all sorts of pragmatic purposes, or discourse functions. Therefore, questions are highly embedded in the speech situation. As, of course, are imperatives and verbs with deictic meanings and so on.

21   Intersubjectivity

Intersubjectivity comes up in the language change literature. Elizabeth Traugott talks about it a lot; so does Halliday. The ideas I have been discussing in this lecture are important for a theory of event structure because they show us that as some verbs draw on situational meanings, we need to locate our theory of event structure in a larger theory of communication. Evidential verbs have argument linking into the speech context, verbs like COME and GO relate to speech context, and so on. Some semantic relations, like force-dynamics ones, link to speech context and they are also recycled in terms of interpersonal behavior, so we have to have a mental model of the communication act in order to understand the meanings of these verbs.

But it is worth noting that the same sorts of ideas about utterances being situated in the communication context have been around for a long time; I am not claiming to be original. The original bit is the claim that this fact requires us not to segment bits of language and separate them off from each other but it requires us to understand language as a seamless web. But the idea that utterances are located in a mental representation of the speech situation, that goes back forever. It goes back at least to Benveniste and Halliday. For example, Halliday and Hasan (1976) distinguish between "ideational," "textual" and "interpersonal" components of the linguistic system. Here is a quote from Traugott (2010: 31) on Halliday: "Halliday has proposed that, most simply put, 'interpersonal' concerns 'clause as exchange' (Halliday 1994: 179), and includes both subjective and intersubjective elements, e.g. modal, and mood-marking elements, vocative, interactive acts of speaking including illocutionary acts, deictic person pronouns, attitudinal lexical items like *splendid*, and prosodic voice features." Illocutionary acts expressions such as *I am telling people to stand up*. If I say *splendid*, I am using an attitudinal lexical item: saying that something is splendid does not mean it is splendid in an objective reality; it means that it is my personal opinion that it is splendid.

22 Conclusions

I gave a number of reasons at the beginning of the lecture for including the speech context in our model of utterances. Meaning is embedded in perceptual information, social categories, and the socially negotiated understanding of perceptual categories. And there are linguistic structures—including tense—which rely on this. Some analyses expect us to relate semantic roles to participants in the speech context. Context is not only necessary for understanding utterances. It is also relevant to lexical semantics and event structure—because of verbs such as COME and GO and because of how complex event structures link to the context in the case of imperatives—as well as being the experiential source of meaning.

Given these conclusions about language and context, we have a further argument for seeing our mental models of language in purely network terms, with no embedding of content within content, and no encapsulation between language and other areas of cognition. I have argued that linguistic structures interact with our mental models of the immediate speech situation; that linguistic structures are scaffolded from other mental models, with the models for relational concepts being our understanding of our own social relationships from birth.

In the course of these lectures, we have deployed very few primitive relations. The main three are the Isa relation of default inheritance and the Argument relation and Value relation which allow us to structure relations and also to classify them. WG is a theory which assume a very simple network—a mindlessly simple network, if you like—with very little structure, and very little in the way of cognitive operations being required to make it possible for us to communicate with language. The theory is respectful of findings from cognitive psychology, and pays attention to the social dimensions of human communication. It can accommodate complex linguistic data sets, and it provides adequate tools for explaining the range of phenomena which are salient when we think about an area of linguistic meaning such as event structure.

In the course of these lectures, we have explored the issue of what events are in the ontology, idiomaticity, how a lexical representation works, evidence for structure in verb meaning, conceptualization and how the network works; the gradient nature of polysemy, events and thematic roles, event classes, *Aktionsarten*, explored case studies of ditransitives and verbs of buying and selling, looked at transitivity alternations, and in this lecture, brought these themes together in terms of language in its situated context. Each of these topics has returned to the idea of language as a network, and each lecture has returned to the nature of networks, as non-encapsulated cognitively plausible models of human language within cognition.

Bibliography

Acedo-Matellán, Victor and Jaume Mateu. 2013. "Satellite-Framed Latin vs. Verb-Framed Romance: A Syntactic Approach." *Probus* 25: 227–265.

Ackema, Peter and Maaike Schoorlemmer. 2006. "Middles." In *The Blackwell Companion to Syntax vol. III*, edited by Martin Everaert and Henk van Riemsdijk, 131–203. Oxford: Basil Blackwell.

Alm-Arvius, Christina. 1993. *The English Verb See: A Study in Multiple Meaning*. Gothenburg: Acta Universitatis Gothoburgensis.

Anderson, John M. 1971. *The Grammar of Case: Towards a Localistic Theory*. Cambridge: Cambridge University Press.

Bach, Emmon. 1986. "The Algebra of Events." *Linguistics and Philosophy* 9: 5–16.

Beavers, John and Andrew Koontz-Garboden. 2012. "Manner and Result in the Roots of Verbal Meaning." *Linguistic Inquiry* 43 (3): 331–369.

Boas, Hans C. 2013. "Constructionist Approaches." In *Oxford Handbook of Construction Grammar*, edited by Thomas Hoffman and Graeme Trousdale, 233–250. Oxford: Oxford University Press.

Bolinger, Dwight. 1977. *Meaning and Form*. London: Longman.

Bresnan, Joan and Tatiana Nikitina. 2009. "The Gradience of the Dative Alternation." In *Reality Exploration and Discovery: Pattern Interaction in Language and Life*, edited by Linda Uyechi and Lian Hee Wee, 161–184. Stanford: CSLI Publications.

Burzio, Luigi. 1981. *Intransitive verbs and Italian auxiliaries*. PhD dissertation, MIT.

Christiansen, Morten and Nick Chater. 2016. *Creating Language: Integrating Evolution, Acquisition, and Processing*. Cambridge, MA: MIT Press.

Copley, Bridget and Heidi Harley. 2014. "Eliminating Causative Entailments with the Force-Theoretic Framework: The Case of The Tohono O'odham Frustrative *Cem*." In *Causation in Grammatical Structures*, edited by Bridget Copley and Fabienne Martin, 120–151. Oxford: Oxford University Press.

Copley, Bridget and Phillip Wolff. 2014. "Theories of Causation Should Inform Linguistic Theory and Vice Versa." In *Causation in Grammatical Structures*, edited by Bridget Copley and Fabienne Martin, 11–57. Oxford: Oxford University Press.

Croft, William A. 1990. "Possible Verbs and the Structure of Events." In *Meanings and Prototypes: Studies on Linguistic Categorization*, edited by Savas L. Tsohatzidis, 48–73. London: Routledge.

Croft, William. 1991. *Syntactic Categories and Grammatical Relations*. Chicago: University of Chicago Press.

Croft, William. 2001. *Radical Construction Grammar*. Oxford: Oxford University Press.

Croft, William. 2003. "Lexical Rules vs. Constructions: A False Dichotomy." In *Motivation in Language: Studies in honour of Günter Radden*, edited by Hubert

Cuyckens, Thomas Berg, René Dirven and Klaus-Uwe Panther, 49–68. Amsterdam: John Benjamins.

Croft, William. 2012. *Verbs: Aspect and Argument Structure.* Oxford: Oxford University Press.

Cutting, John Cooper and Kathryn Bock. 1997. "That's the Way the Cookie Bounces: Syntactic and Semantic Components of Experimentally Elicited Idiom Blends." *Memory and Language* 25 (1): 57–71.

Davidson, Donald. 2001. *Essays on Actions and Events.* Oxford: Oxford University Press.

Dendale, Patrick and Liliane Tasmowski. 2001. "Introduction: Evidentiality and Related Notions." *Journal of Pragmatics* 33: 339–348.

Dowty, David. 1979. *Word Meaning and Montague Grammar.* Dordrecht: Reidel.

Dowty, David. 1991. "Thematic Proto-Roles and Argument Selection." *Language* 67: 547–619.

Dowty, David. 2001. "The Semantic Asymmetry of 'Argument Alternations' (and Why It Matters)." In *Making Sense: From Lexeme to Discourse*, edited by Geart van der Meer and Alice G. B. ter Meulen, 171–186. Groningen: Center for Language and Cognition.

Espinal, M. Teresa and Jaume Mateu. 2010. "On Classes of Idioms and their Interpretation." *Journal of Pragmatics* 42: 1397–1411.

Faller, Martina. 2002. "Semantics and Pragmatics of Evidentials in Cuzco Quechua." PhD diss., Stanford University.

Fillmore, Charles J. 1968. "The Case for Case." In *Universals in Linguistic Theory*, edited by Emmon Bach and Robert Thomas Harms, 1–88. New York: Holt, Rinehart, and Winston.

Fillmore, Charles J. 1982. "Frame Semantics." In *Linguistics in the Morning Calm*, 111–137. Seoul: Hanshin Publishing Co.

Fillmore, Charles J. 1997. *Lectures on Deixis.* Stanford, CA: CSLI Publications.

Fillmore, Charles J. and Beryl T. Atkins. 1992. "Towards a Frame-Based Lexicon: The Semantics of RISK and its Neighbors." In *Frames, Fields, and Contrasts: New Essays in Semantics and Lexical Organization*, edited by Adrienne Lehrer and Eva Feder Kittay, 75–102. Hillsdale, New Jersey: Lawrence Erlbaum Associates.

Fodor, Jerry. 1970. "Three Reasons for Not Deriving 'Kill' from 'Cause to Die'." *Linguistic Inquiry* 1: 429–38.

Frajzyngier, Zygmunt. 1985. "Truth and the Indicative Sentence." *Studies in Language* 9 (2): 243–254.

Frajzyngier, Zygmunt. 1995. "Functional Theory of Complementizers." In *Modality in Grammar and Discourse*, edited by Joan Bybee and Suzanne Fleischman, 473–502. Amsterdam and Philadelphia: John Benjamins.

Francis, Elaine. 1999. "Variation within Lexical Categories." PhD diss., University of Chicago.

Gärdenfors, Peter. 2000. *Conceptual Spaces: The Geometry of Thought*. Cambridge, Mass.: MIT Press.

Gärdenfors, Peter. 2014. *The Geometry of Meaning: Semantics Based on Conceptual Spaces*. Cambridge MA: MIT Press.

Geuder, Wilhelm and Matthias Weisgerber. 2008. "Manner of Movement and the Conceptualization of Force." In *Journée d'étude "Il'y a manière et manière."* Arras, France: Université d'Artois.

Gibbs, Raymond W., Josephine M. Bogdanovich, Jeffrey R. Sykes and Dale J. Barr. 1997. "Metaphor in Idiom Comprehension." *Journal of Memory and Language* 37: 141–154.

Gildea, Daniel and Daniel Jurafsky. 1996. "Learning Bias and Phonological Rule Induction." *Computational Linguistics* 22: 497–530.

Gisborne, Nikolas. 2008. "Dependencies are constructions." In *Constructional Approaches to English Grammar*, edited by Graeme Trousdale and Nikolas Gisborne, 219–255. Berlin: Mouton de Gruyter.

Gisborne, Nikolas. 2010. *The Event Structure of Perception Verbs*. Oxford: Oxford University Press.

Gisborne, Nikolas. 2011. "Constructions, Word Grammar, and Grammaticalization." *Cognitive Linguistics* 22: 155–182.

Gisborne, Nikolas. 2017. "Defaulting to the New Romance Synthetic Future." In *Defaults in Morphological Theory*, edited by Nikolas Gisborne and Andrew Hippisley. Oxford: Oxford University Press.

Gisborne, Nikolas. "Word Grammar Morphology. In *The Oxford Handbook of Morphological Theory*, edited by Jenny Audring and Francesca Mansini, 327–345. Oxford: Oxford University Press.

Gisborne, Nikolas and James Donaldson. 2019. "Thematic roles and events." In *The Oxford Handbook of Event Structure* edited by Robert Truswell, 237–264. Oxford: OUP.

Goldberg, Adele. 1995. *Constructions: A Construction Grammar Approach to Argument Structure*. Chicago: University of Chicago Press.

Goldberg, Adele. 2006. *Constructions at Work*. Oxford: Oxford University Press.

Goldberg, Adele. 2010. "Verbs, Constructions and Semantic Frames." In *Syntax, Lexical Semantics and Event Structure*, edited by Malka Rappaport Hovav, Edit Doron and Ivy Sichel, 39–58. Oxford: Oxford University Press.

Goldberg, Adele and Ray Jackendoff. 2004. "The English Resultative as a Family of Constructions." *Language* 80 (3): 532–568.

Green, Georgia M. 1974. *Semantics and Syntactic regularity*. Bloomington: Indiana University Press.

Gropen, Jess, Steven Pinker, Michelle Hollander, Richard Goldberg, and Ronald Wilson. 1989. "The Learnability and Acquisition of the Dative Alternation in English." *Language* 65 (2): 203–257.

Gruber, Jeffrey S. 1965. "*Studies in Lexical Relations*." PhD diss., MIT.

Halliday, Michael and Ruqaiya Hasan. 1976. *Cohesion in English*. London: Longman.

Halliday, Michael. 1994. *Introduction to Functional Grammar*. 2nd ed. London: Edward Arnold.

Hauser, Mark D., Noam Chomsky and W. Tecumseh Fitch. 2002. "The Faculty of Language: What Is It, Who Has It and How Did It Evolve?" *Science* 298: 1569–1579.

Heycock, Caroline B. 1994. *Layers of predication: the non-lexical syntax of clauses*. New York: Garland.

Holmes, Jasper and Richard Hudson. 2005. "Constructions in Word Grammar." In *Construction Grammars: Cognitive Grounding and Theoretical Extensions*, edited by Jan-Ola Östman and Mirjam Fried, 243–272. Amsterdam: Benjamins.

Holmes, Jasper. 2005. "Lexical Properties of English Verbs." PhD diss., University College London.

Horn, George. 2003. "Idioms, Metaphors and Syntactic Mobility." *Journal of Linguistics* 39: 245–273.

Hudson, Richard. 1984. *Word Grammar*. Oxford: Basil Blackwell.

Hudson, Richard. 1992. "On So-called Double-Object Constructions." *Language* 68: 251–276.

Hudson, Richard. 2007. *Language Networks: Towards a New Word Grammar*. Oxford: Oxford University Press.

Hudson, Richard. 2008. "Lexical Semantics and Syntax: Commercial Transactions Reanalyzed." http://dickhudson.com/wp-content/uploads/2013/07/lss.pdf.

Hudson, Richard. 2010. *An Introduction to Word Grammar*. Cambridge: Cambridge University Press.

Hudson, Richard. 2012. "Cognitive Linguistics and Language Structure." http://dickhudson.com/wp-content/uploads/2013/07/cogLgxlgStr.doc.

Hudson, Richard. 2016. "From Practice to Theory and Back." Paper presented at Burch University, Sarajevo, May.

Iacobini, Claudio and Francesca Masini. 2006. "The Emergence of Verb-Particle Constructions in Italian: Locative and Actional Meanings." *Morphology* 16: 155–188.

Iwata, Seizi. 2006. "Argument Resultatives and Adjunct Resultatives in a Lexical Constructional Account: The Case of Resultatives with Adjectival Result Phrases." *Language Sciences* 28: 449–496.

Jackendoff, Ray. 1972. *Semantic Interpretation in Generative Grammar*. Cambridge, MA: MIT Press.

Jackendoff, Ray. 1983. *Semantics and Cognition*. Cambridge, MA: MIT Press.

Jackendoff, Ray. 1985. "Multiple Subcategorization and the Theta-Criterion: The Case of Climb." *Natural Language and Linguistic Theory* 3: 271–295.

Jackendoff, Ray. 1990. *Semantic Structures*. Cambridge, MA: MIT Press.

Jackendoff, Ray. 1997. *The Architecture of the Language Faculty*. Cambridge, MA: MIT Press.

Jackendoff, Ray. 2008. "Construction After Construction and its Theoretical Challenges." *Language* 84 (1): 8–28.

Jackendoff, Ray. 2011. "Alternative Minimalist Visions of Language." In *Non-Transformational Syntax*, edited by Robert Borsley and Kersti Börjars, 268–296. Oxford: Basil Blackwell.

Kay, Paul and Fillmore, Charles J. 1999. "Construction Grammar and Linguistic Generalizations: The What's X Doing Y? Construction." *Language* 75: 1–33.

Kiparsky, Paul. 1997. "Remarks on Denominal Verbs." In *Complex Predicates*, edited by Alex Alsina, Joan Bresnan and Peter Sells, 473–499. Stanford: CSLI Publications.

Koenig, Jean-Pierre and Anthony R. Davis. 2001. "Sublexical modality and the structure of linguistic semantic representations." *Linguistics and Philosophy* 24: 71–124.

Kratzer, Angelika. 1996. "Severing the External Argument from its Verb." In *Phrase Structure and the Lexicon*, edited by Johan Rooryck and Laurie Zaring, 109–137. Dordrecht: Springer.

Kuiper, Koenraad, Marie-Elaine van Egmond, Gerard Kempen, and Simone Sprenger. 2007. "Slipping on Superlemmas: Multi-Word Lexical Items in Speech Production." *The Mental Lexicon* 2 (3): 313–357.

Lakoff, George. 1977. "Linguistic Gestalts." In *Papers from the Thirteenth Regional Meeting of the Chicago Linguistics Society, April 14–16, Chicago*, 236–287. Chicago: Chicago Linguistics Society, University of Chicago.

Lakoff, George. 1987. *Women, Fire, and Dangerous Things*. Chicago: University of Chicago Press.

Landman, Fred. 1992. "The Progressive." *Natural Language Semantics* 1 (1): 1–32.

LaPolla, Randy. 1990. "Grammatical Relations in Chinese: Synchronic and Diachronic Considerations." PhD diss., University of California, Berkeley.

Lawler, John. 1989. "Lexical Semantics in the Commercial Transaction Frame: Value, WORTH, PRICE, and COST." *Studies in Language* 13: 381–404.

Levin, Beth. 1993. *English Verb Classes and Alternations*. Chicago: University of Chicago Press.

Levin, Beth. 2004. "Verbs and Constructions: Where Next?" Paper presented at the *Western Conference on Linguistics*, University of Southern California, Los Angeles, CA, November 12–14. http://web.stanford.edu/~bclevin/wecol04.pdf.

Levin, Beth and Malka Rappaport Hovav. 1991. "Wiping the Slate Clean: A Lexical Semantic Exploration." *Cognition* 41: 123–151.

Levin, Beth and Malka Rappaport Hovav. 2005. *Argument Realization*. Cambridge: Cambridge University Press.

Levin, Beth and Malka Rappaport Hovav. 2013. "Lexicalized Meaning and Manner/Result Complementarity." In *Subatomic Semantics of Event Predicates*, edited by B. Arsenijević, B. Gehrke, and R. Marín, 49–70. Dordrecht: Springer.

Lyons, John. 1977. *Semantics*. Cambridge: Cambridge University Press.
Markman, Ellen M. and Wachtel, Gwyn F. 1988. "Children's Use of Mutual Exclusivity to Constrain the Meanings of Words." *Cognitive Psychology* 20: 120–157.
Markman, Ellen. 1990. "Constraints Children Place on Word Meanings." *Cognitive Science* 14: 57–77.
Nordström, Jackie. 2014. "Language as a discrete combinatorial system rather than a recursive embedding one." *The Linguistic Review* 31: 151–191.
Nunberg, Geoffrey, Ivan Sag and Thomas Wasow. 1994. "Idioms." *Language* 70: 491–538.
Palmer, F. R. 2001. *Mood and Modality*. 2nd ed. Cambridge: Cambridge University Press.
Parsons, Terence. 1990. *Events in the Semantics of English*. Cambridge, MA: MIT Press.
Parsons, Terence. 1995. "Thematic Relations and Arguments." *Linguistic Inquiry* 26: 635–662.
Perlmutter, David M. 1978. "Impersonal passives and the unaccusative hypothesis." *Proceedings of the Annual Meeting of the Berkeley Linguistic Society* 38: 157–189.
Pesetsky, David. 1995. *Zero Syntax: Experiencers and Cascades*. Cambridge, MA: MIT Press.
Peterson, R. R., C. Burgess, G. S. Dell, and K. L. Eberhard. 2001. "Dissociation Between Syntactic and Semantic Processing During Idiom Comprehension." *Journal of Experimental Psychology: Learning, Memory and Cognition* 90: 1223–1237.
Pethő, Gergely. 2001. "What is Polysemy? A Survey of Current Research and Results." In *Pragmatics and the Flexibility of Word Meaning*, edited by Enikö Nemeth and Károly Bibok, 175–224. Amsterdam: Elsevier.
Pinker, Steven. 1989. *Learnability and Cognition: The Acquisition of Argument Structure*. Cambridge, MA: MIT Press.
Pinker, Steven. 1994. *The Language Instinct*. London: Allen Lane.
Pustejovsky, James. 1991. "The Syntax of Event Structure." *Cognition* 41: 47–81.
Pustejovsky, James. 1995. *The Generative Lexicon*. Cambridge, MA: MIT Pres.
Putnam, Hilary. 1975. "The Meaning of 'Meaning'." In: *Philosophical Papers. Vol. 2: Mind, Language and Reality*, 131–193. Cambridge: Cambridge University Press.
Ramchand, Gillian. 1997. *Aspect and Predication*. Oxford: OUP.
Ramchand, Gillian. 2008. *Verb Meaning and the Lexicon: A First Phase Syntax*. Cambridge: Cambridge University Press.
Rappaport Hovav, Malka and Beth Levin. 1998. "Building Verb Meanings." In *The Projection of Arguments: Lexical and Compositional Factors*, edited by Miriam Butt and Wilhelm Geuder. 97–134. Stanford, CA: CSLI Publications.
Rappaport Hovav, Malka and Beth Levin. 2001. "An Event Structure Account of English Resultatives." *Language* 77: 766–797.
Rappaport Hovav, Malka and Beth Levin. 2008. "The English Dative Alternation: The Case for Verb Sensitivity." *Journal of Linguistics* 44: 129–167.

Rappaport Hovav, Malka and Beth Levin. 2010. "Reflections on Manner/Result Complementarity." In *Syntax, Lexical Semantics, and Event Structure*, edited by Malka Rappaport Hovav, Edit Doron, and Ivy Sichel, 21–38. Oxford: Oxford University Press.

Ravin, Yael and Claudia Leacock. 2000. *Polysemy: Theoretical and Computational Approaches*. Oxford: Oxford University Press.

Rooryck, Johan. 2001. "Evidentiality, Part 1." *Glot International* 5 (4): 125–133.

Rosch, Eleanor. 1975. "Cognitive Representation of Semantic Categories." *Journal of Experimental Psychology* 104: 192–233.

Rosen, Carol. 1981. "The Relational Structure of Reflexive Clauses: Evidence from Italian." PhD diss., Harvard University.

Rosta, Andrew. 1992. "English Mediopassive." *UCL Working Papers in Linguistics* 4: 327–351.

Rothstein, Susan. 2004. *Structuring Events: A Study in the Semantics of Lexical Aspect*. Oxford: Blackwell.

Seuren, Pieter. *The Seuren Blog* (blog). https://pieterseuren.wordpress.com/.

Simon, Daniel. "Psych verbs." University of Edinburgh MSc dissertation.

Slobin, Dan. 2004. "The Many Ways to Search for a Frog: Linguistic Typology and the Expression of Motion Events." In *Relating Events in Narrative. Vol. 2*, edited by Sven Strömqvist and Ludo Verhoeven, 219–257. Mahwah, NJ: Lawrence Erlbaum Associates.

Smith, Carlota S. 1997. *The Parameter of Aspect*. 2nd ed. Springer: New York City.

Sprenger, Simone A., Willem Levelt and Gerard Kempen. 2006. "Lexical Access During the Production of Idiomatic Phrases." *Journal of Memory and Language* 54 (2): 161–184.

Steedman, Mark and Marc Moen. 1998. "Temporal Ontology and Temporal Reference." *Computational Linguistics* 14: 15–28.

Stump, George T. 2001. *Inflectional Morphology: A Theory of Paradigm Structure*. Cambridge: Cambridge University Press.

Sweetser, Eve E. 1990. *From Etymology to Pragmatics: Metaphorical and Cultural Aspects of Semantics Structure*. Cambridge: Cambridge University Press.

Talmy, Leonard. 1975. "Semantics and Syntax of Motion." In *Syntax and Semantics, vol. 4*, edited by John Kimball, 181–238. New York: Academic Press.

Talmy, Leonard. 1976. "Semantic Causative Types." In *Syntax and Semantics, vol. 6: The Grammar of Causative Constructions*, edited by Masayoshi Shibatani, 43–116. New York: Academic Press.

Talmy, Leonard. 1983. "How Language Structures Space." In *Spatial Orientation: Theory, Research and Application*, edited by Herbert L. Pick and Linda P. Acredolo, 225–282. New York: Plenum.

Talmy, Leonard. 1985a. "Lexicalization Patterns: Semantic Structure in Lexical Forms." In *Language Typology and Syntactic Description 3: Grammatical Categories and the Lexicon*, edited by T. Shopen, 57–149. Cambridge: Cambridge University Press.

Talmy, Leonard. 1985b. "Force Dynamics in Language and Thought." *Chicago Linguistic Society* 21 (2): 293–337.

Talmy, Leonard. 1988. "Force-Dynamics in Language and Cognition." *Cognitive Science* 12: 49–100.

Talmy, Leonard. 2000. *Toward a Cognitive Semantics*. Cambridge, MA: MIT Press.

Taylor, John R. 2004a. *Linguistic Categorization*. 3rd ed. Oxford: Oxford University Press.

Taylor, John R. 2004b. "The Ecology of Constructions." In *Studies in Linguistic Motivation*, edited by Günter Radden and Klaus-Uwe Panther, 49–73. Berlin: Mouton de Gruyter.

Tollfree, L. 1999. "South East London English: discrete versus continuous modelling of consonantal reduction." In *Urban voices: Accent studies in the British Isles*, edited by Paul Foulkes and Gerald J. Docherty, 163–184. London: Arnold.

Traugott, Elizabeth and Richard Dasher. 2002. *Regularity in Semantic Change*. Cambridge: Cambridge University Press.

Traugott, Elizabeth. 2010. "Revisiting Subjectification and Intersubjectification." In *Subjectification, Intersubjectification and Grammaticalization*, edited by Kristin Davidse, Lieven Vandelanotte, and Hubert Cuyckens, 29–70. Berlin: De Gruyter Mouton.

Van Valin, Robert D. Jr. 1993. "A Synopsis of Role and Reference Grammar." In *Advances in Role and Reference Grammar*, edited by Robert D. Van Valin Jr., 1–164. Amsterdam/Philadelphia: John Benjamin.

Vandeloise, Claude. 1991. *Spatial Prepositions: A Case Study from French*. Chicago: University of Chicago Press.

Vendler, Z. 1957. "Verbs and Times." *Philosophical Review* 66: 143–160.

Vendler, Z. 1967. *Linguistics in Philosophy*. Ithaca, NY: Cornell University Press.

Verhagen, Arie. 2002. "From Parts to Wholes and Back Again." *Cognitive Linguistics* 13: 403–439.

Wechsler, Stephen. 2001. "An Analysis of English Resultatives Under the Event-Argument Homomorphism Model of Telicity." In *Proceedings of the 3rd Workshop on Text Structure, Austin, Texas, October 13–15*, 1–15. Austin: Department of Linguistics, University of Texas.

Wechsler, Stephen. 2015. *Word Meaning and Syntax*. Oxford: Oxford University Press.

About the Series Editor

Fuyin (Thomas) Li (1963, Ph.D. 2002) received his Ph.D. in English Linguistics and Applied Linguistics from the Chinese University of Hong Kong. He is professor of linguistics at Beihang University, where he organizes *China International Forum on Cognitive Linguistics* since 2004, http://cifcl.buaa.edu.cn/Intro.htm. As the founding editor of the journal *Cognitive Semantics*, brill.com/cose, the founding editor of *International Journal of Cognitive Linguistics*, editor of the series *Distinguished Lectures in Cognitive Linguistics*, brill.com/dlcl, (originally *Eminent Linguists' Lecture Series*), editor of *Compendium of Cognitive Linguistics Research*, and organizer of ICLC-11, he plays an active role in the international expansion of Cognitive Linguistics.

His main research interests involve the Talmyan cognitive semantics, overlapping systems model, event grammar, causality, etc. with a focus on synchronic and diachronic perspective on Chinese data, and a strong commitment to usage-based model and corpus method.

His representative publications include the following: *Metaphor, Image, and Image Schemas in Second Language Pedagogy* (2009), *Semantics: A Course Book* (1999), *An Introduction to Cognitive Linguistics* (in Chinese, 2008), *Semantics: An Introduction* (in Chinese, 2007), *Toward a Cognitive Semantics, Volume I: Concept Structuring Systems* (Chinese version, 2017), *Toward a Cognitive Semantics, Volume II: Typology and Process in Concept Structuring* (Chinese version, 2019).

His personal homepage: http://shi.buaa.edu.cn/thomasli
E-mail: thomasli@buaa.edu.cn; thomaslfy@gmail.com

Websites for Cognitive Linguistics and CIFCL Speakers

All the websites were checked for validity on 20 January 2019

Part 1   Websites for Cognitive Linguistics

1. http://www.cogling.org/
   Website for the International Cognitive Linguistics Association (ICLA)

2. http://www.cognitivelinguistics.org/en/journal
   Website for the journal edited by ICLA, *Cognitive Linguistics*

3. http://cifcl.buaa.edu.cn/
   Website for China International Forum on Cognitive Linguistics (CIFCL)

4. http://cosebrill.edmgr.com/
   Website for the journal *Cognitive Semantics* (ISSN 2352–6408/ E-ISSN 2352–6416), edited by CIFCL

5. http://www.degruyter.com/view/serial/16078?rskey=fw6Q2O&result=1&q=CLR
   Website for the Cognitive Linguistics Research (CLR)

6. http://www.degruyter.com/view/serial/20568?rskey=dddL3r&result=1&q=ACL
   Website for Application of Cognitive Linguistics (ACL)

7. http://www.benjamins.com/#catalog/books/clscc/main
   Website for book series in Cognitive Linguistics by Benjamins

8. http://www.brill.com/dlcl
   Website for Distinguished Lectures in Cognitive Linguistics (DLCL)

9. http://refworks.reference-global.com/
   Website for online resources for Cognitive Linguistics Bibliography

10. http://benjamins.com/online/met/
    Website for Bibliography of Metaphor and Metonymy

11. http://linguistics.berkeley.edu/research/cognitive/
    Website for Cognitive Program in Berkeley

12. https://framenet.icsi.berkeley.edu/fndrupal/
    Website for Framenet

13. http://www.mpi.nl/
    Website for the Max Planck Institute for Psycholinguistics

Part 2   Websites for CIFCL Speakers and Their Research

14. CIFCL Organizer
    Thomas Li, thomasli@buaa.edu.cn; thomaslfy@gmail.com
    Personal homepage: http://shi.buaa.edu.cn/thomasli
    http://shi.buaa.edu.cn/lifuyin/en/index.htm

15. CIFCL 18, 2018
    Arie Verhagen, A.Verhagen@hum.leidenuniv.nl
    http://www.arieverhagen.nl/

16. CIFCL 18, 2018 (CIFCL 12, 2013)
    Stefan Th. Gries, stgries@linguistics.ucsb.edu
    http://www.stgries.info

17. CIFCL 17, 2017
    Jeffrey M. Zacks, jzacks@wustl.edu
    Lab: dcl.wustl.edu
    Personal homepage: https://dcl.wustl.edu/affiliates/jeff-zacks/

18. CIFCL 16, 2016
    Cliff Goddard, c.goddard@griffith.edu.au
    https://www.griffith.edu.au/griffith-centre-social-cultural-research/our-centre/cliff-goddard

19. CIFCL 15, 2016
    Nikolas Gisborne, n.gisborne@ed.ac.uk

20. CIFCL 14, 2014
    Phillip Wolff, pwolff@emory.edu

21. CIFCL 13, 2013 (CIFCL 3, 2006)
    Ronald W. Langacker, rlangacker@ucsd.edu
    http://idiom.ucsd.edu/~rwl/

22. CIFCL 12, 2013 (CIFCL 18, 2018)
    Stefan Th. Gries, stgries@linguistics.ucsb.edu
    http://www.stgries.info

23. CIFCL 12, 2013
    Alan Cienki, a.cienki@vu.nl
    https://research.vu.nl/en/persons/alan-cienki

24. CIFCL 11, 2012
    Sherman Wilcox, wilcox@unm.edu
    http://www.unm.edu/~wilcox

25. CIFCL 10, 2012
    Jürgen Bohnemeyer, jb77@buffalo.edu
    Personal homepage: http://www.acsu.buffalo.edu/~jb77/
    The CAL blog: https://causalityacrosslanguages.wordpress.com/
    The blog of the UB Semantic Typology Lab: https://ubstlab.wordpress.com/

26. CIFCL 09, 2011
    Laura A. Janda, laura.janda@uit.no
    http://ansatte.uit.no/laura.janda/

27. CIFCL 09, 2011
    Ewa Dabrowska, ewa.dabrowska@northumbria.ac.uk

28. CIFCL 08, 2010
    William Croft, wcroft@unm.edu
    http://www.unm.edu/~wcroft

29. CIFCL 08, 2010
    Zoltán Kövecses, kovecses.zoltan@btk.elte.hu

30. CIFCL 08, 2010
    (Melissa Bowerman: 1942–2011)

31. CIFCL 07, 2009
    Dirk Geeraerts, dirk.geeraerts@arts.kuleuven.be
    http://wwwling.arts.kuleuven.be/qlvl/dirkg.htm

32. CIFCL 07, 2009
    Mark Turner, mark.turner@case.edu

33. CIFCL 06, 2008
    Chris Sinha, chris.sinha@ling.lu.se

34. CIFCL 05, 2008
    Gilles Fauconnier, faucon@cogsci.ucsd.edu

35. CIFCL 04, 2007
    Leonard Talmy, talmy@buffalo.edu
    https://www.acsu.buffalo.edu/~talmy/talmy.html

36. CIFCL 03, 2006 (CIFCL 13, 2013)
    Ronald W. Langacker, rlangacker@ucsd.edu
    http://idiom.ucsd.edu/~rwl/

37. CIFCL 02, 2005
    John Taylor, john.taylor65@xtra.co.nz
    https://independent.academia.edu/JohnRTaylor

38. CIFCL 01, 2004
    George Lakoff, lakoff@berkeley.edu
    http://georgelakoff.com/